✳ *Highlights* ✳
of this
Study Guide

✳ Each Chapter of this **Study Guide** includes—

   ✳ Chapter **Introduction**

   ✳ Easy to Read & Understand, Comprehensive **Outline**

   ✳ **True-False** Questions

   ✳ **Fill-In** Questions

   ✳ **Multiple-Choice** Questions

   ✳ **Short Essay** Questions

   ✳ **GamePoints** or **RockOn** Questions—hypothetical fact problems & black letter law questions on key issues

✳ Each Unit of this **Study Guide** ends with—

   ✳ **Cumulative Hypothetical** & corresponding **Multiple-Choice** Questions

   ✳ **Multiple-Choice** Questions covering *Focus on Ethics* sections

✳ This **Study Guide** also contains an **Answer Appendix** with answers to all of the Questions & explanations of the Answers

---

Study Guide

to Accompany

The Legal Environment of Business
Text & Cases—Ethical, Regulatory, Global, and Corporate Issues
Eighth Edition

FRANK B. CROSS
Herbert D. Kelleher
Centennial Professor in Business Law
University of Texas at Austin

ROGER LeROY MILLER
Institute for University Studies
Arlington, Texas

Prepared by

William Eric Hollowell
Member of
U.S. Supreme Court Bar
Minnesota State Bar
Florida State Bar

Roger LeRoy Miller
Institute for University Studies
Arlington, Texas

SOUTH-WESTERN
CENGAGE Learning

Australia · Brazil · Japan · Korea · Mexico · Singapore · Spain · United Kingdom · United States

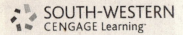
SOUTH-WESTERN
CENGAGE Learning

**Study Guide to Accompany
The Legal Environment of Business:**
TEXT AND CASES
**Ethical, Regulatory, Global, and
Corporate Issues**
Eighth Edition

**Frank B. Cross
Roger LeRoy Miller**

Vice President/Editorial Director:
Jack W. Calhoun

Editor-in-Chief:
Rob Dewey

Senior Acquisitions Editor:
Vicky True-Baker

Senior Developmental Editor:
Jan Lamar

Marketing Director:
Lisa L. Lysne

Marketing Manager:
Laura-Aurora Stopa

Marketing Coordinator:
Nicole Parsons

Production Editor:
Bill Stryker

Content Project Manager:
Anne Sheroff

Senior Media Editor:
Kristen Meere

Manufacturing Buyer:
Kevin Kluck

Editorial Assistant:
Patrick Ian Clark

Senior Art Director:
Michelle Kunkler

For product information and technology assistance, contact us at
**Cengage Learning Academic Resource Center,
1-800-423-0563**
For permission to use material from this text or product, submit all requests online at **www.cengage.com/permissions**
Further permissions questions can be emailed to
permissionrequest@cengage.com

ISBN-13: 978-0-538-46979-1
ISBN-10: 0-538-46979-X

South-Western Cengage Learning
5191 Natorp Blvd.
Mason, OH 45040
USA

Cengage Learning products are represented in Canada by Nelson Education, Ltd.

For your course and learning solutions, visit
www.cengage.com

Purchase any of our products at your local college store or at our preferred online store **www.cengagebrain.com**

Printed in the United States of America
1 2 3 4 5   15 14 13 12 11

Table of Contents

Preface

To the Student

This *Study Guide* is designed to help you read and understand *The Legal Environment of Business,* Eighth Edition.

How the *Study Guide* Can Help You

This *Study Guide* can help you maximize your learning, subject to the constraints and the amount of time you can allot to this course. There are at least six specific ways in which you can benefit from using this guide.

1. The *Study Guide* can help you decide which topics are the most important. Because there are so many topics analyzed in each chapter, many students become confused about what is essential and what is not. You cannot, of course, learn everything; this *Study Guide* can help you concentrate on the crucial topics in each chapter.

2. If you are forced to miss a class, you can use this *Study Guide* to help you learn the material discussed in your absence.

3. There is a possibility that the questions that you are required to answer in this *Study Guide* are representative of the types of questions that you will be asked during examinations.

4. You can use this *Study Guide* to help you review for examinations.

5. This *Study Guide* can help you decide whether you really understand the material. Don't wait until examination time to find out!

6. Finally, the questions in this *Study Guide* will help you develop critical thinking skills that you can use in other classes and throughout your career.

The Contents of the *Study Guide*

The legal environment is sometimes considered a difficult subject because it uses a specialized vocabulary and also takes most people much time and effort to learn. Those who work with and teach legal environment believe that the subject matter is exciting and definitely worthy of your efforts. Your text, *The Legal Environment of Business,* **Eighth Edition,** and this student learning guide have been written for the precise purpose of helping you learn the most important aspects of legal environment. We always try to keep you, the student, in mind.

Every chapter includes the following sections:

1. What This Chapter Is About: You are introduced to the main subject matter of each chapter in this section.

2. Chapter Outline: Using an outline format, the salient points in each chapter are presented.

3. True-False Questions: Ten true-false questions are included for each chapter. Generally, these questions test knowledge of terminology and principles. The answers are given at the back of the book. Whenever an answer is false, the reasons why it is false are presented at the back of the book also.

4. Fill-in Questions: Here you are asked to choose between two alternatives for each space that needs to be filled in. Answers are included at the back of the book.

5. Multiple-Choice Questions: Ten multiple-choice questions are given for each chapter. The answers, along with an explanation, are included at the back of this book.

6. Short Essay Questions: Two essay questions are presented for each chapter.

7. GamePoints or RockOn: Unique hypothetical fact problems on key issues.

How to Use this Study Guide

What follows is a recommended strategy for improving your grade in your legal environment class. It may seem like a lot of work, but the payoffs will be high. Try the entire program for the first three or four chapters. If you then feel you can skip some steps safely, try doing so and see what happens.

For each chapter we recommend you follow the sequence of steps below:

1. Read the What This Chapter Is About and Chapter Outline.

2. Read any of the Concept Summaries that may be included in the chapter you are studying in *The Legal Environment of Business*, **Eighth Edition.**

3. Read about half the textbook chapter (unless it is very long), being sure to underline only the most important topics (which you should be able to recognize after having read no more than two chapter outlines in this *Study Guide*). Put a check mark by the material that you do not understand.

4. If you find the textbook's chapter easy to understand, you might want to finish reading it. Otherwise, rest for a sufficient period before you read the second half of the chapter. Again, be sure to underline only the most important points and to put a check mark by the material you find difficult to understand.

5. After you have completed the entire textbook chapter, take a break. Then read only what you have underlined throughout the entire chapter.

6. Now concentrate on the difficult material, for which you have left check marks. Reread this material and *think about it*; you will find that it is very exciting to figure out difficult material on your own.

7. Now do the True-False Questions, Fill-In Questions, and Multiple-Choice Questions. Compare your answers with those at the back of this book. Make a note of the questions you have missed and find the pages in your textbook upon which these questions are based. If you still don't understand, ask your instructor.

8. If you still have time, do one or both of the essay questions.

9. Before your examination, study your class notes. Then review the chapter outline in the text. Reread the Chapter Outline in this *Study Guide*, then redo all of the questions within each chapter. Compare your answers with the answers at the back of this *Study Guide*. Identify your problem areas and reread the relevant pages in **The Legal Environment of Business, Eighth Edition.** Think through the answers on your own.

If you have followed the strategy outlined above, you should feel sufficiently confident and be relaxed enough to do well on your exam.

Study Skills for *The Legal Environment of Business,* Eighth Edition

Every student has a different way to study. We give several study hints below that we think will help any student to master the textbook **The Legal Environment of Business, Eighth Edition.** These skills involve outlining, marking, taking notes, and summarizing. You may not need to use all these skills. Nonetheless, if you do improve your ability to use them, you will be able to understand more easily the information in **The Legal Environment of Business, Eighth Edition.**

MAKING AN OUTLINE

An outline is simply a method for organizing information. The reason an outline can be helpful is that it shows how concepts relate to each other. Outlining can be done as part of your reading or at the end of your reading, or as a rereading of each section within a chapter before you go on to the next section. Even if you do not believe that you need to outline, our experience has been that the act of *physically* writing an outline for a chapter helps most students to improve greatly their ability to retain the material in **The Legal Environment of Business, Eighth Edition** and master it, thereby obtaining a higher grade in the class, with less effort.

To make an effective outline you have to be selective. Outlines that contain all the information in the text are not very useful. Your objective in outlining is to identify main concepts and to subordinate details to those main concepts. Therefore, your first goal is to *identify the main concepts in each section*. Often the large, first-level headings within your textbook are sufficient as identifiers of the major concepts within each section. You may decide, however, that you want to phrase an identifier in a way that is more meaningful to you. In any event, your outline should consist of several levels written in a standard outline format. The most important concepts are assigned a roman numeral; the second most important a capital letter; the third most important, numbers; and the fourth most important, lower-case letters. Even if you make an outline that is no more than the headings in the text, you will be studying more efficiently than you would be otherwise. As we stated above, the process of physically writing the words will help you master the material.

MARKING A TEXT

From kindergarten through high school you typically did not own your own textbooks. They were made available by the school system. You were told not to mark in them. Now that you own your own text for a course, your learning can be greatly improved by marking your text. There is a trade-off here. The more you mark up your textbook, the less you will receive from your bookstore when you sell it back at the end of the semester. The benefit is a better understanding of the subject matter, and the cost is the reduction in the price you receive for the resale of the text. Additionally, if you want a text that you can mark with your own notations, you necessarily have to buy a new one or a used one that has no markings. Both carry a higher price tag than a used textbook with markings. Again there is a trade-off.

Different Ways of Marking   The most commonly used form of marking is to underline important points. The second most commonly used method is to use a felt-tipped highlighter, or marker, in yellow or some other transparent color. Marking also includes circling, numbering, using arrows, brief notes, or any other method that allows you to remember things when you go back to skim the pages in your textbook prior to an exam.

Why Marking Is Important   Marking is important for the same reason that outlining is—it helps you to organize the information in the text. It allows you to become an *active* participant in the mastery of the material. Researchers have shown that the physical act of marking, just like the physical act of outlining, helps you better retain the material. The better the material is organized in your mind, the more you will remember. There are two types of readers—passive and active. The active reader outlines or marks. Active readers typically do better on exams. Perhaps one of the reasons that active readers retain more is because the physical act of outlining and/or marking requires greater concentration. It is through greater concentration that more is remembered.

Points to Remember When Marking

1. Read one section at a time before you do any extensive marking. You can't mark a section until you know what is important and you can't know what is important until you read the whole section.

2. Don't over mark. Just as an outline cannot contain everything that is in a text (or in a lecture), marking can't be of the whole book. Don't fool yourself into thinking you've done a good job just because each page is filled up with arrows, asterisks, circles, and underlines. When you go back to review the material you won't remember what was important. The key is *selective* activity. Mark each page in a way that allows you to see the most important points at a glance. You can follow up your marking by writing out more in your subject outline.

HOW TO STUDY AND TAKE EXAMS

There is basically one reason why you have purchased the *Study Guide*—to improve your exam grade. By using this *Study Guide* assiduously, you will have the confidence to take your mid-terms and final examinations and to do well. The *Study Guide*, however, should not just be used a day before each exam. Rather, the guide is most helpful if you use it at the time that you read the chapter. That is to say, after you read a chapter in ***The Legal Environment of Business,* Eighth Edition** you should directly go to the appropriate chapter in the *Study Guide*. This systematic review technique is the most effective study technique you can use.

Besides learning the concepts in each chapter as well as possible, there are additional strategies for taking exams. You need to know in advance what type of exam you are going to take—essay or objective or both. You need to know which reading materials and lectures will be covered. For both objective and essay exams (but more importantly for the former) you need to know if there is a penalty for guessing incorrectly. If there is, your strategy will be different: you will usually only mark what you are certain of. Finally, you need to know how much time will be allowed for the exam.

FOLLOWING DIRECTIONS

Students are often in a hurry to start an exam so they take little time to read the instructions. The instructions can be critical, however. In a multiple-choice exam, for example, if there is no indication that there is a penalty for guessing, then you should never leave a question unanswered. Even if there only remains a few minutes at the end of the exam, you should guess for those questions about which you are uncertain.

Additionally, you need to know the weight given to each section of an exam. In a typical multiple-choice exam, all questions have equal weight. In some exams, particularly those involving essay questions, different parts of the exam carry different weights. You should use these weights to apportion your time accordingly. If an essay part of an exam accounts for only 20 percent of the total points on the exam, you should not spend 60 percent of your time on the essay.

You need to make sure you are answering the question correctly. Some exams require a No. 2 lead pencil to fill in the dots on a machine-graded answer sheet. Other exams require underlining or circling. In short, you have to look at the instructions carefully.

Lastly, check to make sure that you have all the pages of the examination. If you are uncertain, ask the instructor or the exam proctor. It is hard to justify not having done your exam correctly because you failed to answer all the questions. Simply stating that you did not have them will pose a problem for both you and your instructor. Don't take a chance. Double check to make sure.

TAKING OBJECTIVE EXAMINATIONS

The most important point to discover initially with any objective test is if there is a penalty for guessing. If there is none, you have nothing to lose by guessing. In contrast, if a half-point is subtracted for each incorrect answer, then you probably should not answer any question for which you are purely guessing.

Students usually commit one of two errors when they read objective-exam questions: (1) they read things into the questions that don't exist, or (2) they skip over words or phrases.

Most test questions include key words such as:

- all
- always
- never
- only

If you miss these key words you will be missing the "trick" part of the question. Also, you must look for questions that are only *partly* correct, particularly if you are answering true/false questions.

Never answer a question without reading all of the alternatives. More than one of them may be correct. If more than one of them seems correct, make sure you select the answer that seems the most correct.

Whenever the answer to an objective question is not obvious, start with the process of elimination. Throw out the answers that are clearly incorrect. Even with objective exams in which there is a penalty for guessing, if you can throw out several obviously incorrect answers, then you may wish to guess among the remaining ones because your probability of choosing the correct answer is high.

Typically, the easiest way to eliminate incorrect answers is to look for those that are meaningless, illogical, or inconsistent. Often test authors put in choices that make perfect sense and are indeed true, but they are not the answer to the question under study.

Acknowledgments

We wish to thank Suzanne Jasin of K & M Consulting for her expert design and composition of this guide.

We welcome comments and criticisms to help us make this guide even more useful. All errors are our sole responsibility.

Roger LeRoy Miller
Eric Hollowell

Chapter 1
Business and Its Legal Environment

WHAT THIS CHAPTER IS ABOUT

The first chapters in Unit 1 provide the background for the entire course. Chapter 1 sets the stage. From this chapter, you must understand that (1) the law is a set of general rules, (2) in applying these general rules, a judge cannot fit a case to suit a rule, but must fit (or find) a rule to suit the case, and (3) in fitting (or finding) a rule, a judge must also supply reasons for the decision.

CHAPTER OUTLINE

I. WHAT IS LAW?

Law consists of enforceable rules governing relationships among individuals and between individuals and their society.

II. BUSINESS ACTIVITIES AND THE LEGAL ENVIRONMENT

The law is split into different topics to make it easier to study, but more than one of those areas of the law can affect individual business decisions. Whether an activity is ethical is an important part of deciding whether to engage in it, but simply complying with the law may not meet all ethical obligations.

III. SOURCES OF AMERICAN LAW

A. CONSTITUTIONAL LAW

The U.S. Constitution distributes power among the branches of government. It is the supreme law of the land. Any law that conflicts with it is invalid. The states also have constitutions, but the federal constitution prevails.

B. STATUTORY LAW

Statutes and ordinances are enacted by Congress and by state and local legislative bodies. Uniform laws (such as the Uniform Commercial Code) and model codes are created by panels of experts and scholars and adopted at the option of each state's legislature.

C. ADMINISTRATIVE LAW

Administrative law consists of the rules and regulations issued by administrative agencies, which derive their authority from the legislative and executive branches of government.

D. CASE LAW AND COMMON LAW DOCTRINES

Case law includes courts' interpretations of constitutional provisions, statutes, and administrative rules. Because statutes often codify common law rules, courts often rely on the common law as a guide to the intent and purpose of a statute. Case law governs all areas not covered by statutes.

IV. THE COMMON LAW TRADITION

The American legal system, based on the decisions judges make in cases, is a common law system, which involves the application of principles applied in earlier cases with similar facts. This system

1

comes from early English courts, which made a distinction between remedies at law and remedies in equity.

A. REMEDIES AT LAW AND REMEDIES IN EQUITY
As a rule, courts grant an equitable remedy only if the remedy at law is inadequate.

1. Remedies at Law
Remedies at law include awards of land, money, and items of value. A jury trial is available only in an action at law.

2. Remedies in Equity
Remedies in equity include decrees of specific performance, injunctions, and rescission. Decisions to award equitable remedies are guided by equitable maxims.

B. THE DOCTRINE OF *STARE DECISIS*
The use of precedent as binding authority in a common law system is the doctrine of *stare decisis*. *Stare decisis* makes the legal system more efficient, just, uniform, stable, and predictable.

1. Departures from Precedent
A judge may decide that a precedent is incorrect if there have been changes in technology, business practices, or society's attitudes.

2. When There Is No Precedent
When there is no precedent, a court may look at other legal principles and policies, social values, or scientific data.

C. LEGAL REASONING

1. Issue-Rule-Application-Conclusion (IRAC)
Legal reasoning requires learning the facts of a case, identifying the issues and the relevant legal rules, applying the rules to the facts, and coming to a conclusion.

2. Forms of Legal Reasoning
In applying an old precedent or establishing a new one, judges use many forms of reasoning—deductive reasoning, linear reasoning, reasoning by analogy, and others—to harmonize their decisions with earlier cases.

V. SCHOOLS OF JURISPRUDENTIAL THOUGHT
Judges interpret and apply the law. When the law is expressed in general terms, there is some flexibility in interpreting it. This interpretation can be influenced by a judge's personal philosophy. Legal philosophies include the following.

A. THE NATURAL LAW SCHOOL
Natural law is a system of moral and ethical principles that are believed to be inherent in human nature and discoverable by humans through the use of their natural intelligence.

B. THE POSITIVIST SCHOOL
Legal positivists believe that there is no higher law than a nation's positive law (the law created by a particular society at a particular point in time). The law is the law and must be obeyed.

C. THE HISTORICAL SCHOOL
Followers of this school focus on legal principles that have been applied in past cases, emphasizing that those principles should be applied strictly in present cases.

D. LEGAL REALISM
Legal realists believe that in making decisions, judges are influenced by their own beliefs, the application of principles should be tempered by each case's circumstances, and extra-legal sources should be consulted.

VI. CLASSIFICATIONS OF LAW

A. SUBSTANTIVE LAW AND PROCEDURAL LAW
Substantive law includes laws that define, describe, regulate, and create rights and duties. *Procedural law* includes rules for enforcing those rights.

B. PRIVATE LAW AND PUBLIC LAW
Private law concerns relationships between private entities. *Public law* addresses the relationship between persons and their government.

C. CIVIL LAW AND CRIMINAL LAW
Civil law regulates relationships between individuals. *Criminal law* regulates relationships between individuals and society.

D. CYBERLAW
Cyberlaw is the emerging body of law (court decisions, new and amended statutes, etc.) that governs cyberspace transactions.

VII. HOW TO FIND PRIMARY SOURCES OF LAW

A. FINDING STATUTORY LAW

1. Publication of Statutes
Federal statutes are arranged by date of enactment in *United States Statutes at Large*. State statutes are collected in similar state publications. Statutes are also published in codified form (the form in which they appear in the federal and state codes) in other publications.

2. Finding a Statute in a Publication
Statutes are usually referred to in their codified form. In the codes, laws are compiled by subject. For example, the *United States Code* (U.S.C.) arranges by subject most federal laws. Each subject is assigned a title number and each statute a section number within a title.

B. FINDING ADMINISTRATIVE LAW

1. Publication of Rules and Regulations
Rules and regulations adopted by federal administrative agencies are published initially in the *Federal Register*. They are also compiled by subject in the *Code of Federal Regulations* (C.F.R.).

2. Finding a Rule or Regulation in a Publication
In the C.F.R., rules and regulations are arranged by subject. Each subject is assigned a title number and each rule or regulation a section number within a title.

C. FINDING CASE LAW

1. Publication of Court Opinions
State appellate court opinions are often published by the state in consecutively numbered volumes. They may also be published in units of the *National Reporter System*, by West Publishing Company. Federal court opinions appear in other West publications.

2. Finding a Court Opinion in a Publication
After a decision is published, it is usually referred to by the name of the case and the volume, name, and page number of one or more reporters (which are often, but not always, West reporters). This information is called the citation.

VIII. HOW TO READ AND UNDERSTAND CASE LAW

A. THE PARTIES

1. **Plaintiff v. Defendant**
   In the title of a case (*Alpha v. Beta*), the *v.* means versus (against). Alpha is the plaintiff (the party who filed the suit) and Beta the defendant. Some appellate courts place the name of the party appealing a decision first, so this case on appeal may be called *Beta v. Alpha*.

2. **Appellant v. Appellee**
   The appellant is the party who appeals a case to another court or jurisdiction from the one in which the case was originally brought. An appellant may be referred to as a petitioner. The appellee is the party against whom an appeal is taken. An appellee may be referred to as a respondent.

B. THE COURT'S OPINION
The opinion contains the court's reasons for its decision, the rules of law that apply, and the judgment.

1. **Unanimous Opinion**
   When more than one judge (or justice) decides a case, and they all agree, a unanimous opinion is written for the whole court.

2. **Majority Opinion**
   If a decision is not unanimous, a majority opinion outlines the views of the majority.

3. **Concurring Opinion**
   A concurring opinion is one in which a judge emphasizes a point that was not emphasized in the unanimous or majority opinion.

4. **Dissenting Opinion**
   A dissenting opinion may be written by a judge who does not agree with the majority. A dissent may form the basis of arguments used years later in overruling the majority opinion.

TRUE-FALSE QUESTIONS

(Answers at the Back of the Book)

____ **1.** Law is a body of enforceable rules governing relationships among individuals and between individuals and their society.

____ **2.** Legal positivists believe that law should reflect universal principles that are part of human nature.

____ **3.** The doctrine of *stare decisis* obligates judges to follow precedents established within their jurisdictions.

____ **4.** Common law develops from rules of law announced in court decisions.

____ **5.** Statutory law is legislation.

____ **6.** A federal statute takes precedence over the U.S. Constitution.

____ **7.** Congress enacted the Uniform Commercial Code for adoption by the states.

____ **8.** Criminal law covers disputes between persons, and between persons and their governments.

____ **9.** In most states, the same courts can grant legal or equitable remedies.

____ **10.** A citation includes the name of the judge who decided the case.

FILL-IN QUESTIONS

(Answers at the Back of the Book)

The common law system, on which the American legal system is based, involves the application of principles applied in earlier cases _____ (with similar facts/whether or not the facts are similar). This use of previous case law, or _____ (precedent/preeminent), is known as the doctrine of *stare decisis*, and _____ (emphasizes a flexible/permits a predictable) resolution of cases.

MULTIPLE-CHOICE QUESTIONS

(Answers at the Back of the Book)

____ **1.** Tonya is a legal positivist. Tonya believes that

  a. the law should be applied the same in all cases in all circumstances.
  b. the law should reflect universal principles that are part of human nature.
  c. the law should strictly follow decisions made in past cases.
  d. the written law of a society at a particular time is most significant.

____ **2.** In a suit between Best Products, Inc., and Central Sales Corporation, the court applies the doctrine of *stare decisis*. This means that the court follows rules of law established by

  a. all courts.
  b. courts of higher rank only.
  c. courts of lower rank only.
  d. no courts.

____ **3.** In a suit between Delta Fishing Company and Rivermouth Trawlers, Inc., the court applies the doctrine of *stare decisis*. This requires the court to find cases that, compared to the case before it, has

  a. entirely different facts.
  b. no facts, only conclusions of law.
  c. precisely identical facts.
  d. similar facts.

____ **4.** In a suit between Retail Sales Company and Shoppers Mall, Inc., the court orders a *rescission*. This is

  a. an action to cancel a contract and return the parties to the positions they held before the contract was made.
  b. an award of damages.
  c. an order to do or refrain from doing a particular act.
  d. an order to perform what was promised.

____ **5.** In a given case, most courts may grant

  a. equitable or legal remedies, but not both.
  b. equitable remedies, legal remedies, or both.
  c. equitable remedies only.
  d. legal remedies only.

____   **6.** The U.S. Constitution takes precedence over

    a. a provision in a state constitution or statute only.
    b. a state supreme court decision only.
    c. a state constitution, statute, and court decision.
    d. none of the choices.

____   **7.** Case law includes interpretations of federal and state

    a. administrative rules and statutes only.
    b. administrative rules, statutes, and constitutions.
    c. constitutions only.
    d. none of the choices.

____   **8.** Civil law concerns

    a. disputes between persons, and between persons and their governments.
    b. only laws that define, describe, regulate, and create rights and duties.
    c. only laws that establish methods for enforcing rights.
    d. wrongs committed against society for which society demands redress.

____   **9.** Michael is a judge. To reason by analogy, Michael compares the facts in one case to

    a. an impartial third party's review.
    b. the facts in another case.
    c. the defendant's arguments.
    d. the plaintiff's hypothetical.

____   **10.** A concurring opinion, written by one of the judges who decide a case before a multi-judge panel, is

    a. an opinion that is written for the entire court.
    b. an opinion that outlines only the views of the majority.
    c. a separate opinion that agrees with the court's ruling but for different reasons.
    d. a separate opinion that does not agree with court's ruling.

SHORT ESSAY QUESTIONS

1. What is the primary function of law?

2. What is *stare decisis*? Why is it important?

GAMEPOINTS
(Answers at the Back of the Book)

1. You see a spot in the market for a video game outlet. You open "GameBox" to profit from local sales, rentals, and exchanges. Hott Games Company promises to ship a certain assortment of games and gear for your grand opening. Despite this contract, Hott does not ship as agreed, and your opener is a bust, costing you a lot of money. Into which category of the law does Hott's breach of your contract fall? Which remedies, if any, are available to you?

2. You're a fan of the "Gods & Warriors" (GW) video game series. On the issue of GWX, you pick up your reserved copy and eagerly put it in your player. Anticipating a great game, you find instead that the graphics are two-dimensional, the response to your commands is slow, and the sound is out of synch. The game has to be rebooted repeatedly in mid-play. Which sources of the law are most likely to afford you an opportunity for relief, and why?

Chapter 2
The Court System

WHAT THIS CHAPTER IS ABOUT

This chapter explains which courts have power to hear what disputes and when. The chapter also covers the judicial process—the application of procedural rules and what happens before, during, and after a civil trial.

CHAPTER OUTLINE

I. THE JUDICIARY'S ROLE IN AMERICAN GOVERNMENT

Under the power of judicial review, the courts can decide whether the laws or actions of the executive branch and the legislative branch are constitutional.

II. BASIC JUDICIAL REQUIREMENTS

A. JURISDICTION

To hear a case, a court must have jurisdiction over (1) the defendant or the property involved and (2) the subject matter.

1. Jurisdiction over Persons or Property

A court has *in personam* (personal) jurisdiction over persons within the court's geographic area. A court has *in rem* jurisdiction over property within its area.

a. Long Arm Statutes

A court's power is limited to the territorial boundaries of the state in which it is located, but in some cases, a state's long arm statute gives a court jurisdiction over a nonresident.

b. Corporate Contacts

A corporation is subject to the jurisdiction of the courts in any state in which it is incorporated, in which it has its main office, or in which it does business.

2. Jurisdiction over Subject Matter

A court of general jurisdiction can decide virtually any type of case. A court's jurisdiction may be limited by the subject of a suit, the amount of money in controversy, or whether a proceeding is a trial or an appeal.

3. Jurisdiction of the Federal Courts

a. Federal Questions

Any suit based on the Constitution, a treaty, or a federal law can originate in a federal court.

b. Diversity of Citizenship

Federal jurisdiction covers cases involving (1) citizens of different states, (2) a foreign government and citizens of a state or of different states, or (3) citizens of a state and citizens or subjects of a foreign government. The amount in controversy must be more than $75,000.

4. Exclusive v. Concurrent Jurisdiction

Exclusive: when cases can be tried only in federal courts or only in state courts. Concurrent: When both federal and state courts can hear a case.

9

B. JURISDICTION IN CYBERSPACE

Whether a court can compel the appearance of a party outside the geographic area of the court's jurisdiction depends on the amount of business the party transacts over the Internet with parties within the court's area ("sliding scale" test). Internationally, the minimum contacts test mentioned above generally applies.

C. VENUE

Venue is concerned with the most appropriate location for a trial.

D. STANDING TO SUE

Standing is the interest (injury or threat) that a plaintiff has in a case. A plaintiff must have standing to bring a suit, and the controversy must be justiciable (real, as opposed to hypothetical or purely academic).

III. THE STATE AND FEDERAL COURT SYSTEMS

A. THE STATE COURT SYSTEMS

1. Trial Courts

Trial courts are courts in which trials are held and testimony is taken.

2. Appellate Courts

Courts that hear appeals from trial courts look at *questions of law* (what law governs a dispute) but not *questions of fact* (what occurred in the dispute), unless a trial court's finding of fact is clearly contrary to the evidence. Decision of a state's highest court on state law is final.

B. THE FEDERAL COURT SYSTEM

1. U.S. District Courts

The federal equivalent of a state trial court of general jurisdiction. There is at least one federal district court in every state. Other federal trial courts include the U.S. Tax Court and the U.S. Bankruptcy Court.

2. U.S. Courts of Appeals

The U.S. (circuit) courts of appeals for twelve of the circuits hear appeals from the federal district courts located within their respective circuits. The court of appeals for the thirteenth circuit (the federal circuit) has national jurisdiction over certain cases.

3. United States Supreme Court

The highest level of the federal court system. The Supreme Court can review any case decided by any of the federal courts of appeals, and it has authority over some cases decided in state courts.

4. Appeals to the Supreme Court

To appeal a case to the Supreme Court, a party asks for a writ of *certiorari*. Whether the Court issues the writ is within its discretion.

IV. JUDICIAL PROCEDURES: FOLLOWING A CASE THROUGH THE COURTS

A. PROCEDURAL RULES

The Federal Rules of Civil Procedure govern trials in federal district court. Each state has its own rules of procedure that apply in its courts, as well as to the federal courts within the state. The litigation process has three phases: pretrial, trial, and posttrial.

B. CONSULT WITH AN ATTORNEY

The time and expense of litigation are important considerations when deciding what course to pursue. Attorney fees can be fixed, may accrue on an hourly or a contingency basis, or may be set by a judge.

V. PRETRIAL PROCEDURES

A. THE PLEADINGS

The pleadings inform each party of the claims of the other and specify the issues in the case. They include the complaint and answer (and counterclaim and reply).

1. The Plaintiff's Complaint

Filed by the plaintiff with the clerk of the trial court (with the proper venue). The complaint contains (1) a statement alleging the facts necessary for the court to take jurisdiction, (2) a short statement of the facts necessary to show that the plaintiff is entitled to a remedy, and (3) a statement of the remedy the plaintiff is seeking.

2. Service of Process

The complaint is delivered to the defendant, with a summons. The summons tells the defendant to answer the complaint and file a copy of the answer with the court and the plaintiff within a specified time (usually twenty to thirty days).

3. Method of Service

Corporations receive service through their officers or registered agents.

4. Waiver of Formal Service of Process

In federal cases, service can be waived.

5. The Defendant's Response

a. Answer

An answer admits the allegations in the complaint or denies them and sets out any defenses.

1) Affirmative Defense

Exists when the defendant admits the truth of the complaint but raises new facts to dismiss the action (for example, the time period for raising the claim has passed).

2) Counterclaim

This is the defendant's claim against the plaintiff, who will have to answer it with a reply, which has the same characteristics as an answer.

b. Motion to Dismiss

This motion alleges that even if the facts in the complaint are true, their legal consequences are such that there is no reason to go on with the suit and no need for the defendant to present an answer.

1) Denial of the Motion

If the court denies the motion, and the defendant does not file a further pleading, a judgment will be entered for the plaintiff.

2) Grant of the Motion

If the court grants the motion, the defendant is not required to answer the complaint. If the plaintiff does not file an amended complaint, a judgment will be entered for the defendant.

c. No Response

Results in a judgment for the plaintiff (who is awarded the relief sought in the complaint).

B. DISMISSALS AND JUDGMENTS BEFORE TRIAL

1. Motion to Dismiss

(See above.) Either party may file a motion to dismiss if they have agreed to settle the case. A court may file such a motion on its own.

2. **Motion for Judgment on the Pleadings**
Any party can file this motion (after the complaint, answer, and any counterclaim and reply have been filed), when no facts are disputed and only questions of law are at issue. A court may consider only those facts stated in the pleadings.

3. **Motion for Summary Judgment**
Any party can file this motion, if there is no disagreement about the facts and the only question is which laws apply to those facts. A court can consider evidence outside the pleadings (for example, sworn statements by witnesses).

C. DISCOVERY

1. **What Discovery Is**
Discovery is the process of obtaining information from the opposing party or from witnesses. Privileged material is safeguarded and only relevant matters are discoverable.

   a. **Discovery Rules**
   Discovery is allowed concerning any information that is relevant to any party's claim or defense. Of course, parties are protected from undue harassment, and privileged or confidential information is protected from disclosure.

   b. **Depositions**
   Sworn testimony, recorded by a court official. Can be used as testimony, if a witness is unavailable, or to impeach (challenge the credibility of) a party or witness who testifies differently at trial.

   c. **Interrogatories**
   A series of written questions for which written answers are prepared and signed under oath. Interrogatories are directed to the plaintiff or the defendant.

   d. **Request for Admissions**
   A written request to a party for an admission of the truth of matters relating to the trial. Any matter admitted is considered to be true.

   e. **Request for Documents, Objects, and Entry on Land**
   A written request to examine documents and other items not in the party's possession.

   f. **Request for Examinations**
   Granted when a party's physical or mental condition is in question.

   g. **Electronic Discovery**
   Relevant information stored electronically cane be the subject of a discovery request.

2. **What Discovery Does**
Discovery allows both parties to learn as much as they can about what to expect at a trial and helps to narrow the issues so that trial time is spent on the main questions.

D. PRETRIAL CONFERENCE

After discovery, the attorneys may meet with the judge to discuss resolving the case or at least to clarify the issues and agree on such things as the number of expert witnesses or the admissibility of certain types of evidence.

E. JURY SELECTION

Most civil matters can be heard by six-person juries. Some trials must be heard by twelve persons.

1. *Voir Dire*
The process by which a jury is selected. The parties' attorneys ask prospective jurors questions to determine whether any are biased or have a connection with a party or a witness.

    2. **Challenges**

      a. **Peremptory Challenge**
      Asking, without providing a reason, that an individual not be sworn in as a juror.

      b. **Challenge for Cause**
      Asking, for a specific reason, that an individual not be sworn in as a juror.

VI. THE TRIAL

A. OPENING STATEMENTS
Each side sets out briefly his or her version of the facts and outlines the evidence that will be presented. The plaintiff goes first.

B. RULES OF EVIDENCE
These rules ensure that evidence presented during a trial is fair and reliable.

C. PRESENTATION OF EVIDENCE

1. Burden of Proof
In a civil case, a plaintiff must prove his or her case by a **preponderance of the evidence** (the claim is more likely to be true than the defendant's). Some claims (such as fraud) must be proved by **clear and convincing evidence** (the truth of the claim is highly probable). Evidence includes the testimony of witnesses.

2. Admissible Evidence
Evidence that is relevant to the matter in question (tends to prove or disprove a fact in question or to establish that a fact or action is more probable or less probable than it would be without the evidence).

3. Inadmissible Evidence
Relevant evidence whose probative value is substantially outweighed by other considerations (the issue has been proved or disproved, or the evidence would mislead the jury, or cause the jury to decide the issue on an emotional basis). Hearsay is not admissible.

4. Examination of Witnesses

    a. **Plaintiff's Evidence**
    After the opening statements, the plaintiff calls and questions the first witness (direct examination); the defendant questions the witness (cross-examination); the plaintiff questions the witness again (redirect examination); the defendant follows (recross-examination). The plaintiff's other witnesses are then called.

    b. **Defendant's Evidence**

      1) **Motion for a Directed Verdict**
      At the conclusion of the plaintiff's case, the defendant can ask the judge to direct a verdict for the defendant on the ground that the plaintiff presented no evidence that would justify granting the plaintiff relief. The judge grants the motion if there is insufficient evidence to raise an issue of fact.

      2) **Defendant's Witnesses**
      If the motion is denied, the defendant calls the witnesses for his or her side of the case (and there is direct, cross-, redirect, and recross-examination). At the end of the defendant's case, either side can move for a directed verdict.

    c. **Rebuttal**
    At the conclusion of the defendant's case, the plaintiff can present a rebuttal (additional evidence to refute the defendant's case).

 d. Rejoinder
 The defendant can refute the plaintiff's rebuttal in a rejoinder.

D. CLOSING ARGUMENTS

Each side summarizes briefly his or her version of the facts, outlines the evidence that supports his or her case, and reveals the shortcomings of the points made by the other party. The plaintiff goes first.

E. JURY INSTRUCTIONS

In a jury trial, the judge instructs (charges) the jury in the law that applies to the case. The jurors may disregard the facts as stated in the charge, but they are not free to ignore the statements of law. (A reviewing court ordinarily remands a case for a new trial if a judge misstates the law in the jury instructions.)

F. JURY VERDICT

In a jury trial, the jury specifies the factual findings and the amount of damages to be paid by the losing party. This is the verdict. After it is announced, the trial is ended, and the jurors are discharged.

VII. POSTTRIAL MOTIONS

A. MOTION FOR A JUDGMENT IN ACCORDANCE WITH THE VERDICT
The prevailing party usually files this motion.

B. MOTION FOR A NEW TRIAL
This motion is granted if the judge believes that the jury erred but that it is not appropriate to grant a judgment for the other side (for example, the jury verdict resulted from a misapplication of the law or misunderstanding of the evidence, or there is newly discovered evidence, misconduct by the parties, or error by the judge).

C. MOTION FOR JUDGMENT *N.O.V.*
The defendant can file this motion, if he or she previously moved for a directed verdict (*n.o.v.* is from the Latin *non obstante veredicto,* "notwithstanding the verdict;" federal courts use "motion for judgment as a matter of law"). The judge will grant this motion if the jury's verdict was unreasonable and erroneous.

VIII. THE APPEAL

A. FILING THE APPEAL
The papers to be filed include—

1. Notice of Appeal
The appellant (the losing party—or the winning party, if that party is dissatisfied with the relief obtained) must file a notice of appeal with the clerk of the trial court within a certain period of time.

2. Record on Appeal
The appellant files in the reviewing court: (1) the pleadings, (2) a transcript of the trial and copies of the exhibits, (3) the judge's rulings on the parties' motions, (4) the arguments of counsel, (5) the jury instructions, (6) the verdict, (7) the posttrial motions, and (8) the judgment order from which the appeal is taken.

3. Brief
The appellant files with the abstract a brief, which contains (1) a short statement of the facts; (2) a statement of the issues; (3) the rulings by the trial court that the appellant contends are erroneous and prejudicial; (4) the grounds for reversal of the judgment; (5) a statement of the applicable law; and (6) arguments on the appellant's behalf, citing applicable statutes and relevant cases.

4. **Reply**
   The appellee (respondent) may file an answering brief.

B. **APPELLATE REVIEW**
   Appellate courts do not usually reverse findings of fact unless they are contradicted by evidence at the trial. An appellate court can **affirm, reverse,** or **modify** a trial court's decision, or **remand** the case to the trial court for further proceedings consistent with the appellate court's opinion.

C. **HIGHER APPELLATE COURTS**
   If the reviewing court is an intermediate appellate court, the case may be appealed to the state supreme court. The state supreme court can affirm, reverse, or remand. If a federal question is involved, the case may be appealed to the United States Supreme Court, which may agree to hear it. Otherwise, the case is ended.

IX. ENFORCING THE JUDGMENT

The court can order a sheriff to seize property owned by the defendant and hold it until the defendant pays the judgment owed to the plaintiff. If the defendant fails to pay, the property can be sold at an auction and the proceeds given to the plaintiff, or the property can be transferred to the plaintiff in lieu of payment.

TRUE-FALSE QUESTIONS

(Answers at the Back of the Book)

____ 1. Under a long arm statute, a state court can compel someone outside the state to appear in the court.

____ 2. Doing substantial business in a jurisdiction over the Internet can be enough to support a court's jurisdiction over a nonresident defendant.

____ 3. The United States Supreme Court is the final authority for any case decided by a state court.

____ 4. Suits involving federal questions originate in federal district courts.

____ 5. Pleadings consist of a complaint, an answer, and a motion to dismiss.

____ 6. In ruling on a motion for summary judgment, a court cannot consider evidence outside the pleadings.

____ 7. An answer may admit or deny the statements or allegations in a complaint.

____ 8. Before a trial, if there are no issues of fact, a court may grant a summary judgment.

____ 9. Only a losing party may appeal to a higher court.

____ 10. A motion for a new trial is granted if a jury verdict is the obvious result of a misapplication of the law.

FILL-IN QUESTIONS

(Answers at the Back of the Book)

Courts of original jurisdiction are _____ (trial/reviewing) courts. Courts of appellate jurisdiction are _____ (trial/reviewing) courts. Trial courts resolve disputes through determining _____ (factual issues/the law) and applying _____ (the facts to the law/ the law to the facts). Reviewing courts most commonly reverse cases on the basis of errors

_____ (of law but not of fact/of fact and of law) committed by lower courts within the same system.

MULTIPLE-CHOICE QUESTIONS

(Answers at the Back of the Book)

____ **1.** Matrix Corporation, which is based in Texas, advertises on the Web. A court in Illinois would be most likely to exercise jurisdiction over Matrix if the firm

a. conducted substantial business with Illinois residents at its site.
b. interacted with any Illinois resident through its Web site.
c. only advertised passively at its Web site.
d. all of the choices.

____ **2.** Centre Hotels Corporation was incorporated in Delaware, has its main office in New Jersey, and does business in New York. Centre is subject to the jurisdiction of

a. Delaware, New Jersey, or New York.
b. Delaware or New Jersey only.
c. Delaware or New York only.
d. New Jersey or New York only.

____ **3.** Saf-T Packaging, Inc., loses its suit against Medico Equipment Corporation. Saf-T's best ground for an appeal is the trial court's interpretation of

a. the conduct of the witnesses during the trial.
b. the credibility of the evidence that Top presented.
c. the dealings between the parties before the suit.
d. the law that applied to the issues in the case.

____ **4.** Jin files a suit against Keyes, and loses. Jin appeals, and loses again. The United States Supreme Court is

a. required to hear the case if Jin appeals again.
b. required to hear the case if Jin lost in a federal court.
c. required to hear the case if Jin lost in a state court.
d. not required to hear the case.

____ **5.** Gulf Coast Realty Company, which is based in Florida, owns commercial property in Georgia. A dispute arises over the ownership of the property with Hashmi, a resident of Alabama. Hashmi files a suit against Gulf Coast Realty in Georgia. In this suit, Georgia has

a. diversity jurisdiction.
b. *in personam* jurisdiction.
c. *in rem* jurisdiction.
d. no jurisdiction.

____ **6.** Levonne sues Mikayla in a state trial court. Levonne loses the suit. If Levonne wants to appeal, the most appropriate court in which to file the appeal is

a. the state appellate court.
b. the nearest federal district court.
c. the nearest federal court of appeals.
d. the United States Supreme Court.

_____ 7. Jasmine and Kedric are involved in an automobile accident. Lyle is a passenger in Kedric's car. Jasmine wants to ask Lyle, as a witness, some questions concerning the accident. Lyle's answers to the questions are given in

    a. a deposition.
    b. a response to interrogatories.
    c. a response to a judge's request at a pretrial conference.
    d. none of the choices.

_____ 8. Rianna files a suit against Salazar. At the trial, after Rianna calls and questions Timor

    a. Rianna calls his second witness.
    b. Rianna questions Timor again.
    c. Salazar calls her first witness.
    d. Salazar questions Timor.

_____ 9. The jury returns a verdict against Natural Reserve Corporation (NRC), in its suit against Overflow Waste, Inc. NRC can file a motion for

    a. a directed verdict.
    b. a judgment on the pleadings.
    c. a new trial or for a judgment notwithstanding the verdict.
    d. summary judgment.

_____ 10. ABC Sales Company wins its suit against DEF Products, Inc. After the entry of a judgment, an appeal may be filed by

    a. ABC only.
    b. Delta only.
    c. either ABC or Delta.
    d. neither ABC nor Delta.

SHORT ESSAY QUESTIONS

1. What is jurisdiction? How does jurisdiction over a person or property differ from subject matter jurisdiction?

2. What permits a court to exercise jurisdiction based on contacts over the Internet?

GAMEPOINTS

(Answers at the Back of the Book)

1. You're playing "AniMax," a video game in which you assume the identity of "Max," a resident of New Jersey with the power to morph into vicious animals to battle a variety of super- and sub-human beings. As a Siberian tiger, you confront a series of deadly reptiles released into the wilds of New York City by "The Trainer." If you were to file a lawsuit against your opponent, in which type of court could you initiate the action?

2. You're a game designer with the Xcite Now Games Corporation. Your company moves from Colorado to Texas to take advantage of the technical talent available in the Austin area. You sell your house and relocate your family, but Xcite Now discharges you less than two months later. You file a suit against the employer for reinstatement or at least damages. You lose the trial and appeal. The appellate court affirms the decision of the trial court. You want to appeal to the United States Supreme Court. Can the Court refuse to hear the case?

Chapter 3
Alternative and Online Dispute Resolution

WHAT THIS CHAPTER IS ABOUT

This chapter outlines alternatives to judicial resolution of legal controversies. These alternatives include negotiation, conciliation, mediation, arbitration, and online dispute resolution.

CHAPTER OUTLINE

I.   THE PROBLEMS OF COST AND COMPLEXITY
Reasons for methods of alternative dispute resolution (ADR) include the complexity of litigation (complex rules), its expense in time and money, and its lack of privacy.

II. THE SEARCH FOR ALTERNATIVES TO LITIGATION
ADR is any procedure or device for resolving disputes other than the traditional judicial process. Besides the solutions outlined elsewhere in this chapter, proposals include—

A. CAPS ON DAMAGE AWARDS
For pain and suffering, to deter some potential litigants from suing.

B. PENALIZING THOSE WHO BRING FRIVOLOUS LAWSUITS
Rule 11 of the Federal Rules of Civil Procedure allows for sanctions against lawyers and litigants who bring frivolous lawsuits in federal courts.

C. CASE-MANAGEMENT PLANS
These require courts to place cases on different tracks, to hear simple cases sooner.

D. POLITICS AND LAW
Congress required the federal courts to develop a plan to cut judicial costs and delays.

E. NEW METHODS AND ARRANGEMENTS
Alternatives to litigation include private forums for dispute resolution, caps on damage awards, penalties against those who bring frivolous lawsuits, and case-management plans.

III. NEGOTIATION AND MEDIATION
Nonadversarial in nature—the goal is to find grounds for agreement.

A. NEGOTIATION
Parties come together informally, with or without attorneys, to try to settle or resolve their differences without involving independent third parties. Forms of ADR associated with negotiation include—

1. Mini-trial
A private proceeding in which attorneys briefly argue each party's case. A third party indicates how a court would likely decide the issue.

19

2. Early Neutral Case Evaluation
Parties select a neutral third party (generally an expert) to evaluate their positions, with no hearing and no discovery. The evaluation is a basis for negotiating a settlement.

3. Summary Jury Trial (SJT)
Like a mini-trial, but a jury renders a nonbinding verdict. Negotiations must follow: If no settlement is reached, either side can seek a full trial.

4. Facilitation
A facilitator assists disputing parties in negotiating, communicating offers, etc. Conciliators sometimes recommend solutions.

B. MEDIATION
Parties come together informally with a mediator, who may propose solutions. A mediator is often an expert in a particular field and charges a fee. Results may or may not be binding.

1. Advantages of Mediation
Few procedural rules; proceedings can be made to fit the parties' needs; the parties reach agreement by consent; the parties select a mediator.

2. Disadvantages of Mediation
The mediator can only help the parties reach a decision, not make a decision for them; no deadline; no threat of sanctions if a party fails to negotiate in good faith.

IV. ARBITRATION
An arbitrator—the third party hearing the dispute—decides the dispute. The decision may (or may not) be legally binding. Disputes are often arbitrated because of an arbitration clause in a contract entered into before the dispute.

A. THE FEDERAL ARBITRATION ACT (FAA) OF 1925
Provides means for enforcing whatever arbitration procedure the parties agree on. Under the FAA, the parties can ask a federal district court to—

1. Compel Arbitration
The FAA enforces any arbitration clause in a contract that involves interstate commerce (which may include business activities only slightly connected to the flow of commerce) [Section 4].

2. Confirm the Arbitrator's Decision
One party obtains a court order directing another party to comply with the terms of the arbitrator's decision [Section 9].

3. Set Aside the Arbitrator's Decision
Grounds are limited to misconduct, fraud, corruption, or abuse of power in the arbitration process; a court will not review the merits of the dispute or the arbitrator's judgment [Section 10]. (See below.)

B. STATE ARBITRATION STATUTES
The states follow the federal approach to enforce voluntary agreements to arbitrate disputes between private parties. Most states require that (1) an agreement to submit a dispute to arbitration be in writing and (2) the submission be within a certain time of the dispute (generally six months).

C. THE ARBITRATION PROCESS
Unless a statute provides otherwise, the rights and duties of the parties are set by their agreement. (For example, by including a choice-of-law clause, they may have the law of a specific state govern their agreement.)

1. **Submission**
   Typically includes identities of the parties, nature of the dispute, monetary amounts involved, place at which arbitration is to occur, and a statement that parties intend to be bound by the arbitrator's award.

2. **The Hearing**
   The parties must decide on the issues and the arbitrator's powers. They may stipulate rules of procedure or have the arbitrator set rules. Typically, the parties present opening arguments and evidence, call and examine witnesses, and present closing arguments.

3. **The Award**
   This is the arbitrator's final decision. Under most statutes, an arbitrator must render an award within thirty days of the close of a hearing. In most states, the award must be in writing but does not need to state findings of fact or conclusions of law.

D. **ENFORCEMENT OF AGREEMENTS TO SUBMIT TO ARBITRATION**
As long as an agreement to submit to arbitration does not compel an illegal act or contravene public policy, a court will enforce it.

1. **The Issue of Arbitrability**
   A court can decide whether or not the parties agreed to submit a particular matter to arbitration (without ruling on the issue in dispute).

2. **Compulsory Arbitration Agreements**
   Generally, mandatory arbitration clauses in employment contracts are enforceable. In consumer contracts, mandatory arbitration clause will not be enforced if, as can occur with adhesion contracts, their enforcement would be unconscionable (manifestly unfair or oppressive).

E. **SETTING ASIDE AN ARBITRATION AWARD**
A losing party may appeal the arbitrator's award to a court.

1. **Fact Findings and Legal Conclusions**
   The arbitrator's factual findings and legal conclusions are normally conclusive. Whether the arbitrator erred is no basis for setting aside an award. A court will not look at the merits of a dispute, the sufficiency of the evidence, or the arbitrator's reasoning.

2. **Public Policy and Illegality**
   No award will be enforced if compliance would result in the commission of a crime, or conflict with or undermine public policy.

3. **Defects in the Arbitration Process**
   An award may be set aside if—

   a. The award was the result of corruption, fraud, or other "undue means" (such as a bribe or *ex parte* communications).

   b. The arbitrator exhibited bias or corruption.

   c. The arbitrator refused to postpone the hearing despite sufficient cause, refused to hear material evidence, or otherwise acted to substantially prejudice the rights of a party.

   d. The arbitrator exceeded his or her powers or failed to use them to make a mutual, final, and definite award.

4. **Waiver**
   A party may forfeit the right to challenge an award by failing to object to a defect in a timely manner.

5. **Conflicts of Law**
   Under the supremacy clause and the commerce clause of the U.S. Constitution, federal law has preeminence over state law. When there is a conflict, state law is preempted by federal

law. Thus, the strong federal policy favoring arbitration can override a state's laws that might be more favorable to litigation.

6. **Choice of Law**
The Federal Arbitration Act has been interpreted to allow parties to choose the law of a specific state to govern their arbitration agreement.

F. DISADVANTAGES OF ARBITRATION
The result can be unpredictable; arbitrators do not have to issue written opinions; arbitrators must decide disputes according to rules provided by the parties; arbitration can be as expensive as litigation; discovery is usually not available.

V.   THE INTEGRATION OF ADR AND COURT PROCEDURES

A. COURT-MANDATED ADR
Many, if not most, federal courts require parties to attempt to settle their differences through ADR before going to trial. Many states refer certain cases to ADR. Some states compel the arbitration of certain disputes.

B. COURT-ANNEXED ARBITRATION
Unlike voluntary arbitration, in court-annexed arbitration—

1. **Certain Disputes Are Not Arbitrable**
Disputes involving title to real estate or a court's equity powers are not arbitrable.

2. **No Discovery Without Court Approval**
After a hearing commences, a party who seeks discovery must usually secure approval from the court that mandated the arbitration.

3. **Rules of Evidence May Be Different**
Most states impose the same rules on arbitration hearings and trials. Others allow all relevant evidence whether or not it would be admissible at trial. Some leave it to the arbitrator to decide.

4. **A Court Can Review an Arbitrated Dispute** *De Novo*
Either party may reject an award for any reason; the case proceeds to trial, and the court considers all the evidence and legal questions as though no arbitration had occurred.

5. **Court Costs and Fees May Be Imposed**
Many statutes impose such expenses on a party who rejects an award but does not improve his or her position by going to trial.

C. COURT-RELATED MEDIATION
Mediation is often used in disputes in employment law, environmental law, product liability, and franchises. Advantages of mediation include lower cost, speed (one or two days), and resolutions that benefit both sides.

VI. ADR FORUMS AND SERVICES

A. NONPROFIT ORGANIZATIONS
The major source of private arbitration services is the American Arbitration Association (AAA). There exist many other state and local nonprofit organizations that provide arbitration services. Many industries—including the insurance, automobile, and securities industries—also now have mediation or arbitration programs to facilitate the timely and inexpensive settlement of claims.

B. FOR-PROFIT ORGANIZATIONS
For-profit organizations also act as mediators or arbitrators.

C. ONLINE ORGANIZATIONS
Many Web sites offer online dispute resolution (ODR) services to help resolve small- to medium-sized business liability claims.

1. **What Law Applies in an ODR Proceeding?**
   Most ODR services do not apply the law of a specific jurisdiction. Results are based on general, common legal principles.

2. **Negotiation and Mediation Services**
   A settlement may be negotiated through blind bidding: one party submits an offer to be shown to the other party if it falls within a previously agreed range. There is a limited time to respond.

D. **ARBITRATION PROGRAMS**
   The federal government set up Internet Corporation for Assigned Names and Numbers (ICANN) as a nonprofit corporation to oversee the distribution of domain names. ICANN has issued rules and authorized organizations to resolve related disputes.

VII. INTERNATIONAL DISPUTE RESOLUTION

To protect themselves, parties to international contracts may include special clauses, including a forum-selection clause (stating which jurisdiction will hear a dispute), a choice-of-law clause (stating which law applies), and an arbitration clause (stating that a dispute must go first to arbitration).

TRUE-FALSE QUESTIONS

(Answers at the Back of the Book)

____ 1. Most lawsuits go to trial.

____ 2. In mediation, a mediator makes a decision on the matter in dispute.

____ 3. A party to an arbitration agreement may never be compelled to arbitrate a dispute.

____ 4. The jury verdict, in a summary jury trial, is binding.

____ 5. A major similarity between negotiation and mediation is that no third parties are involved.

____ 6. In binding arbitration, an arbitrator's decision is usually the final word.

____ 7. In court-annexed arbitration, an award is final.

____ 8. The goal of arbitration is to come to a resolution that benefits both sides in a dispute.

____ 9. A losing party may appeal an arbitrator's award to a court.

____ 10. ADR resolves disputes by any method other than litigation.

FILL-IN QUESTIONS

(Answers at the Back of the Book)

_____ (Arbitration/Mediation/Negotiation) is the settling of a dispute by parties meeting informally, with or without attorneys, to discuss and resolve their differences without the involvement of independent third parties. _____ (Arbitration/Mediation/Negotiation) is the settling of a dispute by parties meeting informally with a third party, _____ (an arbitrator/ a mediator/ a negotiator), who assists the parties in reaching an agreement. _____ (Arbitration/Mediation/Negotiation) is the settling of a dispute by an impartial third party, _____ (an arbitrator/a mediator/a negotiator), who does more than assist the parties in resolving their dispute—he or she renders a decision that may be legally binding.

MULTIPLE-CHOICE QUESTIONS

(Answers at the Back of the Book)

____   1. Gabriella files a suit against Huey. Before going to trial, the parties meet with their attorneys to represent them, to try to resolve the dispute without involving a third party. This is

a. arbitration.
b. litigation.
c. mediation.
d. negotiation.

____   2. Sean files a suit against Tifa. They meet, and their attorneys present the case to a jury. The jury renders a non-binding verdict, after which the parties try to reach an agreement. This is

a. a mini-trial.
b. a summary jury trial.
c. early neutral case evaluation.
d. mediation.

____   3. Flo Irrigation Service submits a claim against Garden Pumps, Inc., to an online dispute resolution forum. An appeal of this dispute may be made to a court by

a. Flo and Garden by mutual agreement only.
b. Flo only.
c. Flo or Garden.
d. Garden only.

____   4. Cobb and Roberts submit their dispute to binding arbitration. A court can set aside the arbitrator's award if

a. Cobb is not satisfied with the award.
b. Roberts is not satisfied with the award.
c. the award involves at least $75,000.
d. the award violates public policy.

____   5. Fleet Feet, Inc., sells to Go! Sporting Goods 1,000 pairs of running shoes. Go! does not pay, claiming the shoes are defective. They agree to mediate the dispute. Go! does not mediate in good faith. The mediator can impose

a. any sanction.
b. any sanction that a court could impose.
c. no sanction.
d. only a sanction that the parties agreed to initially.

____   6. Liability Insurance Corporation and Master Insurance, Inc., cannot agree on which of them should pay a certain claim. They submit their dispute to a mini-trial. The result will be

a. advisory only.
b. legally binding if it is clearly stated in specific terms.
c. legally binding if it is definitely in one party's favor.
d. legally binding if it is fairly balanced between the parties.

____   7. Beach Products, Inc., and Coastal Concessions Company agree to submit their contract dispute to a summary jury trial. The verdict will be

a. advisory only.
b. legally binding if it is clearly stated in specific terms.
c. legally binding if it is definitely in one party's favor.
d. legally binding if it is fairly balanced between the parties.

____ **8.** Fiona files a suit against Gert in a state court that requires the parties to some disputes to attempt arbitration before a trial will be held. In most states, court-annexed arbitration is *not* available if a dispute involves

   a. services.
   b. title to goods.
   c. title to intangible property, such as copyrights or trademarks.
   d. title to real estate.

____ **9.** Dag and Elvie agree to dissolve their corporation but cannot agree on the division of its assets. They decide to arbitrate their dispute. Compared to litigation, the advantages of arbitration include

   a. the finality of the result, which cannot be appealed to a court.
   b. the higher cost, which encourages the parties to "keep it short."
   c. the informality of the proceeding, which includes less complex rules.
   d. the longer delay, which gives the parties time to "cool down."

____ **10.** Kyra and Leon agree to dissolve their partnership but cannot agree on the split of its assets and profits. They decide to mediate the dispute. Compared to arbitration, the advantages of mediation include

   a. the finality of the result, which cannot be appealed to a court.
   b. the higher cost, which encourages the parties to "keep it short."
   c. the longer delay, which gives the parties time to "cool down."
   d. the mutually agreed-to resolution, which can benefit both sides to the dispute.

SHORT ESSAY QUESTIONS

1. What are the principal advantages and disadvantages of using mediation?

2. What are the differences between voluntary and court-annexed arbitration?

GAMEPOINTS

(Answers at the Back of the Book)

1. You create "Faceville," an online game that combines features of a social networking site and a virtual reality environment. Public participation exceeds everyone's expectations, and you assume the presidency of FV Inc. and become one of the Web's newest billionaires. With the success comes a conflict. Garvey, who was your college roommate and friend, claims that he created "Faceville." He agrees to arbitration over this claim. Before the proceeding, the arbitrator meets with Garvey outside your presence. During the proceeding, the arbitrator lets only Garvey argue his side. When the arbitrator awards him $65 million, you're dumbfounded. Later, you learn that Garvey offered to split the proceeds of a favorable award with the arbitrator. What are the bases on which this award might be set aside? Discuss.

2. Before the dispute with Garvey draws to a close, Hildebrand, one of your previous employers, files a suit against you in a state court. Hildebrand contends that "Faceville" was his idea and that during your employment, you purloined the concept and code to create it. The state requires this dispute to be submitted to court-annexed arbitration. What is the difference between *voluntary* arbitration and *court-annexed* arbitration? If, like your dispute with Garvey, this dispute is not resolved in arbitration, or if either Hildebrand or you disagree with the arbitrator's decision, will a court hear the case? Explain.

Chapter 4
Ethics and Business Decision Making

WHAT THIS CHAPTER IS ABOUT

The concepts set out in this chapter include the nature of business ethics and the relationship between ethics and business. Ultimately, the goal of this chapter is to provide you with basic tools for analyzing ethical issues in a business context.

CHAPTER OUTLINE

I. BUSINESS ETHICS

Ethics is the study of what constitutes right and wrong behavior. Ethics focuses on morality and the application of moral principles in everyday life. Business ethics focuses on what constitutes ethical behavior in the world of business. Business ethics is *not* a separate kind of ethics.

A. WHY IS BUSINESS ETHICS IMPORTANT?
An understanding of business ethics is important to the long-run viability of a business, the well being of its officers and directors, and the welfare of its employees.

B. THE MORAL MINIMUM
The minimal acceptable standard for ethical business behavior is compliance with the law. The minimal acceptable standard for ethical business behavior is compliance with the law. But the law does not, and cannot, codify all ethical requirements. An action that is legal may not be ethical. Standards in a company's policies or codes of ethics must also guide decisions.

C. "GRAY AREAS" IN THE LAW
The legality of a particular action is not always clear. Because there are many laws regulating business, it is possible to violate one without realizing it. And there are "gray areas" of the law in which it is difficult to predict how a court will rule. Sometimes, the test may be whether a consequence was "foreseeable." Or a case may involve the law in a new context. The best course is to act responsibly and in good faith.

D. SHORT-RUN PROFIT MAXIMIZATION
In the short run, unethical behavior may lead to increased profits. In the long run, such behavior can lead to costly lawsuits, settlements and other payments, and bad publicity, undercutting profits.

E. THE IMPORTANCE OF ETHICAL LEADERSHIP
Management must set and apply ethical standards to which they are committed. Employees will likely follow their example.

1. Attitude of Top Management
Ethical conduct can be furthered by not tolerating unethical behavior, setting realistic employee goals, and periodic employee review.

27

2. Behavior of Owners and Managers
Those who actively foster unethical or illegal conduct encourage it in others.

F. CREATING ETHICAL CODES OF CONDUCT
Most large corporations have codes of conduct that indicate the firm's commitment to legal compliance and to the welfare of those who are affected by corporate decisions and practices.

1. Ethics Training to Employees
Large firms may emphasize ethics in training programs.

2. The Sarbanes-Oxley Act
The Sarbanes-Oxley Act of 2002 requires firms to set up confidential systems for employees to report suspected illegal or unethical financial practices.

II. ETHICAL TRANSGRESSIONS BY FINANCIAL INSTITUTIONS

A. STOCK BUYBACKS
If the management of a company believes that its stock price is too low, or below "fair value," company funds can be used to buy shares, boosting the price. This benefits corporate executives who have stock options through which they can buy shares at a lower price and sell at the higher price. This is not illegal, but can appear to be improper.

B. EXECUTIVE DECISIONS
A business's decision to overextend itself risks failure and, with an ill-timed expenditure of company funds, can appear to be unethical. For example, American International Group's issuance of policies to guarantee financial contracts led to the company's near failure when too many of the insured events occurred. Its executives' simultaneous spending of company funds on an expensive conference added to the appearance of impropriety.

C. EXECUTIVE BONUSES
Company commissions and bonuses can be paid for conduct that ultimately results in negative consequences for the company. For example, a commission may be paid on the purchase of a risky asset—such as a loan with a significant possibility of default—even after the risk materializes. Such payments contributed to the subprime mortgage crisis of 2007.

III. APPROACHES TO ETHICAL REASONING
Ethical reasoning is the process by which an individual examines a situation according to his or her moral convictions or ethical standards. Fundamental ethical reasoning approaches include the following.

A. DUTY-BASED ETHICS

1. Religious Ethical Standards
Religious standards provide that when an act is prohibited by religious teachings, it is unethical and should not be undertaken, regardless of the consequences. Religious standards also involve compassion.

2. Kantian Ethics
Immanual Kant believed that people should be respected because they are qualitatively different from other physical objects. Kant's *categorical imperative* is that individuals should evaluate their actions in light of what would happen if everyone acted the same way.

3. The Principle of Rights
According to the principle that persons have rights (to life and liberty, for example), a key factor in determining whether a business decision is ethical is how that decision affects the rights of others, including employees, customers and society.

B. OUTCOME-BASED ETHICS: UTILITARIANISM
Utilitarianism is a belief that an action is ethical if it produces the greatest good for the greatest number. This approach is often criticized, because it tends to reduce the welfare of people to plus and minus signs on a cost-benefit worksheet.

C. CORPORATE SOCIAL RESPONSIBILITY

1. Stakeholder Approach
Under this approach, a firm's duty to its shareholders should be weighed against duties to others (employees, etc.) who may have a greater stake in a particular decision.

2. Corporate Citizenship
This theory argues that business firms should pursue goals that society deems important, because firms have so much wealth and power. Some companies publish annual corporate social responsibility—or sustainability, or citizenship—reports to highlight their activities.

3. A Way of Doing Business
Some argue that corporate promotion of social goals should be pursued as a "way of doing business" rather than as a special program. Some suggest that such activities should be relevant and significant to a firm's stakeholders.

4. Employee Recruiting and Retention
A focus on corporate social responsibility can help a firm retain its employees, especially altruistic younger workers.

IV. MAKING ETHICAL DECISIONS
The goal is to ensure that all corporate actors think more broadly about how their decisions and actions will affect other employees, shareholders, customers, and the community. Guidelines include the following.

A. THE LAW
Is the proposed action legal?

B. BUSINESS RULES AND PROCEDURES
Is the proposed action consistent with company policies and procedures?

C. SOCIAL VALUES
Is the proposed action consistent with the "spirit" of the law, even if it is not expressly prohibited?

D. AN INDIVIDUAL'S CONSCIENCE
How does the actor's or decision maker's conscience regard the plan of action? Could the plan survive in the glare of publicity?

E. PROMISES TO OTHERS
Will the action satisfy commitments that have been made to others, inside and outside the corporation?

F. HEROES
How would the actor's or decision maker's hero regard the action?

V. PRACTICAL SOLUTIONS TO CORPORATE ETHICS QUESTIONS
A practical method to investigate and solve ethics problems might include five steps—

A. INQUIRY
Who are the parties, what is the problem, and what are the relevant ethical principles?

B. DISCUSSION
What are the options for action? What are the goals to be attained?

C. DECISION
Can a consensus be reached on the options for action? If so, what is the plan?

D. JUSTIFICATION
What are the reasons for the proposed actions? Will the corporate stakeholders accept those reasons?

E. EVALUATION
Will the solution satisfy corporate, community, and individual values?

VI.   BUSINESS ETHICS ON A GLOBAL LEVEL

There are important ethical differences among, and within, nations. Some countries, for example, largely reject any role for women professionals, which may cause difficulties for American women attempting to do business in those countries.

A. THE MONITORING OF EMPLOYMENT PRACTICES OF FOREIGN SUPPLIERS
Concerns include the treatment of foreign workers who make goods imported and sold in the United States by U.S. firms. Should a U.S firm refuse to deal with certain suppliers or monitor their workplaces to make sure that the workers are not being mistreated?

B. THE FOREIGN CORRUPT PRACTICES ACT
Payments to government officials in exchange for government contracts are not unusual in some countries and are not always considered to be unethical.

1. Prohibition against the Bribery of Foreign Officials
The Foreign Corrupt Practices Act (FCPA) of 1977 prohibits U.S. businesspersons from bribing foreign officials to secure favorable contracts.

2. Accounting Requirements
Accountants may be subject to penalties for making false statements business records or accounts.

3. Penalties
Firms: fines up to $2 million. Individuals: fines up to $100,000 (cannot be paid by the company); imprisonment up to five years.

TRUE-FALSE QUESTIONS

(Answers at the Back of the Book)

____   **1.**   Ethics is the study of what constitutes right and wrong behavior.

____   **2.**   A background in business ethics is as important as knowledge of specific laws.

____   **3.**   The *minimal* acceptable standard for ethical behavior is compliance with the law.

____   **4.**   According to utilitarianism, it does not matter how many people benefit from an act.

____   **5.**   The best course towards accomplishing legal and ethical behavior is to act responsibly and in good faith.

____   **6.**   The ethics of a particular act is always clear.

____   **7.**   To foster ethical behavior among employees, managers should apply ethical standards to which they are committed.

____   **8.**   If an act is legal, it is ethical.

____   **9.**   The roles that women play in other countries can present ethical problems for U.S. firms doing business internationally.

____   **10.**   Bribery of public officials is only an ethical issue.

FILL-IN QUESTIONS

(Answers at the Back of the Book)

_____ (Religious standards/ Kantian ethics/ The principle of rights) provide(s) that when an act is prohibited by religious teachings, it is unethical and should not be undertaken, regardless of the consequences. According to _____ (religious standards/ Kantian ethics/ the principle of rights), individuals should evaluate their actions in light of what would happen if everyone acted the same way. According to _____ (religious standards/ Kantian ethics/ the principle of rights), a key factor in determining whether a business decision is ethical is how that decision affects the rights of others.

MULTIPLE-CHOICE QUESTIONS

(Answers at the Back of the Book)

____ 1. Trent is a marketing executive for Unique Appliance Company. Compared to Trent's personal choices, his actions in the business world require the application of

  a. more complex ethical standards.
  b. simpler ethical standards.
  c. the same ethical standards.
  d. no ethical standards.

____ 2. Darby, an employee of Equipment Sales, Inc., takes a duty-based approach to ethics. Under this standard, Darby believes that she must

  a. achieve the greatest good for the most people.
  b. avoid unethical behavior regardless of the consequences.
  c. conform to society's standards.
  d. place Equipment Sales's interests first.

____ 3. Mikayla, chief financial officer of Napoli Pasta Company, adopts religious ethical standards. These involve an element of

  a. compassion.
  b. cost-benefit analysis.
  c. discretion.
  d. utilitarianism.

____ 4. Reba, an employee of Sterling Credit Bank, takes an outcome-based approach to ethics. With this approach, Reba believes that she must

  a. achieve the greatest good for the most people.
  b. avoid unethical behavior regardless of the consequences.
  c. conform to society's standards.
  d. place Sterling Credit's interests first.

____ 5. Don is a manager with Engineering Aviation Systems. At a company ethics meeting, Don's most effective argument against utilitarianism is that it

  a. gives profits priority over costs.
  b. ignores the practical costs of a given set of circumstances.
  c. justifies human costs that many persons find unacceptable.
  d. requires complex cost-benefit analyses of simple situations.

____ 6. In resolving an ethical problem, in most cases a decision by Oil Production Services, or any business firm, will have a negative effect on

a. one group as opposed to another.
b. the firm's competitors.
c. the government.
d. none of the choices.

____ 7. **Based on a Sample CPA Exam Question.** Ethical standards would most likely be considered violated if Light & Sound Services, Inc., represents to Studio Film Production Company that certain services will be performed for a stated fee, but it is apparent at the time of the representation that

a. Light & Sound cannot perform the services alone.
b. the actual charge will be substantially higher.
c. the actual charge will be substantially lower.
d. the fee is a competitive bid.

____ 8. Stefanie, the president of Thruway Trucking, Inc., tries to ensure that Thruway's actions are legal and ethical. To ensure this result, the best course of Stefanie and Thruway is to act in

a. good faith.
b. ignorance of the law.
c. regard for the firm's shareholders only.
d. their own self interest.

____ 9. Pew, an executive with Black Spot Corporation, follows the "principle of rights" theory, under which an action may be ethical depending on how it affects

a. the right determination under a cost-benefit analysis.
b. the right of Pew to maintain his dignity.
c. the right of Black Spot to make a profit.
d. the rights of others.

____ 10. Treasure Trove, Inc., a U.S. corporation, makes a side payment to the minister of commerce of Tuvalu (an island country in the Pacific Ocean) for a favorable business contract. In the United States, this payment would be considered

a. illegal and unethical.
b. illegal only.
c. neither illegal nor unethical.
d. unethical only.

SHORT ESSAY QUESTIONS

1. What is ethics?

2. What is the difference between legal and ethical standards? How are legal standards affected by ethical standards?

GAMEPOINTS

(Answers at the Back of the Book)

1. You're playing "Sun Ascendant," a video game in which the sun has burned out, and your goal is to accomplish certain tasks, advance to different levels, collect eight "Golden Orbs," and ultimately restart the fire in our sun. The difficulty of mastering the tasks increases at each level. At the fifth level—Mars—you

become stalled. There are Web sites on which players reveal the steps to win the game. Is it ethical to consult these sites? Why or why not?

2. Still playing "Sun Ascendant," you advance no farther than Venus, the seventh level. Frustrated, you purposely damage the game disk and attempt to return it to the game outlet where you bought it. If the seller won't take it back, you vow to complain about the game and the vendor on every gamers' site on the Internet. What are the ethics in this situation? Discuss.

CUMULATIVE HYPOTHETICAL PROBLEM FOR UNIT ONE—INCLUDING CHAPTERS 1–4

(Answers at the Back of the Book)

Computer Data, Inc. (CDI), incorporated and based in California, signs a contract with Eagle Management Corporation, incorporated and based in Arizona, to make and sell customized software to Eagle for resale to consumers. CDI ships defective software to Eagle, which causes losses estimated at $100,000.

____ **1.** Eagle and CDI enter into mediation. In mediation, the parties

    a. may come to an agreement by mutual consent.
    b. must accept a winner-take-all result.
    c. settle their dispute without the assistance of a third party.
    d. submit their dispute to a mediator for a legally binding decision.

____ **2.** Eagle could file a suit against CDI in

    a. Arizona only.
    b. California only.
    c. a federal court only.
    d. Arizona, California, or a federal court.

____ **3.** Eagle files a suit against CDI, seeking the amount of its losses as damages. Damages is a remedy

    a. at law.
    b. in equity.
    c. at law or in equity, depending on how the plaintiff phrases its complaint.
    d. at law or in equity, depending on whether there was any actual "damage."

____ **4.** Federal authorities file charges against CDI, alleging that the shipment of defective software violated a federal statute. CDI asks the court to exercise its power of judicial review. This means that the court can review

    a. the actions of the federal authorities and declare them excessive.
    b. the charges against CDI and declare them unfounded.
    c. the statute and declare it unconstitutional.
    d. the totality of the situation and declare it unethical.

____ **5.** CDI's managers evaluate the shipment of defective software in terms of CDI's ethical obligations, if any. In other words, CDI's managers are considering the firm's

    a. legal liability.
    b. maximum profitability.
    c. optimum profitability.
    d. right or wrong behavior.

QUESTIONS ON THE FOCUS ON ETHICS FOR UNIT ONE— ETHICS AND THE FOUNDATIONS

(Answers at the Back of the Book)

____ **1.** The managers of Standard Products Company (SPC) evaluate its sale of possibly defective goods in terms of its ethical obligations, if any. In other words, the managers are considering SPC's

    a. legal liability.
    b. maximum profitability.
    c. moral minimum.
    d. right or wrong behavior.

____ **2.** If SPC conducts its operations ethically, there will be a likely increase in its

    a. future profits, goodwill, and reputation.
    b. future profits only.
    c. good will only.
    d. reputation only.

____ **3.** If SPC pursues a certain course because its managers believe in the "rightness" of a cause, rather than because the action will increase corporate profits, SPC's position could arguably be

    a. illegal.
    b. maximal.
    c. socially irresponsible.
    d. unethical.

Chapter 5

Constitutional Law

WHAT THIS CHAPTER IS ABOUT

This chapter emphasizes that the Constitution is the supreme law in this country and discusses some of the constitutional limits on the law. Neither Congress nor any state may pass a law in conflict with the Constitution. To sustain a federal law or action, a specific federal power must be found in the Constitution. A state has the inherent power to enact laws that have a reasonable relationship to the welfare of its citizens.

CHAPTER OUTLINE

I. THE CONSTITUTIONAL POWERS OF GOVERNMENT

A. A FEDERAL FORM OF GOVERNMENT

In a federal form of government (the United States), the states form a union and sovereign power is divided between a central authority and the states.

1. Relation between State and Federal Powers

Neither the national government nor a state government is superior to the other except within areas of exclusive authority granted under the Constitution. The courts determine the nature and scope of state and federal powers.

2. The Regulatory Powers of the States

States possess police powers (the right to regulate private activities to protect or promote the public order, health, safety, morals, and general welfare). Statutes covering almost every aspect of life have been enacted under the police powers.

3. Relations among the States

a. The Privileges and Immunities Clauses

Each state must provide the citizens of other states the same privileges and immunities it provides its own citizens. A state cannot treat nonresidents engaged in basic, essential activities differently without substantial justification.

b. The Full Faith and Credit Clause

Property and contract rights established by law in one state must be honored by other states.

B. THE SEPARATION OF THE NATIONAL GOVERNMENT'S POWERS

Under the Constitution, the legislative branch makes the laws, the executive branch enforces the laws, and the judicial branch interprets the laws. Under a checks and balances system, each branch has some power to limit the actions of the other two.

C. THE COMMERCE CLAUSE

The Constitution (Article I, Section 8) gives Congress power to regulate commerce among the states.

35

1. The Commerce Power Today
The national government can regulate every commercial enterprise in the United States. The United States Supreme Court has held, however, that this does not justify regulation of areas that have "nothing to do with commerce."

2. The "Dormant" Commerce Clause
When state laws impinge on interstate commerce, courts balance the state's interest in regulating a certain matter against the burden on interstate commerce. State laws that *substantially* interfere with interstate commerce violate the commerce clause.

D. THE SUPREMACY CLAUSE AND FEDERAL PREEMPTION
The Constitution (Article IV) provides that the Constitution, laws, and treaties of the United States are the supreme law of the land.

1. When Federal and State Laws Are in Direct Conflict
The state law is rendered invalid.

2. Federal Preemption
If Congress chooses to act exclusively in an area in which states have concurrent power, Congress preempts the area (the federal law takes precedence over a state law on the same subject).

E. THE TAXING AND SPENDING POWERS

1. The Taxing Power
The Constitution (Article I, Section 8) gives Congress the power to levy taxes, but Congress may not tax some states and exempt others. Any tax that is a valid revenue-raising measure will be upheld.

2. The Spending Power
The Constitution (Article I, Section 8) gives Congress the power to spend the money it raises with its taxing power. This involves policy choices, with which taxpayers may disagree. Congress can spend funds to promote any objective, so long as it does not violate the Bill of Rights.

II.   BUSINESS AND THE BILL OF RIGHTS
The first ten amendments to the Constitution protect individuals and businesses against some interference by the federal government. Under the due process clause of the Fourteenth Amendment, many rights also apply to the states. In other words, many of the limits apply to both the federal and state governments.

A. LIMITS ON FEDERAL AND STATE GOVERNMENTAL ACTIONS
Under the due process clause of the Fourteenth Amendment, many rights also apply to the states. In other words, many of the limits apply to both the federal and state governments.

B. FREEDOM OF SPEECH
The First Amendment guaranty of freedom of speech applies to the federal and state governments.

1. Reasonable Restrictions
Any form of expression is subject to reasonable restrictions. If a restriction is content neutral (not aimed at suppressing expressive conduct or its message), it will likely be upheld.

2. Protected Speech
This includes symbolic speech—nonverbal expressions, such as gestures, articles of clothing, some acts and so on. Governments can regulate the time, place, and manner of speech.

3. Speech with Limited Protection

    a. Corporate Political Speech
    States can prohibit corporations from using corporate funds for independent expressions of opinion about political candidates.

    b. Commercial Speech
    A state restriction on commercial speech, such as advertising, is valid as long as it (1) seeks to implement a substantial government interest, (2) directly advances that interest, and (3) goes no further than necessary to accomplish its objective.

4. Unprotected Speech

    a. Defamatory Speech
    This is speech that harms the good reputation of another. It can take the form of libel (if it is in writing) or slander (if it is oral).

    b. "Fighting Words"
    These are words that are likely to incite others to violence.

    c. Obscene Speech
    States can ban child pornography. Bans on other materials are often disputed.

    d. Online Obscenity
    Attempts to regulate obscene materials on the Internet have been challenged, and some have been struck as unconstitutional.

C. FREEDOM OF RELIGION
Under the First Amendment, the government may not establish a religion (the establishment clause) nor prohibit the exercise of religion (the free exercise clause).

1. The Establishment Clause
The government cannot show a preference for, or promote or inhibit one religion over another, but must accommodate all religions.

2. The Free Exercise Clause
A law that infringes on the free exercise of religion in public places must be justified by a compelling state interest. A person cannot be compelled to do something contrary to his or her religious practices unless those practices contravene public policy or public welfare.

D. SEARCHES AND SEIZURES
Under the Fourth Amendment, law enforcement and other government officers cannot conduct unreasonable searches or seizures.

1. Search Warrant Required
An officer must obtain a search warrant before searching or seizing private property. It must describe what is to be searched or seized.

    a. Non-business Contexts
    To obtain a warrant, the officer must convince a judge that there is **probable cause** (evidence that would convince a reasonable person a search or seizure is justified).

    b. Business Premises
    To obtain a warrant to inspect business premises, government inspectors must have probable cause, but the standard is different: a general and neutral enforcement plan is enough.

2. No Search Warrant Required
No warrant is required for seizures of spoiled or contaminated food or searches of businesses in highly regulated industries. The same standard sometimes applies in other contexts (such as airline screenings). General manufacturing is not considered a highly regulated industry.

E. SELF-INCRIMINATION
Under the Fifth Amendment, no person can be compelled to give testimony that might subject him or her to a criminal prosecution.

1. Sole Proprietors
Individuals who own their own businesses and have not incorporated cannot be compelled to produce their business records.

2. Partnerships and Corporations
Partnerships and corporations *can* be compelled to produce their business records, even if the records incriminate the persons who constitute the business entity.

III. DUE PROCESS AND EQUAL PROTECTION

A. DUE PROCESS
Both the Fifth and the Fourteenth Amendments provide that no person shall be deprived "of life, liberty, or property, without due process of law."

1. Procedural Due Process
Any government decision to take away the life, liberty, or property of an individual must include procedural safeguards to ensure fairness.

2. Substantive Due Process
Substantive due process focuses on the content (substance) of legislation.

a. Compelling Interest Test
A statute can restrict an individual's fundamental right (such as all First Amendment rights) only if the statute promotes a compelling or overriding governmental interest.

b. Rational Basis Test
Restrictions on rights not regarded as fundamental must relate rationally to a legitimate government purpose. Most business regulations qualify.

B. EQUAL PROTECTION
The Fourteenth Amendment prohibits a state from denying any person "the equal protection of the laws." The due process clause of the Fifth Amendment applies the equal protection clause to the federal government.

1. What Equal Protection Means
Equal protection means that the government must treat similarly situated individuals in a similar manner. If a law distinguishes among individuals, the basis for the distinction (classification) is examined.

a. Strict Scrutiny
A law that inhibits some persons' exercise of a fundamental right or a classification based on a suspect trait must be necessary to promote a compelling state interest.

b. Intermediate Scrutiny
Laws using classifications based on gender or legitimacy must be substantially related to important government objectives.

c. The "Rational Basis" Test
In matters of economic or social welfare, the classification will be considered valid if there is any conceivable rational basis on which it might relate to any legitimate government interest.

2. The Difference between Substantive Due Process and Equal Protection
A law that limits the liberty of *all* persons to do something may violate substantive due process. A law that limits the liberty of only *some* persons may violate equal protection.

IV. PRIVACY RIGHTS

There is no specific guarantee of this right, but it is derived from guarantees in the First, Third, Fourth, Fifth, and Ninth Amendments. There are a number of federal statutes that protect privacy in certain areas, including medical information. Pretending to be someone else or to make false representations—pretexting—to obtain another's confidential phone records is a federal crime.

TRUE-FALSE QUESTIONS

(Answers at the Back of the Book)

____ 1. A federal form of government is one in which a central authority holds all power.

____ 2. The president can hold acts of Congress and of the courts unconstitutional.

____ 3. Congress can regulate any activity that substantially affects commerce.

____ 4. A state law that substantially affects interstate commerce is unconstitutional.

____ 5. When there is a direct conflict between a federal law and a state law, the federal law is invalid.

____ 6. Some constitutional protections apply to businesses.

____ 7. The Bill of Rights protects against various types of interference by the federal government only.

____ 8. Any restriction on commercial speech is unconstitutional.

____ 9. Due process and equal protection are different terms for the same thing.

____ 10. A right to privacy is not specifically guaranteed in the U.S. Constitution.

FILL-IN QUESTIONS

(Answers at the Back of the Book)

Police power is possessed by the _____ (federal government/states). Police power refers to the right of the _____ (federal government/states) to regulate private activities to protect or promote the public order, health, safety, morals, and general welfare. Building codes, licensing requirements, and many other _____ (federal/state) statutes have been enacted under the police power.

MULTIPLE-CHOICE QUESTIONS

(Answers at the Back of the Book)

____ 1. Of the three branches of the federal government provided by the Constitution, the branch that makes the laws is

a. the administrative branch.
b. the executive branch.
c. the judicial branch.
d. the legislative branch.

____ **2.** Tristate Business Corporation markets its products in three states. Under the commerce clause, Congress can regulate

   a. any commercial activity in the United States.
   b. only commercial activities that are in interstate commerce.
   c. only commercial activities that are local.
   d. only activities that have nothing to do with commerce.

____ **3.** Southeast Shipping Company challenges an Alabama statute, claiming that it unlawfully interferes with interstate commerce. A court will likely

   a. balance Alabama's interest in regulating the matter against the burden on interstate commerce.
   b. balance the burden on Alabama against the merit and purpose of interstate commerce.
   c. strike the statute.
   d. uphold the statute.

____ **4.** A Nevada statute bans business entities from making political contributions that individuals can make. A court would likely hold this statute to be

   a. an unconstitutional restriction of speech.
   b. constitutional under the First Amendment.
   c. justified by the need to protect individuals' rights.
   d. necessary to protect state interests.

____ **5.** An Ohio statute bans certain advertising to prevent consumers from being misled. A court would likely hold this statute to be

   a. an unconstitutional restriction of speech.
   b. constitutional under the First Amendment.
   c. justified by the need to protect individuals' rights.
   d. necessary to protect state interests.

____ **6.** Procedures used in Oklahoma and other states in making decisions to take life, liberty, or property are the focus of constitutional provisions covering

   a. equal protection.
   b. procedural due process.
   c. substantive due process.
   d. the right to privacy.

____ **7.** A Vermont statute that limits the liberty of *all* persons to engage in a certain activity may violate constitutional provisions covering

   a. equal protection.
   b. procedural due process.
   c. substantive due process.
   d. the right to privacy.

____ **8.** A Harbor City ordinance restricts most vendors from doing business in a heavily trafficked area. This might be upheld under constitutional provisions covering

   a. equal protection.
   b. procedural due process.
   c. substantive due process.
   d. the right to privacy.

____ **9.** If South Carolina enacts a statute that directly conflicts with a federal law

   a. both laws are invalid.
   b. both laws govern concurrently.
   c. South Carolina's statute takes precedence.
   d. the federal law takes precedence.

____ **10.** The First Amendment protects Nancy and others from

    a. dissemination of obscene materials and speech that harms their good reputations or violates state criminal laws.

    b. dissemination of obscene materials only.

    c. speech that harms their good reputations or violates state criminal laws only.

    d. neither dissemination of obscene materials nor speech that harms their good reputations or violates state criminal laws.

SHORT ESSAY QUESTIONS

1. What is the effect of the supremacy clause?

2. What is the significance of the commerce clause?

GAMEPOINTS

(Answers at the Back of the Book)

1. In the video game "Brainiac," each player solves puzzles and answers questions based on information displayed on the screen. The quicker and more accurate answers score more points. As the creator, developer, and seller of "Brainiac," you hope to sell millions of copies. How does the Constitution affect what you can say in the game's ads?

2. "Trader Vex" is a video game that involves commerce among virtual worlds and their inhabitants in the midst of an intergalactic conflict. The goal is to amass the most goods and money, or their equivalent, and store them in a safe location. If these worlds were the states of the United States, could the national government regulate their trade? Could the states regulate affairs within their borders? If so, and these regulations were in conflict, what would be the result?

Chapter 6
Administrative Law

WHAT THIS CHAPTER IS ABOUT

Administrative agencies regulate virtually every aspect of a business's operation. Agencies' rules, orders, and decisions make up the body of administrative law. How agencies function is the subject of this chapter.

CHAPTER OUTLINE

I. THE PRACTICAL SIGNIFICANCE OF ADMINISTRATIVE LAW

Congress delegates some of its authority to make and implement laws, particularly in highly technical areas, to administrative agencies.

A. ADMINISTRATIVE AGENCIES EXIST AT ALL LEVELS OF GOVERNMENT

Administrative agencies at all levels of government—federal, state, and local—affect all aspects of business—capital structure and financing, employer-employee relations, production and marketing, and more.

B. AGENCIES PROVIDE A COMPREHENSIVE REGULATORY SCHEME

Agencies at different levels of government may cooperate to create and enforce regulations.

II. AGENCY CREATION AND POWERS

A. ENABLING LEGISLATION

To create an agency, Congress passes enabling legislation, which specifies the powers of the agency.

B. TYPES OF AGENCIES

1. Executive Agencies

Includes cabinet departments and their subagencies. Subject to the authority of the president, who can appoint and remove their officers.

2. Independent Regulatory Agencies

Includes agencies outside the major executive departments. Their officers serve for fixed terms and cannot be removed without just cause.

C. AGENCY POWERS AND THE CONSTITUTION

Agency powers include functions associated with the legislature (rulemaking), executive branch (enforcement), and courts (adjudication). Under Article I of the Constitution and the delegation doctrine, Congress has the power to establish agencies, which create *legislative rules* to implement laws and *interpretive rules* to declare policy.

1. Executive Controls

The executive branch exercises control over agencies through the president's powers to appoint federal officers and to veto enabling legislation or congressional attempts to modify an existing agency's authority.

2. Legislative Controls

Congress exercises authority over agency power through enabling legislation and subsequent legislation. Congress can restrict or expand agency power substantively, limit or increase it through funding, or set time limits. Congress can investigate an agency. Individual legislators may affect agency policy through attempts to help their constituents deal with agencies. The Administrative Procedure Act (APA) of 1946 and other laws also act as a check on agency power.

3. Judicial Controls

The APA provides for judicial review of most agency decisions. According to the exhaustion doctrine, a party must have used all potential administrative remedies before filing a suit.

III. THE ADMINISTRATIVE PROCEDURE ACT

Rulemaking, investigation, and adjudication make up the administrative process. The APA imposes procedural requirements that agencies must follow.

A. THE ARBITRARY AND CAPRICIOUS TEST

The APA provides that courts should set aside agency decisions that are "arbitrary, capricious, an abuse of discretion, or otherwise not in accordance with the law." This includes such factors as the following.

1. Failure to provide a rational explanation for a decision.
2. Change in prior policy without an explanation.
3. Consideration of legally inappropriate factors.
4. Failure to consider a relevant factor.
5. Render of a decision plainly contrary to the evidence.

B. RULEMAKING

Rulemaking is the formulation of new regulations. Legislative rules, or substantive rules, are as legally binding as the laws that Congress makes. Interpretive rules are not binding but indicate how an agency will apply a certain statute.

1. Notice of the Proposed Rulemaking

An agency begins by publishing, in the *Federal Register,* a notice that states where and when proceedings will be held, terms or subject matter of the proposed rule, the agency's authority for making the rule, and key information underlying the proposed rule.

2. Comment Period

Interested parties can express their views. An agency must respond to significant comments by modifying the final rule or explaining, in a statement accompanying the final rule, why it did not.

3. The Final Rule

The agency publishes the final rule—the terms of which may differ from the proposed rule—in the *Federal Register*. This final "legislative rule" has binding legal effect unless overturned by a court. The period must be at least thirty days and is often sixty days or more.

C. INFORMAL AGENCY ACTIONS

A rule that only states an agency's interpretation of its enabling statute's meaning is an "interpretative rule" and may be issued without formal rulemaking. These rules impose no direct or binding effect.

IV. JUDICIAL DEFERENCE TO AGENCY DECISIONS

Courts generally defer to an agency's factual judgment on a subject within the area of its expertise and its interpretation of its legal authority.

A. THE HOLDING OF THE *CHEVRON* CASE
When reviewing an agency's interpretation of law, a court should ask (1) whether the enabling statute directly addresses the issue and if not (2) whether the agency's interpretation is reasonable.

B. WHEN COURTS WILL GIVE *CHEVRON* DEFERENCE TO AGENCY INTERPRETATION
The extent of this deference has been much debated. If an agency's decision has resulted from formal rulemaking, it is more likely to be subject to deference.

V. ENFORCEMENT AND ADJUDICATION

A. INVESTIGATION
Agencies must have knowledge of facts and circumstances pertinent to proposed rules. Agencies must also obtain information and investigate conduct to ascertain whether its rules are being violated.

1. Inspections and Tests
Through on-site inspections and testing, agencies gather information to prove a regulatory violation or to correct or prevent a bad condition.

2. Subpoenas
A subpoena *ad testificandum* is an order to a witness to appear at a hearing. A subpoena *duces tecum* is an order to a party to hand over records or other documents. Limits on agency demands for information through these subpoenas, and otherwise, include—

a. An investigation must have a legitimate purpose.
b. The information that is sought must be relevant.
c. Demands must be specific.
d. The party from whom the information is sought must not be unduly burdened by the request.

3. Search Warrants
A search warrant directs an officer to search a specific place for a specific item and present it to the agency.

a. Search Warrants Usually Required
The Fourth Amendment protects against unreasonable searches and seizures by requiring that in most instances a physical search must be conducted under the authority of a search warrant.

b. Some Warrantless Searches Legal
Warrants are not required to conduct searches in businesses in highly regulated industries, in certain hazardous operations, and in emergencies.

B. ADJUDICATION
Adjudication involves the resolution of disputes by an agency.

1. Negotiated Settlements
The purpose of negotiation is (1) for agencies: to eliminate the need for further proceedings and (2) for parties subject to regulation: to avoid publicity and the expense of litigation.

2. Formal Complaints
If there is no settlement, the agency may issue a formal complaint. The party charged in the complaint may respond with an answer. The case may go before an administrative law judge (ALJ).

3. **The Role of an Administrative Law Judge (ALJ)**

   The ALJ presides over the hearing. The ALJ has the power to administer oaths, take testimony, rule on questions of evidence, and make determinations of fact. An ALJ works for the agency, but must be unbiased. Certain safeguards in the APA prevent bias and promote fairness.

4. **Hearing Procedures**

   Procedures vary widely from agency to agency. Agencies exercise substantial discretion over the type of procedures used. A formal hearing resembles a trial, but more items and testimony are admissible in an administrative hearing.

5. **Agency Orders**

   After a hearing, the ALJ issues an initial order. Either side may appeal to the commission that governs the agency and ultimately to a federal appeals court. If there is no appeal or review, the initial order becomes final.

VI. PUBLIC ACCOUNTABILITY

A. FREEDOM OF INFORMATION ACT (FOIA) OF 1966

The federal government must disclose certain records to any person on request. A failure to comply may be challenged in federal district court.

B. GOVERNMENT-IN-THE-SUNSHINE ACT OF 1976

Requires (1) that "every portion of every meeting of an agency" that is headed by a "collegial body" is open to "public observation" and (2) procedures to ensure that the public is provided with adequate advance notice of meetings and agendas (with exceptions).

C. REGULATORY FLEXIBILITY ACT OF 1980

Whenever a new regulation will have a "significant impact upon a substantial number of small entities," the agency must conduct a regulatory flexibility analysis. The analysis must measure the cost imposed by the rule on small businesses and must consider less burdensome alternatives.

D. SMALL BUSINESS REGULATORY ENFORCEMENT FAIRNESS ACT

Under this act, passed in 1996—

1. **Congress Reviews New Federal Regulations**

   Congress reviews new regulations for at least sixty days before they take effect. Opponents have time to present arguments to Congress.

2. **Agencies Must Issue "Plain English" Guides**

   Agencies must prepare guides that explain how small businesses can comply with their regulations.

3. **Regional Boards Rate Federal Agencies**

   The National Enforcement Ombudsman receives comments from small businesses about agencies. Based on the comments, Regional Small Business Fairness Boards rate the agencies.

TRUE-FALSE QUESTIONS

(Answers at the Back of the Book)

_____ 1. Enabling legislation specifies the powers of an agency.

_____ 2. Most federal agencies are part of the executive branch of government.

_____ 3. To create an agency, Congress enacts enabling legislation.

___ **4.** Agency rules are not as legally binding as the laws that Congress enacts.

___ **5.** After an agency adjudication, the administrative law judge's order must be appealed to become final.

___ **6.** Congress has no power to influence agency policy.

___ **7.** The Administrative Procedure Act provides for judicial review of most agency actions.

___ **8.** When a new regulation will have a significant impact on a substantial number of small entities, an analysis must be conducted to measure the cost imposed on small businesses.

___ **9.** Courts generally defer to an agency's findings on facts within the area of its expertise.

___ **10.** An agency cannot conduct a search without a warrant.

FILL-IN QUESTIONS

(Answers at the Back of the Book)

The rulemaking process begins with the publication in the _____ (*Congressional Record/Federal Register*) of a notice of the proposed rulemaking. The agency may conduct a public hearing at which it presents evidence to justify the proposed rule, and _____ (anyone/no one) may present opposing evidence. The agency _____ (must/need not) respond to significant comments. After the hearing, the agency publishes the final draft of the rule in the _____ (*Congressional Record/Federal Register*).

MULTIPLE-CHOICE QUESTIONS

(Answers at the Back of the Book)

___ **1.** Paige, a congressperson, believes a new federal agency is needed to oversee the consumer lending industry. Congress has the power to establish an agency with functions that include

   a. adjudication.
   b. prevarication.
   c. qualification.
   d. regurgitation.

___ **2.** Like other federal agencies, the Environmental Protection Agency may obtain information concerning activities and organizations that it oversees by issuing

   a. a complaint.
   b. a rule.
   c. a subpoena.
   d. a judgment.

___ **3.** In making rules, the procedures of the Equal Employment Opportunity Commission and other federal agencies normally includes a period during which

   a. judges are asked about a proposed rule.
   b. probable violators of a proposed rule are notified and publicized.
   c. the administrators "notice" a problem and "comment" on it.
   d. the public is asked to comment on a proposed rule.

____ **4.** The Occupational Safety and Health Administration (OSHA) issues a subpoena for Precision Systems Corporation to hand over its files. Precision's possible defenses against the subpoena include

    a. OSHA cannot issue a subpoena.
    b. OSHA is a federal agency, but Precision only does business locally.
    c. OSHA's request is not specific enough.
    d. OSHA's request violates Precision's right to privacy.

____ **5.** The Federal Trade Commission (FTC) issues an order relating to the advertising of Discount Mart, Inc. Discount appeals the order to a court. The court may review whether the FTC's action is

    a. arbitrary, capricious, or an abuse of discretion.
    b. discourteous, disrespectful, or dissatisfying to one or more parties.
    c. flippant, wanton, or in disregard of social norms.
    d. impious, non-utilitarian, or in violation of ethical precepts.

____ **6.** The Federal Energy Regulatory Commission (FERC) wants to close a series of its meetings to the public. To open the meetings, Jennifer or any citizen could sue the FERC under

    a. the Freedom of Information Act.
    b. the Government-in-the-Sunshine Act.
    c. the Regulatory Flexibility Act.
    d. no federal or state law.

____ **7.** The U.S. Fish and Wildlife Service orders Elin to stop using a certain type of fishing net from her boat. To appeal this order to a court, Elin must

    a. appeal simultaneously to the agency and the court.
    b. bypass all administrative remedies and appeal directly to the court.
    c. exhaust all administrative remedies.
    d. ignore the agency and continue using the net.

____ **8.** The National Oceanic and Atmospheric Administration (NOAA) is a federal agency. To limit the authority of NOAA, the president can

    a. abolish NOAA.
    b. take away NOAA's power.
    c. refuse to appropriate funds to NOAA.
    d. veto legislative modifications to NOAA's authority.

____ **9.** The Federal Communications Commission (FCC) publishes notice of a proposed rule. When comments are received about the rule, the FCC must respond to

    a. all of the comments.
    b. any significant comments that bear directly on the proposed rule.
    c. only comments by businesses engaged in interstate commerce.
    d. only comments by businesses that will be affected by the rule.

____ **10.** Sol is an administrative law judge (ALJ) for the National Labor Relations Board. In hearing a case, Sol has the authority to make

    a. decisions binding on the federal courts.
    b. determinations of fact.
    c. new laws.
    d. new rules.

Short Essay Questions

1. What are the conditions to judicial review of an agency enforcement action?

2. How does Congress hold agency authority in check?

GamePoints

(Answers at the Back of the Book)

1. You are playing the video game "Risky Hazards," in which your character is an inspector for the Occupational Safety and Health Administration. In one scenario, you enter what appears to be a deserted warehouse to find a small group working in a dimly lit corner. The premises are fraught with hazards—loose wires, dangling ceiling tiles, dripping liquids, locked exit doors. A figure claiming to be a supervisor argues, "You can't come in here during working hours, this is private property, and you didn't give twenty-four-hours notice. Besides, there's no emergency—you need a warrant to come in here." Are any of these points valid? Explain.

2. In the video game "Magic Coffee Beans," your character is the owner of the Tasty Pastry Café. Your objective is to do brisk business profitably and expand to other locations. An inspector for the state equal opportunity agency cites your café for failing to provide access for disabled persons. The cost to comply would undercut your profit. Unable to negotiate a solution to all of the parties' satisfaction, the agency files a formal complaint against the Tasty Pastry. What's next?

Chapter 7
Criminal Law and Cyber Crime

WHAT THIS CHAPTER IS ABOUT

This chapter defines what makes an act a crime, describes crimes that affect business (including cyber crimes), lists defenses to crimes, and outlines criminal procedure. Sanctions for crimes are different from those for torts or breaches of contract. Another difference between civil and criminal law is that an individual can bring a civil suit, but only the government—through a district attorney, for example— can prosecute a criminal.

CHAPTER OUTLINE

I. CIVIL LAW AND CRIMINAL LAW

A. CIVIL LAW
Civil law consists of the duties that exist between persons or between citizens and their governments, excluding the duty not to commit crimes.

B. CRIMINAL LAW
A crime is a wrong against society proclaimed in a statute and, if committed, punishable by society through fines, imprisonment, or death. Crimes are offenses against society as a whole (some torts are also crimes) and are prosecuted by public officials, not victims. In a criminal trial, the state must prove its case beyond a reasonable doubt.

C. CLASSIFICATION OF CRIMES
Felonies are serious crimes punishable by death or by imprisonment in a federal or state penitentiary for more than a year. A crime that is not a felony is a misdemeanor—punishable by a fine or by confinement (in a local jail) for up to a year. Petty offenses are minor misdemeanors.

II. CRIMINAL LIABILITY
Two elements must exist for a person to be convicted of a crime—

A. THE CRIMINAL ACT (*ACTUS REUS*)
A criminal statute prohibits certain behavior—an act of commission (doing something) or an act of omission (not doing something that is a legal duty).

B. STATE OF MIND (INTENT TO COMMIT A CRIME, OR *MENS REA*)
The mental state required to establish criminal guilt depends on the crime.

1. Criminal Negligence or Recklessness
Criminal recklessness is conscious disregard for a substantial and justifiable risk. Criminal negligence is a deviation from the standard of care that a reasonable person would use under the same circumstances—an unjustified, substantial, foreseeable risk that results in harm.

2. Strict Liability and Overcriminalization
Strict liability crimes do not require a wrongful mental state. These include environmental crimes, drug offenses, and other violations affecting public health, safety, and welfare. Critics

51

contend that strict liability is the wrong theory to apply to social problems such as drug abuse.

C. CORPORATE CRIMINAL LIABILITY

1. Liability of the Corporate Entity

A corporation is liable for crimes committed by its agents and employees within the course and scope of employment if the corporation authorized or could have prevented the crime. A corporation may also be liable for failing to perform a duty imposed by law.

2. Liability of Corporate Officers and Directors

Directors and officers are personally liable for crimes they commit and may be liable for the actions of employees under their supervision.

III. TYPES OF CRIMES

A. VIOLENT CRIME

These include murder, rape, assault and battery (see Chapter 12), and *robbery* (forcefully and unlawfully taking personal property from another). They are classified by degree, depending on intent, use of weapons, and the victim's suffering.

B. PROPERTY CRIME

Robbery could also be in this category.

1. Burglary

Burglary is the unlawful entry into a building with the intent to commit a felony.

2. Larceny

Wrongfully taking and carrying away another's personal property with the intent of depriving the owner permanently of the property (without force or intimidation, which are elements of robbery).

a. Property

The definition of property includes computer programs, computer time, trade secrets, cellular phone numbers, long-distance phone time, Internet service, and natural gas.

b. Grand Larceny and Petit Larceny

In some states, grand larceny is a felony and petit larceny a misdemeanor. The difference depends on the value of the property taken.

3. Arson

Arson is the willful and malicious burning of a building (and in some states, personal property) owned by another. Every state has a statute that covers burning a building to collect insurance.

4. Receiving Stolen Goods

The recipient need not know the identity of the true owner of the goods.

5. Forgery

Forgery is fraudulently making or altering any writing in a way that changes the legal rights and liabilities of another is forgery.

6. Obtaining Goods by False Pretenses

This includes, for example, buying goods with a check written on an account with insufficient funds.

C. PUBLIC ORDER CRIME

Examples: public drunkenness, prostitution, gambling, and illegal drug use.

D. WHITE-COLLAR CRIME

1. **Embezzlement**
   Embezzlement is fraudulently appropriating another's property or money by one who has been entrusted with it (without force or intimidation). Withholding taxes collected from employees can constitute embezzlement. Intending to return embezzled property is not a defense.

2. **Mail and Wire Fraud**

   a. **The Crime**
      It is a federal crime to (1) mail or cause someone else to mail something written, printed, or photocopied for the purpose of executing (2) a scheme to defraud (even if no one is defrauded). Also a crime to use wire, radio, or television transmissions to defraud.

   b. **The Punishment**
      Fine of up to $1,000, imprisonment for up to five years, or both. If the violation affects a financial institution, the fine may be up to $1 million, the imprisonment up to thirty years, or both.

3. **Bribery**

   a. **Bribery of Public Officials**
      This is attempting to influence a public official to act in a way that serves a private interest by offering the official a bribe. The crime is committed when the bribe (anything the recipient considers valuable) is offered.

   b. **Commercial Bribery**
      Commercial bribery is attempting, by a bribe, to obtain proprietary information, cover up an inferior product, or secure new business is commercial bribery.

   c. **Bribery of Foreign Officials**
      A crime occurs when attempting to bribe foreign officials to obtain business contracts. The Foreign Corrupt Practices Act of 1977 (see Chapter 4) makes this a crime.

4. **Bankruptcy Fraud**
   Filing a false claim against a debtor; fraudulently transferring assets to favored parties; or fraudulently concealing property before or after a petition for bankruptcy is filed.

5. **Insider Trading**
   Using inside information (information not available to the general public) about a publicly traded corporation to profit from the purchase or sale of the corporation's securities (see Chapter 29).

6. **Theft of Intellectual Property**
   It is a federal crime to steal trade secrets, or to knowingly buy or possess another's stolen secrets. Penalties include up to ten years' imprisonment, fines up to $500,000 (individual) or $5 million (corporation), and forfeiture of property. Piracy—the unauthorized copying of intellectual property—is also a federal crime, punishable by five years' imprisonment and $500,000 or more.

E. **ORGANIZED CRIME**

1. **Money Laundering**
   Transferring the proceeds of crime through legitimate businesses. Financial institutions must report transactions of more than $10,000.

2. **The Racketeer Influenced and Corrupt Organizations Act (RICO) of 1970**
   RICO incorporates by reference twenty-six federal crimes and nine state felonies. Two offenses constitute "racketeering activity."

a. **Activities Prohibited by RICO**
(1) Use income from racketeering to buy an interest in an enterprise, (2) acquire or maintain such an interest through racketeering activity' (3) conduct or participate in an enterprise through racketeering activity, or 4) conspire to do any of the above.

b. **Criminal Liability**
RICO can be used to attack white-collar crime. Penalties include fines of up to $25,000 per violation, imprisonment for up to 20 years, or both.

c. **Civil Liability**
Civil penalties include divestiture of a defendant's interest in a business or dissolution of the business. Private individuals can recover treble damages, plus attorneys' fees.

IV. DEFENSES TO CRIMINAL LIABILITY

A. JUSTIFIABLE USE OF FORCE
People can use as much nondeadly force as necessary to protect themselves, their dwellings, or other property or to prevent a crime. Deadly force can be used in self-defense if there is a reasonable belief that imminent death or serious bodily harm will otherwise result, if the attacker is using unlawful force, and if the defender did not provoke the attack.

B. NECESSITY
A defendant may be relieved of liability if his or her criminal act was necessary to prevent an even greater harm.

C. INSANITY

1. The Model Penal Code Test
Most federal courts and some states use this test: a person is not responsible for criminal conduct if at the time, as a result of mental disease or defect, the person lacks substantial capacity either to appreciate the wrongfulness of the conduct or to conform his or her conduct to the law.

2. The *M'Naughten* Test
Some states use this test: a person is not responsible if at the time of the offense, he or she did not know the nature and quality of the act or did not know that the act was wrong.

3. The Irresistible Impulse Test
Some states use this test: a person operating under an irresistible impulse may know an act is wrong but cannot refrain from doing it.

D. MISTAKE

1. Mistake of Fact
This is a defense if it negates the mental state necessary to commit a crime.

2. Mistake of Law
A person not knowing a law was broken may have a defense if (1) the law was not published or reasonably made known to the public or (2) the person relied on an official statement of the law that was wrong.

E. DURESS
Duress occurs when a threat induces a person to do something that he or she would not otherwise do. Duress can be a defense if the threat is of a danger that is immediate and inescapable.

F. ENTRAPMENT
This occurs when a law enforcement agent suggests that a crime be committed, pressures or induces an individual to commit it, and arrests the individual for it.

G. STATUTES OF LIMITATIONS
A statute of limitation provides that the state has only a certain amount of time to prosecute a crime. Most statutes of limitations do not apply to murder.

H. IMMUNITY
A state can grant immunity from prosecution or agree to prosecute for a less serious offense in exchange for information. This is often part of a plea bargain between the defendant and the prosecutor.

V.   CRIMINAL PROCEDURES

A. CONSTITUTIONAL SAFEGUARDS
Most of these safeguards apply not only in federal but also in state courts by virtue of the due process clause of the Fourteenth Amendment.

1. Fourth Amendment
This amendment provides protection from unreasonable searches and seizures. No warrants for a search or an arrest can be issued without probable cause.

2. Fifth Amendment
No one can be deprived of "life, liberty, or property without due process of law." No one can be tried twice (double jeopardy) for the same offense. No one can be required to incriminate themselves.

3. Sixth Amendment
This amendment guarantees a speedy trial, trial by jury, a public trial, the right to confront witnesses, and the right to a lawyer in some proceedings.

4. Eighth Amendment
This amendment prohibits excessive bail and fines, and cruel and unusual punishment.

B. THE EXCLUSIONARY RULE
Evidence obtained in violation of the Fourth, Fifth, and Sixth Amendments, as well as all "fruit of the poisonous tree" (evidence derived from illegally obtained evidence), must be excluded from trial. The purpose is to deter police misconduct.

C. THE *MIRANDA* RULE

1. Rights
A person in custody to be interrogated must be informed (1) he or she has the right to remain silent, (2) anything said can and will be used against him or her in court, (3) he or she has the right to consult with an attorney, and (4) if he or she is indigent, a lawyer will be appointed.

2. Exceptions
These rights can be waived if the waiver is knowing and voluntary. "Public safety" may warrant admissibility. If other evidence justifies a conviction, it will not be overturned if a confession was coerced. A suspect must assertively state that he or she wants a lawyer, to exercise that right.

D. CRIMINAL PROCESS

1. Arrest
An arrest requires a warrant based on probable cause (a substantial likelihood that the person has committed or is about to commit a crime). To make an arrest without a warrant, an officer must also have probable cause.

2. Indictment or Information
A formal charge is called an **indictment** if issued by a grand jury and an **information** if issued by a government prosecutor.

3. Trial
Criminal trial procedures are similar to those of a civil trial, but the standard of proof is higher: the prosecutor must establish guilt beyond a reasonable doubt.

4. Federal Sentencing Guidelines
These guidelines cover possible penalties for federal crimes. A sentence is based on a defendant's criminal record, seriousness of the offense, and other factors.

VI. CYBER CRIME

Computer crime is a violation of criminal law that involves knowledge of computer technology for its perpetration, investigation, or prosecution.

A. CYBER FRAUD

Fraud (a misrepresentation knowingly made with the intent to deceive another and on which a reasonable person relies to his or her detriment) occurs online via e-mail by false promises of funds or notices of a relative's distress.

1. Online Auction Fraud
This occurs when a buyer pays for an auctioned item but does not receive it, or receives something worth less than the promised article. It can be difficult to pinpoint a fraudulent seller, who may assume multiple identities.

2. Online Retail Fraud
This occurs when a consumer pays for, but does not receive, an item, which may be nonexistent or worthless.

B. CYBER THEFT

Cyber theft occurs when a thief steals data from a computer via the Internet.

1. Identity Theft
Identity theft occurs when a form of identification is stolen and used to access the victim's financial resources. Identity theft is a federal crime. Victims have rights to work with creditors and credit bureaus to remove negative information from credit reports, among other things.

2. Phishing
This occurs when a criminal posing as a legitimate business e-mails an unsuspecting individual to update or confirm personal banking, credit, or other information.

3. Vishing
This variation of phishing involves voice communication—an e-mail requesting a phone call, for example, to relate a credit account password and number.

4. Employment Fraud
A criminal may claim to be an employer to obtain personal information from job seekers who post their resumes online.

5. Credit-Card Crime on the Web
Stolen credit cards are more likely to hurt merchants and issuers because consumers whose cards are stolen are not liable for the costs of subsequent purchases made with the cards. Businesses take further risks by electronically storing customers' credit account numbers, which can be stolen.

C. HACKING

A hacker uses one computer to break into another, often without the knowledge of either computer's owner. A hacker might appropriate a number of computers by secretly installing a program on each to operate as a robot, or bot, and forward a transmission to more computers, creating a botnet.

1. Malware
A bot program, or any software harmful to a computer or its user, is malware. Other examples include a worm, which can reproduce itself and spread from computer to another,

and a virus, which can reproduce but must be attached to a host file to travel between computers.

2. **New Service-Based Hacking Available at Low Cost**
    The business trend of software as a service (SAAS) has been adopted by hackers who rent their crimeware as a service (CAAS) through various Web sites. Those who hire CAAS can target individual groups, if desired, for minimal cost.

3. **Cyberterrorism**
    A cyberterrorist exploits a computer for a serious impact, such as exploding an internal data "bomb" to shut down a central computer or spreading a virus to cripple a computer network. A business might be targeted to steal a customer list or business plans, to sabotage products or services, or to disrupt operations.

D. **PROSECUTING CYBER CRIMES**
    Jurisdictional issues and the anonymous nature of technology can hamper the investigation and prosecution of cyber crimes. For example, a person who commits an act that constitutes a crime in one jurisdiction may have acted from a different jurisdiction, where the act is not a crime. If the act is committed via e-mail, there may not be "sufficient contacts" to support a prosecution.

E. **THE COMPUTER FRAUD AND ABUSE ACT**
    The Counterfeit Access Device and Computer Fraud and Abuse Act of 1984 prohibits cyber theft. The crime consists of (1) accessing a computer without authority and (2) taking data. Penalties include fines and imprisonment for up to twenty years (and civil suits).

TRUE-FALSE QUESTIONS

(Answers at the Back of the Book)

____ 1. Only the government prosecutes criminal defendants.

____ 2. A crime punishable by imprisonment is a felony.

____ 3. Burglary involves taking another's personal property from his or her person or immediate presence.

____ 4. Embezzlement requires physically taking property for another's possession.

____ 5. Stealing computer time is larceny.

____ 6. Offering a bribe is only one element of the crime of bribery.

____ 7. Receiving stolen goods is a crime only if the recipient knows the true owner.

____ 8. Using a fabricated identity to access online funds is identity theft.

____ 9. The appropriate location for a trial can be a key issue in a case involving a cyber crime.

____ 10. A business takes no risk by electronically storing its customers' credit account numbers.

FILL-IN QUESTIONS

(Answers at the Back of the Book)

Specific constitutional safeguards for those accused of crimes apply in all federal courts, and most of them also apply in state courts under the due process clause of the Fourteenth Amendment. The safeguards include (1) the Fourth Amendment protection from _____ (unexpected/unreasonable) searches

and seizures, (2) the Fourth Amendment requirement that no warrants for a search or an arrest can be issued without _____ (probable/possible) cause, (3) the Fifth Amendment requirement that no one can be deprived of "life, liberty, or property without _____ (consent/due process of law)," (4) the Fifth Amendment prohibition against double _____ (immunity/jeopardy), (5) the Sixth Amendment guaranties of a speedy _____ (appeal/trial), _____ _____ (appeal to/trial by) a jury, a public trial, the right to confront _____ (counsel/witnesses), and the right to legal counsel, and (6) the Eighth Amendment prohibitions against excessive _____(bail/bail and fines) and cruel and unusual punishment.

MULTIPLE-CHOICE QUESTIONS

(Answers at the Back of the Book)

____ **1.** Loren is charged with criminal theft. For a conviction, like most crimes, theft requires

a. a guilty conscience and physical symptoms such as sweaty palms.
b. a personal ethics code and a failure to follow its standards.
c. a specified state of mind and performance of a prohibited act.
d. a desire or an ambition, a plan to accomplish a goal, and the motivation to act.

____ **2.** Gwen signs Heidi's name, without her consent, to the back of a check. This is

a. burglary.
b. embezzlement.
c. forgery.
d. larceny.

____ **3.** Newt, a bank teller, deposits into his account checks that bank customers give to him to deposit into their accounts. This is

a. burglary.
b. embezzlement.
c. forgery.
d. larceny.

____ **4.** Grover posts an electric piano for bids on iSell, a Web auction site. Hyapatia makes the highest bid and sends the payment, which Grover receives, but he does not ship the piano. This is online

a. auction fraud.
b. puffery.
c. retail fraud.
d. trickery but not fraud.

____ **5.** Posing as Deft Credit Company, Milo e-mails Lovey, asking her to verify her credit card information through a link in the e-mail. She clicks on the prompt and enters the data. This is

a. employment fraud.
b. phishing.
c. piracy.
d. vishing.

____ **6.** Crissy uses her computer and an online connection to break into Bargain Discount Store's computer network. Crissy is

a. a virus.
b. a hacker.
c. a worm.
d. malware.

___ 7. Jody, a government agent, arrests Kevin for the commission of a crime. Kevin claims that Jody entrapped him. This is a valid defense if Jody

    a. did not tell Kevin that she was a government agent.
    b. pressured Kevin into committing the crime.
    c. set a trap for Kevin, who was looking to commit the crime.
    d. was predisposed to commit a crime.

___ 8. Perla is arrested on suspicion of the commission of a crime. Individuals who are arrested must be told of their right to

    a. confront witnesses.
    b. protection against unreasonable searches.
    c. remain silent.
    d. trial by jury.

___ 9. While away from her business, Kate is arrested on suspicion of commission of a crime. At Kate's trial, under the exclusionary rule

    a. biased individuals must be excluded from the jury.
    b. business records must be excluded from admission as evidence.
    c. illegally obtained evidence must be excluded from admission as evidence.
    d. the arresting officer must be excluded from testifying.

___ 10. Eve is arrested on suspicion of commission of a crime. A grand jury issues a formal charge against her. This is

    a. an arraignment.
    b. an indictment.
    c. an information.
    d. an inquisition.

SHORT ESSAY QUESTIONS

1. What are some of the significant differences between criminal law and civil law?

2. What constitutes criminal liability under the Racketeer Influenced and Corrupt Organizations Act, and what are the penalties?

GAMEPOINTS

(Answers at the Back of the Book)

1. In the video game "Xtreme Climb," your avatar is making an ascent up the highest peak in the United States, when a yeti—an abominable snowman—leaps from an outcropping and tosses your climbing companion from the precipice. The yeti howls into the wind and stomps along the ledge towards your avatar. Which crimes described in this chapter, if any, has the yeti committed? Explain.

2. You're playing "Not Me," a video game in which your identity has been stolen and is in use by someone else. Your credit is being depleted and your bank accounts are being bled dry. What methods are most likely being used to rob you?

Chapter 8
International Law in a Global Economy

WHAT THIS CHAPTER IS ABOUT

This chapter notes sources of international law, some of the ways in which U.S. businesspersons do business in foreign countries, and how that business is regulated. The chapter concludes with a look at some aspects of national legal systems.

CHAPTER OUTLINE

I. **INTERNATIONAL LAW**
To facilitate commerce, sovereign nations agree to be governed in certain respects by international law.

A. **SOURCES OF INTERNATIONAL LAW**

1. **International Customs**
These are customs that evolved among nations in their relations with each other. "[E]vidence of a general practice accepted as law" [Article 38(1) of the Statute of the International Court of Justice].

2. **Treaties and International Agreements**
A treaty is an agreement or contract between two or more nations that must be authorized and ratified by the supreme power of each nation. A bilateral agreement occurs when only two nations form an agreement; multilateral agreements are those formed by several nations.

3. **International Organizations**
Composed mainly of nations (such as the United Nations); usually established by treaty; such entities adopt resolutions that require particular behavior of nations (such as the 1980 United Nations Convention on Contracts for the International Sale of Goods).

B. **COMMON LAW AND CIVIL SYSTEMS**
Legal systems are generally divided into common law and civil law systems.

1. **Common Law Systems**
Common law systems are based on case law. These systems exist in countries that were once a part of the British Empire (such as Australia, India, and the United States). *Stare decisis* requires following precedent unless otherwise necessary.

2. **Civil Law Systems**
Civil law systems are based on codified law (statutes). Courts interpret the code and apply the rules without developing their own laws. Civil law systems exist in most European nations, and in Latin American, African, and Asian countries.

3. **Islamic Law Systems**
In an Islamic legal system, the law is influenced by *sharia*, the religious law of Islam. Some Middle Eastern countries have codified *sharia* and enforce it through national court systems.

61

C. INTERNATIONAL PRINCIPLES AND DOCTRINES

The following are based on courtesy and respect and are applied in the interest of maintaining harmony among nations.

1. The Principle of Comity

One nation defers and gives effect to the laws and judicial decrees of another country, so long as those laws and judicial decrees are consistent with the law and public policy of the accommodating nation.

2. The Act of State Doctrine

The judicial branch of one country will not examine the validity of public acts committed by a recognized foreign government within its own territory. This doctrine applies in cases of—

a. Expropriation

This occurs when a government seizes a privately owned business or goods for a proper public purpose and pays just compensation.

b. Confiscation

This occurs when a government seizes private property for an illegal purpose or without just compensation. In a suit on this ground, the defendant must show that a taking was an expropriation, not a confiscation.

3. The Doctrine of Sovereign Immunity

This doctrine exempts foreign nations from the jurisdiction of domestic courts. In the United States, the Foreign Sovereign Immunities Act (FSIA) of 1976 exclusively governs the circumstances in which an action may be brought against a foreign nation. Generally, the plaintiff must show that the defendant is not entitled to sovereign immunity.

a. When Is a Foreign State Subject to U.S. Jurisdiction?

When it has waived its immunity, when the action is based on commercial activity in the U.S. by the foreign state, or when the foreign state has committed a tort or violated certain international laws [Section 1605].

b. What Entities Fall within the Category of Foreign State?

A political subdivision and an instrumentality (an agency or entity acting for the state) [Section 1603].

c. What Is a Commercial Activity?

Courts decide whether an activity is governmental or commercial.

II. DOING BUSINESS INTERNATIONALLY

A. EXPORTING

The simplest way to do business internationally is to export to foreign markets. Direct exporting: signing a sales contract with a foreign buyer. Indirect exporting: selling directly to consumers through a foreign agent or foreign distributor.

B. MANUFACTURING ABROAD

A domestic firm can establish a manufacturing plant abroad by—

1. Licensing

A firm may license its technology to a foreign manufacturer to avoid the process, product, or formula being pirated. The foreign firm agrees to keep the technology secret and to pay royalties for its use.

2. Franchising

Franchising (see Chapter 17) is a form of licensing in which the owner of a trademark, trade name, or copyright conditions its use in the selling of goods or services.

3. Investing in a Wholly Owned Subsidiary or a Joint Venture
When a wholly owned subsidiary is established, the domestic firm retains ownership of the foreign facilities and control over the entire operation. In a joint venture, a domestic firm and one or more foreign firms share ownership, responsibilities, profits, and liabilities.

III. REGULATION OF SPECIFIC BUSINESS ACTIVITIES

A. INVESTMENT PROTECTIONS
When a government confiscates property without just compensation, few remedies are available. Many countries guarantee compensation to foreign investors in their constitutions, statutes, or treaties. Some countries provide insurance for their citizens' investments abroad.

B. EXPORT CONTROLS

1. Restricting Exports
Under the U.S. Constitution, Congress cannot tax exports, but may set export quotas. Under the Export Administration Act of 1979, restrictions can be imposed on the flow of technologically advanced products and technical data.

2. Stimulating Exports
Devices to stimulate exports include export incentives and subsidies.

C. IMPORT CONTROLS
Laws prohibit, for example, importing illegal drugs and agricultural products that pose dangers to domestic crops or animals.

1. Quotas and Tariffs
Quotas limit how much can be imported. Tariffs are taxes on imports (usually a percentage of the value, but can be a flat rate per unit).

2. Antidumping Duties
A tariff (duty) may be assessed on imports to prevent *dumping* (sales of imported goods at "less than fair value," usually determined by prices in the exporting country).

D. TRADE AGREEMENTS THAT MINIMIZE TRADE BARRIERS

1. The World Trade Organization (WTO)
This the principal instrument for regulating international trade. Each member country agrees to grant *normal-trade-relations (NTR) status* to other members (the most favorable treatment with regard to trade).

2. The European Union (EU)
The EU is a regional trade association that minimizes trade barriers among its member nations.

3. The North American Free Trade Agreement (NAFTA)
NAFTA created a regional trading unit consisting of Mexico, the United States, and Canada. The goal is to eliminate tariffs in the region on substantially all goods over a period of fifteen to twenty years, while retaining tariffs on goods imported from other countries.

4. The Central American-Dominican Republic Free Trade Agreement (CAFTA-DR)
CAFTA-DR aims to reduce tariffs and improve market access among Costa Rica, Dominican Republic, El Salvador, Guatemala, Honduras, Nicaragua, and the United States.

IV. U.S. LAWS IN A GLOBAL CONTEXT

A. U.S. ANTITRUST LAWS
For U.S. courts to exercise jurisdiction over a foreign entity under U.S. antitrust laws, a violation must (1) have a substantial effect on U.S. commerce or (2) constitute a *per se* violation (see

Chapter 27). Foreign governments and persons·can also sue U.S. firms and persons for antitrust violations.

B. INTERNATIONAL TORT CLAIMS
The Alien Tort Claims Act (ATCA) of 1789 allows foreign citizens to bring suits in U.S. courts for injuries allegedly caused by violations of international tort law. Some cases have involved violations of human rights, including torture and discrimination. Some have alleged environmental crimes.

C. ANTIDISCRIMINATION LAWS
U.S. employers must abide by U.S. employment discrimination laws (see Chapter 22) unless to do so would violate the laws of the country in which their workplace is located.

TRUE-FALSE QUESTIONS

(Answers at the Back of the Book)

____ **1.** All nations must give effect to the laws of all other nations.

____ **2.** Under the act of state doctrine, foreign nations are subject to the jurisdiction of U.S. courts.

____ **3.** Under the doctrine of sovereign immunity, foreign nations are subject to the jurisdiction of U.S. courts.

____ **4.** The Foreign Sovereign Immunities Act states the circumstances in which the United States can be sued in foreign courts.

____ **5.** A member of the World Trade Organization must usually grant other members most-favored nation status, with regard to trade.

____ **6.** U.S. courts cannot exercise jurisdiction over foreign entities under U.S. antitrust laws.

____ **7.** Legal systems are generally divided into criminal law and civil law systems.

____ **8.** U.S. employers with workplaces abroad must generally comply with U.S. discrimination laws.

____ ·**9.** Foreign citizens can bring suits in U.S. courts for injuries allegedly caused by violations of international tort law.

____ **10.** Congress cannot tax exports.

FILL-IN QUESTIONS

(Answers at the Back of the Book)

_____ (A confiscation/An expropriation) occurs when a national government seizes a privately owned business or privately owned goods for a proper public purpose. _____ _____ (A confiscation/An expropriation) occurs when the taking is made for an illegal purpose. When ____ _____ (a confiscation/an expropriation) occurs, the government pays just compensation. When _____ (a confiscation/an expropriation) occurs, the government does not pay just compensation.

MULTIPLE-CHOICE QUESTIONS

(Answers at the Back of the Book)

____ **1.** Lightspeed, Inc., makes supercomputers that feature advanced technology. To inhibit Lightspeed's export of its products to other countries, Congress can

    a. confiscate all profits on exported supercomputers.
    b. expropriate all profits on exported supercomputers.
    c. set quotas on exported supercomputers.
    d. tax exported supercomputers.

____ **2.** Kenya issues bonds to finance the construction of an international airport. Kenya sells some of the bonds in the United States to Lacy. A terrorist group destroys the airport, and Kenya refuses to pay interest or principal on the bonds. Lacy files suit in a U.S court. The court will hear the suit

    a. if Kenya's acts constitute a confiscation.
    b. if Kenya's acts constitute an expropriation.
    c. if Kenya's selling bonds is a "commercial activity."
    d. under no circumstances.

____ **3.** To obtain new computers, Liberia accepts bids from U.S. firms, including Macro Corporation and Micro, Inc. Macro wins the contract. Alleging impropriety in the awarding of the contract, Micro files a suit in a U.S. court against Liberia and Macro. The court may decline to hear the suit under

    a. the act of state doctrine.
    b. the doctrine of sovereign immunity.
    c. the Export Administration Act.
    d. the World Trade Organization.

____ **4.** An Australian seller and a U.S. buyer form a contract that the buyer breaches. The seller sues in an Australian court and wins damages, but the buyer's assets are in the United States. If a U.S. court enforces the judgment, it will be because of

    a. the act of state doctrine.
    b. the doctrine of sovereign immunity.
    c. the principle of comity.
    d. the World Trade Organization.

____ **5.** General Auto Corporation makes cars in the United States. To boost the sales of General Auto and other domestic automakers, Congress can

    a. neither set quotas nor tax imports.
    b. only set quotas on imports.
    c. only tax imports.
    d. set quotas and tax imports.

____ **6.** The United States has a common law legal system. Common law systems are based on

    a. administrative rules and regulations.
    b. case law.
    c. codified law.
    d. executive pronouncements.

_____ **7.** France has a civil law legal system. Civil law systems are based on

   a. administrative rules and regulations.
   b. case law.
   c. codified law.
   d. executive pronouncements.

_____ **8.** United Oil, Inc., is a U.S. firm, doing business in the United States and in other nations, including Venezuela. Venezuela seizes the property of United Oil, without paying just compensation. This is

   a. a confiscation.
   b. a dumping.
   c. a licensing.
   d. an expropriation.

_____ **9.** Global Construction, Inc., is a U.S. firm. Helen, a U.S. citizen, works for Global in a country outside the United States. Inez, a citizen of a foreign country, also works for Global outside the United States. Helen and Inez believe that they are being harassed on the job, in violation of U.S. law. This law protects

   a. Helen and Inez.
   b. Helen only.
   c. Inez only.
   d. neither Helen nor Inez.

_____ **10.** High Sierra Lumber Company, a U.S. firm, signs a contract with Izo, Ltd., a Japanese company, to give Izo the right to sell High Sierra's products in Japan. This is

   a. a distribution agreement.
   b. a joint venture.
   c. direct exporting.
   d. licensing.

SHORT ESSAY QUESTIONS

1. In what ways may a company conduct international business?

2. How does the Foreign Sovereign Immunities Act affect commercial activities by foreign governments?

GAMEPOINTS

(Answers at the Back of the Book)

1. In the video game "Business Planet," your avatar flies in a private jet around the world, making deals. The play involves the application of legal doctrines, economic principles, and cultural values to outwit competitors in global markets and profit handsomely. In an Asian city, Won Thieu Tre, Ltd., offers your avatar a deal that promises a 200 percent profit. Your avatar immediately accepts. Won Thieu Tre fails to pay, however, and you file a suit in the game in a U.S. court. The defendant claims "sovereign immunity." What does this mean?

2. Still playing "Business Planet," you warehouse a variety of raw materials and other resources on your firm's property in Indonesia in anticipation of enterprising contracts with local outfits in the economically booming Far East. A political party hostile to Western influence ascends to power and seizes these assets. Your avatar protests, asking for compensation. The government responds that if you were entitled to anything, the profit that you have already accrued is enough. Could you recover more in a U.S. court? Why or why not?

CUMULATIVE HYPOTHETICAL PROBLEM
FOR UNIT TWO—INCLUDING CHAPTERS 5–8

(Answers at the Back of the Book)

GPS, Inc., designs and sells the technology for advanced global positioning systems that can be used to pinpoint the location of virtually any person or object.

____ 1. As a for-profit corporation that does business in interstate commerce, GPS may be subject to regulations issued by

    a. federal administrative agencies only.
    b. federal agencies or state agencies in states in which Corrosive does business.
    c. neither federal nor state agencies.
    d. state agencies in states in which Corrosive does business only.

____ 2. During an investigation into GPS's activities, a court orders GPS to provide its business records. As a corporation, GPS can

    a. be compelled to provide only records that do *not* incriminate its officers.
    b. be compelled to provide records that incriminate its officers.
    c. refuse to provide records that incriminate its officers.
    d. refuse to provide *any* business records.

____ 3. After the investigation into GPS's activities, some of its officers are suspected of having committed crimes. As a corporation, GPS can

    a. be fined or denied certain privileges if it is held criminally liable.
    b. be imprisoned if it is held criminally liable.
    c. be fined, denied privileges, or imprisoned if it is held criminally liable.
    d. not be found to be criminally liable.

____ 4. Congress enacts a law that affects GPS, which challenges the law on the basis of equal protection. This means that GPS claims the law

    a. does not include sufficient procedural safeguards.
    b. limits the liberty of *all* persons in a way that is unconstitutional.
    c. limits the liberty of *some* persons in a way that is unconstitutional.
    d. unduly burdens interstate commerce.

____ 5. A dispute arises between GPS and Fong, Ltd., a Chinese firm. GPS obtains a judgment in a U.S. court against Fong. Whether this judgment will be enforced by a court in China depends on the Chinese court's application of

    a. the act of state doctrine.
    b. the doctrine of sovereign immunity.
    c. the principle of comity.
    d. the World Trade Organization.

QUESTIONS ON THE FOCUS ON ETHICS FOR UNIT TWO— THE PUBLIC AND INTERNATIONAL ENVIRONMENT

(Answers at the Back of the Book)

Quality Unlimited Info Company (QUIC) collects and sells personal data about individuals to businesses.

____   1.   In some countries, QUIC tailors its data and marketing to those countries' censorship requirements. In ethical terms, QUIC's actions may

      a.   constitute cyber theft.
      b.   suppress freedom of speech.
      c.   transgress the arbitrary and capricious standard.
      d.   undermine the principle of sovereign immunity.

____   2.   QUIC wants to use its resources to influence the political process with respect to issues that do not relate to QUIC's business. QUIC's state attempts to block this use of resources. In a challenge to the state's action, under the First Amendment the most important question is whether

      a.   QUIC and other corporations are protected by the free speech clause.
      b.   QUIC should leverage political power through its economic skills.
      c.   QUIC's speech is political in nature.
      d.   QUIC's speech relates to an economic matter.

____   3.   The Environmental Protection Agency (EPA) may inspect QUIC's plant

      a.   only if a regulatory violation is occurring.
      b.   only if QUIC is in an industry subject to extensive regulation.
      c.   only if the EPA is obtaining private information for regulatory purposes.
      d.   under no circumstances.

Chapter 9
Contract Formation

WHAT THIS CHAPTER IS ABOUT

Contract law concerns the formation and keeping of promises, the excuses our society accepts for breaking such promises, and what promises are considered contrary to public policy and therefore legally void. This chapter introduces the basic terms and concepts of contract law.

CHAPTER OUTLINE

I. AN OVERVIEW OF CONTRACT LAW

A. SOURCES OF CONTRACT LAW
Contract law is common law, which governs all contracts except when statutes or administrative regulations have modified or replaced it. Statutory law—particularly the Uniform Commercial Code (UCC)—governs all contracts for sales of goods.

B. THE FUNCTION OF CONTRACT LAW
Contract law ensures compliance with a promise and entitles a nonbreaching party to relief when a contract is breached. All contractual relationships involve promises, but all promises do not establish contractual relationships. Most contractual promises are kept, because keeping a promise is generally in the mutual self-interest of the promisor and the promisee.

C. DEFINITION OF A CONTRACT
A **contract** is a promise for the breach of which the law gives a remedy or the performance of which the law recognizes as a duty (that is, an agreement that can be enforced in court). A contract may be formed when two or more parties promise to perform or to refrain from performing some act now or in the future. A party who does not fulfill his or her promise may be subject to sanctions, including damages or, in some circumstances, being required to perform the promise.

D. THE OBJECTIVE THEORY OF CONTRACTS
Intent to enter into a contract is judged by objective (outward) facts as interpreted by a reasonable person, rather than by a party's subjective intent. Objective facts include (1) what a party says when entering into a contract, (2) how a party acts or appears, and (3) circumstances surrounding a deal.

E. ELEMENTS OF A CONTRACT

1. Requirements of a Valid Contract

a. Agreement
This requirement includes an offer and an acceptance. One party must offer to enter into a legal agreement, and another party must accept the offer.

b. Consideration
Promises must be supported by legally sufficient and bargained-for consideration.

c. Contractual Capacity
This includes characteristics that qualify the parties to a contract as competent.

69

    d. Legality
    A contract's purpose must be to accomplish a goal that is not against public policy.

  2. Defenses to the Enforceability of a Contract

    a. Genuineness of Assent
    The apparent consent of both parties must be genuine.

    b. Form
    A contract must be in whatever form the law requires (some contracts must be in writing).

II. TYPES OF CONTRACTS

Each category signifies a legal distinction regarding a contract's formation, performance, or enforceability.

A. CONTRACT FORMATION

1. Bilateral versus Unilateral Contracts
Bilateral contract—a promise for a promise (to accept the offer, the offeree need only promise to perform). *Unilateral contract*—a promise for an act (the offeree can accept only by completing performance, but once performance has substantially begun, the offeror cannot revoke the offer).

2. Formal versus Informal Contracts
Formal contract—a special form or method of creation is required for enforcement. *Informal contract*—a contract that is not formal (certain contracts must be in writing, however).

3. Express versus Implied-in-Fact Contracts
Express contract—the terms of the agreement are fully and explicitly stated in words (oral or written). *Implied contract*—implied from the conduct of the parties.

B. CONTRACT PERFORMANCE

Executed contract—a contract that has been fully performed on both sides. *Executory contract*—a contract that has not been fully performed by one or more of the parties.

C. CONTRACT ENFORCEABILITY

Valid contract—has all elements necessary to entitle at least one party to enforce it. *Void contract*—produces no legal obligations on the part of any of the parties. *Voidable contract*—valid contract that can be avoided by one or more of the parties. *Unenforceable contract*—contract that cannot be enforced because of certain legal defenses.

III. AGREEMENT

A. REQUIREMENTS OF THE OFFER

An offer is a promise or commitment to do or refrain from doing some specified thing in the future. The elements for an offer to be effective are—

1. Intention
The offeror must intend to be bound by the offer. Intent is determined by what a reasonable person in the offeree's position would conclude the offeror's words and actions meant.

    a. Expressions and Statements That Are Not Offers
    These include (1) expressions of opinion, (2) statements of intention, (3) preliminary negotiations, and (4) advertisements, catalogues, price lists, and circulars.

    b. Agreements to Agree
    An agreement to agree to a material term of a contract at some future date may be enforced if the parties clearly intended to be bound and agreed on all essential terms, and no disputed issues remain. The emphasis is on the parties' intent rather than on form.

2. **Definiteness of Terms**
All major terms must be stated with reasonable definiteness in the offer (or, if the offeror directs, in the offeree's acceptance). Courts are sometimes willing to supply a missing term when the parties have clearly manifested an intent to form a contract.

3. **Communication of the Offer**
The offer must be communicated to the offeree.

B. TERMINATION OF THE OFFER

1. **Termination by Action of the Parties**

   a. **Revocation of the Offer by the Offeror**
   The offeror can revoke an offer by express repudiation or by performance of acts that are inconsistent with the offer and that are made known to the offeree. A revocation becomes effective when the offeree or offeree's agent actually receives it.

   b. **Option Contracts and Other Irrevocable Offers**
   An *option contract* is a promise to hold an offer open for a specified period of time in return for a payment (if no time is specified, a reasonable time is implied). An offer may be irrevocable if the offeree justifiably relies on it to his or her detriment. A merchant's firm offer may be irrevocable (see Chapter 11).

   c. **Rejection of the Offer by the Offeree**
   An offer may be rejected by words or conduct evidencing an intent not to accept the offer. Asking about an offer is not rejecting it. Rejection is effective only on its receipt by the offeror or the offeror's agent.

   d. **Counteroffer by the Offeree**
   The offeree's attempt to include different terms is a rejection of the original offer and a simultaneous making of a new offer. The *mirror image rule* requires the acceptance to match the offer exactly.

2. **Termination by Operation of Law**

   a. **Lapse of Time**
   An offer terminates when the time specified in the offer has passed. The time begins to run when the offeree receives the offer, not when it is sent. If no time is specified, the offer terminates at the end of a reasonable period, as determined by the circumstances.

   b. **Other Events**
   An offer can be terminated by destruction of the subject matter of the offer, the death of incompetence of either party, or a statute or court decision that makes the offer illegal.

C. ACCEPTANCE

1. **Unequivocal Acceptance**
The offeree must accept the offer unequivocally. Silence can constitute acceptance if the offeree (1) takes the benefit of offered services after an opportunity to reject them, or (2) had prior dealings with the offeror that led the offeror to believe silence would be acceptance.

2. **Communication of Acceptance**
A bilateral contract is formed when acceptance is communicated (must be timely). In a unilateral contract, communication is unnecessary, unless the offeror requests notice or has no adequate means of determining if the act has been performed.

3. **Mode and Timeliness of Acceptance**
An acceptance is timely if it is made before the offer is terminated.

   a. **The Mailbox Rule**
   Acceptance is effective on dispatch when sent by whatever means is authorized by the offeror. This is the *mailbox rule*.

b. Authorized Means of Acceptance
Specific means can be stated in the offer or authorized by facts or by law. If an offeror specifies an exclusive means, a contract is not formed unless the offeree uses it. If the offeror does not specify a certain means, the offeree can accept by any medium reasonable under the circumstances (the same means the offeror used to communicate the offer or a faster means).

c. Substitute Method of Acceptance
An acceptance sent by unauthorized means is effective on receipt.

IV. CONSIDERATION
Consideration is the value given in return for a promise.

A. ELEMENTS OF CONSIDERATION

1. Legally Sufficient Value
Something of legal value must be given in exchange for a promise. It may be a return promise. If it is performance, it may be (1) an act (other than a promise); (2) a forbearance (refraining from action); or (3) the creation, modification, or destruction of a legal relation.

2. Bargained-for Exchange
The promise must induce the value, and the value must induce the promise. Situations that lack this element include "past" consideration (promises made with respect to events that have already taken place are unenforceable).

3. Adequacy of Consideration
Generally, a court will not evaluate adequacy (the fairness of a bargain), unless its absence indicates fraud, duress, incapacity, undue influence, or a lack of bargained-for exchange.

B. AGREEMENTS THAT LACK CONSIDERATION

1. Preexisting Duty
A promise to do what one already has a legal duty to do is not consideration. But if a party runs into extraordinary difficulties that were unforeseen when a contract was formed, an agreement to pay more may be enforced. Also, parties can rescind a contract to the extent it is executory.

2. Past Consideration
A promise made in return for an event that has already occurred lacks consideration.

C. PROMISSORY ESTOPPEL
Under the doctrine of **promissory estoppel** (detrimental reliance), a person who relies on the promise of another may be able to recover in the absence of consideration if—

1. The promise was clear and definite.
2. The reliance is justifiable.
3. The promisor knew or had reason to believe that the promisee would likely rely on the promise, and the reliance induced a change of a substantial and definite character.
4. Justice will be better served by enforcement of the promise.

V. CAPACITY
Persons who are minors, intoxicated, or mentally incompetent but not yet adjudicated officially as such, have capacity to enter into a contract; but they can normally avoid liability under the contract.

VI. LEGALITY

A. CONTRACTS CONTRARY TO STATUTE

1. Contracts to Commit a Crime
A contract to commit a crime is illegal. If the contract is rendered illegal by statute after it has been entered into, the contract is discharged.

2. Usury
Every state sets rates of interest charged for loans (with exceptions for certain business deals). Charging a higher rate is usury—some states allow recovery of the principal plus interest; other states allow recovery of the principal but no interest; a few states permit no recovery.

3. Gambling
All states regulate gambling (any scheme that involves distribution of property by chance among persons who pay for the chance to receive the property). Some states do not enforce gambling debts. Issues include whether one state can regulate its residents who gamble through gaming sites based elsewhere and whether betting on fantasy sports is gambling.

4. Licensing Statutes
All states require certain professionals to obtain licenses. If the purpose is to raise revenue, a contract with an unlicensed practitioner normally will be enforceable. If the purpose is to protect the public from unlicensed practitioners, such a contract will be unenforceable.

B. CONTRACTS CONTRARY TO PUBLIC POLICY

1. Contracts in Restraint of Trade

a. Prohibited Contracts
Contracts that restrain trade, adversely affect the public, or violate an antitrust statute.

b. Covenant Not to Compete
Acceptable if reasonable, determined by the time and size of area in which the party agrees not to compete. (In the sale of a business, it must also be a separate agreement.) To prevent undue hardship courts in some states convert the terms into reasonable ones and enforce the covenants.

2. Unconscionable Contracts or Clauses
A bargain that is unfairly one-sided is unconscionable.

a. Procedural Unconscionability
This relates to a party's lack of knowledge or understanding of contract terms because of small print, "legalese," etc. An adhesion contract (drafted by one party for his benefit) may be held unconscionable.

b. Substantive Unconscionability
This relates to the parts of a contract that are so unfairly one-sided they "shock the conscience" of the court.

3. Exculpatory Clauses
This is a contract clause that absolves a party of negligence or other wrong. Often held to be unconscionable, but may be enforced if the party seeking its enforcement is not involved in a business important to the public interest (health clubs, amusement parks).

VII. VOLUNTARY CONSENT

A. MISTAKES
It is important to distinguish between mistakes made in judgment as to value or quality and mistakes made as to facts. Only the latter have legal significance.

1. Bilateral (Mutual) Mistakes
When both parties make a mistake as to a material fact, either party can rescind the contract. The same rule applies if the parties attach materially different meanings to a word or term in the contract that may be subject to more than one reasonable interpretation.

2. Unilateral Mistakes of Fact
A unilateral mistake as to a material fact does not afford a mistaken party relief. Exceptions: include (1) if the other party knows or should know of the mistake or (2) if the mistake is due to a mathematical error and is done inadvertently and without gross negligence.

B. FRAUDULENT MISREPRESENTATION
If an innocent party is fraudulently induced to enter into a contract, the contract normally can be avoided. Fraud consists of: (1) misrepresentation of a material fact, (2) an intent to deceive, and (3) the innocent party's justifiable reliance on the misrepresentation. To collect damages, a party must also have suffered an injury.

C. UNDUE INFLUENCE
Occurs when a contract enriches a party at the expense of another dominated by the enriched party. The contract is voidable. Essentially, the party taken advantage of does not exercise free will.

D. DURESS
Involves forcing a party to enter into a contract by threatening the party with an act that is wrongful or illegal. Threatening to exercise a legal right or taking advantage of another's economic need (unless the party exacting the price also creates the need) does not give rise to duress.

VIII. THE STATUTE OF FRAUDS
The Statute of Frauds stipulates what types of contracts must be in writing to be enforceable. If a contract is not in writing, it is not void but the Statute of Frauds is a defense to its enforcement.

A. CONTRACTS THAT MUST BE IN WRITING TO BE ENFORCEABLE
(1) Contracts involving interests in land, (2) contracts that cannot be performed within one year of formation, (3) collateral promises, (4) promises in consideration of marriage, and (5) contracts for sales of goods priced at $500 or more (see Chapter 11).

B. EXCEPTION
Some courts apply the doctrine of promissory estoppel to allow parties to recover under oral contracts that would otherwise be unenforceable under the Statute of Frauds.

IX. THIRD PARTY RIGHTS

A. ASSIGNMENTS
The transfer of a contract right to a third person is an assignment.

1. Rights That Cannot Be Assigned
Rights cannot be assigned if a statute prohibits assignment, a contract is personal (unless all that remains is a money payment), the assignment materially increases or alters the risk or duties of the obligor, or the contract provides that it cannot be assigned.

2. Exceptions
A contract cannot prevent an assignment of (1) a right to receive money, (2) rights in real property, (3) rights in negotiable instruments (checks and notes), or (4) a right to receive damages for breach of a sales contract or for payment of an amount owed under the contract (even if the contract prohibits it).

B. DELEGATIONS
Duties are not assigned; they are delegated. A delegation does not relieve the delegator of the obligation to perform if the delegatee fails to perform.

1. Duties That Cannot Be Delegated
Any duty can be delegated unless (1) performance depends on the personal skill or talents of the obligor, (2) special trust has been placed in the obligor, (3) performance by a third party will vary materially from that expected by the obligee, or (4) the contract prohibits it.

2. Effect of a Delegation
The obligee must accept performance from the delegatee, unless the duty is one that cannot be delegated. If the delegatee fails to perform, the delegator is still liable.

C. THIRD PARTY BENEFICIARIES

There are two types of third party beneficiaries: intended and incidental. An intended beneficiary is one for whose benefit a contract is made; if the contract is breached, he or she can sue the promisor. The benefit that an incidental beneficiary receives from a contract between other parties is unintentional; an incidental beneficiary cannot enforce the contract.

TRUE-FALSE QUESTIONS

(Answers at the Back of the Book)

____ 1. All promises are legal contracts.

____ 2. An agreement includes an offer and an acceptance.

____ 3. A contract not to compete is never enforceable.

____ 4. A contract providing that one party is to pay another "a fair share of the profits" is enforceable.

____ 5. Inadequate consideration may indicate fraud, duress, or undue influence.

____ 6. A promise to do what one already has a legal duty to do is not legally sufficient consideration.

____ 7. A minor may generally disaffirm a contract entered into with an adult.

____ 8. Under a mistake of fact, a contract can sometimes be avoided.

____ 9. A contract for a transfer of an interest in land need not be in writing to be enforceable.

____ 10. Acceptance is timely if it is made before an offer terminates.

FILL-IN QUESTIONS

(Answers at the Back of the Book)

Whether or not a party intended to enter into a contract is determined by the _____ (objective/subjective) theory of contracts. The theory is that a party's intention to enter into a contract is judged by _____ (objective/subjective) facts as they would be interpreted by a reasonable person. Relevant facts include: (1) what the party said; (2) what the party _____ (did/secretly believed); and (3) the _____ (circumstances surrounding/party's personal thoughts concerning) the transaction. Generally, courts examine facts in _____ (a particular transaction/similar transactions) to determine whether the parties made a contract and, if so, what its terms are.

MULTIPLE-CHOICE QUESTIONS

(Answers at the Back of the Book)

____ 1. Gio questions whether there is consideration for his contract with Huey. Consideration has two elements—there must be a bargained-for exchange and the value of whatever is exchanged must be

a. adequately sufficient.
b. definitely sufficient.
c. economically sufficient.
d. legally sufficient.

____ **2.** Stuart claims that he and Trina entered into a contract. The intent to enter into a contract is determined with reference to

    a. the conscious theory of contracts.
    b. the objective theory of contracts.
    c. the personal theory of contracts.
    d. the subjective theory of contracts.

____ **3.** Echo enters into an implied-in-fact contract with Flip. The parties' conduct

    a. defines the contract's terms.
    b. determines the facts.
    c. factors in the implications of the contract.
    d. is irrelevant in terms of the facts.

____ **4.** Rena, a sixteen-year-old minor, buys a car from Super Autos and wrecks it. To disaffirm the contract and satisfy a duty of restitution, Rena must

    a. neither return the car nor pay for the damage.
    b. only return the car.
    c. only pay for the damage.
    d. return the car and pay for the damage.

____ **5.** Metro Airport asks for bids on a construction project. Metro estimates that the cost will be $2,000,000. Most bids are about $2,000,000, but Nash Builders bids $1,800,000. In adding a column of figures, Nash mistakenly omitted a $150,000 item. If Metro accepts Nash's bid

    a. Metro can enforce the contract if the errors were material.
    b. Metro can enforce the contract if the errors were unilateral.
    c. Nash can avoid the contract if Metro had reason to know of the mistake.
    d. Nash can avoid the contract if the errors were the result of negligence.

____ **6.** Jo offers to buy Ky's textbook for $60. Ky accepts and hands the book to Jo. The transfer and delivery of the book constitute performance. With respect to Jo's promise, this performance is

    a. consideration, because Jo sought it for her promise, and Ky gave it in exchange for that promise.
    b. consideration, because performance always constitutes consideration.
    c. not consideration, because Ky already had a duty to hand the textbook to Jo.
    d. not consideration, because performance never constitutes consideration.

____ **7.** Before opening her new sports merchandise store, Miley places an ad in the newspaper showing cross-training shoes at certain prices. Within hours of opening for business, the store is sold out of some of the shoes. In this situation Miley has made

    a. a bilateral contract with the people reading the ad.
    b. an invitation seeking offers from people who might read the ad.
    c. an offer to the people reading the ad.
    d. a unilateral contract with the people reading the ad.

____ **8.** Urban Properties, Inc., makes an offer in a letter to Vita to sell a certain lot for $50,000, with the offer to stay open for thirty days. Vita would prefer to pay $40,000, if Urban would sell at that price. To leave room for negotiation without rejecting the offer, Vita should reply

    a. "I will not pay $50,000."
    b. "Will you take $40,000?"
    c. "I will pay $40,000."
    d. "I will pay $45,000."

   9. Saf-T Storage Company and Tristate Trucking Inc. enter into an oral contract for the sale of a warehouse. Before Tristate takes possession, this contract is enforceable by

     a. neither Saf-T nor Tristate.
     b. Saf-T only.
     c. Saf-T or Tristate.
     d. Tristate only.

   10. Kelly contracts with Liu, a financial planner who is required by the state to have a license. Liu does not have a license. Their contract is enforceable if

     a. Kelly does not know that Liu is required to have a license.
     b. Liu does not know that he is required to have a license.
     c. the purpose of the statute is to protect the public from unlicensed practitioners.
     d. the purpose of the statute is to raise government revenue.

SHORT ESSAY QUESTIONS

1. What are the basic elements of a contract?

2. What are the elements of fraudulent misrepresentation?

ROCKON

(Answers at the Back of the Book)

1. You own a small club—Sammy D's—that features local musicians. On Tuesday night, you post a notice promising to pay $100 to any musician who takes to the stage for one hour. Tyler steps up to the mic and opens a sixty-minute set with a cover of the Beatles tune "I Saw Her Standing There." Do you have to pay Tyler $100? Explain.

2. Suppose, in the previous question, that your notice did not promise to pay but simply publicized "Tuesday Tune Night" and offered stage time to any musician who wished to perform. Uri entertains your patrons for an hour with a polished, professional hip hop repertoire, and then asks you for a percentage of the club's receipts for that hour. Do you have to pay?

Chapter 10
Contract Performance, Breach, and Remedies

WHAT THIS CHAPTER IS ABOUT

This chapter begins with a discussion of performance and discharge of contracts. Performance of a contract discharges it. Discharging a contract terminates it. Breach of contract is the failure to perform what a party is under a duty to perform. When this happens, the nonbreaching party can choose one or more remedies.

CHAPTER OUTLINE

I. DISCHARGE BY PERFORMANCE

Most contracts are discharged by performance—the parties' doing what they promised to do.

A. CONDITIONS

If performance is contingent on a condition and the condition is not satisfied, the obligations of the parties are discharged.

B. TENDER OF PERFORMANCE

Tender (an unconditional offer to perform by one who is ready, willing, and able to do so) can accomplish performance. If performance has been tendered and the other party refuses to perform, the party making the tender can sue for breach.

C. TYPES OF PERFORMANCE

1. Complete Performance

Complete performance occurs when express conditions are fully satisfied in all aspects.

2. Substantial Performance

a. Confers Most of the Benefits Promised

To qualify as substantial, performance must not vary greatly from that promised in the contract and must create substantially the same benefits.

b. Entitles the Other Party to Damages

Substantial performance by one party entitles the other party to damages for the failure to comply with the contract.

3. Performance to the Satisfaction of Another

a. Personal Satisfaction of One of the Parties

When the subject matter of the contract is personal, performance must actually satisfy the party (a condition precedent).

b. Satisfaction of a Reasonable Person

Most contracts need only be performed to the satisfaction of a reasonable person.

79

    c. Satisfaction of a Third Party
When the satisfaction of a third party is required, most courts require the work to be satisfactory to a reasonable person. Some require the personal satisfaction of the third party.

D. MATERIAL BREACH OF CONTRACT
A breach of contract is the nonperformance of a contractual duty. It is material when performance is not at least substantial; the nonbreaching party is excused from performing. If a breach is minor (not material), the nonbreaching party's duty to perform may be suspended until the breach is remedied.

E. ANTICIPATORY REPUDIATION
This is when, before either party has a duty to perform, one party refuses to perform.

    1. Damages and a Similar Contract
Anticipatory repudiation can discharge the nonbreaching party, who can sue to recover damages immediately and can also seek a similar contract elsewhere.

    2. Retraction Is Possible
Until the nonbreaching party treats a repudiation as a breach, the repudiating party can retract his or her repudiation by proper notice.

F. TIME FOR PERFORMANCE
If a specific time is stated, the parties must usually perform by that time. If time is stated to be vital or construed to be "of the essence," it is a condition of the contract. If no time is stated, a reasonable time is implied, and a delay will not affect the performing party's right to payment.

II. DISCHARGE BY AGREEMENT

A. DISCHARGE BY RESCISSION
Rescission is the process by which a contract is canceled and the parties are returned to the positions they occupied prior to forming it.

    1. Executory Contracts
Contracts that are executory on both sides can be rescinded.

        a. Requirements for Rescission
The parties must make another agreement, which must satisfy the legal requirements for a contract. Their promises not to perform are consideration for the second contract.

        b. Form of Rescission
Rescission is enforceable if oral (even if the original agreement was in writing), unless it is subject to the UCC and the contract requires written rescission.

    2. Executed Contracts
Contracts that are executed on one side can be rescinded only if the party who has performed receives consideration to call off the deal.

B. DISCHARGE BY NOVATION
This occurs when the parties to a contract and a new party get together and agree to substitute the new party for one of the original parties. Requirements are (1) a previous valid obligation, (2) an agreement of all the parties to a new contract, (3) the extinguishment of the old obligation (discharge of the prior party), and (4) a new, valid contract.

C. DISCHARGE BY SETTLEMENT AGREEMENT
Parties to a contract can execute a new agreement with different terms. The new agreement can expressly or impliedly revoke and discharge the previous contract's obligations.

D. DISCHARGE BY ACCORD AND SATISFACTION
To discharge by accord and satisfaction, the parties must agree to accept performance that is different from the performance originally promised.

1. **Accord**
An accord is an executory contract to perform an act that will satisfy an existing duty. An accord suspends, but does not discharge, the duty.

2. **Satisfaction**
Satisfaction is the performance of the accord, and discharges the original contract.

3. **If the Obligor Refuses to Perform**
The obligee can sue on the original obligation or seek specific performance of the accord.

III.   DISCHARGE BY OPERATION OF LAW

A. ALTERATION OF THE CONTRACT
An innocent party can treat a contract as discharged if the other party materially alters a term (such as quantity or price) without consent.

B. STATUTES OF LIMITATIONS
Statutes of limitations limit the period during which a party can sue based on a breach of contract. An action for the breach of a contract for a sale of goods must be commenced within four years after the breach occurs, whether the innocent party knows of the breach [UCC 2–725]. The parties can shorten this period to one year but cannot extend it.

C. BANKRUPTCY
A discharge in bankruptcy (see Chapter 30) will bar enforcement of most of a debtor's contracts.

D. IMPOSSIBILITY OR IMPRACTICABILITY OF PERFORMANCE

1. **Objective Impossibility of Performance**
Performance is objectively impossible in the unforeseeable event of—

   a. A party's death or incapacity.

   b. Destruction of the specific subject matter.

   c. A change in law that makes performance illegal.

2. **Temporary Impossibility**
An event that makes it temporarily impossible to perform will suspend performance until the impossibility ceases.

3. **Commercial Impracticability**
Performance may be excused if it becomes significantly more difficult or expensive than contemplated when the contract was formed.

4. **Frustration of Purpose**
A contract will be discharged if unforeseeable, supervening circumstances make it impossible to attain the purpose the parties had in mind.

IV.   BREACH OF CONTRACT AND REMEDIES

A. DAMAGES
Damages compensate a nonbreaching party for the loss of a bargain and, under special circumstances, for additional losses. Generally, the party is placed in the position he or she would have occupied if the contract had been performed.

1. **Compensatory Damages**
Compensatory damages compensate the injured party for the loss of the bargain (for injuries arising directly from the loss). Incidental damages (expenses that are caused directly by a breach of contract such as those incurred to obtain performance from another source) may also be recovered.

a. Standard Measure
The measurement of compensatory damages varies by type of contract. The standard measure is the difference between the value of the promised performance and the actual performance, less any loss that the injured party could have avoided.

b. Sale of Goods
The usual measure is the difference between the contract price and the market price. When a buyer breaches and the seller has not yet produced the goods, the measure is instead normally lost profits on the sale.

c. Sale of Land
In most states, the measure of damages is the difference between the contract and market prices of the land. In some states, when a seller breaches a contract and the breach is not deliberate, the buyer recovers only the down payment and expenses, placing him or her in the position occupied before the sale, not the benefit of the bargain.

d. Construction Contracts
The measure depends on which party breaches and when.

1) Owner's Breach Before, During, or After Construction
Contractor can recover (1) before construction: only profits (contract price, less cost of materials and labor); (2) during construction: profits, plus cost of partial construction; (3) after construction: the contract price, plus interest.

2) Contractor's Breach
Owner can recover for (1) failing to begin: cost, above contract price, to complete; (2) stopping mid-project: cost of completion; (3) late completion: costs related to loss of use.

2. Consequential Damages
These are damages giving an injured party the entire *benefit* of the bargain—foreseeable losses caused by special circumstances beyond the contract. The breaching party must know (or have reason to know) that special circumstances will cause the additional loss.

3. Punitive Damages
Punitive damages are designed to punish a wrongdoer and to deter similar, future conduct. They normally are not awarded in a breach of contract action.

4. Nominal Damages
These damages (such as $1) establish that a party acted wrongfully even if no loss resulted.

B. MITIGATION OF DAMAGES
Generally, an injured party has a duty to mitigate damages. For example, persons whose jobs have been wrongfully terminated have a duty to seek other jobs. The damages they receive are their salaries, less the income they received (or would have received) in similar jobs.

C. LIQUIDATED DAMAGES PROVISIONS
A liquidated damages provision in a contract specifies a certain amount to be paid on a breach.

1. Liquidated Damages versus Penalties
If a provision is construed as a penalty, it will not be enforced.

2. Enforceability
There are two requirements for an enforceable liquidated damages provision: (1) when the contract was made, it must have been difficult to estimate the damages that would be incurred on a breach and (2) the amount set as damages must be reasonable (not excessive).

D. EQUITABLE REMEDIES

1. **Rescission and Restitution**
Rescission is an action to undo, or cancel, a contract—to return nonbreaching parties to the positions they occupied prior to the transaction. Available if fraud, mistake, duress, or failure of consideration occurs. The rescinding party must give prompt notice to the breaching party.

   a. **Restitution**
   To rescind a contract, the parties must make restitution by returning to each other goods, property, or money previously conveyed. Restitution is also available in other actions.

   b. **Restitution Is Not Limited to Rescission Cases**
   Restitution is available in other actions, such as when money or property is transferred due to a mistake, incapacity, or fraud.

2. **Specific Performance**
This remedy calls for the performance of the act promised in the contract.

   a. **When Specific Performance Is Available**
   Damages must be an inadequate remedy. If goods are unique, a court will decree specific performance. Specific performance is granted to a buyer in a contract for the sale of land (land is unique).

   b. **When Specific Performance Is Not Available**
   Contracts for a sale of goods (other than unique goods) rarely qualify, because substantially identical goods can be bought or sold elsewhere. Courts normally refuse to grant specific performance of personal service contracts.

3. **Reformation**
This remedy is used when the parties have imperfectly expressed their agreement in writing. It allows the contract to be rewritten to reflect the parties' true intentions.

E. **ELECTION OF REMEDIES DOCTRINE**
A nonbreaching party must choose which remedy to pursue. This doctrine has been eliminated in contracts for sales of goods [UCC 2–703, 2–711]—UCC remedies are cumulative (see Chapter 11).

F. **WAIVER OF BREACH**
A nonbreaching party may be willing to accept a defective performance of the contract. This relinquishment of a right to full performance is a waiver. A waiver keeps the contract going, but the nonbreaching party can recover damages caused by defective or less-than-full performance.

G. **CONTRACT PROVISIONS LIMITING REMEDIES**

1. **Exculpatory Clauses**
A provision excluding liability for fraudulent or intentional injury or for illegal acts will not be enforced. An exculpatory clause for negligence contained in a contract made between parties who are in roughly equal bargaining positions usually will be enforced.

2. **Limitation-of-Liability Clauses**
A clause excluding liability for negligence may be enforced.

TRUE-FALSE QUESTIONS

(Answers at the Back of the Book)

____ 1. Complete performance occurs when a contract's conditions fully occur.

____ 2. A material breach of contract does not excuse the nonbreaching party from further performance.

____ **3.** An executory contract cannot be rescinded.

____ **4.** Objective impossibility discharges a contract.

____ **5.** If a contract does not require a certain time for performance, a reasonable time will be implied.

____ **6.** Damages are designed to compensate a nonbreaching party for the loss of a bargain.

____ **7.** Liquidated damages are uncertain in amount.

____ **8.** On a breach of contract, a nonbreaching party has a duty to mitigate damages that he or she suffers.

____ **9.** Consequential damages are foreseeable damages that arise from a party's breach of a contract.

____ **10.** Specific performance is the usual remedy when one party has breached a contract for a sale of goods.

FILL-IN QUESTIONS

(Answers at the Back of the Book)

The usual measure of compensatory damages under a contract for a sale of goods is the difference between _____ (the contract price and the market price/the market price and lost profits on the sale). The usual remedy for a seller's breach of a contract for a sale of real estate is _____ (specific performance/rescission and restitution). If this remedy is unavailable or if the buyer breaches, in most states the measure of damages is the difference between _____ (the contract price and the market price/the market price and lost profits on the sale).

MULTIPLE-CHOICE QUESTIONS

(Answers at the Back of the Book)

____ **1.** Town Delivery Service contracts with Pizza! Pie! to deliver its goods to customers. This contract will, like most contracts, be discharged by

    a. accord and satisfaction.
    b. agreement.
    c. operation of law.
    d. performance.

____ **2.** Ric and Skye contract for the sale of Ric's business. Skye makes a down payment, and Ric gives her the keys to one of his stores. Before the contract is fully performed, however, they agree to return the money and keys, and cancel the sale. This is

    a. a material breach.
    b. an accord and satisfaction.
    c. a novation.
    d. a rescission.

____ **3.** Carlotta contracts with Darlene to act as her personal financial planner. Carlotta's duties under this contract will be discharged if

    a. Darlene declares bankruptcy.
    b. it becomes illegal for Eve to provide the service.
    c. the cost of providing the service doubles.
    d. none of the choices.

____ 4. Dion contracts to build a store for Ella for $500,000, with payments to be in installments of $50,000 as the work progresses. Dion finishes the store except for a cover over a compressor on the roof. A cover can be installed for $500. Ella refuses to pay the last installment. If Dion's breach is not material

    a. both parties have claims against each other.
    b. Dion has a claim against Ella for $50,000, but Ella has no claim against Dion.
    c. Ella has a claim against Dion for the failure to cover the compressor, but Dion has no claim against Ella.
    d. neither party has a claim against the other.

____ 5. Finnegan and Ewan want Dribble to replace Finnegan as a party to their contract. They can best accomplish this by agreeing to

    a. an accord and satisfaction.
    b. an assignment.
    c. a novation.
    d. a nullification.

____ 6. Cavendish contracts to deliver Bagels & More's products to its customers for $1,500, payable in advance. Bagels pays the money, but Cavendish fails to perform. Bagels can

    a. obtain restitution of the $1,000 but not rescind the contract.
    b. recover nothing nor rescind the contract.
    c. rescind the contract and obtain restitution of the $1,000.
    d. rescind the contract only.

____ 7. Soda Fountain Supplies Corporation contracts to sell to Tasty Malts, Inc., six steel mixers for $5,000. When Soda Fountain fails to deliver, Tasty Malts buys mixers from Dairy Appliance Company, for $6,500. Tasty Malts' measure of damages is

    a. $6,500.
    b. $5,000.
    c. $1,500 plus incident al damages.
    d. nothing.

____ 8. Olivia contracts with Pinky to buy a credenza for $1,500. Olivia tells Pinky that if the goods are not delivered on Monday, she will lose $2,000 in business. Pinky ships the credenza late. Olivia can recover

    a. $3,500.
    b. $2,000.
    c. $1,500.
    d. nothing.

____ 9. Billie agrees to sell an acre of land to Cliburn for $5,000. Billie fails to go through with the deal, when the market price of the land is $7,000. If Cliburn cannot obtain the land through specific performance, he may recover

    a. $7,000.
    b. $5,000.
    c. $2,000.
    d. nothing.

____ 10. Doctors Hospital, Inc., contracts with E-Services Company to maintain Doctors' computers. Their contract provides that E-Services will pay Doctors $500 for each day that E-Services is late in responding to a service request. If Doctors sues to enforce this clause, Doctors will

    a. lose, because the clause is a liquidated damages clause, which violates public policy.
    b. lose, unless the clause is determined to be a penalty.
    c. win, because the clause is a liquidated damages clause, which is always enforceable.
    d. win, unless the clause is determined to be a penalty.

SHORT ESSAY QUESTIONS

1. What effect does a material breach have on the nonbreaching party? What is the effect of a nonmaterial breach?

2. What are damages designed to do in a breach of contract situation?

ROCKON

(Answers at the Back of the Book)

1.   You're the owner of Joystick Productions, a recording company with an eclectic catalog of musical and dramatic works. The artists can present unique challenges to Joystick's technology—even the classical and spoken-word performers often push the envelope to its limits. You contract with Outside the Box, Inc., to build and program a digital recording system that doesn't require pushing buttons, clicking switches, or manipulating a mouse, but responds instead to gestures and voices. Images are to be selected on a screen by the movement of your hand in the air. Operations are to be controlled by such commands as, "Record now" and "Cut." The system that Outside the Box delivers nearly meets the specifications—only its voice recognition capability fails to perform as promised. What effect does this failure have on Joystick's obligation to pay?

2.   You and your heavy metal band Rigid contract with Blitz Festivals, Inc., a regional concert promoter, to perform June 16 in an amphitheatre at the McCloud County Fair for a total of $8,500. The community pressures the fair sponsors to stage acts with broader name-recognition than your band, despite the greater expense, in an effort to draw larger crowds. Blitz then reneges on its deal with you—"What can we do? Our hands are tied. You guys aren't big enough." You find another gig for that date, playing in Tavern on the Commons, a small club, for $4,250. If you successfully sue Blitz for breach, how much might you recover?

Chapter 11
Sales, Leases, and E-Contracts

WHAT THIS CHAPTER IS ABOUT

The Uniform Commercial Code (UCC) provides a framework of rules to deal with all the phases arising in an ordinary sales transaction from start to finish—from sale to payment. This chapter outlines the principles of UCC Article 2 and Article 2A, e-contracts, and the United Nations Convention on Contracts for the International Sale of Goods.

CHAPTER OUTLINE

I. THE SCOPE OF ARTICLE 2—THE SALE OF GOODS
Article 2 governs contracts for sales of goods.

A. WHAT IS A SALE?
A *sale* is "the passing of title from the seller to the buyer for a price" [UCC 2–106(1)]. The price may be payable in money, goods, services, or land.

B. WHAT ARE GOODS?
Goods are tangible and movable. Legal disputes concern the following—

1. Goods Associated with Real Estate
Goods include minerals or the like and structures, if severance from the land is by the seller (but not if the buyer is to do it); growing crops or timber to be cut; and other "things attached" to realty but capable of severance without material harm to the land [UCC 2–107].

2. Goods and Services Combined
Services are not included in the UCC. If a transaction involves both goods and services, a court determines which aspect is dominant under the predominant-factor test.

C. WHO IS A MERCHANT?
UCC 2–104: Special rules apply to those who (1) deal in goods of the kind involved; (2) by occupation, hold themselves out as having knowledge and skill peculiar to the practices or goods involved in the transaction; (3) employ a merchant as a broker, agent, or other intermediary.

II. THE SCOPE OF ARTICLE 2A—LEASES
Article 2A governs contracts for leases of goods. A *lease agreement* is the bargain of the lessor and lessee, in their words and deeds, including course of dealing, usage of trade, and course of performance [UCC 2A–103(k)].

III. THE FORMATION OF SALES AND LEASE CONTRACTS
The following sections summarize how UCC provisions *change* the effect of the common law of contracts.

A. OFFER
Verbal exchanges, correspondence, and the actions of the parties may not reveal exactly when a binding contractual obligation arises. An agreement sufficient to constitute a contract can exist even if the moment of its making is undetermined [UCC 2–204(2), 2A–204(2)].

1. **Open Terms**

   A sales or lease contract will not fail for indefiniteness even if one or more terms are left open, as long as: (1) the parties intended to make a contract and (2) there is a reasonably certain basis for the court to grant an appropriate remedy [UCC 2–204(3), 2A–204((3)].

   a. **Open Price Term**

      If the parties have not included a price term, a court will set a reasonable price at the time for delivery [UCC 2–305(1)]. If, through the fault of one of the parties, a price is not fixed, the other party can fix a reasonable price or treat the contract as canceled [UCC 2–205(3)].

   b. **Open Payment Term**

      If the payment is not specified, payment is due at the time and place at which the buyer will receive the goods [UCC 2–310(a)].

   c. **Open Delivery Term**

      If a delivery term is not specified, delivery is at the seller's place of business (or, if no place of business, the seller's residence) [UCC 2–308(a)].

   d. **Open Quantity Term**

      If the quantity term is left open, a court will have no basis for determining a remedy [UCC 2–306]. Requirements and output contracts are exceptions.

2. **Merchant's Firm Offer**

   If a merchant gives assurances in a signed writing that an offer will remain open, the offer is irrevocable, without consideration for the stated period of time, or if no definite period is specified, for a reasonable period (not more than three months) [UCC 2–205, 2A–205].

B. ACCEPTANCE

Generally, acceptance of an offer to buy or sell goods may be made in any reasonable manner and by any reasonable means. Acceptance may be by either a prompt shipment of goods or a promise to ship [UCC 2–206(1)(b)].

1. **Shipment of Nonconforming Goods**

   Shipment of nonconforming goods is both an acceptance and a breach unless the seller seasonably notifies the buyer that the nonconforming shipment does not constitute an acceptance and is offered only as an accommodation.

2. **Communication of Acceptance**

   To accept a unilateral offer, the offeree must notify the offeror of performance within a reasonable time [UCC 2–206(2), 2A–206(2)].

3. **Additional Terms**

   If the offeree's response indicates a definite acceptance of the offer, a contract is formed, even if the acceptance includes terms in addition to, or different from, the original offer [UCC 2–207(1)].

   a. **When Both Parties Are Merchants**

      Additional terms are part of the contract unless (1) the offer expressly states no other terms; (2) they materially alter the original contract; or (3) the offeror objects to the modified terms in a timely fashion [UCC 2–207(2)].

   b. **When the Parties Act As If They Have a Contract**

      Regardless of what parties write down, they have a contract according to their conduct [UCC 2–207(3)]. This means that a court can strike any terms on which the parties do not agree [UCC 2–207(3)].

C. CONSIDERATION

An agreement modifying a contract or lease needs no consideration to be binding [UCC 2–209(1), 2A–208(1)]. Modification must be sought in good faith [UCC 1–203].

D. THE STATUTE OF FRAUDS
To be enforceable, a sales contract must be in writing if the goods are $500 or more and a lease if the payments are $1,000 or more [UCC 2–201, 2A–201].

1. Sufficiency of the Writing and Its Terms
A writing is sufficient if it indicates that a contract was intended and it is signed by the party against whom enforcement is sought. It is not enforceable beyond the quantity of goods in the writing. Other terms can be proved by oral testimony.

2. Special Rules for Contracts between Merchants
The requirement of a writing is satisfied if one merchant sends a signed written confirmation to the other, unless the merchant who receives the confirmation gives written notice of objection within ten days of receipt.

3. Exceptions
An oral contract for a sale or lease that should otherwise be in writing will be enforceable if [UCC 2–201(3), 2A–201(4)] (1) manufacture of special goods has begun, (2) party against whom enforcement is sought admits in court proceedings a contract was made, or (3) payment is made and accepted or goods are received and accepted (enforceable to that extent).

IV. TITLE, RISK, AND INSURABLE INTEREST

A. IDENTIFICATION
Identification is the designation of goods as the subject matter of the contract. For an interest in goods to pass from seller to buyer or lessor to lessee, the goods must (1) exist and (2) be identified as the goods subject to the contract. This gives a buyer the right to obtain insurance and to recover from third parties who damage the goods (and sometimes from the seller).

B. WHEN TITLE PASSES
Parties can agree on when and under what conditions title will pass. If they do not specify a time, title passes on delivery [UCC 2–401(2)]. Delivery terms determine when this occurs.

1. Shipment Contracts
If the seller is required or authorized to ship goods by carrier, title passes at time and place of shipment [UCC 2–401(2)(a)]. All contracts are shipment contracts unless they say otherwise.

2. Destination Contracts
If the seller is required to deliver goods to a certain destination, title passes when the goods are tendered there [UCC 2–401(2)(b)].

3. Delivery without Movement of the Goods
If a buyer is to pick up goods, passing title turns on whether a seller must give a document of title (bill of lading, warehouse receipt).

a. When a Document of Title Is Required
Title passes when and where the document is delivered. The goods do not need to move (for example, they can stay in a warehouse).

b. When No Document of Title Is Required
If the goods have been identified, title passes when and where the contract was made. If the goods have not been identified, title does not pass until identification [UCC 2–401(3)].

C. RISK OF LOSS
By agreement, parties can generally control when risk of loss passes from seller to buyer. Otherwise, the question of who suffers a financial risk if goods are damaged, destroyed, or lost is resolved mostly under UCC 2–509 and 2A–219.

1. Delivery with Movement of the Goods—Carrier Cases
When goods are to be delivered by truck or other paid transport—

a. Shipment Contracts
Risk passes to the buyer or lessee when the goods are delivered to a carrier [UCC 2–509(1)(a), 2A–219(2)(a)].

b. Destination Contracts
Risk passes to the buyer or lessee when the goods are tendered to the buyer at the destination [UCC 2–509(1)(b), 2A–219(2)(b)].

2. Delivery without Movement of the Goods
When goods are to be picked up by the buyer or lessee—

a. If the Seller or Lessor Is a Merchant
Risk passes only on the buyer's or lessee's taking possession of the goods.

b. If the Seller or Lessor Is Not a Merchant
Risk passes on tender of delivery [UCC 2–509(3), 2A–219(c)].

c. If a Bailee Holds the Goods
Risk passes when (1) the buyer receives a negotiable document of title for the goods, (2) the bailee acknowledges the buyer's (or in the case of a lease, the lessee's) right to the goods, or (3) the buyer receives a nonnegotiable document of title, presents the document to the bailee, and demands the goods. If the bailee refuses to honor the document, the risk remains with the seller [UCC 2–503(4)(b), 2–509(2), 2A–219(2)(b)].

3. Breach of a Sales or Lease Contract
Generally, the party in breach bears the risk of loss.

a. When the Seller or Lessor Breaches
Risk passes to the buyer or lessee when the defects are cured or the buyer or lessee accepts the goods in spite of the defects [UCC 2–510(2), 2A–220(1)].

b. When the Buyer or Lessee Breaches
Risk shifts to the buyer or lessee (if the goods have been identified), where it stays for a commercially reasonable time after the seller or lessor learns of the breach. The buyer or lessee is liable only to the extent of any deficiency in seller or lessor's insurance [UCC 2–510(3), 2A–220(2)].

D. INSURABLE INTEREST
A buyer or lessee has an insurable interest in goods the moment they are identified to the contract [UCC 2–501(1), 2A–218(1)]. A seller or lessor has an insurable interest in goods as long as he or she retains title or holds a security interest in the goods [UCC 2–501(2), 2A–218(3)].

V. PERFORMANCE OF SALES AND LEASE CONTRACTS
The UCC imposes on the performance of all sales or lease contract an obligation of good faith (honesty, and in the case of a merchant the observance of reasonable commercial standards of fair dealing in the trade) [UCC 2–103(b)].

A. OBLIGATIONS OF THE SELLER OR LESSOR
A seller or lessor must have and hold conforming goods for the buyer or lessee and give notice reasonably necessary to enable the buyer or lessee to take delivery [UCC 2–503(1), 2A–508(1)].

1. Tender of Delivery
Tender must occur at a reasonable hour, in a reasonable manner, and the goods must be available for a reasonable time [UCC 2–503(1)(a)]. Goods must be tendered in a single delivery unless parties agree otherwise [UCC 2–612, 2A–510] or a party can request delivery in lots [UCC 2–307].

2. Place of Delivery
Parties may agree on a destination, or the contract or circumstances may indicate a place.

    a. Seller's Place of Business

    If the contract does not designate a place of delivery, and the buyer is to pick up the goods, the place is the seller's place of business or if none, the seller's residence [UCC 2–308].

    b. Identified Goods That Are Not at the Seller's Place of Business

    Wherever they are is the place of delivery [UCC 2–308].

3. The Perfect Tender Rule

A seller or lessor must deliver goods in conformity with every detail of the contract. If goods or tender fail in any respect, the buyer or lessee can accept the goods, reject them, or accept part and reject part [UCC 2–601, 2A–509]. Exceptions include—

    a. Cure

        1) Within the Contract Time for Performance

        If nonconforming goods are rejected, the seller or lessor can notify the buyer or lessee of an intention to repair, adjust, or replace the goods and can then do so within the contract time for performance [UCC 2–508, 2A–513].

        2) After the Time for Performance

        The seller or lessor can cure if there are reasonable grounds to believe the nonconformance would be acceptable.

        3) Substantially Restricts the Buyer's Right to Reject

        If the buyer or lessee refuses goods but does not disclose the nature of the defect, he or she cannot later assert the defect as a defense if it is one that could have been cured [UCC 2–605, 2A–514].

    b. Substitution of Carriers

    When an agreed-on manner of delivery becomes impracticable or unavailable through no fault of either party, a commercially reasonable substitute is sufficient [UCC 2–614(1)].

    c. Commercial Impracticability

    Delay or nondelivery is not a breach if performance is impracticable "by the occurrence of a contingency the nonoccurrence of which was a basic assumption on which the contract was made" [UCC 2–615(a), 2A–405(a)]. Seller must give notice.

    d. Destruction of Identified Goods

    When goods are destroyed (through no fault of a party) before risk passes, parties are excused from performance [UCC 2–613(a), 2A–221]. If goods are only partially destroyed, a buyer can treat a contract as void or accept damaged goods with a price allowance.

    e. Assurance and Cooperation

    A party with reasonable grounds to believe that the other will not perform may demand adequate assurance, suspend his or her own performance, and with no assurance within thirty days treat the contract as repudiated [UCC 2–609, 2A–401]. When required cooperation is not forthcoming, the other party can do whatever is reasonable, including holding the uncooperative party in breach [UCC 2–311(3)(b)].

B. OBLIGATIONS OF THE BUYER OR LESSEE

The buyer or lessee must make payment at the time and place he or she receives the goods unless the parties have agreed otherwise [UCC 2–310(a), 2A–516(1)].

1. Payment

Payment can be by any means agreed on between the parties [UCC 2–511].

2. Right of Inspection

The buyer or lessee can verify, before making payment, that the goods are what were contracted for. There is no duty to pay if the goods are not as ordered [UCC 2–513(1),

2A–515(1)]. Inspection can be in any reasonable place, time and manner, determined by custom of the trade, practice of the parties, and so on [UCC 2–513(2)].

3. Acceptance
Acceptance is presumed if a buyer or lessee has a reasonable opportunity to inspect and fails to reject in a reasonable time [UCC 2–606, 2–602, 2A–515]. A buyer or lessee can accept by words or conduct. Under a sales contract, a buyer can accept by any act (such as using or reselling the goods) inconsistent with the seller's ownership [UCC 2–606(1)(c)].

4. Partial Acceptance
If some of the goods do not conform to the contract, and the seller or lessor has failed to cure, a buyer or lessee can accept only the conforming goods, but not less than a single commercial unit [UCC 2–601(c), 2A-509(1)].

C. ANTICIPATORY REPUDIATION
A party can (1) treat a repudiation as a final breach by pursuing a remedy or (2) wait, hoping that the repudiating party will decide to honor the contract [UCC 2–610, 2A–402]. If the party decides to wait, the breaching party can retract the repudiation [UCC 2–611, 2A–403].

VI. REMEDIES FOR BREACH OF SALES AND LEASE CONTRACTS

A. REMEDIES OF THE SELLER OR LESSOR

1. When the Goods Are in the Possession of the Seller or Lessor
Before goods are delivered to the buyer or lessee, the seller or lessor has the following remedies.

a. The Right to Cancel the Contract
After the seller or lessor has notified the buyer or lessee of the cancellation, the seller or lessor's obligations are discharged and he or she can pursue remedies available for breach [UCC 2–703(f), 2A–523(1)(a)].

b. The Right to Withhold Delivery
This remedy is available when a buyer or lessee wrongfully rejects or revokes acceptance of the goods, fails to pay, or repudiates part of the contract [UCC 2–703(a), 2A–523(1)(c)]. If the breach results from the buyer or the lessee's insolvency, the seller or lessor can refuse to deliver unless the buyer or lessee pays in cash [UCC 2–702(1), 2A–525(1)].

c. The Right to Resell or Dispose of the Goods
The seller or lessor can hold the buyer or lessee liable for any loss [UCC 2–703(d), 2–706(1), 2A–523(1)(e), 2A–527(1)]. The seller must timely notify the buyer unless the goods are perishable or will rapidly decline in value [UCC 2–706(2), (3)].

d. The Right to Recover the Purchase Price or Lease Payments Due
This remedy is available if the seller or lessor is unable to resell or dispose of the goods [UCC 2–709(1), 2A–529(1)].

e. The Right to Recover Damages for the Buyer's Nonacceptance
If a buyer or lessee repudiates a contract or wrongfully refuses to accept, the seller or lessor can recover the difference between the contract price and the market price (at the time and place of tender), plus incidental damages. If the market price is less than the contract price, the seller or lessor gets lost profits [UCC 2–708, 2A–528].

2. When the Goods Are in Transit
A seller or lessor can stop delivery of goods if (1) buyer or lessee is insolvent or (2) buyer or lessee is solvent but in breach (if the quantity shipped is a carload, a truckload, or larger) [UCC 2–705, 2A–526].

3. When the Goods Are in the Possession of the Buyer or Lessee

a. **The Right to Recover the Purchase Price or Lease Payments Due**
   A seller or lessor has the right to recover the purchase price or the payments due under the lease contract, plus incidental damages, if the buyer or lessee has accepted the goods but refuses to pay for them [UCC 2–709(1), 2A–529(1)].

b. **The Right to Reclaim the Goods**
   A seller has the right to reclaim the goods when the buyer is insolvent and has not paid for them. This remedy is available to a lessor if a lessee is in default [UCC 2A–525(2)].

B. REMEDIES OF THE BUYER OR LESSEE

1. **When the Seller or Lessor Refuses to Deliver the Goods**

   a. **The Right of Cover**
      A buyer or lessee can obtain cover (substitute goods) and then sue for damages. The measure of damages is the difference between the cost of cover and the contract price, plus incidental and consequential damages, minus expenses saved by the breach [UCC 2–712, 2–715, 2A–518, 2A–520].

   b. **The Right to Replevy Goods**
      The buyer or lessee can replevy goods subject to the contract if the seller or lessee has repudiated or breached it and the buyer or lessee is unable to cover [UCC 2–716(3), 2A–521(3)].

   c. **The Right to Recover Damages**
      The measure is the difference between the contract price and, when buyer or lessee learned of the breach, the market price (at the place of delivery), plus incidental and consequential damages, minus expenses saved by the breach [UCC 2–713, 2A–519].

2. **When the Seller or Lessor Delivers Nonconforming Goods**

   a. **The Right to Reject the Goods**
      If the goods or tender fail to conform in any respect, the buyer or lessee can reject them, in whole or in part [UCC 2–601, 2A–509]. The buyer or lessee can then cover or cancel.

      1) **Timeliness and Reason for Rejection Required**
         Rejection must be within a reasonable time, and the seller or lessor must be notified and told of the defect [UCC 2–602(1), 2–605, 2A–509(2), 2A–514].

      2) **Duties of a Merchant Buyer or Lessee**
         If the buyer or lessee is a merchant, he or she must follow the instructions of the seller or lessor in regard to the goods [UCC 2–603, 2A–511].

   b. **The Right to Revoke Acceptance**
      Acceptance can be revoked if a nonconformity substantially impairs the value, the seller or lessor is notified within a reasonable time after the nonconformity is or should have been discovered, and—

      1) Acceptance was based on a reasonable assumption that the nonconformity would be cured, and it has not been cured within a reasonable period of time [UCC 2–608(1)(a), 2A–517(1)(a)], or

      2) The buyer or lessee did not discover the nonconformity before acceptance, because it was difficult or because assurances made by the seller or lessor that the goods conformed kept the buyer or lessee from inspecting [UCC 2–608(1)(b), 2A–517(1)(b)].

   c. **The Right to Recover Damages for Accepted Goods**
      Notice of a breach must be within a reasonable time [UCC 2–607, 2A–516]. The measure of damages is the difference between value of goods as accepted and value if they had been as promised [UCC 2–714(2), 2A–519(4)].

C. ADDITIONAL PROVISIONS AFFECTING REMEDIES

A seller and buyer can expressly provide for remedies in addition to, in lieu of, or otherwise different from those provided in the UCC [UCC 2–719(1), 2A–503(1)]. Any remedy can be made exclusive (at least until it fails in its essential purpose) [UCC 2–719(2), 2A–503(2)].

VII. SALES AND LEASE WARRANTIES

A. WARRANTIES OF TITLE

1. Sellers

Sellers warrant (1) they have good title to the goods and transfer of title is rightful [UCC 2–312(1)(a)]; (2) goods are free of a security interest or other lien of which buyer has no knowledge [UCC 2–312(1)(b)]; and (3) goods are free of any third person's patent, trademark, or copyright claims [UCC 2–312(3)].

2. Lessors

Lessors warrant (1) no third party will interfere with the lessee's use of the goods and (2) the goods are free of any third person's patent, trademark, or copyright claims [UCC 2A–211].

B. EXPRESS WARRANTIES

1. When Express Warranties Arise

Seller or lessor warrants that goods will conform to [UCC 2–313, 2A–210] (1) affirmations or promises of fact (on a label or in a contract, an ad, a brochure, etc.); (2) descriptions (for example, on a label or in a contract, an ad, a brochure, etc.); and (3) samples or models.

2. Statements of Opinion and Value

A statement that relates to the value or worth of goods or a statement of opinion or recommendation about goods is not an express warranty [UCC 2–313(2), 2A–210(2)], unless seller or lessor is an expert and gives an opinion as an expert.

C. IMPLIED WARRANTIES

An implied warranty is derived by implication or inference from the nature of a transaction or the relative situations or circumstances of the parties.

1. Implied Warranty of Merchantability

This warranty automatically arises in every sale or lease of goods by a merchant who deals in such goods. Goods that are merchantable are "reasonably fit for the ordinary purposes for which such goods are used" [UCC 2–314, 2A–212].

2. Implied Warranty of Fitness for a Particular Purpose

Arises when a seller or lessor knows or has reason to know particular purpose for which buyer or lessee will use goods and knows buyer or lessee is relying on seller or lessor to select suitable goods [UCC 2–315, 2A–213]. Goods can be merchantable but not fit for a particular purpose.

3. Implied Warranty—Dealing, Performance, or Trade Usage

When the parties know a well-recognized trade custom, it is inferred that they intended it to apply to their contract [UCC 2–314, 2A–212].

VIII. E-CONTRACTS

Disputes arising from contracts entered into online concern the terms and assent to those terms.

A. ONLINE OFFERS

1. Displaying the Offer

Terms should be conspicuous and clearly spelled out. On a Web site, this can be done with a link to a separate page that contains the details.

2. Provisions to Include

Subjects that might be covered include remedies, forum selection, choice-of-law, arbitration, payment, taxes, refund and return policies, disclaimers, and privacy policies. An online offer should also include a mechanism by which an offeree can affirmatively indicate assent (such as an "I agree" box to click on).

B. ONLINE ACCEPTANCES

1. Click-On Agreements

This occurs when a buyer, completing a transaction on a computer, indicates his or her assent to be bound by the terms of the offer by clicking on a button that says, for example, "I agree." The terms may appear on a Web site through which a buyer obtains goods or services, or on a computer screen when software is loaded.

2. Shrink-Wrap Agreements

This is an agreement whose terms are expressed inside a box in which a product is packaged. Usually, the agreement is not between a seller and a buyer, but a manufacturer and the product's user. Terms generally concern warranties, remedies, and other issues.

a. Shrink-Wrap Agreements and Enforceable Contract Terms

Courts often enforce shrink-wrap agreements, reasoning that the seller proposed an offer that the buyer accepted after an opportunity to read the terms. Also, it is more practical to enclose the full terms of sale in a box.

b. Shrink-Wrap Terms That May Not Be Enforced

If a court finds that the buyer learned of the shrink-wrap terms *after* the parties entered into a contract, the court might conclude that those terms were proposals for additional terms, which were not part of the contract unless the buyer expressly agreed to them.

3. Browse-Wrap Terms

These do not require a user to assent to the terms before going ahead with an online transaction. Offerors of these terms generally assert that they are binding without the user's active consent. Critics argue that a user should at least be required to navigate past the terms before they should be considered binding.

C. E-SIGNATURES

1. State Laws Governing E-Signatures

Most states have laws governing e-signatures, although the laws are not uniform. The Uniform Electronic Transactions Act (UETA), issued in 1999, was an attempt by the National Conference of Commissioners on Uniform State Laws and the American Law Institute to create more uniformity.

2. Federal Law on E-Signatures and E-Documents

In 2000, Congress enacted the Electronic Signatures in Global and National Commerce (E-SIGN) Act to provide no contract, record, or signature may be denied legal effect solely because it is in an electronic form.

IX. INTERNATIONAL SALES CONTRACTS

The 1980 United Nations Convention on Contracts for the International Sale of Goods (CISG) governs contracts for the international sale of goods.

A. APPLICABILITY OF THE CISG

The CISG is to international sales contracts what UCC Article 2 is to domestic sales contracts (except the CISG does not apply to consumer sales). The CISG applies when the parties to an international sales contract do not specify in writing the precise terms of their contract.

B. A COMPARISON OF CISG AND UCC PROVISIONS

1. The Mirror Image Rule

The terms of the acceptance must mirror those of the offer [Art. 19].

2. Irrevocable Offers

An offer is irrevocable if the offeror states that it is or if the offeree reasonably relies on it as being irrevocable. The offer is irrevocable even without a writing and consideration [Art. 16(2)].

C. REMEDIES FOR BREACH

The CISG provides remedies similar to the UCC's, including, in appropriate circumstances, damages (difference between contract and market prices), consequential damages, the right to avoid a contract, and the right to specific performance.

TRUE-FALSE QUESTIONS

(Answers at the Back of the Book)

____ 1. Under the UCC, a sale occurs when title passes from a seller to a buyer for a price.

____ 2. The UCC governs sales of goods, services, and real estate.

____ 3. If goods fail to conform to a contract in any way, a buyer or lessee can accept or reject the goods.

____ 4. If a seller is a merchant, the risk of loss passes when a buyer takes possession of the goods.

____ 5. If a contract for a sale of goods is missing a term, the contract will not be enforceable.

____ 6. Unless the parties agree otherwise, a buyer or lessee must pay for goods in advance.

____ 7. If a buyer wrongfully refuses to accept conforming goods, the seller can recover damages.

____ 8. If a seller wrongfully refuses to deliver conforming goods, the buyer can recover damages.

____ 9. Promises of fact made during the bargaining process are express warranties.

____ 10. A click-on agreement is not normally enforced.

FILL-IN QUESTIONS

(Answers at the Back of the Book)

_____ (F.A.S./F.O.B.) means that delivery is at a seller's expense to a specific location—the place of shipment or a place of destination. When the term is _____ (F.A.S./F.O.B.) place of shipment, risk passes when the seller puts the goods into a carrier's possession. When the term is _____ (F.A.S./F.O.B.) place of destination, risk passes when the seller tenders delivery. _____ (F.A.S./F.O.B.) requires a seller at his or her own expense and risk to deliver goods alongside the ship that will transport them at which point risk passes.

MULTIPLE-CHOICE QUESTIONS

(Answers at the Back of the Book)

____ 1. Frozen Cow, Inc., agrees to sell ice cream to Gordo Stadium Concessions. Before the time for performance, Frozen Cow tells Gordo that it will not deliver. This is

a. anticipatory repudiation.
b. perfect tender.
c. rejection of performance.
d. revocation of acceptance.

____ **2.** Mall Stores Corporation sends its purchase order form to Neat Displays, Inc., for shelving. Neat responds with its own form. Additional terms in Neat's form automatically become part of the parties' contract

   a. under any circumstances.
   b. under no circumstances.
   c. unless Mall objects to the new terms within a reasonable period of time.
   d. unless Neat indicates otherwise before shipping the goods.

____ **3.** Calibrate Corporation agrees to ship one hundred scientific calculators to GR8 Equations, Inc. Before the calculators arrive at GR's laboratory, they are lost. The most important factor in determining who bears the risk of loss is

   a. how the calculators were lost.
   b. the contract's shipping terms.
   c. the method by which the calculators were shipped.
   d. title to the calculators.

____ **4.** Omni Architects buys ten drafting desks from Precision Supply, Inc. They agree to ship the computers "F.O.B. Omni" via Quik2U Trucking Company. The desks are lost in transit. The loss is suffered by

   a. Omni (the buyer).
   b. Precision (the seller).
   c. Quik2U (the carrier).
   d. not Omni, Precision, or Quik2U.

____ **5.** Red Apples Corporation agrees to sell forty cases of apples to Sweet Fruit, Inc., under a shipment contract. Red gives the apples to Refrigerated Trucking, Inc. (RTI), which delivers them to Sweet. Title passed when

   a. Red agreed to sell the goods.
   b. Red gave the goods to RTI.
   c. RTI delivered the goods to Sweet.
   d. Sweet exercised dominion over the goods.

____ **6.** City Soccer League contracts to buy goods from Ben's Sports. Ben's wrongfully fails to deliver the goods. City can recover damages equal to the difference between the contract and market prices

   a. at the time the contract was made.
   b. at the time and place of tender.
   c. when City learned of the breach.
   d. when City files a suit against Ben's.

____ **7.** Delta Grocers, Inc., agrees to buy 10,000 potatoes from Bayou Farms. Only half of the shipment conforms to the contract, but conforming potatoes are in short supply in the market. Bayou's best course is to

   a. accept the entire shipment.
   b. accept the conforming goods and sue for the difference between the contract price and cost of cover.
   c. reject the entire shipment and sue for specific performance.
   d. suspend payment and wait to see if Eagle will tender conforming goods.

____   8.   Lorena buys a scooter from Mooch's Motor Sales, which agrees to keep the scooter until Lorena picks it up. Before she gets it, it is stolen. The loss is suffered by

a. Lorena (the buyer) and Mooch's (the seller).
b. Lorena only.
c. Mooch's only.
d. neither Lorena nor Mooch's.

____   9.   Falcon Skis, Inc., makes and sells skis. In deciding whether the skis are merchantable, a court would consider whether

a. Falcon violated any government regulations.
b. the skis are a quality product.
c. the skis are fit for the ordinary purpose for which such goods are used.
d. the skis are made in an efficient manner.

____   10. BroadBand Company agrees to sell software to Ally from BroadBand's Web site. To complete the deal, Ally clicks on a button that, with reference to certain terms, states, "I agree." Ally does not, however, read the terms. The parties have

a. a binding contract that does not include the terms.
b. a binding contract that includes only the terms to which Holly later agrees.
c. a binding contract that includes the terms.
d. no contract.

STARBUCKS COFFEE COMPANY
INTERNATIONAL SALES CONTRACT
APPLICATIONS

(Answers at the Back of the Book)

The following hypothetical situation and multiple-choice questions relate to your text's fold-out exhibit of the international sales contract used by Starbucks Coffee Company. In that contract, Starbucks orders five hundred tons of coffee at $10 per pound from XYZ Company.

____   1.   Starbucks and XYZ would have an enforceable contract even if they did *not* state in writing

a. the amount of coffee ordered.
b. the price of the coffee.
c. the amount of coffee ordered and the price of the coffee.
d. none of the choices.

____   2.   If Starbucks and XYZ did not include a "DESCRIPTION" of the coffee as "High grown Mexican Altura," then the delivered coffee must met

a. Starbuck's subjective expectations of their quality.
b. Starbuck's description of the goods in ads, on labels, and so on.
c. XYZ's description of the goods in ads, on labels, and so on.
d. XYZ's subjective belief in their quality.

____   3.   Starbucks's incentive to pay on time, according to the terms of this contract, is the clause titled

a. CLAIMS.
b. GUARANTEE.
c. PAYMENT.
d. PRICE.

____ **4.** XYZ's incentive to deliver coffee that conforms to the contract is the clause titled

    a. CLAIMS.
    b. GUARANTEE.
    c. PAYMENT.
    d. PRICE.

____ **5.** Under this contract, until the coffee is delivered to its destination, the party who bears the risk of loss is

    a. Bonded Public Warehouse.
    b. Green Coffee Association.
    c. Starbucks.
    d. XYZ.

SHORT ESSAY QUESTIONS

1. For purposes of the UCC, who is a merchant?

2. What is the difference between the implied warranty of merchantability and the implied warranty of fitness for a particular purpose?

RockOn

(Answers at the Back of the Book)

1. For the Summer Solstice Symphonic Symposia—a series of workshops for composers and musicians—you order fifty Tundra-brand cellos from The String Instrument Source, Inc. The Source confirms your order in writing. On the last day to ship the order, the seller realizes that it does not have enough Tundra cellos in stock and ships Unitone cellos instead, with a note stating that the Unitone instruments are an accommodation. Is The Source in breach? Discuss.

2. As a sound engineer, you agree orally to custom design and build a system for Cato, the newest pop star, for his upcoming European tour at the price of $250,000. You complete the project for $180,000, but Cato says that he no longer needs the system and refuses to pay for it. Unable to sell the unique system, you incur storage costs of $6,000. Can you recover damages? If so, how much?

Chapter 12
Torts and Cyber Torts

What This Chapter Is About

The law of **torts** is concerned with wrongful conduct by one person that causes injury to another. *Tort* is French for "wrong." For acts that cause physical injury or that interfere with physical security and freedom of movement, tort law provides remedies, typically damages (money).

This chapter outlines intentional torts, negligence, and strict liability. These categories include torts that are specifically related to business and cyber torts.

Chapter Outline

I. THE BASIS OF TORT LAW

Two notions serve as the basis of all torts: wrongs and compensation. Tort law recognizes that some acts are wrong because they cause injuries to others. A tort action is a *civil* action in which one person brings a personal suit against another, usually for damages.

A. THE PURPOSE OF TORT LAW

The purpose is to provide remedies for the violation of protected interests, including personal safety, property, privacy, family relations, reputation, and dignity.

B. DAMAGES AVAILABLE IN TORT ACTIONS

Compensatory damages compensate a person for actual losses. Punitive damages are intended to punish a wrongdoer and deter others from similar wrongdoing.

1. Compensatory Damages

Special damages cover quantifiable losses, such as medical expenses, lost wages, irreplaceable items, and damaged property. *General damages* are for non-monetary harm, such as pain and suffering, loss of reputation, and loss or impairment of mental or physical capacity.

2. Punitive Damages

These are awarded only when wrongful conduct is particularly egregious or reprehensible. Punitive damages are subject to the limits of the due process clause of the U.S. Constitution.

C. TORT REFORM

The tort law system has been criticized as encouraging trivial and unfounded lawsuits, excessive damage awards, and costly changes in response (such as doctors' ordering unnecessary tests).

1. Federal Level

At the federal level, the Class Action Fairness Act (CAFA) of 2005 shifted jurisdiction over cases involving large numbers of plaintiffs and large amounts of potential awards to the federal courts.

2. State Level

At the state level, about half of the states have limited damages—or banned punitive damages—especially in medical malpractice cases.

II. INTENTIONAL TORTS AGAINST PERSONS

These torts involve acts that were intended or could be expected to bring about consequences that are the basis of the tort. A tortfeasor (one committing a tort) must intend to commit an act, the consequences of which interfere with the personal or business interests of another in a way not permitted by law.

A. ASSAULT AND BATTERY

1. Assault

Assault is an intentional act that creates in another person a reasonable apprehension or fear of immediate harmful or offensive contact.

2. Battery

Battery is an intentional and harmful or offensive physical contact. Physical injury need not occur. The reasonable person standard determines whether the conduct is offensive.

3. Compensation

A plaintiff may be compensated for emotional harm or loss of reputation resulting from a battery, as well as for physical harm.

4. Defenses to Assault and Battery

An individual who is defending his or her life or physical well-being can claim self-defense. An individual can claim defense of others if he or she acted reasonably to protect others who were in real or apparent danger.

B. FALSE IMPRISONMENT

1. What False Imprisonment Is

False imprisonment is the intentional confinement or restraint of another person without justification. Confinement can be by physical barrier, physical restraint, or threat of physical force.

2. Merchants' Privilege to Detain

In some states, a merchant is justified in delaying suspected shoplifters if there is probable cause. The detention must be done in a reasonable manner and for only a reasonable time.

C. INTENTIONAL INFLICTION OF EMOTIONAL DISTRESS

This consists of an act that amounts to extreme and outrageous conduct resulting in severe emotional distress in another. Stalking is one way to commit it. Repeated annoyance, with threats, is another.

D. DEFAMATION

Defamation is wrongfully hurting another's good reputation through false statements of fact. Doing it orally is slander. Doing it in writing is libel.

1. The Publication Requirement

The statement must be published (communicated to a third party). Anyone who republishes or repeats a defamatory statement is liable.

2. Damages for Libel

Because libelous statements are written, can be circulated widely, and are typically a result of deliberation, general damages are presumed. Showing an actual injury is not required.

3. Damages for Slander

Because slander has a temporary quality, special damages must be proved. Proof of injury—actual economic loss—is required. The exceptions are when one falsely states that a person has a loathsome disease, has committed improprieties in a profession or trade, has committed or been imprisoned for a serious crime, or is unchaste or has engaged in serious sexual misconduct.

4. Defenses to Defamation

a. Truth
The statement is true. It must be true in whole, not in part.

b. Privileged Speech
The statement is privileged: absolute (made in a judicial or legislative proceeding) or qualified (for example, made by one corporate director to another and was about corporate business).

c. Public Figures
The statement is about a public figure, made in a public medium, and related to a matter of general public interest. To recover damages, a public figure must prove a statement was made with actual malice (knowledge of its falsity or reckless disregard for the truth).

E. INVASION OF PRIVACY
A person must have a reasonable expectation of privacy. The invasion must be highly offensive. Four acts qualify:

1. The use of a person's name, picture, or other likeness for commercial purposes without permission. (This is appropriation—see below.)

2. Intrusion on an individual's affairs or seclusion.

3. Publication of information that places a person in a false light.

4. Public disclosure of private facts about an individual that an ordinary person would find objectionable.

F. APPROPRIATION
This is the use of one person's name or likeness by another, without permission and for the benefit of the user. An individual's right to privacy includes the right to the exclusive use of his or her identity.

1. Degree of Likeness
The use of a person's name may be enough to impose liability.

2. Right of Publicity as a Property Right
A person's financial interest in the commercial exploitation of his or her identity is protected.

G. FRAUDULENT MISREPRESENTATION
Fraud is the use of misrepresentation and deceit for personal gain. Opinions and puffery (seller's talk) are not fraud. The elements of fraudulent misrepresentation—

1. **Misrepresentation** of material facts or conditions with knowledge that they are false or with reckless disregard for the truth.

2. **Intent** to induce another to rely on the misrepresentation.

3. **Justifiable reliance** by the deceived party.

4. **Damages** suffered as a result of reliance.

5. **Causal connection** between the misrepresentation and the injury.

H. ABUSIVE OR FRIVOLOUS LITIGATION
Persons have a right not to be sued unless there is a legally just and proper reason. Torts related to abusive litigation include malicious prosecution (suing out of malice without probable cause) and abuse of process (using a legal process in an improper manner or to accomplish a purpose for which it was no t designed). The latter does not require proof of malice or a loss in a prior legal proceeding.

III. BUSINESS TORTS
Torts involving wrongful interference with business rights generally fall into these two categories.

A. WRONGFUL INTERFERENCE WITH A CONTRACTUAL RELATIONSHIP

1. The Intent Factor
Any lawful contract can be the basis for this action. The plaintiff must prove that the defendant actually induced the breach of a contractual relationship, not merely that the defendant reaped the benefits of a broken contract.

2. Requirements
There are three elements: (1) a valid, enforceable contract between two parties, (2) a third party's knowledge of the contract, and (3) the third party's intentionally causing one of the parties to break the contract.

B. WRONGFUL INTERFERENCE WITH A BUSINESS RELATIONSHIP

1. An Example
If there are two yogurt stores in a mall, placing an employee of Store A in front of Store B to divert customers to Store A constitutes the tort of wrongful interference with a business relationship.

2. Requirements
The elements of this action are (1) an established business relationship, (2) a third party's use of predatory methods to end the relationship, and (3) damages.

C. DEFENSES TO WRONGFUL INTERFERENCE
There is no liability if the interference was permissible. Bona fide competitive behavior is a privileged interference even if it results in the breaking of a contract. The public policy that favors free competition in advertising outweighs the instability that competitive activity might cause in contractual relations.

IV. INTENTIONAL TORTS AGAINST PROPERTY

A. TRESPASS TO LAND
This occurs if a person, without permission, enters onto, above, or below the surface of another's land; causes anything to enter onto the land; or remains on the land or permits anything to remain on it.

1. Trespass Criteria, Rights, and Duties
Posted signs *expressly* establish trespass. Entering onto property to commit an illegal act *impliedly* does so. Trespassers are liable for any property damage. Owners may have a duty to post notice of any danger.

2. Defenses against Trespass to Land
Defenses against trespass include that the trespass was warranted or that the purported owner had no right to possess the land in question.

B. TRESPASS TO PERSONAL PROPERTY
This occurs when an individual unlawfully harms the personal property of another or interferes with an owner's right to exclusive possession and enjoyment. Defenses include that the interference was warranted.

C. CONVERSION
Conversion is an act depriving an owner of personal property without permission and without just cause. Conversion is the civil side of crimes related to theft. Buying stolen goods is conversion.

D. DISPARAGEMENT OF PROPERTY
Disparagement of property occurs when economically injurious falsehoods are made about another's product or ownership of property. It is a general term for torts that can be specifically referred to as slander of quality (product) or slander of title (ownership of property).

V. NEGLIGENCE

An act that does not constitute an intentional tort because the element of intent is missing may constitute negligence.

A. THE DEFINITION OF NEGLIGENCE

1. What Negligence Is

Negligence is a party's failure to live up to a required duty of care, causing another to suffer injury. The breach of the duty must create a risk of certain harmful consequences, whether or not that was the intent of the party who committed the breach.

2. The Elements of Negligence

(1) A duty of care, (2) breach of the duty of care, (3) damage or injury as a result of the breach, and (4) the breach causes the damage or injury.

B. THE DUTY OF CARE AND ITS BREACH

A failure to comply with a duty of care may consist of an act or its omission.

1. The Reasonable Person Standard

The measure of the duty of care is the reasonable person standard (how a reasonable person would have acted in the same circumstances).

2. The Duty of Landowners

Owners, including retailers and other businesspersons, are expected to use reasonable care (guard against some risks and warn of others) to protect persons, such as customers and other invitees, coming onto their property. Obvious risks may provide an exception.

3. The Duty of Professionals

A professional's duty is consistent with his or her knowledge, skill, and intelligence, including what is reasonable for that professional. These include accountants, attorneys, and physicians.

4. Factors for Determining a Breach of the Duty of Care

These factors include the nature of the act (whether it is outrageous or commonplace), the manner in which the act is performed (cautiously versus heedlessly), and the nature of the injury (whether it is serious or slight).

5. No Duty to Rescue

Failing to rescue a stranger in peril is not a breach of a duty of care.

C. CAUSATION

1. Is There Causation in Fact?

The breach of the duty of care must cause the injury—that is, "but for" the wrongful act, the injury would not have occurred.

2. Was the Act the Proximate, or Legal, Cause of the Injury?

There must be a connection between the act and the injury strong enough to justify imposing liability. Generally, the harm or the victim of the harm must have been foreseeable in light of all of the circumstances.

D. THE INJURY REQUIREMENT AND DAMAGES

To recover damages, a party must have suffered a loss, harm, wrong, or invasion of a protected interest. Compensatory damages are the norm, but punitive damages may be awarded if a defendant was grossly negligent (acted with reckless disregard for the consequences).

VI. DEFENSES TO NEGLIGENCE

Besides the following defenses, a defendant might assert that a plaintiff failed to prove one of the required elements of negligence.

A. ASSUMPTION OF RISK
A person who voluntarily enters into a risky situation, aware of the risk, cannot recover.

1. Express or Implied Assumption of Risk
The risk can be assumed by express agreement or implied by the plaintiff's knowledge of the risk and subsequent conduct. This does not include a risk different from or greater than the risk normally involved in the situation.

2. When Courts Do Not Apply Assumption of Risk
This does not apply in emergencies or when a statute protects a class of people from harm and a member of the class is injured by the harm (such as a workers' compensation statute).

B. SUPERSEDING CAUSE
A superseding intervening force breaks the connection between the breach of the duty of care and the injury or damage. Taking a defensive action (such as swerving to avoid an oncoming car) does not break the connection. Nor does someone else's attempt to rescue the injured party.

C. CONTRIBUTORY OR COMPARATIVE NEGLIGENCE

1. Contributory Negligence
In a few states, a plaintiff cannot recover for an injury if he or she was negligent.

2. "Pure" Comparative Negligence
In most states, the plaintiff's and the defendant's negligence is compared and liability pro-rated.

3. Modified Comparative Fault
Under a "50 percent" rule, a plaintiff recovers nothing if he or she is determined to have been more than 50 percent at fault. Under a "51 percent" rule, a plaintiff recovers nothing if he or she is determined to have been more than half (51 percent or more) at fault.

VII. SPECIAL NEGLIGENCE DOCTRINES AND STATUTES

A. *RES IPSA LOQUITUR*
If negligence is very difficult to prove, a court may infer it, and the defendant must prove he or she was not negligent. This is only if the event causing the harm is one that normally does not occur in the absence of negligence and is caused by something within the defendant's control.

B. NEGLIGENCE *PER SE*
A person who violates a statute providing for a criminal penalty is liable when the violation causes another to be injured, if (1) the statute sets out a standard of conduct, and when, where, and of whom it is expected; (2) the injured person is in the class protected by the statute; and (3) the statute was designed to prevent the type of injury suffered.

C. "DANGER INVITES RESCUE" DOCTRINE
A person who endangers another is liable for injuries to third persons attempting to rescue the endangered party.

D. SPECIAL NEGLIGENCE STATUTES
Good Samaritan statutes protect persons (especially medical personnel) who aid others from being sued for negligence. Dram shop acts impose liability on tavern owners or bartenders for injuries caused by intoxicated persons who are served by them. A statute may impose liability on social hosts for acts of their guests.

VIII. CYBER TORTS
Cyber torts are torts committed in cyberspace.

A. IDENTIFYING THE AUTHOR OF ONLINE DEFAMATION
To discover the identity of a person who posts a defamatory remark, a party generally must obtain a court order.

B. LIABILITY OF INTERNET SERVICE PROVIDERS
Under the Communications Decency Act (CDA) of 1996, Internet service providers (ISPs) are not liable for the defamatory remarks of those who use their services.

C. THE SPREAD OF SPAM
Spam is junk e-mail.

1. State Regulation of Spam
Most states regulate spam. Many of these require the senders to tell recipients how to opt out of future mailings. Increasingly, states are passing laws to prohibit spam.

2. The Federal CAN-SPAM Act

a. What Is Preempted
The Controlling the Assault of Non-Solicited Pornography and Marketing (CAN-SPAM) Act preempts state antispam statutes except for those that prohibit deceptive e-mailing practices.

b. What Is Permitted
The CAN-SPAM Act permits the use of unsolicited commercial e-mail.

c. What Is Prohibited
The act prohibits certain spamming activities, including the use of false return addresses and other misleading or deceptive information. Also prohibited are "dictionary attacks"—sending messages to randomly generated e-mail addresses—and "harvesting" e-mail addresses from Web sites.

3. The U.S. Safe Web Act

a. Cooperation
The Undertaking Spam, Spyware, and Fraud Enforcement with Enforcers Beyond the Borders (U.S. Safe Web) Act of 2006 allows the Federal Trade Commission (FTC) to cooperate and share information with foreign agencies investigating and prosecuting Internet fraud, spamming, and spyware.

b. Safe Harbor
Internet service providers (ISPs) have a "safe harbor"—immunity from liability—for supplying information to the FTC concerning unfair or deceptive conduct in foreign jurisdictions.

TRUE-FALSE QUESTIONS

(Answers at the Back of the Book)

_____ 1. To commit an intentional tort, a person must intend the consequences of his or her act or know with substantial certainty that certain consequences will result.

_____ 2. A reasonable apprehension or fear of harmful or offensive contact in the distant future is an assault.

_____ 3. A defamatory statement must be communicated to a third party to be actionable.

_____ 4. Puffery is fraud.

_____ 5. Conversion is wrongfully taking or retaining an individual's personal property and placing it in the service of another.

_____ 6. An _ordinary_ person standard determines whether allegedly negligent conduct resulted in a breach of a duty of care.

____ **7.** Malicious prosecution occurs when a party files a suit out of malice, with or without probable cause.

____ **8.** Bona fide competitive behavior can constitute wrongful interference with a contractual relationship.

____ **9.** An Internet service provider is not normally liable for its users' defamatory remarks.

____ **10.** A wrongful act need not actually be the cause of an injury for liability on a theory of negligence.

FILL-IN QUESTIONS

(Answers at the Back of the Book)

1. Basic defenses to _____ (negligence/intentional torts) include comparative negligence, contributory negligence, and assumption of risk.

2. One who voluntarily and knowingly enters into a risky situation normally cannot recover damages. This is the defense of _____ (contributory negligence/ assumption of risk).

3. When both parties' failure to use reasonable care combines to cause injury, in some states the injured party's recovery is prorated according to his or her own negligence. This is _____ (comparative/contributory) negligence.

MULTIPLE-CHOICE QUESTIONS

(Answers at the Back of the Book)

____ **1.** Driving a car negligently, Rollo crashes into a phone pole. The pole falls, smashing through the roof of a house, killing Silky. But for Rollo's negligence, Silky would not have died. Regarding the death, the crash is the

    a. cause in fact.
    b. intervening cause.
    c. proximate cause.
    d. superseding cause.

____ **2.** Melvin, a wholesale dairy products salesperson, follows Nadine, another wholesale dairy products salesperson, as he contacts his customers. Melvin solicits each of Nadine's customers. Melvin is most likely liable for

    a. appropriation.
    b. assault.
    c. conversion.
    d. wrongful interference with a business relationship.

____ **3.** Stefano, an engineer, supervises the construction of a new house. When the house collapses due to faulty construction, the injured parties sue Stefano. As a professional, he is held to the same standard of care as

    a. ordinary persons.
    b. other engineers.
    c. other professionals, including accountants, attorneys, and physicians.
    d. the injured parties.

____ 4. Ricardo sends a letter to Stefanie in which he falsely accuses her of embezzling from her employer Teeth & Gums Dental Clinic. This is defamation only if the letter is read by

   a. a public figure.
   b. any third person.
   c. Stefanie.
   d. Stefanie's employer.

____ 5. Nina is injured in a truck accident and sues Owen, alleging negligence. Owen claims that Nina was driving carelessly. Comparative negligence may reduce Nina's recovery

   a. even if Nina was only slightly at fault.
   b. only if Nina was as equally at fault as Owen.
   c. only if Nina was less at fault than Owen.
   d. only if Nina was more at fault than Owen.

____ 6. Online World (OW) is an Internet service provider. Publicity Now!, Inc., spams OW's customers, some of who then cancel OW's services. Publicity Now! may be liable for

   a. battery.
   b. conversion.
   c. infliction of emotional distress.
   d. trespass to personal property.

____ 7. Lonnie drives across Myra's land. This is a trespass to land only if

   a. Lonnie damages the land.
   b. Lonnie does not have Myra's permission to drive on her land.
   c. Lonnie makes disparaging remarks about Myra's land.
   d. Myra is aware of Lonnie's driving on her land.

____ 8. Petra believes that Quinn is about to hit her. To prevent harmful contact, Petra hits Quinn. If Quinn sues Petra, she can most likely successfully claim

   a. defense of others.
   b. intentional infliction of emotional distress.
   c. self-defense.
   d. no defense.

____ 9. Ricky accuses Sara of fraud. Normally, the reliance giving rise to fraud is based on a statement of

   a. delusion.
   b. fact.
   c. opinion.
   d. puffery.

____ 10. To protect its customers and other business invitees, Grocers Market must warn them of

   a. all dangers.
   b. hidden dangers.
   c. obvious dangers.
   d. no dangers.

SHORT ESSAY QUESTIONS

1. What is a *tort*?

2. What are the elements of a cause of action based on negligence?

GAMEPOINTS

(Answers at the Back of the Book)

1.   The game "StreetFight" features martial contests between two or more players, with the winner of the bouts "owning the street." You're playing the game with Tom, who's losing every bout, when he suddenly grabs the playing device from your hands, raises it as if to strike you, and says, "If I lose one more time, we're gonna take this outside." Which torts set out in this chapter, if any, might Tom have committed? Why?

2.   . You're playing "Prince of Peril," a video game in which your avatar travels the universe, engaging nasty villains and taking on fantastic risks at incredible odds to "honor the imperial duty of care." In one encounter, your avatar leaps from his space cruiser to battle a pair of Saturnian Neanderthals. The cruiser collides with an orbiting space station that veers off course, enters the Earth's atmosphere, bursts into flames, and crashes into an oil refinery in Louisiana. The earth-shaking concussion causes a nearby silo to collapse onto Twyla, a bystander. Applying the principles set out in this chapter, can Twyla recover from the Prince of Peril?

Chapter 13
Strict Liability and Product Liability

WHAT THIS CHAPTER IS ABOUT

Strict liability is liability for injury imposed for reasons other than fault. Manufacturers, processors, and sellers may be liable to consumers, users, and bystanders for physical harm or property damage caused by defective goods. This is *product liability*.

CHAPTER OUTLINE

I. STRICT LIABILITY

A. ABNORMALLY DANGEROUS ACTIVITIES

The basis for imposing strict liability on an abnormally dangerous activity is that the activity creates an extreme risk. Balancing the risk against the potential for harm, it is fair to ask the person engaged in the activity to pay for injury caused by that activity. Abnormally dangerous activities—

1. Involve potentially serious harm to persons or property.
2. Involve a high degree of risk that cannot be completely guarded against by the exercise of reasonable care.
3. Are activities not commonly performed in the area in which damage or an injury occurs.

B. OTHER APPLICATIONS OF STRICT LIABILITY

A person who keeps a dangerous animal is strictly liable for any harm inflicted by the animal. Strict liability is also a theory applicable in product liability cases.

II. PRODUCT LIABILITY

Product liability may be based on negligence, misrepresentation, strict liability, or warranty law.

A. PRODUCT LIABILITY BASED ON NEGLIGENCE

If the failure to exercise reasonable care in the making or marketing of a product causes an injury, the basis of liability is negligence.

1. Manufacturer's Duty of Care

Due care must be exercised in designing, assembling, and testing a product; selecting materials; inspecting and testing products bought for use in the final product; and placing warnings on the label to inform users of dangers of which an ordinary person might not be aware.

2. Privity of Contract between Plaintiff and Defendant Is Not Required

B. PRODUCT LIABILITY BASED ON MISREPRESENTATION

There may liability for a misrepresentation if it (1) is of a material fact, (2) is intended to induce a buyer's reliance, (3) the buyer relies on it, and (4) there is an injury. Fraudulent misrepresenta-

111

tion occurs when the misrepresentation is done knowingly or with reckless disregard for the facts.

III. STRICT PRODUCT LIABILITY

A defendant may be liable for the result of an act regardless of intention or exercise of reasonable care.

A. STRICT PRODUCT LIABILITY AND PUBLIC POLICY

Public policy assumes that (1) consumers should be protected from unsafe products, (2) manufacturers and distributors should not escape liability solely for lack of privity, and (3) sellers and lessors are in a better position to bear the cost of injuries caused by their products.

B. THE REQUIREMENTS FOR STRICT PRODUCT LIABILITY

Under the *Restatement (Second) of Torts*, Section 402A—

1. **Product Is in a Defective Condition When the Defendant Sells It**

2. **Defendant Is Normally in the Business of Selling the Product**

3. **Defect Makes the Product Unreasonably Dangerous**
   A product may be so defective as to be unreasonably dangerous if either—

   a. **Product Is Dangerous beyond the Ordinary Consumer's Expectation**
      There may have been a flaw in the manufacturing process that led to some defective products being marketed, or a perfectly made product may not have had adequate warning on the label.

   b. **Manufacturer Failed to Use a Less Dangerous, Economically Feasible Alternative**
      A manufacturer may have failed to design a safe product.

4. **Plaintiff Incurs Harm to Self or Property by Use of the Product**

5. **Defect Is the Proximate Cause of the Harm**

6. **Product Was Not Substantially Changed after It Was Sold**
   Between the time the product was sold and the time of the injury.

C. PRODUCT DEFECTS

The *Restatement (Third) of Torts: Products Liability* categorizes defects as—

1. **Manufacturing Defects**
   A manufacturing defect occurs when a product departs from its intended design even though all possible care was taken (strict liability).

2. **Design Defects**
   A design defect exists when a foreseeable risk of harm posed by a product could have been reduced by use of a reasonable alternative design and the omission makes the product unreasonably unsafe. A court would consider such factors as consumer expectations and warnings.

3. **Inadequate Warnings**
   A warning defect occurs when a reasonable warning could have reduced a product's foreseeable risk of harm and the omission makes the product unreasonably unsafe. Factors include the content and comprehensibility of a warning, and the expected users.

D. MARKET-SHARE LIABILITY

In some cases, some courts hold that all firms that manufactured and distributed a certain product during a certain period are liable for injuries in proportion to the firms' respective shares of the market.

E. OTHER APPLICATIONS OF STRICT PRODUCT LIABILITY

1. **Strict Liability Protects Bystanders**
   All courts extend strict liability to cover injured bystanders (limited in some cases to those whose injuries are reasonably foreseeable).

2. **Strict Liability Extends to Suppliers**
   Suppliers of component parts may be liable for injuries caused by defective products.

IV. DEFENSES TO PRODUCT LIABILITY

A. ASSUMPTION OF RISK
In some states, this is a defense if (1) plaintiff knew and appreciated the risk created by the defect and (2) plaintiff voluntarily engaged in the risk, event though it was unreasonable to do so.

B. PRODUCT MISUSE
The use must not be the one for which the product was designed, and the misuse must not be reasonably foreseeable.

C. COMPARATIVE NEGLIGENCE (FAULT)
Most states consider a plaintiff's actions in apportioning liability.

D. COMMONLY KNOWN DANGERS
Failing to warn against such a danger is not ground for liability.

E. KNOWLEDGEABLE USER
Failing to warn a *knowledgeable* user of a danger that is commonly known to such users is not ground for liability.

F. STATUTES OF LIMITATIONS AND REPOSE
A statute of limitations provides that an action must be brought within a specified period of time after the cause of action accrues (after some damage occurs or after a harmed party discovers the damage). A statute of repose limits the time in which a suit can be filed. It runs from an earlier date and for a longer time than a statute of limitations.

TRUE-FALSE QUESTIONS

(Answers at the Back of the Book)

____ 1. Strict liability is imposed for reasons other than fault.

____ 2. A requirement for a suit based on strict liability is the defendant's intent to affect certain results.

____ 3. A requirement for *any* suit based on strict liability is a failure to exercise due care.

____ 4. The doctrine of strict liability applies only to abnormally dangerous activities.

____ 5. Privity of contract is required to bring a product liability suit based on negligence.

____ 6. A requirement for a *product liability* suit based on strict liability is a failure to exercise due care.

____ 7. In many states, the plaintiff's negligence may be raised as a defense in a product liability suit based on strict liability.

____ 8. Product liability is imposed only if a defect in the design or construction of a product causes an injury.

____ 9. A manufacturer has a duty to warn about risks that are obvious or commonly known.

____ 10. Assumption of risk can be raised as a defense in a product liability suit.

FILL-IN QUESTIONS

(Answers at the Back of the Book)

1. Basic defenses to _____ (negligence/intentional torts) include comparative negligence, contributory negligence, and assumption of risk.

2. One who voluntarily and knowingly enters into a risky situation normally cannot recover damages. This is the defense of _____ (contributory negligence/ assumption of risk).

3. When both parties' failure to use reasonable care combines to cause injury, in some states the injured party's recovery is prorated according to his or her own negligence. This is _____ (comparative/ contributory) negligence.

MULTIPLE-CHOICE QUESTIONS

(Answers at the Back of the Book)

____ **1.** The design of a bridge built by Suspension Engineering, Inc., is defective and soon after completion it begins to sway in the wind. Everyone stays off, except Rory, who wants to show off. Rory falls from the bridge and sues Suspension, who can raise the defense of

a. assumption of risk.
b. commonly known danger.
c. product misuse.
d. knowledgeable user.

____ **2.** Kitchensharp Products, Inc. (KPI), makes knifes and other utensils. Louella is injured while using a KPI knife, and sues KPI for product liability based on negligence. KPI could successfully defend against the suit by showing that

a. Louella's injury resulted from a commonly known danger.
b. Louella misused the knife in a foreseeable way.
c. KPI did not sell the knife to Louella.
d. the knife was not altered after KPI sold it.

____ **3.** StandUp Tools, Inc., makes and sells tools. Tifa is injured as a result of using a StandUp tool. She sues StandUp for product liability based on strict liability. To succeed, Tifa must prove that StandUp

a. was in privity of contract with Tifa.
b. did not use care with respect to the tool.
c. misrepresented a material fact regarding the tool on which Tifa relied.
d. none of the choices.

____ **4.** Yard Work, Inc., makes and sells garden tools. Under the *Restatement (Second) of Torts*, a tool could be unreasonably dangerous

a. only if, in making the tool, Yard Work failed to use a less dangerous but economically feasible alternative.
b. only if the tool is dangerous beyond the ordinary consumer's expectation.
c. if, in making the tool, Yard Work failed to use a less dangerous but economically feasible alternative or if the tool is dangerous beyond the ordinary consumer's expectation.
d. none of the above.

___ **5.** Misha is in a Sip n' Snak store when a bottle of Hi Cola on a nearby shelf explodes, injuring her. She can recover from the manufacturer of Hi Cola only if she can show that

    a. she did not assume the risk of the explosive bottle of Hi Cola.
    b. she intended to buy the explosive bottle of Hi Cola.
    c. she was injured due to a defect in the product.
    d. the manufacturer failed to use due care in making the bottle of Hi Cola.

___ **6.** Vivid Vid, Inc., designs and manufacturers DVD players. In a product liability suit based on negligence, Vivid could be liable for violating its duty of care with respect to

    a. a player's design only.
    b. a player's design or manufacture.
    c. a player's manufacture only.
    d. neither a player's design nor its manufacture.

___ **7.** Gears, Inc., makes bicycles. Hope is injured while riding a Gears bike and files a suit against the maker for product liability based on misrepresentation. To succeed, Hope must show that

    a. Gears did not use due care with respect to making the bike.
    b. Gears misrepresented a material fact regarding the bike, on which Hope relied.
    c. Hope did not abuse or misuse the bike.
    d. Hope was in privity of contract with Gears.

___ **8.** Implosive Mining Company engages in blasting operations. This is subject to strict liability because

    a. blasting is a dangerous activity.
    b. blasting is a negligent activity.
    c. Implosive is a mining company.
    d. mining can be done without blasting.

___ **9.** Roadway Construction, Inc., uses dynamite in its projects. Sven stores household chemicals in the garage. Most likely liable for any injury caused by an abnormally dangerous activity is

    a. neither Roadway nor Sven.
    b. Roadway and Sven.
    c. Roadway only.
    d. Sven only.

___ **10.** Cliff owns Deconstruction Corporation (DC), a demolition company. A demolition by a DC crew injures Eli, a passerby. Under the doctrine of strict liability, Cliff must pay for Eli's injury

    a. only if Eli's injury was not reasonably foreseeable.
    b. only if Eli's injury was reasonably foreseeable.
    c. only if the DC crew was at fault.
    d. whether or not the DC crew was at fault.

SHORT ESSAY QUESTIONS

1. What distinguishes strict liability as a theory for recovery in a product liability case from other bases for recovery?

2. How defective must a product be to support a cause of action in strict liability in a product liability suit?

ROCKON

1.   You manage the careers of musicians, including Baker Charlie, a blues rock group of rising fame. Zot! Corp. makes electrical equipment—amplifiers, microphones, and so on. You buy Zot! equipment for Baker Charlie's six-month U.S. tour. During the first performance, a surge of power through a microphone electrocutes the lead singer Dawg. An inexpensive resistor added to the microphone during its manufacture would have prevented the surge. You claim that Zot! committed negligence. Zot! argues that Dawg was not in privity, and besides, he assumed the risk. Who's most likely to prevail? Why?

2.   You buy a grand piano from Piano Showcase that was sold to the retailer by Quality Wholesale, Inc., which bought it from its manufacturer Raven Corp. While you are adjusting a rug under one of the piano's feet, it collapses on you, causing bodily injuries. You file a suit in strict product liability against the seller, the wholesaler, and the maker. Can you recover damages without proof of negligence? Explain.

Chapter 14
Intellectual Property and Internet Law

WHAT THIS CHAPTER IS ABOUT

Intellectual property consists of the products of intellectual, creative processes. The law of trademarks, patents, copyrights, and related concepts protect many of these products (such as inventions, books, software, movies, and songs). This chapter outlines these laws, including their application in cyberspace.

CHAPTER OUTLINE

I. TRADEMARKS AND RELATED PROPERTY

A. STATUTORY PROTECTION OF TRADEMARKS
The Lanham Act protects trademarks at the federal level. Many states also have statutes that protect trademarks.

1. What Is a Trademark?
A distinctive mark, motto, device, or emblem that a manufacturer stamps, prints, or otherwise affixes to the goods it produces to distinguish them from the goods of other manufacturers.

2. The Federal Trademark Dilution Act of 1995
Prohibits dilution (unauthorized use of marks on goods or services, even if they do not compete directly with products whose marks are copied).

B. TRADEMARK REGISTRATION
A trademark may be registered with a state or the federal government. Trademarks do not need to be registered to be protected.

1. Requirements for Federal Registration
A trademark may be filed with the U.S. Patent and Trademark Office on the basis of (1) use or (2) the intent to use the mark within six months (which may be extended to thirty months).

2. Renewal of Federal Registration
Between the fifth and sixth years and then every ten years (twenty years for marks registered before 1990).

C. TRADEMARK INFRINGEMENT
This occurs when a trademark is copied to a substantial degree or used in its entirety by another.

D. DISTINCTIVENESS OF THE MARK
The extent to which the law protects a trademark is normally determined by how distinctive it is, with the purpose of reducing the likelihood that consumers will be confused by similar marks.

1. **Strong Marks**
Fanciful, arbitrary, or suggestive marks are considered most distinctive.

2. **Descriptive Terms, Geographic Terms, and Personal Names**
Descriptive terms, geographic terms, and personal names are not inherently distinctive and are not protected until they acquire a secondary meaning (which means that customers associate the mark with the source of a product)

3. **Generic Terms**
Terms such as *bicycle* or *computer* receive no protection, even if they acquire secondary meaning.

E. **SERVICE, CERTIFICATION, AND COLLECTIVE MARKS**
Laws that apply to trademarks normally also apply to—

1. **Service Marks**
Used to distinguish the services of one person or company from those of another. Registered in the same manner as trademarks.

2. **Certification Marks**
Used by one or more persons, other than the owner, to certify the region, materials, mode of manufacture, quality, or accuracy of the owner's goods or services.

3. **Collective Marks**
Certification marks used by members of a cooperative, association, or other organization.

F. **TRADE DRESS**
Trade dress is the image and appearance of a product, and has the same protection as trademarks.

G. **COUNTERFEIT GOODS**
Counterfeit goods copy or imitate trademarked goods but are not genuine.

1. **The Stop Counterfeiting in Manufactured Goods Act**
This act makes it a crime to intentionally traffic in counterfeit goods or services, or use a counterfeit mark on or in connection with goods or services. The act covers counterfeit labels, stickers, packaging, and similar items, whether or not they are attached to goods.

2. **Counterfeiting Penalties**
These include fines of up to $2 million and imprisonment of up to ten years (more for repeat offenders). Forfeiture of counterfeit products and the payment of restitution to a trademark holder or other victim can be imposed.

H. **TRADE NAMES**
These indicate a business's name. Trade names cannot be registered with the federal government but may be protected under the common law if they are used as trademarks or service marks.

II. **CYBER MARKS**

A. **DOMAIN NAME REGISTRATION**
The Internet Corporation for Assigned Names and Numbers (ICANN) oversees the Internet domain registration system and facilitates the resolution of domain name disputes. To protect genuine marks, businesses sometimes register thousands of misspelled names.

B. **ANTICYBERSQUATTING LEGISLATION**
Disputes over domain names often involve cybersquatting or typosquatting. The Anticybersquatting Consumer Reform Act (ACRA) of 1999 amended the Lanham Act to make cybersquatting clearly illegal. Damages may be awarded.

1. Cybersquatting
Cybersquatting occurs when a person registers a domain name that is the same as, or confusingly similar to, another's mark and offers to sell it to the authentic mark's owner.

2. Typosquatting
This occurs when a person registers a misspelling of a mark that he or she does not own.

C. META TAGS
Meta tags are words in a Web site's key-word field that determine the site's appearance in search engine results. Using others' marks as tags without permission constitutes trademark infringement.

D. DILUTION IN THE ONLINE WORLD
Using a mark, without permission, in a way that diminishes its distinctive quality is dilution. Tech-related cases have concerned the use of marks as domain names and spamming under another's logo.

E. LICENSING
Licensing is permitting a party to use a mark, copyright, patent, or trade secret for certain purposes, which may need to include the maintenance of quality to protect the licensor's rights. Use for other purposes is a breach of the license agreement.

III. PATENTS

A. WHAT A PATENT IS
A grant from the federal government that conveys and secures to an inventor the exclusive right to make, use, and sell an invention for a period of twenty years (fourteen years for a design).

B. SEARCHABLE PATENT DATABASES
Searchable patent databases are important to a business to inventory its assets or to study trends in an industry or a technology, which may help to develop a business strategy or evaluate a job applicant.

C. WHAT IS PATENTABLE?
An invention, discovery, or design must be genuine, novel, useful, and not obvious in light of the technology of the time to be patented. A patent is given to the first person to invent a product, not to the first person to file for a patent.

1. Patents for Software
The basis for software is often a mathematical equation or formula, which is not patentable, but a patent can be obtained for a process that incorporates a computer program.

2. Patents for Business Processes
Business processes are patentable (laws of nature, natural phenomena, and abstract ideas are not).

D. PATENT INFRINGEMENT
Making, using, or selling another's patented design, product, or process without the patent owner's permission is infringement. (Making and selling a patented product in another country is not.)

E. REMEDIES FOR PATENT INFRINGEMENT
A patent owner may obtain an injunction, damages, an order for destruction of all infringing copies, attorneys' fees, and court costs.

IV. COPYRIGHTS

A. WHAT A COPYRIGHT IS
An intangible right granted by statute to the author or originator of certain literary or artistic productions. Protection is automatic; registration is not required.

B. COPYRIGHT PROTECTION

Protection lasts for the life of the author plus 70 years. Copyrights owned by publishing houses expire 95 years from the date of publication or 120 years from the date of creation, whichever is first. For works by more than one author, copyright expires 70 years after the death of the last surviving author.

C. WHAT IS PROTECTED EXPRESSION?

To be protected, under Section 102 of the Copyright Act a work must meet these requirements—

1. Fit a Certain Category

It must be a (1) literary work; (2) musical work; (3) dramatic work; (4) pantomime or choreographic work; (5) pictorial, graphic, or sculptural work; (6) film or other audiovisual work; or (7) a sound recording. The Copyright Act also protects computer software and architectural plans.

2. Be Fixed in a Durable Medium

From which it can be perceived, reproduced, or communicated.

3. Be Original

A compilation of facts (formed by the collection and assembling of preexisting materials of data) is copyrightable if it is original.

D. WHAT IS NOT PROTECTED

Ideas, facts, and related concepts are not protected. If an idea and an expression cannot be separated, the expression cannot be copyrighted.

E. COPYRIGHT INFRINGEMENT

A copyright is infringed if a work is copied without the copyright holder's permission. A copy does not have to be exactly the same as the original—copying a substantial part of the original is enough.

1. Penalties

Actual damages (based on the harm to the copyright holder); damages under the Copyright Act, not to exceed $150,000; and criminal proceedings (which may result in fines or imprisonment).

2. Exception—Fair Use Doctrine

The Copyright Act permits the fair use of a work for purposes such as criticism, news reporting, teaching (including multiple copies for classroom use), scholarship, or research. Factors in determining whether a use is infringement include the effect of the use on the market for the work.

F. COPYRIGHT PROTECTION FOR SOFTWARE

The Computer Software Copyright Act of 1980 protects the binary object code (the part of a software program readable only by computer); the source code (the part of a program readable by people); and the program structure, sequence, and organization. Protection does not extend to a program's "look and feel"—the general appearance, command structure, video images, menus, windows, and other displays.

V. COPYRIGHTS IN DIGITAL INFORMATION

Copyright law requires the copyright holder's permission to sell a "copy" of a work. This is important in cyberspace because the nature of the Internet means that data is "copied" before being transferred online—loading a file or program into a computer's random access memory (RAM) is making a "copy."

A. PIRACY, PROFIT, AND CRIME

It is a crime to exchange pirated, copied, copyrighted materials, even if no profit is realized from the exchange, and to copy works for personal use without the owners' authorization.

B. **THE DIGITAL MILLENNIUM COPYRIGHT ACT OF 1998**
This act imposes penalties on anyone who circumvents encryption software or other technological anti-piracy protection. Also prohibits the manufacture, import, sale, or distribution of devices or services for circumvention. ISPs are not liable for their customers' violations.

C. **MP3 AND FILE-SHARING TECHNOLOGY**
MP3 file compression and music file sharing occur over the Internet through peer-to-peer (P2P) networking. Doing this without the permission of the owner of the music's copyright is infringement.

VI. TRADE SECRETS

A. **WHAT A TRADE SECRET IS**
Trade secrets include customer lists, formulas, plans, research and development, pricing information, marketing techniques, production techniques, and generally anything that provides an opportunity to obtain an advantage over competitors who do not know or use it.

B. **TRADE SECRET PROTECTION**
Protection of trade secrets extends both to ideas and their expression. Liability extends to those who misappropriate trade secrets by any means. Trade secret theft is a violation of the common law and most states' statutes (based on the Uniform Trade Secrets Act), and a federal crime (under the Economic Espionage Act of 1996).

C. **TRADE SECRETS IN CYBERSPACE**
The nature of technology (especially e-mail) undercuts a firm's ability to protect its confidential information, including trade secrets.

VII. INTERNATIONAL PROTECTION

A. **THE BERNE CONVENTION**
The Berne Convention is an international copyright treaty.

1. **For Citizens of Countries That Have Signed the Berne Convention**
If, for example, an American writes a book, the copyright in the book is recognized by every country that signed the convention.

2. **For Citizens of Other Countries**
If a citizen of a country that has not signed the convention publishes a book first in a country that has signed, all other countries that have signed recognize that author's copyright.

B. **THE TRIPS AGREEMENT**
Trade-Related Aspects of Intellectual Property Rights (TRIPS) Agreement is part of the agreement creating the World Trade Organization (WTO). Each member nation must not discriminate (in administration, regulation, or adjudication of intellectual property rights) against the rights' owners.

C. **THE MADRID PROTOCOL**
Under this treaty, a U.S. company wishing to register its trademark abroad can submit a single application and designate other member countries in which they would like to register the mark.

TRUE-FALSE QUESTIONS

(Answers at the Back of the Book)

____ 1. To obtain a patent, an applicant must show that an invention is genuine, novel, useful, and not obvious in light of current technology.

____ 2. To obtain a copyright, an author must show that a work is genuine, novel, useful, and not a copy of a current copyrighted work.

___   **3.** In determining whether the use of a copyrighted work is infringement under the fair use doctrine, one factor is the effect of that use on the market for the copyrighted work.

___   **4.** A personal name is protected under trademark law if it acquires a secondary meaning.

___   **5.** A formula for a chemical compound is not a trade secret.

___   **6.** A trade name, like a trademark, can be registered with the federal government.

___   **7.** A copy must be exactly the same as an original work to infringe on its copyright.

___   **8.** Only the *intentional* use of another's trademark is trademark infringement.

___   **9.** Using another's trademark in a domain name without permission violates federal law.

___   **10.** Trademark dilution requires proof that consumers are likely to be confused by the unauthorized use of the mark.

FILL-IN QUESTIONS

(Answers at the Back of the Book)

Copyright protection is automatic for the life of the author of a work plus _____ (70/95/120) years. Copyrights owned by publishing houses expire _____ (70/95/120) years from the date of the publication of a work or _____ (70/95/120) years from the date of its creation, whichever is first. For works by more than one author, a copyright expires _____ (70/95/120) years after the death of the last surviving author.

MULTIPLE-CHOICE QUESTIONS

(Answers at the Back of the Book)

___   **1.** Johnnycakes, Inc., uses Pattycake Corporation's patented formula in Johnnycakes's recipe for a similar product, without Pattycake's permission. This is

  a. copyright infringement.
  b. patent infringement.
  c. trademark infringement.
  d. none of the choices.

___   **2.** Omega, Inc., uses a trademark on its products that no one, including Omega, has registered with the government. Under federal trademark law, Omega

  a. can register the mark for protection.
  b. cannot register a mark that has been used in commerce.
  c. is guilty of trademark infringement.
  d. must postpone registration until the mark has been out of use for three years.

___   **3.** Tony owns Tonio's, a pub in a small town in Iowa. Universal Dining, Inc., opens a chain of pizza places in California called "Tonio's" and, without Tony's consent, uses "toniosincalifornia" as part of the URL for the chain's Web site. This is

  a. copyright infringement.
  b. cybersquatting.
  c. trademark dilution.
  d. none of the choices.

_____ **4.** The graphics used in "Grave Raiders," a computer game, are protected by

    a. copyright law.
    b. patent law.
    c. trademark law.
    d. trade secrets law.

_____ **5.** Production techniques used to make "Grave Raiders," a computer game, are protected by

    a. copyright law.
    b. patent law.
    c. trademark law.
    d. trade secrets law.

_____ **6.** Tech Corporation uses USA, Inc.'s trademark in Tech's ads without USA's permission. This is

    a. copyright infringement.
    b. patent infringement.
    c. trademark infringement.
    d. none of the choices.

_____ **7.** Clothes made by workers who are members of the Clothes Makers Union are sold with tags that identify this fact. This is

    a. a certification mark.
    b. a collective mark.
    c. a service mark.
    d. trade dress.

_____ **8.** Isabel invents a new type of light bulb and applies for a patent. If Isabel is granted a patent, the invention will be protected

    a. for 10 years.
    b. for 20 years.
    c. for the life of the inventor plus 70 years.
    d. forever.

_____ **9.** Data Corporation created and sells "Economix," financial computer software. Data's copyright in Economix is best protected under

    a. the Berne Convention.
    b. the Madrid Protocol.
    c. the Paris Convention.
    d. the TRIPS Agreement.

_____ **10.** National Media, Inc. (NMI), publishes _Opinion_ magazine, which contains an article by Paula. Without her permission, NMI puts the article into an online database. This is

    a. copyright infringement.
    b. patent infringement.
    c. trademark infringement.
    d. none of the choices.

SHORT ESSAY QUESTIONS

1. What does a copyright protect?

2. What is a trade secret and how is it protected?

GAMEPOINTS

(Answers at the Back of the Book)

1.   You create a new video game-playing device that you call "The Gem." Its revolutionary twist on other game devices is that The Gem can respond to a player's eye movements, making a handheld joystick or similar control almost unnecessary. At this point, is The Gem protected by trademark, patent, or copyright law? If not, how could this protection be obtained?

2.   For The Gem, you write and develop "Rock Roles," a game that allows players to perform in a virtual rock band. Can "Rock Roles" be marketed with a thousand songs uploaded without the copyright owners' permission? Would this be "fair use"? Explain.

Chapter 15
Creditor-Debtor Relations and Bankruptcy

WHAT THIS CHAPTER IS ABOUT

This chapter sets out the rights and remedies available to a creditor, when a debtor defaults, under laws other than federal bankruptcy law. This chapter also covers bankruptcy law. Congressional authority to regulate bankruptcies comes from Article I, Section 8, of the U.S. Constitution. Bankruptcy law (1) protects a debtor by giving him or her a fresh start and (2) ensures equitable treatment to creditors competing for a debtor's assets.

CHAPTER OUTLINE

I. **LAWS ASSISTING CREDITORS**

  A. **LIENS**
  A lien is a claim against property to satisfy a debt or to protect a claim for payment of a debt.

   1. **Mechanic's Liens**
   A creditor can file this lien on real property when a person contracts for labor, services, or materials to improve the property but does not pay.

     a. **When a Creditor Must File a Mechanic's Lien**
     A creditor must file the lien within a specific period, measured from the last date on which materials or labor was provided (usually within 60 to 120 days).

     b. **If the Owner Does Not Pay**
     The property can be sold to satisfy the debt. Notice of the foreclosure and sale must be given to the debtor in advance.

   2. **Artisan's Liens**
   This is a security device by which a creditor can recover from a debtor for labor and materials furnished in the repair of personal property.

     a. **The Creditor Must Possess the Property**
     The lien terminates if possession is voluntarily surrendered, unless the lienholder records notice of the lien in accord with state statutes.

     b. **If the Owner Does Not Pay**
     The property can be sold to satisfy the debt. Notice of the foreclosure and sale must be given to the debtor in advance.

   3. **Judicial Liens**

     a. **Writ of Attachment**
     Attachment is a court-ordered seizure and taking into custody of property before the entry of a final judgment for a past-due debt.

125

1) After a Court Issues a Writ of Attachment
A sheriff or other officer seizes nonexempt property. If the creditor prevails at trial, the property can be sold to satisfy the judgment.

2) Limitations
The due process clause of the Fourteenth Amendment limits a court's power to authorize seizure of a debtor's property without notice to the debtor or a hearing on the facts.

b. Writ of Execution
A writ of execution is an order, usually issued by a clerk of court, directing the sheriff to seize and sell any of the debtor's nonexempt property within the court's geographical jurisdiction.

1) First, the Creditor Must Obtain a Judgment against the Debtor
If the debtor does not pay, proceeds from the sale pay the judgment. The debtor can redeem the property any time before it is sold.

2) Limitations
Because of laws that exempt a debtor's homestead and designated items of personal property, many judgments are uncollectible.

B. GARNISHMENT
Garnishment occurs when a creditor collects a debt by seizing property of the debtor (such as wages or money in a bank account) that a third party (such as an employer or a bank) holds.

1. Garnishment Proceedings
The creditor obtains a judgment against the debtor and serves it on the third party (the garnishee) so that, for example, part of the debtor's paycheck will be paid to the creditor.

2. Laws Limiting the Amount of Wages Subject to Garnishment
In some states, a creditor must go back to court for a separate order of garnishment for each pay period. Both federal and state laws limit the amount of money that can be garnished from a debtor's weekly take-home pay. State limits are often higher.

C. CREDITORS' COMPOSITION AGREEMENTS
A *creditors' composition agreement* is a contract between a debtor and his or her creditors for discharge of the debtor's liquidated debts on payment of a sum less than that owed.

II.   SURETYSHIP AND GUARANTY

A. SURETYSHIP
Suretyship is a promise by a third person to be responsible for a debtor's obligation. The promise does not have to be in writing. A surety is primarily liable—a creditor can demand payment from the surety the moment the debt is due.

B. GUARANTY
A guaranty is a promise to be secondarily liable for the debt or default of another. A guarantor pays only after the debtor defaults and the creditor has made an attempt to collect from the debtor. A guaranty must be in writing unless the main-purpose exception applies (see Chapter 15). A guaranty may be continuing (to cover a series of transactions), unlimited or limited in time and amount, and absolute (immediate liability on the debtor's default) or conditional (liability only a certain event).

C. ACTIONS RELEASING THE SURETY AND THE GUARANTOR

1. Material Change to the Contract between Debtor and Creditor
Without obtaining the consent of the surety (guarantor), a surety is discharged completely or to the extent the surety suffers a loss.

2. Principal Obligation Is Paid or Valid Tender Is Made

    3. **Surrender or Impairment of Collateral**
       Without the surety's (guarantor's) consent, this action on the part of the creditor releases the surety to the extent of any loss suffered.

  D. **DEFENSES OF THE SURETY AND THE GUARANTOR**

    1. **Most of the Principal Debtor's Defenses**
       Defenses that cannot be used: debtor's incapacity, bankruptcy, and statute of limitations.

    2. **Surety or Guarantor's Own Defenses**

  E. **RIGHTS OF THE SURETY AND THE GUARANTOR**
    If the surety (guarantor) pays the debt—

    1. **The Right of Subrogation**
       A surety (guarantor) may seek any remedies that were available to the creditor against the debtor.

    2. **The Right of Reimbursement**
       A surety is entitled to receive from a debtor all outlays made on behalf of the suretyship arrangement.

    3. **The Right of Contribution**
       A surety who pays more than his or her proportionate share on a debtor's default is entitled to recover from co-sureties.

III. PROTECTION FOR DEBTORS

  A. **EXEMPTED REAL PROPERTY**
    Each state allows a debtor to keep the family home (in some states only if the debtor has a family) in its entirety or up to a specified amount. The Bankruptcy Abuse Prevention and Consumer Protection Act of 2005 limits the use of these exemptions.

  B. **EXEMPTED PERSONAL PROPERTY**
    This includes household furniture up to a specified dollar amount; clothing and other possessions; a vehicle (or vehicles); certain animals; and equipment that the debtor uses in a business or trade.

IV. BANKRUPTCY LAW

  A. **BANKRUPTCY COURTS**
    Bankruptcy proceedings are held in federal bankruptcy courts under the authority of the federal district courts, to which rulings can be appealed. Anyone liable to a creditor can declare bankruptcy (insolvency is not required).

  B. **TYPES OF BANKRUPTCY RELIEF**
    The Bankruptcy Code is in Title 11 of the U.S.C.. Chapters 1, 3, and 5 include definitions and provisions governing case administration, creditors, debtors, and estates. Chapter 7 provides for liquidation. Chapter 11 governs reorganizations. Chapters 12 and 13 provide for the adjustment of debts by parties with regular incomes (family farmers under Chapter 12).

  C. **SPECIAL REQUIREMENTS FOR CONSUMER DEBTORS**
    A clerk of court must provide consumer-debtors (those whose debts arise primarily from purchases of goods for personal or household use) with certain information (details in the text).

V. LIQUIDATION PROCEEDINGS (CHAPTER 7)
This is the most familiar type of bankruptcy proceeding. A debtor declares his or her debts and gives all assets to a trustee, who sells the nonexempt assets and distributes the proceeds to creditors.

A. WHO CAN FILE FOR A LIQUIDATION
Any "person"—individuals, partnerships, and corporations (spouses can file jointly)—except railroads, insurance companies, banks, savings and loan associations, and credit unions.

B. VOLUNTARY BANKRUPTCY

1. The Debtor Receives Credit Counseling
A debtor must receive credit counseling from an approved nonprofit agency within 180 days (six months) before filing a petition.

2. The Debtor Files a Petition with the Court
A husband and wife may file jointly.

3. The Debtor Files Schedules (Lists) with the Court
Within 45 days, a debtor must file forms that list (1) creditors and the debt to each, (2) the debtor's financial affairs, (3) the debtor's property, (4) current income and expenses, (5) payments from employers within the previous 60 days, (6) a certificate proving the receipt of credit counseling, (7) an itemized calculation of monthly income, and (8) the debtor's most recent federal tax return.

4. The Debtor's Attorney Files an Affidavit
The debtor's attorney, if there is one, must attest to a reasonable attempt to verify the accuracy of the debtor's petition and schedules.

5. The Court or Other Party "of Interest" Asks for More Information
Copies of later federal tax returns may be required. A debtor may need to verify his or her identity.

6. The Court May Dismiss a Petition for Substantial Abuse under the "Means Test"

a. If the Debtor's Family Income Exceeds the Median Family Income in the Geographic Area
Abuse may be presumed, and a creditor can file a motion to dismiss the petition, under this "means test." A debtor can rebut the presumption by showing "special circumstances."

b. If the Debtor's Family Income Does *Not* Exceed the Median Family Income in the Geographic Area
A court can dismiss a petition for bad faith or another factor—for example, that the debtor seeks only an advantage over creditors and his or her financial situation does not warrant a discharge of debts.

7. Other Grounds on which the Court May Dismiss a Petition
If the debtor has been convicted of a crime of violence or drug trafficking, a victim can file a motion to dismiss. Failing to pay post-petition domestic support may also result in a dismissal.

8. Filing of the Petition Constitutes an Order for Relief
The clerk of the court must give the trustee and creditors notice within twenty days.

C. INVOLUNTARY BANKRUPTCY
A debtor's creditors can force the debtor into bankruptcy proceedings.

1. Who Can Be Forced into Involuntary Proceedings
A debtor with twelve or more creditors, three or more of whom (with unsecured claims of at least $14,425) file a petition. A debtor with fewer than twelve creditors, one or more of whom (with a claim of $14,425) files. Not a farmer or a charitable institution.

2. When an Order for Relief Will Be Entered

If the debtor does not challenge the petition, the debtor is generally not paying debts as they come due, or a receiver, assignee, or custodian took possession of the debtor's property within 120 days before the petition was filed.

D. AUTOMATIC STAY

When a petition is filed, an automatic stay suspends all action by creditors against the debtor.

1. Exceptions

These include domestic support obligations (owed to a spouse, former spouse, debtor's child, child's parent or guardian, or the government), related proceedings, securities regulation investigations, property tax liens, prior eviction actions, and withholding to repay retirement account loans.

2. Limitations

a. Request for Relief

A creditor or other party "in interest" can ask for relief from the automatic stay, which then expires in 60 days, unless the court extends it.

b. Secured Debts—Adequate Protection Doctrine

This doctrine protects secured creditors by requiring payments, or other collateral or relief, to the extent that the stay may cause the value of their collateral to decrease.

c. Secured Debts—Other Protection

The stay on secured debts may expire within 30 days of a petition if the debtor had a petition dismissed within the prior year. Two dismissed petitions require a finding of good faith in the current filing before the stay takes effect. A stay on secured property terminates 45 days after the creditors' meeting if the debtor does not redeem the property or reaffirm the debt.

E. BANKRUPTCY ESTATE

1. What Property Is Included in the Debtor's Estate

Interests in property presently held; community property; property transferred in a transaction voidable by the trustee; proceeds and profits; certain after-acquired property; interests in gifts, inheritances, property settlements, and life insurance death proceeds to which the debtor becomes entitled within 180 days after filing.

2. What Property Is Not Included

Property acquired after the filing of the petition except as noted above. Also, withholdings for employee benefit plan contributions are excluded.

F. THE TRUSTEE

After the order for relief, an interim trustee is appointed to preside over the debtor's property until the first meeting of creditors, when a permanent trustee is elected. A trustee's duty is to collect and reduce to money the property of the estate and distribute the proceeds.

1. The Trustee's Duties

a. Initial Duties

A trustee must state whether a filing constitutes substantial abuse under the "means test" (see above) within ten days of the creditors' meeting, notify creditors within five days, and file a motion to dismiss or convert to Chapter 11 (or explain why not) within forty days).

b. Duty with Respect to Domestic Support Obligations

A trustee must provide a party to whom this support is owed with certain information.

2. The Trustee's Powers

a. The Right to Possession of the Debtor's Property
The trustee also can require persons holding a debtor's property when a petition is filed to give the property to the trustee.

b. The Strong-Arm Power
The trustee's position is equivalent in rights to that of certain other parties. A trustee has strong-arm power—the same right as a lien creditor who could have levied execution on the debtor's property.

c. Avoidance Powers
A trustee has specific powers to set aside a transfer of the debtor's property. These powers include any voidable rights and the power to avoid preferences, certain statutory liens, and fraudulent transfers.

d. Liens on the Debtor's Property
A trustee can avoid the fixing of certain statutory liens on a debtor's property.

e. The Debtor Shares Most of the Avoidance Powers
If a trustee does not act to enforce a right, the debtor can.

3. Voidable Rights
A trustee can use any ground—including fraud, duress, incapacity, and mutual mistake—that a debtor can use to obtain return of the debtor's property.

4. Preferences
A trustee can recover a debtor's payment or transfer of property made to a creditor within ninety days before the petition in preference to others.

a. Preferences to Insiders
Transfers to insiders within a year of the petition can be recovered, but the debtor's insolvency at the time of the transfer must be proved.

b. Transfers That Do Not Constitute Preferences
Payment for services rendered within ten to fifteen days before payment is not considered a preference. A consumer-debtor can transfer any property to a creditor up to a certain amount without it constituting a preference. Domestic-support debts and transfers under a credit-counseling service's negotiated schedule are excepted.

5. Fraudulent Transfers
A trustee can avoid fraudulent transfers made within two years of a petition's filing or if they were made with intent to delay, defraud, or hinder a creditor. Transfers for less than reasonably equivalent consideration may also be avoided if, by making them, a debtor became insolvent, was left in business with little capital, or intended to incur debts that he or she could not pay.

G. EXEMPTIONS

1. Federal Law
Federal law exempts such property as interests in a residence to $21,625, a motor vehicle to $3,450, certain household goods to $11,525, tools of a trade to $2,175, and retirement and education savings accounts, and the rights to receive Social Security, domestic support, and other benefits.

2. State Law
Most states preclude the use of federal exemptions; others allow a debtor to choose between state and federal. State exemptions may include different value limits and exempt different property.

H. THE HOMESTEAD EXEMPTION
To use this exemption, a debtor must have lived in the state for two years before filing a petition. If the home was acquired within the previous three and a half years, the exemption is limited to

$146,450. In certain cases of substantial abuse and criminal or tortuous acts, no amount is exempt.

I. CREDITORS' MEETING AND CLAIMS
Within "not less than twenty days or more than forty days," the court calls a meeting of creditors, at which the debtor answers questions. Within ninety days of the meeting, a creditor must file a proof of claim if its amount is disputed. If the debtor's schedules list a claim as liquidated, proof is not needed.

J. DISTRIBUTION OF PROPERTY
Any amount remaining after the property is distributed to creditors is turned over to the debtor.

1. Secured Creditors
If collateral is surrendered, a secured party can accept it in full satisfaction of the debt or sell it, apply the proceeds to the debt, and become an unsecured creditor for the difference.

2. Unsecured Creditors
Paid in the order of priority. Each class is paid before the next class is entitled to anything. The order of priority is—

a. Claims for domestic support obligations (subject to certain administrative costs).
b. Administrative expenses (court costs, trustee and attorney fees).
c. In an involuntary bankruptcy, expenses incurred by a debtor in the ordinary course of business.
d. Unpaid wages, salaries, and commissions earned within ninety days of a petition.
e. Unsecured claims for contributions to employee benefit plans.
f. Claims by farmers and fishers against storage or processing facilities.
g. Consumer deposits.
h. Taxes due to the government.
i. Claims of general creditors.

K. DISCHARGE

1. Exceptions—Debts That May Not Be Discharged
Claims for back taxes, amounts borrowed to pay back taxes, goods obtained by fraud, debts that were not listed in a petition, domestic support, student loans, certain cash advances, and others.

2. Objections—Debtors Who May Not Receive a Discharge
Those who conceal property with intent to hinder, delay, or defraud creditors; who fail to explain a loss of assets; who have been granted a discharge within eight years prior to filing a petition; or who fail to attend a debt management class (unless no class is available).

3. Effect of a Discharge
A discharge voids any judgment on a discharged debt and prohibits any action to collect a discharged debt. A co-debtor's liability is not affected.

4. Revocation of a Discharge
A discharge may be revoked within one year if the debtor was fraudulent or dishonest during the bankruptcy proceedings.

L. REAFFIRMATION OF DEBT
A debtor's agreement to pay a dischargeable debt can be made only after certain disclosures and before a discharge is granted, usually requires court approval, and will be denied if it will cause undue hardship. The debtor can rescind a reaffirmation within sixty days or before a discharge is granted, whichever is later.

VI. REORGANIZATIONS (CHAPTER 11)
The creditors and debtor formulate a plan under which the debtor pays a portion of the debts, is discharged of the rest, and continues in business.

A. WHO IS ELIGIBLE FOR RELIEF UNDER CHAPTER 11

Any debtor (except a stockbroker or a commodities broker) who is eligible for Chapter 7 relief is eligible under Chapter 11. With some exceptions, the same principles apply that govern liquidation proceedings (automatic stay, etc.).

B. WHY A CASE MAY BE DISMISSED

A case may be dismissed if this is in the creditors' best interest, there is no reasonable likelihood of rehabilitation, a debtor is unable to affect a plan, or there is an unreasonable delay. Creditors may prefer a *workout* (a privately negotiated settlement) to bankruptcy.

C. DEBTOR IN POSSESSION

On entry of an order for relief, a debtor continues in business as a debtor in possession (DIP).

1. If Gross Mismanagement Is Shown

The court may appoint a trustee (or receiver) to operate the business. This may also be done if it is in the best interests of the estate.

2. The DIP's Role Is Similar to That of a Trustee in a Liquidation

The DIP can avoid pre-petition preferential payments and fraudulent transfers and decide whether to cancel pre-petition executory contracts.

D. CREDITORS' COMMITTEES

A committee of unsecured creditors is appointed to consult with the trustee or DIP. Other committees may represent special-interest creditors. Some small businesses can avoid creditors' committees.

E. THE REORGANIZATION PLAN

1. Who Can File a Plan

Only a debtor can file within the first 120 days (180 days in some cases) after the date of an order for relief. Any other party can file if a debtor does not meet the deadline or fails to obtain creditor consent within 180 days. A court may extend these time periods.

2. What the Plan Must Do

Be fair and equitable ("in the best interests of the creditors"); designate classes of claims and interests; specify the treatment to be afforded the classes; and provide an adequate means for execution; and provide for the payment of tax claims over a fine-year period.

3. The Plan Is Submitted to Creditors for Acceptance

Each class adversely affected by a plan must accept it (two-thirds of the total claims must approve). If only one class accepts, the court may confirm it under the Code's cram-down provision if the plan does not discriminate unfairly against any creditors.

4. Discharge

A plan is binding on confirmation. Claims are not discharged if they would be denied in a liquidation proceeding. An individual debtor is not discharged until a plan's completion.

VII. INDIVIDUALS' REPAYMENT PLANS (CHAPTER 13)

A. WHO IS ELIGIBLE

Individuals (not partnerships or corporations) with regular income and unsecured debts of less than $360,475 or secured debts of less than $1,081,400 are eligible.

B. FILING THE PETITION

A Chapter 13 case can be initiated by voluntary filing of a petition or by conversion of a Chapter 7 case. A debtor must act in good faith at the time of the filing of the plan and the petition. A trustee is appointed.

C. AUTOMATIC STAY

The automatic stay applies to consumer debts but not business debts or domestic-support obligations.

D. **THE REPAYMENT PLAN**

Only a debtor can file a plan, which must provide for (1) turnover to the trustee of the debtor's future income, (2) full payment of all claims entitled to priority, and (3) the same treatment of each claim within a particular class.

1. **Confirmation of the Plan**

A court will confirm a plan (1) if the secured creditors accept it, (2) if it provides that secured creditors retain their liens until there is full payment or a discharge, or (3) if a debtor surrenders property that secures claims to the creditors. Also, a creditor with a purchase-money security interest in a car bought within 910 days before a filing must be paid in full.

2. **Payments under the Plan**

The time for payment is five years if a debtor's income exceeds the state's median under the "means test" (see above) and three years if it does not. Payments must be timely, or the court can convert the case to a liquidation or dismiss the petition.

E. **DISCHARGE**

After completion of payments, debts provided for by the plan are discharged. Many debts (tax claims, domestic support obligations, student loans, and others) are not dischargeable. A discharge obtained by fraud can be revoked within one year.

VIII. FAMILY-FARMER AND FAMILY-FISHERMAN PLANS (CHAPTER 12)

The procedures and requirements under Chapter 12 are nearly identical to those under Chapter 13. Eligible debtors include family farmers and fishermen.

A. **FAMILY FARMERS**

A family farmer is one whose gross income is at least 50 percent farm dependent and whose debts are at least 50 percent farm related (total debt must not exceed $3,792,650). A partnership or closely held corporation (at least 50 percent owned by a farm family) can also qualify.

B. **FAMILY FISHERMEN**

A family fisherman is one whose gross income is at least 50 percent dependent on commercial fishing and whose debts are at least 80 percent related to commercial fishing (total debt must not exceed $1,757,475). A partnership or closely held corporation (at least 50 percent owned by a farm family) can also qualify.

TRUE-FALSE QUESTIONS

(Answers at the Back of the Book)

____ 1. A mechanic's lien involves personal property.

____ 2. An employer can dismiss an employee due to garnishment.

____ 3. A writ of attachment is a court order to seize a debtor's property *before* the entry of a final judgment in a creditor's lawsuit against the debtor.

____ 4. A surety or guarantor is discharged from his or her obligation when the principal debtor pays the debt.

____ 5. A surety cannot use defenses available to the debtor to avoid liability on an obligation to a creditor.

____ 6. A debtor must be insolvent to file a voluntary petition under Chapter 7.

____ 7. With some exceptions, the same principles cover liquidations and reorganizations.

____ 8. Under Chapter 13, the automatic stay applies only to consumer debt, not business debt.

_____ **9.** When a business debtor files for Chapter 11 protection, the debtor is not allowed to continue in business.

_____ **10.** No small business can avoid creditors' committees under Chapter 11.

FILL-IN QUESTIONS

(Answers at the Back of the Book)

A _____ (contract of suretyship/guaranty contract) is a promise to a creditor made by a third person to be responsible for a debtor's obligation. A _____ (guarantor/surety) is primarily liable: the creditor can hold the _____ (guarantor/surety) responsible for payment of the debt when the debt is due, without first exhausting all remedies against the debtor. A _____ (contract of suretyship/guaranty contract) also includes a promise to answer for a principal's obligation, but a _____ (guarantor/surety) is secondarily liable—that is, the principal must first default, and ordinarily, a creditor must have attempted to collect from the principal, because ordinarily a debtor would not otherwise be declared in default.

MULTIPLE-CHOICE QUESTIONS

(Answers at the Back of the Book)

_____ **1.** Davy borrows money from EZ Credit, Inc. Davy defaults. To use attachment as a remedy EZ must first

    a. be unable to collect the amount of a judgment against Davy.
    b. file a suit against Davy.
    c. lose a suit against Davy.
    d. succeed in a suit against Davy.

_____ **2.** Niles's $2,500 debt to Otmar is past due. To collect money from Niles's wages to pay the debt, Otmar can use

    a. an order of receivership.
    b. a writ of attachment.
    c. a writ of execution.
    d. garnishment.

_____ **3.** Eli owes Fatima $200,000. A court awards Fatima a judgment in this amount. To satisfy the judgment, Eli's home is sold at public auction for $150,000. The state homestead exemption is $50,000. Fatima gets

    a. $0.
    b. $50,000.
    c. $100,000.
    d. $150,000.

_____ **4.** Eager Biz Company wants to borrow money from Finance State Bank. The bank insists that Gwen, Eager's president, agree to be personally liable for payment if Eager defaults. Gwen agrees. She is

    a. a guarantor and a surety.
    b. a guarantor only.
    c. a surety only.
    d. neither a guarantor nor a surety.

____ 5. Ismail and Jody agree to act as guarantors on a loan made by Keenan. Keenan defaults on the payments and Jody refuses to pay. If Ismail pays the debt, he can recover from

    a. Keenan and Jody under the right of reimbursement.
    b. Keenan and Jody under the right of proportionate liability.
    c. Keenan under the right of subrogation and Jody under the right of contribution.
    d. neither Keenan nor Jody.

____ 6. Dixie and Elbert make down payments on goods to be received from Feeble Furniture Store. Before the goods are delivered, Feeble files for bankruptcy. Besides consumers like Dixie and Elbert, Feeble owes wages to its employees and taxes to the government. The order in which these debts will be paid is

    a. consumer deposits, unpaid wages, and taxes.
    b. taxes, consumer deposits, and unpaid wages.
    c. unpaid wages, consumer deposits, and taxes.
    d. unpaid wages, taxes, and consumer deposits.

____ 7. Ciera is the sole proprietor of Dinero Café, which owes debts in an amount more than Ciera believes she and the café can repay. The creditors agree that liquidating the business would not be in their best interests. To stay in business, Ciera could file for bankruptcy under

    a. Chapter 7 only.
    b. Chapter 11 only.
    c. Chapter 13 only.
    d. Chapter 11 or Chapter 13.

____ 8. Carlotta files a Chapter 7 petition for a discharge in bankruptcy. She may be denied a discharge if she

    a. fails to explain a loss of assets.
    b. fails to list a debt.
    c. owes back taxes.
    d. owes domestic support payments.

____ 9. Vance files a bankruptcy petition under Chapter 7 to have his debts discharged. Assuming Vance passes the appropriate test, the debts most likely to be discharged include claims for

    a. back taxes accruing within three years before the petition was filed.
    b. certain fines and penalties payable to the government.
    c. domestic support.
    d. student loans, if the payment would impose undue hardship on Bob.

____ 10. Riche Niche Stores, Inc., files for bankruptcy. A corporation can file a petition for bankruptcy under

    a. Chapter 7 only.
    b. Chapter 11 only.
    c. Chapter 13 only.
    d. Chapter 7 or Chapter 11.

SHORT ESSAY QUESTIONS

1. What is a lien? What are the ways in which a lien can arise? What is a lienholder's priority compared to other creditors?

2. Compare Chapters 7, 11, 12, and 13, discussing, for each chapter, the purpose or function, who is eligible for relief, whether proceedings can be initiated voluntarily or involuntarily, procedures leading to discharge, and the advantages.

GAMEPOINTS

(Answers at the Back of the Book)

1.   The story and the art of the video game "Erase against Time" imitates a graphic novel. Players are required to quickly find and obliterate each other's weapons, which are non-traditional in appearance and operation. You find the game so compelling that you ignore everything else, including the payment of your debts. Eventually, your creditors take action, levying mechanic's and artisan's liens. How can they recover payment through these liens? Do they have to notify you?

2.   You start an enterprise to create, develop, and sell video games. But you have an inadequate business plan and lack sufficient financing. Your attempt to cover these mistakes by maxing out credit cards and failing to pay bills only leads to more debt. You have a total of ten unsecured creditors, including Grouper & Halibut, Accountants, whom you owe $15,000. Can Grouper & Halibut file an involuntary Chapter 11 bankruptcy petition against you? Why or why not?

Chapter 16
Mortgages and Foreclosures
after the Recession

WHAT THIS CHAPTER IS ABOUT

The focus of this chapter is on the terms of a mortgage, the different types of mortgage loans available, the characteristics of mortgage fraud, and the law's requirements, prohibitions, penalties, and rewards for each.

CHAPTER OUTLINE

I. MORTGAGES

An individual who buys real property typically borrows the funds from a financial institution to pay for it. A mortgage is a written instrument that gives the creditor an interest in, or a line on, the property as security for the payment.

A. TYPES OF MORTGAGES

A mortgage loan is a contract. A down payment is a part of the purchase price paid in cash. In many cases, borrowers under adjustable-rate mortgages, interest-only mortgages, and balloon mortgages hope to refinance (pay off the original mortgage and obtain a new one on better terms).

1. Fixed-Rate Mortgages

A fixed-rate mortgage is a standard mortgage with a fixed rate of interest. Payments are the same for its duration. The interest rate may be based on the borrower's credit history, credit score, income, and debts.

2. Adjustable-Rate Mortgages (ARMs)

The interest rate on an adjustable-rate mortgage changes periodically. The rate may begin low and fixed. After a certain time, and at certain intervals, the rate adjusts. The adjustment consists of a specified number of points added to an index rate. Most ARMs limit the amount that the rate can increase over the duration of the loan.

3. Interest-Only (IO) Mortgages

An interest-only mortgage gives a borrower the option to pay only the interest portion of the monthly payments for an initial, limited time. The size of the payments then increases to include the principal. The interest on an IO mortgage may be fixed-rate or adjustable.

4. Subprime Mortgages

A subprime mortgage is a loan to a borrower who does not qualify for a standard mortgage. Because subprime borrowers default at a higher rate, subprime mortgages carry higher rates of interest. A subprime mortgage may be a fixed-rate, adjustable-rate, or interest-only loan.

5. Balloon Mortgages

A balloon mortgage starts with low payments for a specified period, with the balance of the loan due at the end. Borrowers often refinance balloon mortgages on their due dates.

137

6. Hybrid and Reverse Mortgages
A hybrid mortgage starts as a fixed-rate mortgage and converts into an ARM. A reverse mortgage pays an existing homeowner for the equity in a home. The reverse mortgage is repaid when the home is sold.

B. HOME EQUITY LOANS
Home equity is the portion of a home's value that is not subject to a mortgage. As a loan is paid, equity accrues. A home equity loan is secured by this amount, which can be seized if the loan is not repaid. A home equity is subordinate to a mortgage loan.

C. CREDITOR PROTECTION

1. Insurance and Perfection
Creditors can protect their interests through—

a. *Private mortgage insurance.* If the debtor defaults, the insurer reimburses the creditor for a portion of the loan.

b. *Recording a mortgage in the appropriate county office.* This On the debtor's default, a creditor who has not recorded his or her interest may have the priority of an unsecured creditor.

2. Statute of Frauds
A mortgage must be in writing to be enforceable, but it is not otherwise required to follow a particular form.

3. Important Mortgage Provisions
Terms may include—

a. Loan terms—the amount, the interest rate, the period of repayment, and others.
b. Provisions for the maintenance of the property.
c. A statement obligating the borrower to maintain homeowners' insurance.
d. A list of the borrower's non-loan financial obligations—property taxes and so on.
e. A provision for the borrower's payment of regular and ordinary expenses associated with the property—taxes, insurance, and other assessments—through the lender.

II. REAL ESTATE FINANCING LAW
Congress and the Federal Reserve Board impose disclosure requirements and certain prohibitions on lenders to protect borrowers from improper lending practices.

A. PREDATORY LENDING AND OTHER IMPROPER PRACTICES

1. Fraud
Predatory lending practices that occur during the loan origination process include failing to disclose terms, providing misleading information, and lying.

2. Steering and Targeting
A lender manipulates a borrower into a loan that benefits the lender but is not the best loan for the borrower.

3. Loan Flipping
A lender convinces a borrower to refinance soon after a mortgage term begins.

B. THE TRUTH-IN-LENDING ACT (TILA)
The Truth-in-Lending Act (TILA) of 1968 requires lenders to disclose the terms of a loan in clear, readily understandable language so that borrowers can make rational choices. In real estate transactions, TILA applies only to residential loans.

1. Required Disclosures
Disclosure must be made on standardized forms and based on uniform formulas. Certain loans—ARMs, reverse mortgages, open-ended home equity loans, and high-interest loans—have special requirements. For all loans, terms that must be disclosed include—

      a.   Loan principal.
      b.   Interest rate at which the loan is made.
      c.   Annual percentage rate (APR), which is the actual cost of the loan on a yearly basis.
      d.   All fees and costs associated with the loan.

  2. **Prohibitions and Requirements**
     Prepayment penalties cannot be charged on most subprime mortgages and home equity loans. A lender cannot coerce an appraiser into misstating the value of property on which a loan is to be issued. A loan cannot be advertised as fixed-rate if its rate or payment amounts fluctuate.

      a.   **Right to Rescind**
         A mortgage cannot be finalized until seven or more days after a borrower receives TILA paperwork. A borrower has the right to rescind a mortgage within three business days (Sunday is the only non-business day). If a lender does not provide the required disclosures, the rescission period runs for three years.

      b.   **Written Representations**
         The disclosure requirements apply to written materials but not oral representations.

C. **PROTECTION FOR HIGH-COST MORTGAGE LOAN RECIPIENTS**
    The Home Ownership and Equity Protection Act (HOEPA) of 1994 amended TILA to create a special category of high-cost and high-fee mortgage products. Rules for the loans are in Regulation Z (enacted by the Federal Reserve Board to implement TILA).

  1. **Which Loans Are Covered?**
     The rules apply to loans for which—

      a.   The APR exceeds the interest rate on Treasury securities of comparable maturity by more than 8 percentage points for a first mortgage and 10 points for a second mortgage.
      b.   The total fees exceed 8 percent of the loan amount or a dollar amount based on the consumer price index, whichever is larger.

  2. **Special Consumer Protections**

      a.   **Disclosures**
         In addition to the TILA disclosures, HOEPA requires lenders to disclose—

         1)   The APR, the regular payment amount, and any balloon payments.
         2)   For a loan with a variable interest rate, the possibility that the rate and payment amounts may increase and to what potential maximum the increase may be.
         3)   The borrower's option not to complete the loan simply because of the disclosures or the signing of a loan application.
         4)   The possible loss of the home financed by the loan if the borrower defaults.

      b.   **Prohibitions**
         HOEPA prohibits lenders from—

         1)   Requiring a balloon payment on a loan with a term of five years or less.
         2)   Issuing a loan that results in negative amortization (this occurs when payments do not cover the interest due and the difference is added to the principal, thus increasing the balance).

  3. **Remedies and Liabilities**
     On a lender's material failure to disclose, a consumer may receive damages in an amount equal to all finance charges and fees paid. On a lender's failure to comply with HOEPA, the borrower's right to rescind is extended to three years.

D. **PROTECTION FOR HIGHER-PRICED MORTGAGE LOANS**
    Higher-Priced Mortgage Loans (HPMLs) are a second category of expensive loans under Regulation Z.

1. **Requirements to Qualify**
   To qualify as an HPML, a mortgage must—

   a. Secure a borrower's principal home.
   b. Have, if the loan is a *first lien*, an APR that exceeds the average prime offer rate for a comparable transaction by 1.5 percentage points or more.
   c. Have, if the loan is a *subordinate lien*, an APR that exceeds the average prime offer rate for a comparable transaction by 3.5 percentage points or more.
   d. Not be a mortgage for initial construction, a bridge loan (a temporary loan with a term of one year or less), a home equity line of credit, and a reverse mortgage.

2. **Special Protections for Consumers**
   For an HPML loan, a lender—

   a. Cannot base a loan on the value of a borrower's home without verifying the borrower's ability to repay it. This can be done through a review of the borrower's financial records—tax returns, bank account statements, payroll records, and credit obligations.
   b. Cannot impose prepayment penalties on a loan for longer than two years.
   c. Cannot impose any prepayment penalties on a loan if the source to pay them is a refinancing by the lender.
   d. Must establish an escrow account for a borrower's insurance and tax payments for a first mortgage.
   e. Cannot structure a loan to evade these protections.

III. FORECLOSURES

If a borrower defaults, or fails to pay a loan, the lender can foreclose on the mortgaged property. The foreclosure process allows a lender to repossess and auction the property. A foreclosure can be expensive and remains on a borrower's credit report for seven years.

A. HOW TO AVOID FORECLOSURE

1. **Forbearance and Workout Agreements**

   a. *Forbearance*—the postponement of part or all of the payments of a loan in danger of foreclosure. This may be based on a borrower's securing a new job, selling the property, or some other factor.

   b. *Workout*—a voluntary attempt to cure a default. A workout agreement sets out the parties' rights and responsibilities (for example, a lender may agree to delay foreclosure in exchange for a borrower's financial information).

2. **Housing and Urban Development Assistance**
   An interest-free loan may be obtained from the U.S. Department of Housing and Urban Development (HUD) to bring the mortgage current. A loan must be between four and twelve months delinquent, and the borrower must be able to make full payments. A HUD loan is a subordinate lien that comes due when the property is sold.

3. **Short Sales**
   A short sale is a sale of the property for less than the balance due on a mortgage loan. A borrower—who typically must show some hardship—sells the property with the lender's consent. The lender gets the proceeds. If the lender does not forgive the balance, the borrower owes the deficiency. A short sale mitigates some costs but can affect a borrower's credit rating.

4. **Sale and Leaseback**
   An investor may buy a property and lease it back to its former owner for less than the mortgage payments. The seller-owner pays off the mortgage with the sale proceeds.

5. **Home Affordable Modification Program**
   The U.S. Treasury Department's Home Affordable Modification Program (HAMP) encourages private lenders to modify mortgages to lower the monthly payments of borrowers in default (to 31 percent of the debtor's gross monthly income). HAMP may share a lender's costs to modify a loan and provides other incentives.

   a. **Determination If a Homeowner Qualifies**
      To qualify for a HAMP modification—

      1) A loan must have originated on or before January 1, 2009.
      2) A home must be its owner's primary residence and must be occupied by its owner.
      3) A loan's unpaid balance must not exceed $729,750 for a single-unit property.
      4) A homeowner must be facing verifiable financial hardship.
      5) Mortgage payments must be more than sixty days late or a homeowner must be at risk of imminent default.

   b. **Steps Taken to Alleviate the Mortgage Burden**
      A loan is restructured by adding delinquencies—unpaid interest, taxes, or insurance premiums—to the principal and cutting the interest rate so that a borrower's payments are 31 percent of his or her gross monthly income. If the rate would be less than 2 percent, a lender can re-amortize the loan, extending the payments for up to forty years.

6. **Voluntary Conveyance**
   A deed in lieu of foreclosure conveys property to a lender in satisfaction of a mortgage. The lender thereby avoids the time, risk, and expense of foreclosure. The borrower avoids foreclosure's negative effects. This option works best when the property's value is close to the outstanding loan principal and there are no other loans on it.

7. **Friendly Foreclosure**
   This occurs when a homeowner agrees to submit to a court's jurisdiction, waive any defenses and the right to appeal, and cooperate with the lender. This can create certainty as to the finality of the transaction with respect to others with a financial interest in the property.

8. **Prepackaged Bankruptcy**
   A prepackaged bankruptcy allows a borrower to negotiate the terms with his or her creditors in advance. This effort can save all of the parties' time and expense.

B. **THE FORECLOSURE PROCEDURE**
A formal foreclosure extinguishes a borrower's equitable right of redemption. The two most common types of foreclosure are judicial foreclosure and power of sale foreclosure. In the former—available in all states—a court supervises the process. In the latter—available in only a few states—a lender forecloses on and sells the property without court supervision.

1. **Acceleration Clauses**
   An acceleration clause allows a lender to call an entire loan due, even if only one payment is missed. Without this clause in a mortgage contract, a lender might have to foreclose on smaller amounts over a period of time as individual payments are missed.

2. **Notice of Default (NOD) and of Sale**
   Filing a notice of default with the appropriate state office initiates a foreclosure. The borrower is put on notice to take steps to pay the loan and cure the default. If this does not occur, the lender gives a notice of sale to the borrower, posts it on the property, files it with the county, and announces it in a newspaper. The property is then sold at auction on the courthouse steps.

3. Deficiency Judgments

If sale proceeds do not cover the amount of the loan, the lender can ask a court for a deficiency judgment. Some states do not permit deficiency judgments for mortgaged residential property.

C. REDEMPTION RIGHTS

1. Equitable Right of Redemption

In all states, a borrower can buy the property after default by paying the amount of the debt, plus interest and costs, *before* the foreclosure sale.

2. Statutory Right of Redemption

In some sates, a borrower can buy the property *after* a judicial foreclosure and sale of the property at auction to a third party. The borrower pays the redemption price, plus taxes, interest, and assessments. This right may exist for up to a year after the sale. Some states allow the borrower to retain possession of the property until the redemption period ends.

TRUE-FALSE QUESTIONS

(Answers at the Back of the Book)

____ 1. Steering and targeting occur when a lender convinces a homeowner to refinance soon after obtaining a mortgage.

____ 2. The loan that a lender provides to enable a borrower to purchase real property is a recession.

____ 3. In any case, a borrower has up to seven business days to rescind a mortgage.

____ 4. Federal disclosure requirements apply only to written materials that a mortgage lender provides.

____ 5. Foreclosure allows a lender to legally repossess and auction off the property securing a loan.

____ 6. The annual percentage rate is the mortgage interest rate offered to the least qualified borrowers as established by a survey of potential borrowers.

____ 7. There are additional disclosure requirements for a loan that carries a high rate of interest or entails high fees for the borrower.

____ 8. A lender can make a higher-priced mortgage loan based on the value of the consumer's home without verifying the consumer's ability to repay the loan.

____ 9. On foreclosure, if a mortgage is not paid within a reasonable time after a notice of default, the property securing the loan can be sold without notice to the buyer.

____ 10. A deficiency judgment requires a borrower to pay the debt remaining after collateral is sold.

FILL-IN QUESTIONS

(Answers at the Back of the Book)

A standard mortgage with an unchanging rate of interest is _____ (a fixed-rate/an adjustable-rate/an interest-only) mortgage. A mortgage in which the rate of interest paid by the borrower changes periodically is _____ (a fixed-rate/an adjustable-rate/an interest-only) mortgage. A mortgage under which the borrower can choose to pay only the interest portion of the monthly payment for a specified period of time is _____ (a fixed-rate/an adjustable-rate/an interest-only) mortgage.

A loan made to a borrower who does not qualify for a standard mortgage is a _____ (home equity loan/hybrid mortgage/subprime mortgage). A loan that starts as a fixed-rate mortgage and then converts into an adjustable-rate mortgage is a _____ (home equity loan/hybrid mortgage/subprime mortgage). A loan for which the lender accepts the borrower's equity in his or her home as collateral, which can be seized if the loan is not repaid on time, is a _____ (home equity loan/hybrid mortgage/subprime mortgage).

MULTIPLE-CHOICE QUESTIONS

(Answers at the Back of the Book)

____ **1.** New England Bank provides a loan to enable Martine to buy real property. This loan is

a. a down payment
b. a mortgage.
c. a short sale.
d. a workout agreement.

____ **2.** Pacific Bank provides Ogden with a standard mortgage with an unchanging rate of interest to buy a home. Payments on the loan remain the same for the duration of the mortgage. This is

a. a fixed-rate mortgage.
b. an adjustable-rate mortgage.
c. an interest-only mortgage.
d. a violation of the law.

____ **3.** Selma borrows $125,000 from Riverview Credit Union to buy a home. Among the terms that must be disclosed under federal law is the annual percentage rate. This is

a. the actual cost of the loan on a yearly basis.
b. the average prime offer rate.
c. the interest rate at which the loan is made.
d. the loan principal.

____ **4.** Igor applies to Hometown Mortgage Company for $80,000 to buy a home. Hometown steers Igor toward an adjustable-rate mortgage even though he qualifies for a fixed-rate mortgage. This is

a. a short sale.
b a subprime mortgage.
c. loan flipping.
d. steering and targeting.

____ **5.** Lizette borrows $110,000 from Main Street Bank to buy a home. Federal law regulates primarily

a. mortgage terms that must be disclosed in writing.
b. oral representations with respect to the terms of a loan.
c. the lowest prices for which real property can be sold.
d. who can buy real property, where they can buy it, and why.

____ **6.** Dylan borrows $150,000 from Countywide Credit Union to buy a home. By recording the mortgage, Countywide protects its

a. priority against a previously filed lien on the property.
b. priority against any party with an earlier claim to the property.
c. rights against Dylan.
d. rights against the claims of later buyers of the property.

____ 7. Bayside Credit Corporation makes mortgage loans to consumers secured by their principal homes. For a Bayside loan to qualify as a Higher-Priced Mortgage Loan (HPML), its annual percentage rate must exceed, by a certain amount,

a. the average prime offer rate for a comparable transaction.
b. the consumer's income-to-debt ratio.
c. the percentage of income that a consumer can devote to its payment.
d. the projected increase in market value of the consumer's home.

____ 8. Upstate Bank has made mortgage loans to consumers that qualify for the Home Affordable Modification Program (HAMP), which offers incentives to lenders to change the terms of certain loans. The purpose of HAMP is to

a. convey property through lenders to consumers who can afford it.
b. force lenders to forgive all high-risk mortgages.
c. reduce monthly payments to levels that homeowners can pay.
d. transfer affordable property to investors to lease to consumers.

____ 9. Duke borrows $150,000 from Community Bank to buy a home. If he fails to make payments on the mortgage, the bank has the right to repossess and auction off the property securing the loan. This is

a. a short sale.
b. forbearance.
c. foreclosure.
d. the equitable right of redemption.

____ 10. Shirley borrows $100,000 from Ridgetop Credit Union to buy a home, which secures the loan. Three years into the term, she stops making payments on it. Ridgetop repossesses and auctions off the property to Toby. The sale proceeds are not enough to cover the unpaid amount of the loan. In most states, Ridgetop can ask a court for

a. a deficiency judgment.
b. a reverse mortgage.
c. a short sale.
d. nothing.

SHORT ESSAY QUESTIONS

1. How does the law protect borrowers from the lending practices that led to the recent recession?

2. What protection exists for borrowers who take out high-cost, high-fee, or higher-priced mortgages from the lending practices that led to the recession?

GAMEPOINTS

(Answers at the Back of the Book)

1. In the video game "Block x Block," your avatar Blockhead is the executive loan officer for Alpha Mortgage & Credit Company. At this point in the game, Carlotta asks to borrow funds from Alpha to start a new business. She has $100,000 equity in her home. You offer her a $75,000 loan for ten years at an interest rate of 4.25. She accepts. On the day of the closing, a fifteen-year Treasury bond is yielding 2.25 percent. Carlotta pays $4,000 in fees to Alpha. Six weeks later, she sells her interest in the new business to Darwin and wants to rescind the Alpha loan. Which federal law covers this loan? On what basis—if any—might she be able to rescind it?

2. Still playing "Block x Block" your avatar is approached by Edgar. Earlier, Blockhead approved a loan to Edgar to buy a home. The amount was $110,000 at a fixed rate of 5.25 percent with a thirty-tear term secured by the home. Now, having paid $7,500 of the mortgage, Edgar says that he lost his job and wants to defer the payments on the mortgage for six months when he will start a new job. In the current market, the value of Edgar's home has decreased to $85,000. What are methods by which Blockhead could recover the outstanding amount of the mortgage for Alpha?

CUMULATIVE HYPOTHETICAL PROBLEM FOR UNIT THREE—INCLUDING CHAPTERS 9–16

(Answers at the Back of the Book)

Drake, Egon, and Flip pool their resources to create and sell video game software. They do business under the name "Game Life" (GL).

____ **1.** To protect the rights that GL has in the games it produces, GL's best protection is offered by

    a. bankruptcy law.
    b. intellectual property law.
    c. sales law.
    d. tort law.

____ **2.** GL sends e-mail to Hoe & Rake, an accounting firm, offering to contract for its services for a certain price. The offer is sent on June 1 and is seen by Hoe on June 2. The offer states that it will be open until July 1. This offer

    a. cannot be revoked because it is a firm offer.
    b. cannot be revoked because it is an option contract.
    c. could have been revoked only before Hoe saw it.
    d. may be revoked any time before it is accepted.

____ **3.** I2I Game Centers writes to GL to order GL's most popular gaming software, which I2I plans to sell to its customers. GL writes to accept but adds a clause providing for interest on any overdue invoices (a common practice in the industry). If there is no further communication between the parties

    a. GL has made a counteroffer.
    b. there is a contract but without GL's added term.
    c. there is a contract that includes GL's added term.
    d. there is no contract because I2I did not expressly accept the added term.

____ **4.** In the previous question, GL ships defective software to I2I, which sells it to customers. The defective software causes losses estimated at $100,000. With respect to I2I, GL likely violated principles of

    a. bankruptcy law.
    b. creditor-debtor law.
    c. intellectual property law.
    d. tort law.

____ **5.** After I2I's losses are publicized, GL loses business and files a voluntary petition in bankruptcy under Chapter 11. A reorganization plan is filed with the court. The court will confirm the plan if it is accepted by

    a. GL.
    b. GL's secured creditors.
    c. GL's shareholders.
    d. GL's unsecured creditors.

QUESTIONS ON THE FOCUS ON ETHICS FOR UNIT THREE—THE COMMERCIAL ENVIRONMENT

(Answers at the Back of the Book)

____ **1.** Jinsey and Kyla enter into a contract for Kyla's services. The contract includes an exculpatory clause. Whether this clause is unconscionable is determined by

a. a court.
b. Jinsey only.
c. Kyla only.
d. UCC 2–311.

____ **2.** Lemon Motors Corporation makes and sells cars and other vehicles. Mick operates a Web site with the domain name "lemonmotorssucks.com." In Lemon's suit against Mick, his best defense is that this domain is protected by

a. copyright law.
b. Mick's freedom of speech.
c. Mick's privacy rights.
d. trademark law.

____ **3.** Creekside Credit Union lends money to Barton, taking a security interest in his assets. Later, Barton files a bankruptcy petition. From the bank's point of view, once Barton is in bankruptcy, his assets have

a. diminished value, or no value.
b. enhanced, or greater, value.
c. the same value as before the petition.
d. unique value.

Chapter 17
Sole Proprietorships, Franchises, and Partnerships

WHAT THIS CHAPTER IS ABOUT

This chapter briefly outlines the features of a sole proprietorship (the most common form of business), reviews the features of partnerships, and discusses franchises, which are widely used to seek profits.

CHAPTER OUTLINE

I. **SOLE PROPRIETORSHIPS**
The simplest form of business—the owner is the business.

   A. **ADVANTAGES OF THE SOLE PROPRIETORSHIP**
These include that the proprietor takes all the profits; this organization is easier to start than others (few legal forms involved); the form has more flexibility (the proprietor is free to make all decisions); and the owner pays only personal income tax on profits.

   B. **DISADVANTAGES OF THE SOLE PROPRIETORSHIP**
These include that the proprietor has all the risk (unlimited liability for all debts); there is limited opportunity to raise capital; and the business dissolves when the owner dies.

II. **FRANCHISES**
A franchise is any arrangement in which the owner of a trademark, a trade name, or a copyright has licensed others to use it in selling goods or services.

   A. **TYPES OF FRANCHISES**

     1. **Distributorship**
This is when a manufacturer licenses a dealer to sell its product (such as an automobile dealer). Often covers an exclusive territory.

     2. **Chain-Style Business Operation**
This occurs when a franchise operates under a franchisor's trade name and is identified as a member of a group of dealers engaged in the franchisor's business (such as most fast-food chains). The franchisee must follow standardized or prescribed methods of operations, and may be obligated to obtain supplies exclusively from the franchisor.

     3. **Manufacturing Arrangement**
This type exists when a franchisor transmits to the franchisee the essential ingredients or formula to make a product (such as Coca-Cola), which the franchisee makes and markets according to the franchisor's standards.

   B. **LAWS GOVERNING FRANCHISING**

1. **Federal Protection of Franchisees in Certain Industries**

   a. **Automobile Dealers' Franchise Act of 1965**
   The Automobile Dealers' Franchise Act protects dealership franchisees from manufacturers' bad faith termination of their franchises.

   b. **Petroleum Marketing Practices Act (PMPA) of 1979**
   The PMPA prescribes the grounds and conditions under which a gasoline station franchisor may terminate or decline to renew a franchise.

   c. **Antitrust Laws**
   These laws may apply if there is an anticompetitive agreement (see Chapter 47).

   d. **Federal Trade Commission (FTC) Franchise Rule**
   Franchisors must disclose material facts necessary to a prospective franchisee's making an informed decision concerning a franchise. This must be in writing, but it may be made available online.

2. **State Protection for Franchisees**
   Similar to federal law. State deceptive practices acts may apply, as may Article 2 of the Uniform Commercial Code.

C. **THE FRANCHISE CONTRACT**
A franchise relationship is created by a contract between the franchisor and the franchisee.

   1. **Payment for the Franchise**
   A franchisee pays (1) a fee for the franchise license, (2) fees for products bought from or through the franchisor, (3) a percentage of sales, and (4) a percentage of advertising and administrative costs.

   2. **Business Premises**
   The agreement may specify whether the premises for the business are leased or purchased and who is to supply equipment and furnishings.

   3. **Location of the Franchise**
   The franchisor determines the territory to be served and its exclusivity. The implied covenant of good faith and fair dealing may apply to a dispute over territorial rights.

   4. **Business Organization**
   A franchisor may specify requirements for the form and capital structure of the franchisee's business.

   5. **Quality Control**
   A franchisor may specify standards of operation (such as quality standards) and personnel training methods. Too much control may result in a franchisor's liability for torts of a franchisee's employees.

   6. **Pricing Arrangements**
   A franchisor may require a franchisee to buy certain supplies from the franchisor at an established price. A franchisor may also suggest retail prices for the goods that the franchisee sells.

D. **FRANCHISE TERMINATION**
Determined by the parties. Usually, termination must be "for cause" (such as breach of the agreement, etc.) and notice must be given. A franchisee must be given reasonable time to wind up the business.

   1. **Wrongful Termination**
   Important in determining whether termination is wrongful is whether it occurred in bad faith, whether the contract's relevant provisions are unconscionable, and so on.

2. The Importance of Good Faith and Fair Dealing
Courts generally try to balance the rights of both parties and provide a remedy if the franchisor acted unfairly. If termination occurred in the normal course of business and reasonable notice was given, however, termination was not likely wrongful.

III. PARTNERSHIPS
A partnership arises from an agreement between two or more persons to carry on a business for profit.

A. AGENCY CONCEPTS AND PARTNERSHIP LAW
Agency principles (see Chapter 19) apply to all partnerships.

B. THE UNIFORM PARTNERSHIP ACT
The Uniform Partnership Act (UPA) governs partnerships.

C. DEFINITION OF PARTNERSHIP
A partnership is "an association of two or more persons to carry on as co-owners a business for profit" [UPA 101(6)]. The intent to associate is a key element. A corporation can be a partner [UPA 101(10)].

D. WHEN DOES A PARTNERSHIP EXIST?
There are three essential elements—

1. A sharing of profits or losses.
2. A joint ownership of the business.
3. An equal right in the management of the business.

E. RECEIPT OF PROFITS AND PARTNERSHIP STATUS
A partnership does not exist if profits are received as payment of—[UPA 202(c)(3)]

1. A debt by installments or interest on a loan.
2. Wages of an employer or for the services of an independent contractor.
3. Rent to a landlord.
4. An annuity to a surviving spouse or representative of a deceased partner.
5. A sale of the goodwill of a business or property.

F. JOINT PROPERTY OWNERSHIP AND PARTNERSHIP STATUS
The joint ownership of property is not enough to create a partnership. Sharing profits from the ownership does not by itself establish a partnership (although sharing profits *and* losses does).

G. ENTITY VERSUS AGGREGATE
Under the UPA, a partnership is treated as an entity [UPA 201, 307(a). A partnership can own property as an entity, and sue and be sued in the firm name.

H. TAX TREATMENT OF PARTNERSHIPS
For federal income tax purposes, a partnership is regarded as an aggregate of individual partners.

I. PARTNERSHIP FORMATION
A partnership agreement generally states the intention to create a partnership, contribute capital, share profits and losses, and participate in management.

1. The Partnership Agreement
The agreement can be oral, written, or implied by conduct. Some must be in writing under the Statute of Frauds (see Chapter 9). Partners can agree to any term that is not illegal or contrary to public policy.

2. Duration of the Partnership
A partnership for a term ends on a specific date or the completion of a particular project. Dissolution without consent of all partners before the end of the term is a breach of the agree-

ment. If there is no fixed term, a partnership is at will, and any partner can dissolve the firm at any time.

3. Partnership by Estoppel

When parties who are not partners hold themselves out as partners and make representations that third persons rely on to deal with them, liability is imposed. A partner who misrepresents a non-partner's status is also liable (and the non-partner's acts may bind the partnership).

J. PARTNERSHIP OPERATION

1. RIGHTS OF PARTNERS

a. Management

1) In Ordinary Matters, the Majority Rules

All partners have equal rights to manage the firm [UPA 401(e)]. Each has one vote.

2) When Unanimous Consent Is Required

Unanimous consent is required to [UPA 301(2), 401(j)]—

a) Alter the essential nature of the firm's business or capital structure.
b) Admit new partners or enter a new business.
c) Assign property into a trust for the benefit of creditors.
d) Dispose of the firm's goodwill.
e) Confess judgment against the firm or submit firm claims to arbitration.
f) Undertake any act that would make conduct of partnership business impossible.
g) Amend partnership articles.

b. Interest in the Partnership

Unless the partners agree otherwise, profits and losses are shared equally [UPA 401(b)].

c. Compensation

Doing partnership business is a partner's duty and not compensable.

d. Inspection of Books

A partner has a right to complete information concerning the conduct of partnership business [UPA 403]. Partnership books must be kept at the principal business office.

e. Accounting of Partnership Assets or Profits

An accounting can be called for voluntarily or compelled by a court. Formal accounting occurs by right in connection with dissolution. A partner also has the right to an accounting to resolve claims among the partners or with the partnership.

f. Property Rights

Property acquired by a partnership is normally partnership property [UPA 203, 204]. A partner can use this property only on the firm's behalf [UPA 401(g)]. A partner is not a co-owner of this property and has no interest in it that can be transferred (although a partner can assign his or her right to a share of the profits) [UPA 501]. A partner's interest is subject to a judgment creditor's lien, attachable through a charging order [UPA 504].

2. DUTIES AND LIABILITIES OF PARTNERS

a. Fiduciary Duties

A partner owes the firm and its partners duties of loyalty and care [UPA 404].

1) Duty of Care

A partner must refrain from "grossly negligent or reckless conduct, intentional misconduct, or a knowing violation of law" [UPA 404(c)].

2) Duty of Loyalty
A partner must account to the firm for "any property, profit, or benefit" in the conduct of its business or from a use of its property, and refrain from dealing with the firm as an adverse party or competing with it [UPA 404(b)].

3) Breach and Waiver of Fiduciary Duties
These duties cannot be waived and partners must comply with the obligations of good faith and fair dealing, but a partner may pursue his or her own interests without automatically violating these duties. [UPA 103(b). 404(d)].

b. Authority of Partners
Each partner is an agent of the partnership in carrying out its usual business, unless designated otherwise.

1) The Scope of Implied Powers
Partners exercise all implied powers necessary and customary to carry on the business.

2) Authorized versus Unauthorized Actions
A partner cannot act purportedly on behalf of the partnership outside the scope of the business (by, for example, selling partnership assets without consent).

c. Liability of Partners

1) Joint Liability
In some states, partners are only jointly liable for partnership obligations, including contracts [UPA 306(a)]. This does not include debts arising from torts, and a creditor must sue all of the partners together (though each may be held liable individually).

2) Joint and Several Liability
In most states, partners are jointly and severally liable for all partnership obligations, including contracts, torts, and breaches of trust [UPA 306(a)] (though a creditor must first try to collect a partnership debt from the firm). A partner who commits a tort must reimburse the partnership for any damages it pays.

3) Liability of Incoming Partners
A newly admitted partner is liable for partnership debts incurred before his or her admission only to the extent of his or her interest in the partnership [UPA 306(b)].

K. DISSOCIATION OF A PARTNER
Dissociation occurs when a partner ceases to be associated in the carrying on of the partnership business. The partner can have his or her interest bought by the firm, which otherwise continues in business.

1. Events Causing Dissociation
Dissociation occurs when a partner give notices and withdraws, declares bankruptcy, assigns his or her interest, dies, becomes incompetent, or is expelled by the firm or by a court. Other events can be specified in the partnership agreement [UPA 601].

2. Wrongful Dissociation
Dissociation is wrongful if it is in breach of the partnership agreement, or occurs before the expiration of its term or completion of its undertaking [UPA 602]. A partner who wrongfully dissociates is liable to the partnership and to the other partners for damages caused by the dissociation.

3. Effects of Dissociation

a. The Partner
A partner's right to participate in the firm's business ends [UPA 603]. The duty of loyalty ends. The duty of care continues only with respect to events that occurred before dissociation, unless the partner participates in winding up the firm's business.

b. The Partnership
The partner's interest in the firm must be purchased according to the rules in UPA 701. To avoid liability for obligations under a theory of apparent authority, a partnership should notify its creditors of a partner's dissociation and file a statement of dissociation in the appropriate state office [UPA 704].

L. PARTNERSHIP TERMINATION
Termination is caused by any change in the relations of the partners that shows unwillingness or inability to carry on partnership business [UPA 801]. To continue the business, a partner can organize a new partnership.

1. Dissolution
Dissolution terminates the right of the partnership to exist as a going concern, but the firm remains long enough to wind up its affairs.

a. Dissolution by Agreement
Partners can agree to dissolve the partnership at any time. A partnership dissolves on the occurrence of an event specified in the partnership agreement for its dissolution.

b. Dissolution by Operation of Law
A partnership for a definite term or undertaking is dissolved when the term expires or the undertaking is accomplished. A partnership is dissolved if an event occurs that makes it impossible to continue lawfully, although the partners can continue if they change the nature of the business [UPA 801(4)].

c. Dissolution by Judicial Decree
A court can dissolve a partnership for commercial impracticality, a partner's improper conduct, or other circumstances [UPA 801(5)].

2. Winding Up and Distribution of Assets
This involves collecting and preserving partnership assets, paying debts, and accounting to each partner for the value of his or her interest. No new obligations can be created on the firm's behalf.

a. Distribution of Assets
Priorities for a partnership's assets are (1) payment of debts, including those owed to partner and non-partner creditors, and (2) return of capital contributions and distribution of profits to partners.

b. If the Partnership's Liabilities Are Greater Than Its Assets
The general partners bear the losses in the same proportion in which they shared the profits.

3. Partnership Buy-Sell Agreements
Partners may agree that one or more partners may buy out the others—who buys what, under what circumstances, and at what price. If a partner's dissociation does not result in dissolution, a buy-out of his or her interest is mandatory [UPA 701] at basically the price as he or she would get on dissolution.

TRUE-FALSE QUESTIONS

(Answers at the Back of the Book)

____   **1.**   In a sole proprietorship, the owner and the business are entirely separate.

____   **2.**   In a sole proprietorship, the owner receives all of the profits.

____   **3.**   The income of a sole proprietorship is taxed to the owner as personal income.

_____ **4.** A franchisee is not subject to the franchisor's control in the area of product quality.

_____ **5.** There is no state law covering franchises.

_____ **6.** There are no federal laws covering franchises.

_____ **7.** A partnership is an association of two or more persons to carry on, as co-owners, a business for profit.

_____ **8.** A general partner is not personally liable for partnership debts if its assets are insufficient to pay its creditors.

_____ **9.** A partnership is usually considered a legal entity apart from its owners.

_____ **10.** Unless a partnership agreement specifies otherwise, profits are shared in the same ratio as capital contributions.

FILL-IN QUESTIONS

(Answers at the Back of the Book)

In most states, partners _____ (are/are not) subject to joint and several liability on partnership debts, contracts, and torts. This means that a third party may sue _____ (one or more/only all) of the partners on a partnership _____ (obligation/tort). If the third party does not sue all of the partners, the liability of those partners who are not sued _____ (is/is not) extinguished. The third party's release of one partner _____ (does not release/releases) the other partners.

MULTIPLE-CHOICE QUESTIONS

(Answers at the Back of the Book)

_____ **1.** Roman owns Solo Enterprises, a sole proprietorship. Roman's liability for the obligations of the business is

a. limited by state statute.
b. limited to the amount of his original investment.
c. limited to the total amount of capital Roman invests in the business.
d. unlimited.

_____ **2.** Flik invests in a franchise with Gas Up! Service Stations, Inc. Gas Up! requires Flik to buy Gas Up! products for every phase of the operation. Flik's best argument to challenge this requirement is that it violates

a. an implied covenant of good faith and fair dealing.
b. antitrust laws.
c. the Federal Trade Commission's Franchise Rule.
d. the U.S. Franchise Agency's Purchase and Sale Regulations.

_____ **3.** Bowie invests in a franchise with Copy Centers, Inc. The franchise agreement may require Bowie to pay a percentage of Copy's

a. administrative and advertising expenses.
b. administrative expenses only.
c. advertising expenses only.
d. neither administrative nor advertising expenses.

____ **4.** Fridley buys a franchise from Global Services, Inc. In their agreement, Global may specify

a. neither requirements for the form of business nor standards of operation.
b. requirements for the form of business and standards of operation.
c. requirements for the form of business only.
d. standards of operation only.

____ **5.** Von buys a franchise from Windward Parasail Corporation. If their agreement is like most franchise agreements, it will allow Windward to terminate the franchise

a. for any reason only with notice.
b. for any reason without notice.
c. for cause only.
d. under no circumstances.

____ **6.** Raven, the owner of Skyline Sales, a sole proprietorship, wants to increase the business's capital without sacrificing control. This can be attained most successfully by

a. borrowing funds.
b. bringing in partners.
c. issuing stock.
d. selling the business.

____ **7.** Delilah is a partner in Estelinda Group. Delilah's dissociation will cause

a. the automatic termination of the firm's legal existence.
b. the immediate maturity of all partnership debts.
c. the partnership's buyout of Dina's interest in the firm.
d. the temporary suspension of all partnership business.

____ **8.** Cosmo holds himself out as a partner of Dayton Associates, a partnership, even though he has no connection to the firm. Cosmo obtains a loan based on the misrepresentation. Cosmo's default on the loan results in

a. Cosmo and Dayton's joint liability for the amount.
b. Cosmo's sole liability for the amount.
c. Delta's sole liability for the amount.
d. neither Cosmo's nor Dayton's liability.

____ **9.** Honi owns Impresario Imports. She hires Jordan as a salesperson, agreeing to pay $10.00 per hour, plus a commission of 10 percent of his sales. The term is one year. Honi and Jordan are

a. not partners, because Jordan does not have an ownership interest or management rights.
b. not partners, because the pay includes an hourly wage.
c. not partners, because the pay includes only a 10-percent commission.
d. partners for one year.

____ **10.** Kris is admitted to an existing partnership. A partnership debt incurred before the date of her admission comes due. Kris is

a. not liable for the debt.
b. only liable for the debt to the amount of her capital contribution.
c. personally liable only to the extent that the other partners do not pay the debt.
d. personally liable to the full extent of the debt.

SHORT ESSAY QUESTIONS

1. What are the rights of partners in a partnership?

2. How do franchise agreements generally delegate price and quality controls over the franchisee's business?

GamePoints

(Answers at the Back of the Book)

1. You're playing "Solo," a video game in which the goal is to amass as much personal profit from the investment of your time and money in your business enterprise as possible. At the start of the game, your business is small—your avatar is your only "employee"—and you expect to make little or no profit for at least a couple of "years." Your competitors include seemingly heartless corporate money mongers and faceless government bureaucrats, whose only reason for existence appears to be to prevent your success. Which form of business organization are you most likely to choose at the start? Why? What are its disadvantages? How can you raise additional capital without losing control of your outfit?

2. The video game "Phantasm" requires two or more players who confront malicious phenomena—ghosts, zombies, and so on—and combine their abilities to capture the bad guys for delivery to university research centers. In the game, you orally agree with your partner to pursue this adventure for five years, with the profits to be split 60/40. If this were a real partnership, would the agreement be enforceable? Should the terms be in writing? Explain.

Chapter 18
Limited Liability Companies and Limited Partnerships

WHAT THIS CHAPTER IS ABOUT

This chapter sets out the law relating to relatively new business organizations: limited liability companies (LLCs), limited liability partnerships (LLPs), limited partnerships, and limited liability limited partnerships (LLLPs). The chief features of these business forms are limited liability and tax advantages.

CHAPTER OUTLINE

I. **THE LIMITED LIABILITY COMPANY**
    A limited liability company (LLC) is a hybrid form of business enterprise. State statutes govern LLCs. Despite some similarities among these state laws, less than one-fifth of the states have adopted the Uniform Limited Liability Company Act (ULLCA).

    A. **TAXATION OF THE LLC**
        An LLC is taxed as a partnership unless it chooses to be taxed as a corporation.

    B. **THE NATURE OF THE LLC**
        An LLC offers the limited liability of a corporation [ULLCA 303]. Courts may pierce the LLC veil to hold members liable for the firm's obligations.

    C. **THE FORMATION OF THE LLC**
        Articles of organization must be filed with the state. Certain information is required. The business's name must include and LLC designation.

    D. **JURISDICTIONAL REQUIREMENTS**
        An LLC is a citizen of every state of which its members are citizens.

    E. **ADVANTAGES OF THE LLC**

        1. **Limited Liability**
            An LLC offers the limited liability of the corporation—the liability of its members is limited to the amount of their investments.

        2. **Flexibility in Taxation**
            An LLC offers the tax advantages of a partnership. LLCs with two or more members can elect to be taxed as either a partnership or a corporation. If no choice is made, an LLC is taxed as a partnership. One-member LLCs are taxed as sole proprietorships unless they elect to be taxed as corporations.

        3. **Management and Foreign Investors**
            An LLC has flexibility in terms of its management and operations (see below). Foreign investors may become LLC members, which encourages investment.

157

F. DISADVANTAGES OF AN LLC

Until uniform statutes are adopted by most states, an LLC with multistate operations may face difficulties. To be treated as a partnership for tax purposes, an LLC must have at least two members.

II.   MANAGEMENT AND OPERATION OF AN LLC

A. MANAGEMENT OF AN LLC

In a member-managed LLC, all members participate in management [ULLCA 404(a)]. In a manager-managed LLC, the members designate a group of persons (member or not) to manage the firm. These managers owe the fiduciary duties of loyalty and care to the LLC and in some states to its members [ULLCA 409(a), (h)].

B. THE LLC OPERATING AGREEMENT

Members decide how to operate the business. Provisions relate to management, division of profits, transfer of membership, what events trigger dissolution, and so on. In the absence of an agreement, LLC statutes govern.

1. A Writing Is Preferred

An operating agreement is not required in all states and if required may not need to be in writing. But a written agreement protects members' interests if there is a dispute or if an LLC statute is contrary to their intent.

2. Partnership Law May Apply

If there is no operating agreement or LLC statute, the principles of partnership law apply. This may give the members broad authority to bind the LLC.

C. OPERATING PROCEDURES

The operating agreement may specify procedures for making decisions. If it does not, choosing and removing managers is done by majority vote [ULLCA 404(b)(3)]. Details concerning meetings and voting rights may also be included. If not, in some states, each member has one vote.

III.   DISSOCIATION AND DISSOLUTION OF AN LLC

A member has the power to dissociate from an LLC but may not have the right to do so. Events that trigger dissociation include withdrawal, expulsion by other members or a court, bankruptcy, incompetence, and death.

A. EFFECT OF DISSOCIATION

The dissociating member loses the right to participate in management and to act as agent for the LLC. The other members can buy his or her interest for a fair value (within 120 days under the ULLCA).

B. DISSOLUTION

The remaining members can continue or dissolve the LLC, unless the operating agreement provides otherwise. A court can order dissolution if, for example, the members have acted illegally. An LLC is bound by the reasonable acts of its members during the winding up process. Proceeds are distributed to LLC creditors (including members) first, to capital contributors second, and to members third.

IV.   LIMITED LIABILITY PARTNERSHIPS

A limited liability partnership (LLP) enjoys the tax advantages of a partnership, while partners avoid personal liability for the wrongdoing of other partners.

A. FORMATION OF AN LLP

The appropriate form must be filed with a central state agency. The business's name must include "Limited Liability Partnership" or "LLP." Annual reports must be filed with the state [UPA 1001, 1002, 1003].

B. LIABILITY IN AN LLP
The UPA exempts partners in an LLP from personal liability for any partnership obligation, "whether arising in contract, tort, or otherwise" [UPA 306(c)].

1. Liability outside the State of Formation
Most states apply the law of the state in which the LLP was formed [UPA 1101].

2. Sharing Liability among Partner
A partner who commits a wrongful act is liable for the results, as is any other partner who committed the act. Some states provide that each partner is liable only up to the proportion of his or her responsibility for the result.

V. LIMITED PARTNERSHIPS
Limited partnerships must include at least one general partner and one or more limited partners. General partners assume management responsibility and liability for all partnership debts.

A. FORMATION OF A LIMITED PARTNERSHIP
Formation of a limited partnership is a public, formal proceeding: there must be two or more partners (at least one of whom is a general partner), and a certificate of limited partnership must be signed and filed with a designated state official (typically the secretary of state).

B. LIABILITIES OF PARTNERS IN A LIMITED PARTNERSHIP
General partners assume liability for all partnership debts. A limited partner is liable only to the extent of any contribution that is promised to the firm or any part of a contribution that was withdrawn [RULPA 502]. But participating in management results in a limited partner's personal liability for partnership debt, if creditors knew of participation [RULPA 303].

C. RIGHTS AND DUTIES IN A LIMITED PARTNERSHIP
Limited partners have essentially the same rights as general partners—a right of access to the partnership books and other information regarding partnership business.

D. DISSOCIATION AND DISSOLUTION

1. General Partners—Dissolution
Dissociation in any form—retirement, death, or mental incompetence—of a general partner dissolves the firm, unless continued by all other partners [RULPA 801]. Illegality, expulsion, or bankruptcy of a general partner dissolves a firm.

2. Limited Partners—No Dissolution
Death or assignment of interest of a limited partner does not dissolve the firm [RULPA 702, 704, 705], nor does personal bankruptcy.

3. Court Decree—Dissolution
A limited partnership can be dissolved by court decree [RULPA 802].

4. Priority to Assets on Dissolution
(1) Creditors, including partners who are creditors; (2) partners and former partners receive unpaid distributions of partnership assets and, except as otherwise agreed, a return on their contributions and amounts proportionate to their share of distributions [RULPA 804].

E. LIMITED LIABILITY LIMITED PARTNERSHIPS
This form is similar to a limited partnership, except that the liability of all partners in a limited liability limited partnership (LLLP) is limited to the amount of their investment in the firm.

TRUE-FALSE QUESTIONS

(Answers at the Back of the Book)

____   1.   Forming a limited liability company does not require the filing of any documents in a state office.

____   **2.** A limited liability company is a citizen of every state of which its members are citizens.

____   **3.** A limited liability company does not offer the limited liability of a corporation.

____   **4.** In a limited liability company, members do not have to participate in its management.

____   **5.** Most limited liability company (LLC) statutes provide that unless the members agree otherwise, all profits of the LLC will be divided equally.

____   **6.** Unless a partnership agreement specifies otherwise, profits are shared in the same ratio as capital contributions.

____   **7.** The death of a *limited* partner dissolves a limited partnership.

____   **8.** In a limited liability partnership, no partner is exempt from personal liability for partnership obligations.

____   **9.** In a limited partnership, the liability of a *limited* partner is limited to the amount of capital he or she invests in the partnership.

____   **10.** In a limited liability limited partnership, the liability of a *general* partner is limited to the amount of capital he or she invests in the partnership.

FILL-IN QUESTIONS

(Answers at the Back of the Book)

Unless the participants agree otherwise, all of the _____ (members/shareholders) of a _____ (limited liability company/joint stock company) may participate in management without assuming liability for the obligations of the firm. In contrast, the _____ (members/shareholders) of a _____ (limited liability company/joint stock company) may be personally liable for the debts of the firm whether or not they participate in the firm's management.

MULTIPLE-CHOICE QUESTIONS

(Answers at the Back of the Book)

____   **1.** Ebsen and Flossy form Eb & Flo, LLC, a limited liability company (LLC), to contract for the installation of custom plumbing and piping. One advantage of an LLC is that it may be taxed as

    a. a corporation.
    b. a partnership.
    c. a sole proprietorship.
    d. a syndicate.

____   **2.** Lonny is a member of Magna Management, a limited liability company that manages commercial properties for their owners. Lonny is liable for the firm's debts

    a. in proportion to the total number of members.
    b. to the extent of his capital contribution.
    c. to the extent that the other members do not pay the debts.
    d. to the full extent of the debts.

____ 3. Cal and Dyson form Elemeno Construction, a limited liability company, to design and make prefabricated housing. They can participate in its management

    a. only to the extent that they assume personal liability for the firm's debts.
    b. only to the extent of the amount of their investment in the firm.
    c. to any extent.
    d. to no extent.

____ 4. Rhianna and Stuart form Toons, LLC, a limited liability company (LLC), to market anime-related merchandise. A disadvantage of an LLC is that

    a. its income is double taxed.
    b. its members are subject to personal liability for the firm's debts.
    c. its members cannot participate in its management.
    d. state laws concerning limited liability companies are not yet uniform.

____ 5. Organic Farms, LLC, is a limited liability company. Its members hire outside managers to operate the LLC. These managers owe Organic Farms

    a. a duty of care only.
    b. a duty of loyalty only.
    c. fiduciary duties of care and loyalty.
    d. neither a duty of care nor a duty loyalty.

____ 6. Elton is a limited partner in Destiny Tours, a limited partnership. Collection Credit Company, a Destiny creditor, claims that Eton is subject to personal liability for Destiny's debts because Elton has the right, as a limited partner to take control of the firm. Collection Credit is correct about

    a. Elton's liability only.
    b. Elton's right to control the firm only.
    c. Elton's liability and Elton's right to control the firm.
    d. none of the choices.

____ 7. Jack and Kiley form J&K, a limited partnership. Jack is a general partner. Kiley is a limited partner. Dissolution of the firm would result from Kiley's

    a. assignment of her interest in the firm to a third party only.
    b. assignment of her interest, bankruptcy, or death.
    c. bankruptcy or death only.
    d. none of the choices.

____ 8. Drs. Lucas and Mikayla are partners in a medical clinic, which is organized as a limited liability partnership. Lucas manages the clinic. A court holds Mikayla liable in a malpractice suit. Lucas is liable

    a. in no way.
    b. in proportion to the total number of partners in the firm.
    c. to the extent of her capital contribution.
    d. to the full extent of the liability.

____ 9. Breck is a general partner in Chumley Investments, a limited partnership. Breck pays personal income taxes on

    a. all of Chumley's income.
    b. his share of Chumley's income.
    c. none of Chumley's income.
    d. only the amount of Chumley's income that is actually paid to him.

___ **10.** Mib, Nate, and Opal want to form a limited partnership. A limited partnership must have at least

     a. no specific number of any type of partner.
     b. one general partner and one limited partner.
     c. one general partner and two limited partners.
     d. two general partners and one limited partner.

SHORT ESSAY QUESTIONS

1. What are the advantages of doing business as a limited liability company?

2. Describe the characteristics of limited partnerships—creation, sharing of profits and losses, liability, capital contribution, management, duration, assignment, and priorities on liquidation.

GAMEPOINTS

(Answers at the Back of the Book)

1. You are playing "Team Up," a video game in which the play consists of choosing athletes for a fantasy sports team to compete with other teams for a championship title. Before selecting your team's players, you form the team's organization, Super Sport LLC. You are Super Sport's sole member. According to the principles discussed in this chapter, how would the firm's profits be taxed? Can a "non-member" manage the day-to-day business of the firm? If one of your players assaults a fan during a game, could you be held fully liable?

2. You are playing "Business Buddy," a video game in which the play consists of two or more players who operate as partners to buy, sell, and trade commodities—oil, corn, swine, and other animals, vegetables, and minerals—in global markets. One of your "buddies" is your cousin Melvin. Your agreement states that you are the "Lone General Partner" with the sole authority to bind the partnership to contracts with others. Without your knowledge, however, Melvin tells the Greater Asian Goatherds Association that he represents your firm and contracts to buy a large herd of goats. Is your partnership bound to this contract? If so, to what extent are you and Melvin personally liable?

Chapter 19
Corporations

WHAT THIS CHAPTER IS ABOUT

This chapter covers corporate classifications, formation, and the rights and responsibilities of all participants—directors, officers, and shareholders. Most corporations are formed under state law, and most states follow some version of the Revised Model Business Corporation Act (RMBCA).

CHAPTER OUTLINE

I. THE NATURE AND CLASSIFICATION OF CORPORATIONS

A. CORPORATE PERSONNEL
Shareholders elect a board of directors, which is responsible for overall management and hires corporate officers to run daily operations.

B. THE LIMITED LIABILITY OF SHAREHOLDERS
The key feature of a corporation is the limit of its owners' liability, for corporate obligations, to the amounts of their investments in the firm. Of course, a lender may require otherwise or a court may "pierce the corporate veil" (see below).

C. CORPORATE EARNINGS AND TAXATION
Corporations can retain corporate profits or pass them on to shareholders in the form of dividends. Profits that are not distributed are retained earnings and can be invested for higher profits, which may cause the price of the stock to rise, benefiting shareholders.

1. Corporate Taxation
Corporate profits are taxed twice—as income to the corporation and, when distributed as dividends, as income to the shareholders.

2. Holding Companies
A holding company (or parent company) holds the shares of another company. Such firms are often established in offshore no-tax or low-tax jurisdictions. A corporation whose shares are held in a holding company may transfer cash and other investments to be taxed in that jurisdiction.

D. TORTS AND CRIMINAL ACTS
A corporation is liable for the torts committed by its agents within the course and scope of employment. A corporation may be held liable for the crimes of its employees and agents if the punishment for the crimes can be applied to a corporation.

E. CLASSIFICATION OF CORPORATIONS

1. Domestic, Foreign, and Alien Corporations
A corporation is a *domestic* corporation in the state in which it incorporated, a *foreign* corporation in other states, and an *alien* corporation in other countries. A foreign corporation normally must obtain a certificate of authority to do business in any state except its home state.

163

2. Public and Private Corporations
A *public* corporation is formed by the government to meet a political or governmental purpose (the U.S. Postal Service, AMTRAK). A *private* corporation is created for private benefit and is owned by private persons.

3. Nonprofit Corporations
These are corporations formed without a profit-making purpose (private hospitals, educational institutions, charities, and religious organizations).

4. Close Corporations
A close corporation is exempt from most of the nonessential formalities of corporate operation (bylaws, annual meetings, etc. [RMBCA 7.32]). To qualify, a firm must have a limited number of shareholders, and restrict its issue and transfer of stock.

a. Management of a Close Corporation
Resembles that of a sole proprietorship or a partnership—one or a few shareholders usually hold the positions of directors and officers.

b. Transfer of Shares in Close Corporations
Often restricted by stipulating that shareholders offer their shares to the corporation or other shareholders before offering them to outsiders.

5. S Corporations

a. Qualification Requirements
Must be a domestic corporation; must not be a member of an affiliated group of corporations; shareholders must be individuals, estates, or certain trusts; must have 100 or fewer shareholders; can have only one class of stock; no shareholder can be a nonresident alien.

b. Benefits
Shareholders can use corporate losses to offset other income; only a single tax on corporate income is imposed at individual income tax rates at the shareholder level (even if it is not distributed).

6. Professional Corporations
Generally subject to the law governing ordinary corporations.

a. Limited Liability
A shareholder in a professional corporation is protected from liability for torts (except malpractice) committed by other members.

b. Unlimited Liability
A court might regard a professional corporation as a partnership, in which each partner may be liable for the malpractice of the others.

II. CORPORATE FORMATION

A. PROMOTIONAL ACTIVITIES
Promoters take the first steps in organizing a corporation: issue a prospectus (see Chapter 29) and secure the corporate charter (see below). Promoters are personally liable on preincorporation contracts until the corporation assumes the contract by novation (see Chapter 10).

B. INCORPORATION PROCEDURES

1. Select the State of Incorporation
Some states offer more advantageous tax or incorporation provisions.

2. Secure the Corporate Name

a. **Must Include Words That Disclose Corporate Status**
All state require that a name include *Corporation, Incorporated, Limited, Company,* or and abbreviation of one of these terms.

b. **Cannot Infringe on Another's Trademark Rights**
States review corporate names to avoid duplication and deception. A name should also be able to serve as a domain name.

3. **Prepare the Articles of Incorporation**
The articles include basic information about the corporation and serve as a primary source of authority for its organization and functions.

a. **Shares of the Corporation**
The amount of stock authorized for issuance; its valuation; and other information as to equity, capital, and credit must be outlined.

b. **Registered Office and Agent**
Usually, the registered office is the principal office of the corporation; the agent is a person designated to receive legal documents on behalf of the corporation.

c. **Incorporators**
Incorporators (some states require only one) must sign the articles when they are submitted to the state; often this is the only duty, and they need have no other interest in the corporation.

d. **Duration and Purpose**
A corporation can have perpetual existence in most states. The intended business activities of the corporation must be specified. Stating a general corporate purpose is usually sufficient.

e. **Internal Organization**
Management structure can be described in bylaws later.

4. **File the Articles with the State**
The articles of incorporation are sent to the appropriate state official (usually the secretary of state). Many states issue a certificate of incorporation authorizing the corporation to conduct business.

C. **FIRST ORGANIZATIONAL MEETING TO ADOPT BYLAWS**
The incorporators or the board; the business conducted depends on state law, the nature of the corporation's business, the provisions of the articles, and the wishes of the promoters. Adoption of the bylaws is the most important function of the first organizational meeting.

D. **IMPROPER INCORPORATION**
On the basis of improper incorporation, a person attempting to enforce a contract or bring a tort suit against the corporation could seek to make the shareholders personally liable. If a corporation seeks to enforce a contract, the defaulting party who learns of a defect in incorporation may be able to avoid liability.

1. *De Jure* **Corporations**
Occurs if there is substantial compliance with all requirements for incorporation. In most states, the certificate of incorporation is evidence that all requirements have been met, and neither the state nor a third party can attack the corporation's existence.

2. *De Facto* **Corporations**
The existence of a corporation cannot be challenged by third persons (except the state) if (1) there is a statute under which the firm can be incorporated, (2) the parties made a good faith attempt to comply with it, and (3) the firm has attempted to do business as a corporation. Some states do not apply this doctrine.

3. Corporation by Estoppel

If an association that is neither an actual corporation nor a *de facto* or *de jure* corporation holds itself out as being a corporation, it will be estopped from denying corporate status in a suit by a third party.

III. CORPORATE POWERS

A. EXPRESS POWERS

Express powers are in (in order of priority) the U.S. Constitution, state constitution, state statutes, articles of incorporation, bylaws, and board resolutions.

B. IMPLIED POWERS

A corporation has the *implied* power to perform all acts reasonably appropriate and necessary to accomplish its purposes.

C. *ULTRA VIRES* DOCTRINE

Ultra vires acts are beyond the purposes stated in the articles. Earlier cases involved contracts (which generally were enforced [RMBCA 3.04]). Now, courts usually allow any legal action a firm takes to profit shareholders, and a declining number of cases are brought mostly against nonprofit or municipal corporations.

IV. PIERCING THE CORPORATE VEIL

When a corporate owners use the entity to perpetuate a fraud, circumvent the law, or in some other way accomplish an illegitimate objective, a court will pierce the corporate veil.

A. FACTORS THAT LEAD COURTS TO PIERCE THE CORPORATE VEIL

Situations that may cause a court to disregard the corporate veil include—

1. A party is tricked or misled into dealing with the corporation rather than the individual.
2. The corporation is set up never to make a profit or always to be insolvent, or it is too thinly capitalized.
3. The corporation is formed to evade an existing legal obligation.
4. Statutory corporate formalities are not followed.
5. Personal and corporate interests are commingled to the extent that the corporation has no separate identity. Loans to the firm, for example, must be in good faith and for fair value.

B. A POTENTIAL PROBLEM FOR CLOSELY HELD CORPORATIONS

The potential for corporate formalities to be overlooked, or for other circumstances to occur that may lead a court to pierce the corporate veil, is especially great in a closely held corporation.

C. THE ALTER EGO THEORY

A court may pierce the corporate veil on the later ego theory—that the corporation was not operated as a separate entity from the person or group who dominated and controlled it—to avoid injustice or fraud.

V. DIRECTORS AND OFFICERS

A. ROLES OF DIRECTORS AND OFFICERS

The board of directors governs a corporation. Officers handle daily business.

1. Management Responsibilities

These include major policy and financial decisions; appointment, supervision, pay, and removal of officers and other managerial employees.

2. Election of Directors

    a. **Number of Directors**
Set in a corporation's articles or bylaws. Corporations with fewer than fifty shareholders can eliminate the board of directors.

    b. **How Directors Are Chosen**
The first board (appointed by the incorporators or named in the articles) serves until the first shareholders' meeting. Shareholders by majority vote (see below) elect subsequent directors.

    c. **Removal of Directors**
Shareholder action can remove a director for cause (or the board may have the power). In most states, a director cannot be removed without cause, unless shareholders have reserved the right.

3. **Compensation of Directors**
Nominal sums may be paid to directors, and there is a trend to provide more. Directors may set their own compensation [RMBCA 8.11]. A director who is also a corporate officer is an inside director. A director who does not hold a management position is an outside director.

4. **Board of Directors' Meetings**

    a. **Formal Minutes and Notice**
A board conducts business by holding formal meetings with recorded minutes. The dates for regular meetings are usually set in the articles and bylaws or by board resolution, and no other notice is required. Telephone or e-conferencing is possible [RMBCA 8.20].

    b. **Quorum Requirements and Voting**
Quorum requirements vary. If the firm specifies none, in most states a quorum is a majority of the number of directors authorized in the articles or bylaws [RMBCA 8.24]. Voting is done in person, one vote per director.

5. **Rights of Directors**

    a. **Participation**
A director has a right to participate in corporate business. Special meetings require notice to all directors [RMBCA 8.23].

    b. **Inspection**
A director has a right of inspection, which means access to all corporate books and records to make decisions.

    c. **Indemnification**
Most states permit a corporation to indemnify a director for costs and fees in defending against corporate-related lawsuits. Many firms buy insurance to cover indemnification [RMBCA 8.51].

6. **Committees of the Board of Directors**

    a. **Executive Committee**
Most states permit a board to elect an executive committee from among the directors to handle management between board meetings. The committee is limited to ordinary business matters.

    b. **Audit Committee**
Selects, compensates, and oversees independent public accountants who audit the firm's financial records under the Sarbanes-Oxley Act of 2002.

    c. **Nominating Committee**
Chooses candidates on which shareholders vote for the board of directors [RMBCA 8.25].

d. **Compensation Committee**
Sets salaries and benefits for executives and may determine directors' compensation.

e. **Litigation Committee**
Decides whether to pursue litigation on behalf of the corporation.

B. CORPORATE OFFICERS AND EXECUTIVES

The board hires officers and other executive employees. Officers act as corporate agents (see Chapter 20). The rights of corporate officers and other high-level managers are defined by employment contracts. Normally, the board can remove officers at any time (but the firm could be liable for breach of contract). Officers' duties are the same as those of directors.

C. DUTIES AND LIABILITIES OF DIRECTORS AND OFFICERS

Directors and officers are fiduciaries of the corporation.

1. Duty of Care

Directors and officers must act in good faith, in what they consider to be the best interests of the corporation, and with the care that an ordinarily prudent person would exercise in similar circumstances.

a. **Duty to Make Informed and Reasonable Decisions**
Directors must be informed on corporate matters and act in accord with their knowledge and training. A director can rely on information furnished by competent officers, or others, without being accused of acting in bad faith or failing to exercise due care [RMBCA 8.30].

b. **Duty to Exercise Reasonable Supervision**
Directors must exercise reasonable supervision when work is delegated.

c. **Dissenting Directors**
Directors must attend board meetings; if not, he or she should register a dissent to actions taken (to avoid liability for mismanagement).

d. **The Business Judgment Rule**
Honest mistakes of judgment and poor business decisions do not make directors and officers liable to the firm for poor results. There can be no bad faith, fraud, or breach of fiduciary duties. The decision must be within the director's managerial authority and the power of the corporation. The director or officer must—

1) Take reasonable steps to become informed.
2) Have a reasonable basis for a decision.
3) Have no personal conflict of interest with the corporation on the matter.

2. Duty of Loyalty

Directors and officers cannot use corporate funds or confidential information for personal advantage. Specifically, they cannot—

a. Compete with the corporation.
b. Usurp a corporate opportunity.
c. Have an interest that conflicts with the interest of the corporation.
d. Engage in insider trading (see Chapter 41).
e. Authorize a corporate transaction that is detrimental to minority shareholders.
f. Sell control over the corporation.

3. Disclosure of Potential Conflicts of Interest

Directors and officers must disclose fully any conflict of interest that might occur in a deal involving the corporation. A contract may be upheld if it was fair and reasonable to the firm when it was made, there was full disclosure of the interest of the officers or directors involved, and it was approved by a majority of disinterested directors or shareholders.

4. **Liability of Directors and Officers**
Directors and officers are personally liable for their torts and crimes, and may be liable for those of subordinates (under the "responsible corporate officer" doctrine or the "pervasiveness of control" theory). The corporation is liable for such acts when committed within the scope of employment.

VI. SHAREHOLDERS

A. SHAREHOLDERS' POWERS
Shareholders own the corporation, approve fundamental corporate changes, and elect and remove directors.

B. SHAREHOLDERS' MEETINGS
Regular meetings must occur annually; special meetings can be called to handle urgent matters. Notice must occur at least ten days and not more than sixty days before a meeting [RMBCA 7.05]. Notice of a special meeting must state the purpose.

1. Proxies
Rather than attend a meeting, shareholders normally authorize third parties to vote their shares. A proxy may be revocable and may have a time limit.

2. Shareholder Proposals
When a firm submits proxy materials to its shareholders (via mail or Web site posting), it must allow them to vote on pending policy proposals.

C. SHAREHOLDER VOTING

1. Quorum Requirements
At the meeting, a quorum must be present. A majority vote of the shares present is required to pass resolutions. Fundamental changes require a higher percentage.

2. Voting Techniques
Each common shareholder has one vote per share. The articles can exclude or limit voting rights.

a. Cumulative Voting
The number of members of the board to be elected multiplied by the total number of voting shares is the number of votes a shareholder has and can be cast for one or more nominees.

b. Shareholder Voting Agreements
A group of shareholders can agree to vote their shares together. A shareholder can vote by proxy. Any person can solicit proxies.

c. Voting Trust
Exists when legal title (recorded ownership on the corporate books) is transferred to a trustee to vote the shares. The shareholder retains all other ownership rights.

D. RIGHTS OF SHAREHOLDERS

1. Stock Certificates
Notice of shareholder meetings, dividends, and corporate reports are distributed to owners listed in the corporate books, not on the basis of possession of stock certificates (which most states do not require).

2. Preemptive Rights
These rights usually apply only to additional, newly issued stock sold for cash (not treasury shares) and must be exercised within a specified time (usually thirty days). When new shares

are issued, each shareholder is given *stock warrants* (transferable options to acquire a certain number of shares at a stated price) [RMBCA 6.30].

3. Dividends
Dividends can be paid in cash, property, or stock. Once declared, a cash dividend is a corporate debt.

a. Sources of Funds
Dividends are payable only from (1) retained earnings, (2) current net profits, or (3) surplus.

b. Illegal Dividends
A dividend paid while a corporation is insolvent is illegal and must be repaid if the shareholders knew that it was illegal when they received it. Directors may be personally liable for paying such a dividend.

c. Failure to Declare a Dividend
Shareholders can ask a court to compel a declaration of a dividend, but to succeed, the directors' conduct must be an abuse of discretion.

4. Inspection Rights
Shareholders (or their attorney, accountant, or agent) can inspect and copy corporate books and records for a proper purpose, if the request is made in advance [RMBCA 16.02]. This right can be denied to prevent harassment or to protect confidential corporate information.

5. Transfer of Shares
Restrictions on transferability must be noted on the face of stock certificates, and must be reasonable.

6. Shareholder's Derivative Suit
If directors fail to take appropriate action to redress a wrong inflicted on the corporation by a third party—ninety days after a shareholders' demand in writing that the directors ac—shareholders can sue in the corporate name to redress the wrong. Any recovery normally goes into the corporate treasury.

E. LIABILITY OF SHAREHOLDERS
In most cases, if a corporation fails, shareholders lose only their investment. Exceptions include—

1. Watered Stock
In most cases, a shareholder who receives watered stock (stock sold by a corporation for less than par value) must pay the difference to the corporation. In some states, such shareholders may be liable to creditors of the corporation for unpaid corporate debts.

2. Breach of Fiduciary Duty
A single shareholder (or a few acting together) who owns enough shares to control the corporation owes a fiduciary duty to the minority shareholders and creditors when they sell their shares.

VII. MAJOR BUSINESS FORMS COMPARED
The appropriate form for doing business depends on an enterprise's characteristics, tax status, and goals.

TRUE-FALSE QUESTIONS
(Answers at the Back of the Book)

____ 1. In some states, a close corporation can operate without formal shareholders' or directors' meetings.

___ **2.** A corporation is liable for the torts of its agents or officers committed within the course and scope of their employment.

___ **3.** An officer is a fiduciary of a corporation.

___ **4.** Preemptive rights entitle shareholders to bring a derivative suit against the corporation.

___ **5.** Only certain funds are legally available for paying dividends.

___ **6.** Damages recovered in a shareholder's derivative suit are paid to the shareholder who filed the suit.

___ **7.** Generally, shareholders are not personally responsible for the debts of the corporation.

___ **8.** Directors, but not officers, owe a duty of loyalty to the corporation.

___ **9.** The business judgment rule makes a director liable for losses to the firm in most cases.

___ **10.** Shareholders may vote to remove members of the board of directors.

FILL-IN QUESTIONS

(Answers at the Back of the Book)

Those who, for themselves or others, take the preliminary steps in organizing a corporation are _____ (promoters/incorporators). These persons enter into contracts with professionals, whose services are needed in planning the corporation, and are personally liable on these contracts, _____ (unless/even if) the third party issues a release or the corporation assumes the contract. A person who applies to the state on behalf of the corporation to obtain its certificate of incorporation is _____ (a promoter/an incorporator). This person _____ (must/need not) have any interest in the corporation.

MULTIPLE-CHOICE QUESTIONS

(Answers at the Back of the Book)

___ **1.** Blaine and Cory want to incorporate to buy, play, sell, and trade video games. The first step in the incorporation procedure is to

a. file the articles of incorporation.
b. hold the first organizational meeting.
c. obtain a corporate charter.
d. select a state in which to incorporate.

___ **2.** Responsibility for the overall management of Fashionista Stores, Inc., a corporation, is entrusted to

a. the board of directors.
b. the corporate officers and managers.
c. the owners of the corporation.
d. the promoters of the corporation.

____ **3.** Daystar Company is a private, for-profit corporation that (1) was formed to market business office software, (2) is owned by ten shareholders, (3) is subject to double taxation, and (4) has made no public offering of its shares. Daystar is

a. a close corporation.
b. a nonprofit corporation.
c. an S corporation.
d. a professional corporation.

____ **4.** Koz is a shareholder of Lil' Biz Company, Inc. A court might "pierce the corporate veil" and hold Koz personally liable for Lil's debts

a. if Koz's personal interests commingle with Lil's interests to the extent it has no separate identity.
b. if Lil' calls too many shareholders' meetings.
c. if Lil' is overcapitalized.
d. under no circumstances.

____ **5.** The management of Orchards & Vines, Inc., is at odds with the shareholders over some recent decisions. The shareholders may file a shareholders' derivative suit to

a. compel dissolution of Orchards & Vines.
b. compel payment of a properly declared dividend.
c. enforce a right to inspect corporate records.
d. recover damages from the management for an *ultra vires* act.

____ **6.** Jeans & Sweats Corporation uses cumulative voting in its elections of directors. Keno owns 3,000 shares. At an annual meeting at which three directors are to be elected, Keno may cast for any one candidate

a. 1,000 votes.
b. 3,000 votes.
c. 9,000 votes.
d. 27,000 votes.

____ **7.** HomeBase Corporation invests in intrastate businesses. In HomeBase's state, as in most states, the minimum number of directors that must be present before its board can transact business is

a. all of the directors authorized in the articles.
b. a majority of the number authorized in the articles or bylaws.
c. any odd number.
d. one.

____ **8.** Perla is a director of Quik Purchasing Corporation. Without informing Quik, Perla goes into business with Rapid Buys, Inc., to compete with Quik. This violates

a. the business judgment rule.
b. the duty of care.
c. the duty of loyalty.
d. none of the choices.

____ **9.** Dylan and Evette are officers of Fullfit Clothing Corporation. As officers, their rights are set out in

a. international agreements.
b. state corporation statutes.
c. the firm's certificate of authority.
d. the officers' employment contracts.

___ **10.** Robin is a director of Sherwood Forest Company. Robin has a right to

    a. compensation.
    b. dividends.
    c. inspect corporate books and records.
    d. transfer shares.

SHORT ESSAY QUESTIONS

1. How do the duty of care and the duty of loyalty govern the conduct of directors and officers in a corporation?

2. What are the rights of the shareholders of a corporation?

GAMEPOINTS

(Answers at the Back of the Book)

1. In the video game "Corporate Cowboy," your task is to investigate complaints of wrongdoing on the part of corporate directors and officers, decide whether there is a violation of the law, and deal with the wrongdoers accordingly. Jane, a shareholder of Goodly Corporation, alleges that its directors decided to invest heavily in the firm's growth in negligent reliance on its officers' faulty financial reports. This caused Goodly to borrow to meet its obligations, resulting in a drop in its stock price. Are the directors liable? Why or why not?

2. You are playing the video game "Conflict of Interest" in which you accrue points by correctly spotting corporate misconduct, skillfully battling against it, and successfully righting the wrong. Your chief opponent is the game's avatar. Ellen, a shareholder of Finagle, Inc., asks you to help her right a wrong suffered by the firm as a result of an act by Bernie, one of the firm's directors and officers. Can Ellen sue Bernie on Finagle's behalf? If so, and Bernie is held liable, who recovers the damages? What defense is the game's avatar likely to assert on Bernie's behalf?

CUMULATIVE HYPOTHETICAL PROBLEM FOR UNIT FOUR—INCLUDING CHAPTERS 17–19

(Answers at the Back of the Book)

Fern, Gigi, and Ho are sole proprietors who decide to pool their resources to produce and maintain an Internet game site, "we-World."

___ **1.** Fern, Gigi, and Ho decide to form a partnership. They transfer their business assets and liabilities to the firm and start business on May 1, 2010. The parties execute a formal partnership agreement on July 1. The partnership began its existence

    a. on May 1.
    b. on July 1.
    c. when each partner's individual creditors consented to the asset transfer.
    d. when the parties initially decided to form a partnership.

___ **2.** After six months in operation, Fern, Gigi, and Ho decide to change the form of their partnership to a limited partnership. To form a limited partnership, they must

    a. accept limited liability for all of the partners.
    b. create the firm according to specific statutory requirements.
    c. designate one general partner to be a limited partner.
    d. each make a capital contribution.

____   **3.** Fern, Gigi, and Ho's we-World is very successful. In March 2012, they decide to incorporate. The articles of incorporation must include all of the following except

a. the name of a registered agent.
b. the name of the corporation.
c. the names of the incorporators.
d. the names of the initial officers.

____   **4.** Fern is a director of we-World. Fern has a right to

a. compensation.
b. participation.
c. preemption.
d. none of the choices.

____   **5.** The board of directors of we-World announces a cash dividend. This dividend may *not* be paid from

a. accumulated surplus.
b. gross profits.
c. net profits.
d. retained earnings.

QUESTIONS ON THE FOCUS ON ETHICS FOR UNIT FOUR— ETHICS AND THE BUSINESS ENVIRONMENT

(Answers at the Back of the Book)

____   **1.** Hollis is an officer with Imprints, Inc., a corporate-logo, screen-printing service. Hollis finds herself in a position to acquire assets that would benefit Imprints if acquired in its name. If Hollis usurps this opportunity, she may violate the duty of

a. acting in one's own interest.
b. agency.
c. care.
d. loyalty.

____   **2.** Chico is a director of Blammo Motorbikes Corporation. Normally, Chico owes fiduciary duties only to

a. himself.
b. Blammo's creditors.
c. Blammo's personnel.
d. Blammo's shareholders.

____   **3.** Brad is an employee of Chloe, a franchisee of Diners Restaurants, Inc. The franchisor may be liable for ad's torts committed within the scope of his employment under the principles of

a. acting in one's own interest.
b. agency.
c. care.
d. loyalty.

Chapter 20
Agency

WHAT THIS CHAPTER IS ABOUT

This chapter covers agency relationships, including how they are formed and the duties involved. Agency relationships are essential to a corporation, which can function and enter into contracts only through its agents.

CHAPTER OUTLINE

I. AGENCY RELATIONSHIPS

In an agency relationship, the parties agree that the agent will act on behalf and instead of the principal in negotiating and transacting business with third persons.

A. EMPLOYER-EMPLOYEE RELATIONSHIPS
Normally, all employees who deal with third parties are deemed to be agents. Statutes covering workers' compensation and so on apply only to employer-employee relationships.

B. EMPLOYER–INDEPENDENT CONTRACTOR RELATIONSHIPS
Those who hire independent contractors have no control over the details of their physical performance. Independent contractors can be agents.

C. DETERMINING EMPLOYEE STATUS
The greater an employer's control over the work, the more likely it is that the worker is an employee. Another key factor is whether the employer withholds taxes from payments to the worker and pays unemployment and Social Security taxes covering the worker.

II. FORMATION OF THE AGENCY RELATIONSHIP

Consideration is not required. A principal must have capacity to contract, but anyone can be an agent. An agency can be created for any legal purpose.

A. AGENCY BY AGREEMENT
Normally, an agency must be based on an agreement that the agent will act for the principal. Such an agreement can be an express written contract or can be implied by conduct.

B. AGENCY BY RATIFICATION
A person who is not an agent (or who is an agent acting outside the scope of his or her authority) may make a contract on behalf of another (a principal). If the principal approves or affirms that contract by word or by action, an agency relationship is created by ratification (see Chapter 32).

C. AGENCY BY ESTOPPEL

1. The Principal's Actions
When a principal causes a third person to believe that another person is his or her agent, and the third person deals with the supposed agent, the principal is estopped to deny the agency relation.

2. The Third Party's Reasonable Belief
The third person must prove that he or she reasonably believed that an agency relationship existed and that the agent had authority—that an ordinary, prudent person familiar with business practice and custom would have been justified in concluding that the agent had authority.

D. AGENCY BY OPERATION OF LAW
A court may find an agency relationship in the absence of a formal agreement. This may occur in family relationships or in an emergency, when the agent's failure to act outside the scope of his or her authority would cause the principal substantial loss.

III. DUTIES OF AGENTS AND PRINCIPALS
An agency relationship is fiduciary.

A. AGENT'S DUTIES TO THE PRINCIPAL

1. Performance
An agent must use reasonable diligence and skill (the degree of skill of a reasonable person under similar circumstances), unless an agent claims special skills (such as those of an accountant), in which case the agent is expected to use those skills.

2. Notification
An agent must notify the principal of all matters concerning the agency. Notice to the agent is considered to be notice to the principal.

3. Loyalty
An agent must act solely for the principal's benefit (not in the interest of the agent or a third party).

a. Confidentiality
Any information or knowledge acquired through the agency relationship is confidential. It cannot be disclosed during the agency or after its termination.

b. Agent's Loyalty Must Be Undivided
An agent employed by a principal to buy cannot buy from himself or herself, and an agent employed to sell cannot become the purchaser, without the principal's consent.

4. Obedience
When an agent acts on behalf of the principal, the agent must follow all lawful instructions of the principal. Exceptions include emergencies and instances in which instructions are not clearly stated.

5. Accounting
An agent must keep and make available to the principal an account of everything received and paid out on behalf of the principal. An agent must keep separate accounts for the principal's funds.

B. PRINCIPAL'S DUTIES TO THE AGENT

1. Compensation
A principal must pay an agent for services rendered (unless the agent does not act for money). Payment must be timely. If no amount has been agreed to, the principal owes the customary amount for such services.

2. Reimbursement and Indemnification
A principal must (1) reimburse the agent for money paid at the principal's request or for necessary expenses and (2) indemnify an agent for liability incurred because of authorized acts.

3. **Cooperation**

A principal must cooperate with and assist an agent in performing his or her duties. The principal must do nothing to prevent performance.

4. **Safe Working Conditions**

A principal must provide safe working conditions.

C. RIGHTS AND REMEDIES OF AGENTS AND PRINCIPALS

For every duty of a principal, an agent has a corresponding right, and vice versa. An agent also has the right to perform without interference by the principal. Remedies for breach of the agency relationship follow normal contract and tort remedies, including damages, termination of the agency, injunction, and accounting.

IV. SCOPE OF AN AGENT'S AUTHORITY

A principal's liability in a contract with a third party arises from the authority given the agent to enter contracts on the principal's behalf.

A. EXPRESS AUTHORITY

1. **Equal Dignity Rule**

In most states, if the contract being executed is or must be in writing, the agent's authority must also be in writing.

a. **Exception—Executive Officer Doing Ordinary Business**

A corporate executive doing ordinary business does not need written authority from the corporation.

b. **Exception—Agent Acting in the Presence of the Principal**

In this case, the agent does not need written authority.

2. **Power of Attorney**

A power of attorney can be special or general. An ordinary power terminates on the incapacity or death of the person giving it. A durable power is not affected by the principal's incapacity.

B. IMPLIED AUTHORITY

Conferred by custom, can be inferred from the position an agent occupies, or is implied as reasonably necessary to carry out express authority.

C. APPARENT AUTHORITY AND ESTOPPEL

An agent has apparent authority when a principal, by word or action, causes a third party reasonably to believe that an agent has authority, though the agent has no authority. The principal may be estopped from denying it if the third party changes position in reliance.

D. EMERGENCY POWERS

If an emergency demands action by the agent, but the agent is unable to communicate with the principal, the agent has emergency power.

E. RATIFICATION

A principal can ratify an unauthorized contract or act, if he or she has the capacity and is aware of all material facts. Ratification can be done expressly or impliedly (by accepting the benefits of a transaction). An entire transaction must be ratified; a principal cannot affirm only part.

1. **Effect of Ratification Without Knowing All the Facts**

If the third party acts in reliance to his or her detriment on the apparent ratification, the principal can repudiate but must reimburse the third party's costs.

2. **Effect of Ratification**

Ratification binds the principal to the agent's act and treats it as if it had been authorized from the outset.

3. Effect of No Ratification

There is no contract binding the principal; the third party's agreement with the agent is an unaccepted offer; the agent may be liable to the third party for misrepresenting his or her authority.

4. Requirements for Ratification

The requirements for ratification are—

a. The agent acted on behalf of an identified principal who later ratified the action.
b. The principal must know all of the material facts. If not, the contract can be rescinded
c. The principal must affirm the agent's act in its entirety.
d. The principal must have the capacity to authorize the transaction when the agent engages in it and the principal ratifies it. The third party must also have capacity
e. The principal's ratification must occur before the third party withdraws from the deal.
f. The principal must follow the same formalities to ratify the contract as would have been needed to authorize it initially.

V. LIABILITY FOR CONTRACTS

Who is liable to third parties for contracts formed by an agent?

A. DEFINITIONS

1. Disclosed Principal

A principal whose identity is known by the third party when the contract is made.

2. Unidentified Principal

A principal whose identity is not known by the third party, but the third party knows the agent is or may be acting for a principal when the contract is made.

3. Undisclosed Principal

A principal whose identity is totally unknown by the third party, who also does not know that the agent is acting in an agency capacity at the time of the contract.

B. IF AN AGENT ACTS WITHIN THE SCOPE OF HIS OR HER AUTHORITY

1. Disclosed Principal

If a principal's identity is known to a third party when an agent makes a contract, the principal is liable. The agent is not liable.

2. Unidentified Principal

The principal is liable. In most states, the agent is also liable (but is entitled to indemnification by the principal).

3. Undisclosed Principal

The principal and the agent are liable. Exceptions—

a. The principal was expressly excluded as a party in the contract.
b. The contract is a negotiable instrument (check or note).
c. The performance of the agent is personal to the contract.

C. IF THE AGENT HAS NO AUTHORITY

The principal is not liable in contract to a third party. The agent is liable, for breach of the implied warranty of authority (not on breach of the contract), unless the third party knew the agent did not have authority.

D. ACTIONS BY E-AGENTS

E-agents include semi-autonomous computer programs capable of executing specific tasks. How much authority do e-agents have? Generally, any party who uses an e-agent is bound by the e-agent's operations whether or not the principal was aware of them. In some circumstances, the third party with whom the e-agent deals can avoid the transaction.

VI. LIABILITY FOR AGENT'S TORTS AND CRIMES

An agent is liable to third parties for his or her torts. Is the principal also liable?

A. PRINCIPAL'S TORTIOUS CONDUCT

A principal may be liable for harm resulting from the principal's negligence or recklessness (giving improper instructions; authorizing the use of improper materials or tools; establishing improper rules; or failing to prevent others' tortious conduct while they are on the principal's property or using the principal's equipment, materials, or tools).

B. PRINCIPAL'S AUTHORIZATION OF AGENT'S TORTIOUS CONDUCT

A principal who authorizes an agent to commit a tortious act may be liable.

C. LIABILITY FOR AGENT'S MISREPRESENTATION

1. Fraudulent Misrepresentation

If a principal has given an agent authority to make statements and the agent makes false claims, the principal is liable. If an agent appears to be acting within the scope of authority in taking advantage of a third party, the principal who placed the agent in that position is liable.

2. Innocent Misrepresentation

When a principal knows that an agent does not have all the facts but does not correct the agent's or the third party's impressions, the principal is liable.

D. LIABILITY FOR AGENT'S NEGLIGENCE

Under the doctrine of *respondeat superior*, an employer is liable for harm caused (negligently or intentionally) to a third party by an employee acting within the scope of employment, without regard to the personal fault of the employer. This is known as *vicarious liability*.

1. The Scope of Employment

Performing work assigned by the employer or engaging in conduct subject to the employer's control are acts within the scope of employment. Conduct not intended by the employee to serve any purpose of the employer is outside the scope of employment.

2. The Distinction between a "Detour" and a "Frolic"

If a servant takes a detour from his master's business, the master is liable for any ensuing tort. If the servant is on a frolic of his or her own, however, the master is not responsible.

3. Travel and Commuting

The travel of those whose jobs require it is considered within the scope of employment for the duration of the trip, including the return. An employee going to and from work or meals is usually considered outside the scope of employment.

4. Notice of Dangerous Conditions

An employer is charged with knowledge of dangerous conditions that concern the employment situation and that an employee discovers.

5. Borrowed Servants

An employer who lends the services of an employee to a third party may be liable for the employee's negligence, depending on who had the right to control the employee at the time.

E. LIABILITY FOR AGENT'S INTENTIONAL TORTS

Generally, an employer is not liable for an agent's intentional tort because a tort normally has no connection to the agency relation.

1. Employer's Liability for Agent's Torts outside the Scope of Employment

An employer who knows or should know that an employee has a propensity for committing tortious acts is liable for the acts even if they are outside the scope of employment. Also, an employer is liable for permitting an employee to engage in reckless acts that can injure others.

2. **Agent's Liability for His or Her Own Torts**
An employee is liable for his or her own torts. An employee who commits a tort at the employer's direction can be liable with the employer, even if he or she was unaware of the wrongfulness.

F. **LIABILITY FOR INDEPENDENT CONTRACTOR'S TORTS**
An employer is not liable for harm caused to a third person by the tortious act of an independent contractor (except in cases of hazardous activities such as blasting operations, the transportation of highly volatile chemicals, and the use of poisonous gases, in which strict liability is imposed).

G. **LIABILITY FOR AGENT'S CRIMES**
A principal is not liable for an agent's crime, unless the principal participated. In some jurisdictions, a principal may be liable for an agent's violating, in the course and scope of employment, such regulations as those governing sanitation, prices, weights, and the sale of liquor.

VII. TERMINATION OF AN AGENCY

A. **TERMINATION BY ACT OF THE PARTIES**

1. **Lapse of Time**
An agency agreement may specify the time period during which the agency relationship will exist. If so, the agency ends when that time expires. If no definite time is stated, an agency continues for a reasonable time and can be terminated at will by either party.

2. **Purpose Achieved**
An agent can be employed to accomplish a particular objective. If so, the agency automatically ends when the objective is accomplished.

3. **Occurrence of a Specific Event**
An agency can be created to terminate on the occurrence of a certain event. If so, the agency automatically ends when the event occurs.

4. **Mutual Agreement**
Parties can cancel their agency by mutually agreeing to do so.

5. **At the Option of One Party**
Both parties have the *power* to terminate an agency, but they may not have the *right* and may therefore be liable for breach of contract.

a. **Agency at Will—Principal Must Give Reasonable Notice**
To allow the agent to recoup expenses and, in some cases, to make a normal profit.

b. **Agency Coupled with an Interest—Irrevocable**
This agency is created for the benefit of the agent, who acquires a beneficial interest in the subject matter, and thus it is not equitable to permit a principal to terminate at will. Also, it is not terminated by the death of either the principal or the agent.

c. **Not an Agency Coupled with an Interest—May Be Revocable**
An agency coupled with an interest should not be confused with an agency in which the agent derives only proceeds or profits (such as a commission) from the sale of the subject matter. This is revocable by the principal, subject to any contract between the parties.

B. **TERMINATION BY OPERATION OF LAW**

1. **Death or Insanity**
Death or insanity of either party automatically and immediately ends an agency. Knowledge of the death is not required.

2. Impossibility
When the specific subject matter of an agency is destroyed or lost, the agency terminates. When it is impossible for the agent to perform the agency lawfully because of a change in the law, the agency terminates.

3. Changed Circumstances
When an event occurs that has such an unusual effect on the subject matter of the agency that the agent can reasonably infer that the principal will not want the agency to continue, the agency terminates.

4. Bankruptcy
Bankruptcy of the principal or the agent usually terminates an agency. In some circumstances, as when the agent's financial status is irrelevant to the purpose of the agency, the agency relationship may continue.

5. War
When the principal's country and the agent's country are at war with each other, the agency is terminated.

C. NOTICE OF TERMINATION

1. Notice Required
If the parties themselves terminate the agency, the principal must inform any third parties who know of the agency that it has ended.

a. Agent's Authority Continues
An agent's actual authority continues until the agent receives notice of termination. An agent's apparent authority continues until the third person is notified (from any source).

b. What the Principal Must Do
The principal is expected to notify directly any third person the principal knows has dealt with the agent. For third persons aware of the agency but who have not dealt with the agent, constructive notice is sufficient.

c. Form of the Notice
No particular form is required unless the agent's authority is written, in which case it must be revoked in writing, and the writing must be shown to all who saw the written authority.

2. No Notice Required
If an agency terminates by operation of law, there is no duty to notify third persons, unless the agent's authority is coupled with an interest.

TRUE-FALSE QUESTIONS

(Answers at the Back of the Book)

____ 1. Employees who deal with third parties are agents of their employers.

____ 2. An agent owes his or her principal a duty to act in good faith.

____ 3. An agent who fails to use reasonable diligence and skill in acting on behalf of his or her principal may be liable for breaching a duty of performance.

____ 4. A *disclosed* principal is liable to a third party for contracts made by the agent acting within the scope of authority.

____ 5. A principal is not liable for harm caused to a third party by an agent acting in the scope of employment.

____ 6. An *undisclosed* principal is liable to a third party for contracts made by an agent acting within the scope of authority.

____ 7. Both parties to an agency have the right to terminate the agency at any time.

____ 8. If a principal does not ratify an otherwise unauthorized contract, the principal is not bound.

____ 9. An e-agent is a person.

____ 10. When an agent enters into a contract on behalf of a principal, the principal must ratify the contract to be bound.

FILL-IN QUESTIONS

(Answers at the Back of the Book)

An agent's use of reasonable diligence and skill is part of the agent's duty of _____ (obedience/performance). Informing a principal of all material matters that come to the agent's attention concerning the subject matter of the agency is an aspect of the agent's duty of _____ (accounting/notification). Acting solely for the benefit of the principal and not in the interest of the agent or a third party is part of the agent's duty of _____ (loyalty/performance). Following all lawful and clearly stated instructions of the principal is an aspect of the agent's duty of _____ (loyalty/obedience). If an agent is required to keep and make available to the principal a record of all property and money received and paid out on behalf of the principal, this is part of the agent's duty of _____ (accounting/notification).

MULTIPLE-CHOICE QUESTIONS

(Answers at the Back of the Book)

____ 1. Elman is an officer for Fizzy Frothy Corporation. When acting for Fizzy in ordinary business situations, Elman is

a. an agent.
b. an agent and a principal.
c. a principal.
d. neither an agent nor a principal.

____ 2. Campbell is a salesperson for DownRiver Enterprises, Inc. In determining whether Campbell is DownRiver's employee or an independent contractor, the most important factor is

a. the degree of control that DownRiver exercises over Campbell.
b. the distinction between DownRiver's business and Campbell's occupation.
c. the length of the working relationship between DownRiver and Campbell.
d. the method of payment.

____ 3. Estimable Finance Company hires Flotilda, who holds herself out as possessing special accounting skills, to act as its agent. As an agent, Flotilda must use the degree of skill or care expected of

a. an average, unskilled person.
b. a person having those special skills.
c. a reasonable person.
d. Estimable Company.

___ **4.** Gregg, a salesperson at Hubris Electronics store, tells Irma, a customer, "Buy your home theatre system here, and I'll set it up for less than what Hubris would charge." Irma buys the system, Gregg sets it up, and Irma pays Gregg, who keeps the money. Gregg has breached the duty of

   a. loyalty.
   b. notification.
   c. obedience.
   d. performance.

___ **5.** Juicy Beverage Company hires Keith to manage one of its kiosks. Although their employment agreement says nothing about Keith being able to hire employees to work in the kiosk, Keith has this authority. This is

   a. apparent authority.
   b. express authority.
   c. imaginary authority.
   d. implied authority.

___ **6.** Metro Movie Company employs Nora as an agent. To terminate her authority, Metro must notify

   a. Nora and third parties who know of the agency relationship.
   b. only Nora.
   c. only third parties who know of the agency relationship.
   d. the public generally.

___ **7.** Midwest Mining, Inc., employs Nick as an agent. Nick enters into a contract with Oceana Resources Company within the scope of his authority but without disclosing that he is acting as Midwest's agent. Midwest does not perform. Oceana can recover from

   a. Midwest only.
   b. Midwest or Nick.
   c. Nick only.
   d. no one.

___ **8.** Questa Products Company requires its customers to pay by check. Ray, a Quality agent, tells customers that they can pay him with cash. Questa learns of Ray's collections, but takes no action to stop them. Ray steals some of the cash. Questa may be liable for the loss under the doctrine of

   a. apparent authority.
   b. express authority.
   c. imaginary authority.
   d. implied authority.

___ **9.** Swifty Delivery Company employs Taesha as a driver. While acting within the scope of employment, Taesha causes an accident in which Vaughn is injured. Vaughn can recover from

   a. neither Swifty nor Taesha.
   b. Swifty only.
   c. Swifty or Taesha.
   d. Taesha only.

___ **10.** Wendy contracts with Zip-It Investments, Inc., to act as Zip-It's agent in a fraudulent scheme. Wendy does not successfully complete the scheme. Zip-It can recover from Wendy for breach of

   a. contract.
   b. implied warranty.
   c. performance.
   d. none of the choices.

SHORT ESSAY QUESTIONS

1.   What are the chief differences among the relationships of principal and agent, employer and employee, and employer and independent contractor? What are the factors that indicate whether an individual is an employee or an independent contractor?

2.   Identify and describe the categories of authority by which an agent can bind a principal and a third party in contract.

GAMEPOINTS

(Answers at the Back of the Book)

From the throne room in your base station on Alpha Centauri—in the video game "Galactic Empire"—you dispatch your loyal, obedient minions to use their diligence and skill to loot the universe on your behalf and return with the treasure for its accounting and their compensation. Applying the agency principles outlined in this chapter, answer the following questions.

1.   One minion, Delilah, does not return with gems and gold, but brings back three contracts. Acting within the scope of her authority, she contracted with Evon, who knew your identity at the time; Felipe, who knew that Delilah was acting on behalf of someone but not whom; and Giorgio, who did not know that Delilah was acting on anyone's behalf. For which contracts, if any, are you liable? For which contracts, if any, is Delilah liable?

2.   A different minion, Hotspur, steals the treasure chest of a giant Cyclops from an asteroid orbiting a distant star. Launching quickly to escape from the celestial body, Hotspur's space pod negligently bangs into the Cyclops, who is injured. If the Cyclops files a suit against you, can there be a recovery for the injury?

Chapter 21
Employment Relationships

WHAT THIS CHAPTER IS ABOUT

This chapter outlines the most significant laws regulating employment relationships. Other significant laws regulating the workplace—those prohibiting employment discrimination—are dealt with in Chapter 25.

CHAPTER OUTLINE

I. EMPLOYMENT AT WILL
Under this doctrine, either the employer or the employee may terminate an employment relationship at any time and for any reason (unless a contract or the law provides to the contrary).

A. EXCEPTIONS TO THE EMPLOYMENT-AT-WILL DOCTRINE

1. Exceptions Based on Contract Theory
Some courts have held that an implied contract exists between an employer and an employee (if, for example, a personnel manual states that no employee will be fired without good cause). A few states have held all employment contracts contain an implied covenant of good faith.

2. Exceptions Based on Tort Theory
Discharge may give rise to a tort action (based on fraud, for example) for wrongful discharge.

3. Exceptions Based on Public Policy
An employer may not fire a worker for reasons that violate a public policy of the jurisdiction (for example, for refusing to violate the law). This policy must be expressed clearly in statutory law. Some state and federal statutes protect whistleblowers from retaliation.

B. WRONGFUL DISCHARGE
An employer cannot fire an employee in violation of an employment contract or a federal or state statute. If so, the employee may bring an action for wrongful discharge.

II. WAGE AND HOUR LAWS
Davis-Bacon Act of 1931 requires "prevailing wages" for employees of some government contractors. Walsh-Healey Act of 1936 requires minimum wage and overtime for employees of some government contractors. Fair Labor Standards Act of 1938 (FLSA) covers all employees and regulates—

A. CHILD LABOR
Children under fourteen can deliver newspapers, work for their parents, and work in entertainment and agriculture. Children fourteen and older cannot work in hazardous occupations.

B. MINIMUM WAGES
Under federal or state law, a specified amount (periodically revised) must be paid to employees in covered industries. Tipped employees and those who are customarily provided food or lodging may be subject to different wage calculations but the minimums are the same.

185

C. OVERTIME PROVISIONS AND EXEMPTIONS

Employees who work more than forty hours per week must be paid no less than one and a half times their regular pay for all hours over forty. Executives, administrative employees, professional employees, outside salespersons, and computer employees are exempt if their pay exceeds a certain amount, their duties do not include certain types of work, and they meet other requirements.

III. LAYOFFS

Restructuring an operation or downsizing a workforce means a layoff.

A. THE WORKER ADJUSTMENT AND RETRAINING NOTIFICATION (WARN) ACT OF 1988

Employers with at least one hundred full-time workers must provide sixty-days' notice before imposing a mass layoff or closing a plant that employs more than fifty full-time workers.

1. Mass Layoff

This is a reduction in force that, during any thirty-day period, results in an employment loss of at least 33 percent of the full-time employees at a single job site and at least fifty employees, or at least five hundred full-time employees. An employment loss is a layoff that exceeds six months or a reduction in hours of more than 50 percent in each month of any six-month period.

2. Notification Requirements

Workers, including part-time and seasonal workers, or their union representative must be notified. State and local agencies must also be notified. This gives workers time to look for new jobs and state agencies time to provide retraining and other resources. Employers can avoid giving notice by staggering layoffs over many months or many job sites.

3. Remedies for Violations

These include fines of up to $500 per day. Employees can recover up to sixty-days' back pay and job benefits, plus attorneys' fees. Discrimination claims are possible (see Chapter 25).

B. STATE LAWS REQUIRING LAYOFF NOTICES

Many states have similar or stricter notice requirements that cover more employers and employees.

IV. FAMILY AND MEDICAL LEAVE ACT (FMLA) OF 1993

Employers with fifty or more employees must provide them with up to twelve weeks of family or medical leave during any twelve-month period.

A. COVERAGE AND APPLICATION

Public and private employers are covered. Key employees, part-time employees, and those who have worked less than twelve months during the previous seven years are not covered. The purposes of the leave must be to care for new children (family leave), or close relatives or themselves with a serious health condition (medical leave). The leave can be extended in military-related situations.

B. BENEFITS AND PROTECTIONS

Employers must continue health-care coverage for an employee during the leave, and guarantee employment in the same, or a comparable, position when the employee returns to work.

C. EMPLOYER VIOLATIONS

Remedies for violations include damages, job reinstatement, promotion, costs, and fees.

V. WORKER HEALTH AND SAFETY

A. THE OCCUPATIONAL SAFETY AND HEALTH ACT OF 1970

This act provides for workplace safety standards—employers have a general duty to keep workplaces safe—with record-keeping, reporting, notice, and inspection requirements. The Occupational Safety and Health Administration (OSHA) administers the act. Penalties are limited, but an employer may also be prosecuted under state law.

B. STATE WORKERS' COMPENSATION LAWS

State laws establish procedure for compensating workers injured on the job. Often excluded are domestic workers, agricultural workers, temporary employees, and employees of common carriers.

1. Workers' Compensation Requirements

There must be an employment relationship, and the injury must be accidental and occur on the job or in the course of employment. An employee must notify the employer of an injury (usually within thirty days), and file a claim with a state agency within a certain period (sixty days to two years) from the time the injury is first noticed.

2. Workers' Compensation and Litigation

An employee's acceptance of benefits bars the employee from suing for injuries caused by the employer's negligence.

VI. INCOME SECURITY

A. SOCIAL SECURITY

The Social Security Act of 1935 provides for payments to persons who are retired, widowed, disabled, etc. Employers and employees must contribute under the Federal Insurance Contributions Act (FICA).

B. MEDICARE

A health insurance program administered by the Social Security Administration for people sixty-five years of age and older and for some under sixty-five who are disabled.

C. PRIVATE PENSION PLANS

The Employee Retirement Income Security Act (ERISA) of 1974 empowers the U.S. Department of Labor to oversee operators of private pension funds. The Pension Benefit Guaranty Corporation (PBGC) pays benefits to participants if their plans cannot.

1. Vesting

Generally, employee contributions to pension plans vest immediately; employee rights to employer contributions vest after five years.

2. Investing

Pension-fund managers must be cautious in investing and must diversify investments to minimize the risk of large losses.

D. UNEMPLOYMENT COMPENSATION

The Federal Unemployment Tax Act of 1935 created a state system that provides unemployment compensation to eligible individuals. A worker must have left his or her job for good cause—not misconduct—be willing and able to work, and be actively seeking employment

E. COBRA

The Consolidated Omnibus Budget Reconciliation Act (COBRA) of 1985 prohibits the elimination of a worker's medical, optical, or dental insurance coverage on the voluntary or involuntary termination or reduction in hours of the worker's employment.

1. Procedures

Except for those fired for gross misconduct, a worker can decide whether to continue coverage. Coverage must be continued for up to eighteen months (twenty-nine, if the worker is disabled).

2. Payment

A worker who opts to continue coverage must pay a premium plus an administrative fee. Penalties for violations include up to 10 percent of the annual cost of the group plan or $500,000, whichever is less.

F. EMPLOYER-SPONSORED GROUP HEALTH PLANS

Under the Health Insurance Portability and Accountability Act (HIPAA), employers who provide health insurance cannot exclude persons with certain preexisting conditions and are restricted in their collection and use of employees' health information.

VII. EMPLOYEE PRIVACY RIGHTS

A right to privacy has been inferred from constitutional guarantees provided by the First, Third, Fourth, Fifth, and Ninth Amendments to the Constitution. Tort law, state constitutions, and some federal and state statutes also provide some privacy rights.

A. ELECTRONIC MONITORING

1. Employee Privacy Protection

Privacy rights are protected at common law (invasion of privacy) and under the U.S. Constitution and state constitutions. The courts generally weigh an employer's interests against an employee's reasonable expectation of privacy, which may depend on whether the employee knows of the monitoring.

2. The Electronic Communications Privacy Act (ECPA) of 1986

Electronic monitoring may violate this act, which prohibits the intentional interception of any electronic communication or the intentional disclosure or use of the information obtained by the interception. A "business-extension exception" permits employers to monitor communications in the ordinary course of business (though not personal communications without consent).

3. Stored Communications

Intentional, unauthorized access to stored electronic communications is prohibited.

B. OTHER TYPES OF MONITORING

1. Lie-Detector Tests

Under the Employee Polygraph Protection Act of 1988, most employers cannot, among other things, require, request, or suggest that employees or applicants take lie-detector tests, except when investigating theft, including theft of trade secrets.

2. Drug Testing

a. Protection for the Privacy Rights of Private Employees

Some state constitutions may prohibit private employers from testing for drugs. State statutes may restrict drug testing by private employers. Other sources of protection include collective bargaining agreements and tort actions for invasion of privacy (see Chapter 4).

b. Protection for Government Employees

Constitutional limitations (the Fourth Amendment) apply. Drug tests have been upheld when there was a reasonable basis for suspecting employees of using drugs, or when drug use could threaten public safety.

3. Genetic Testing

Employers cannot use the results of genetic tests of employees and applicants to make decisions about hiring, firing, placement, or promotion under the Genetic Information Nondiscrimination Act of 2008.

TRUE-FALSE QUESTIONS

(Answers at the Back of the Book)

____ **1.** Drug testing by private employers is permitted.

____ **2.** There are no exceptions to the employment "at will" doctrine.

____ **3.** Employers are required to establish retirement plans for their employees.

____ **4.** Federal wage-hour laws cover all employers engaged in interstate commerce.

____ **5.** Whistleblower statutes protect employers from workers' disclosure of the employer's wrongdoing.

____ **6.** Under federal law, employers can monitor employees' personal communications.

____ **7.** Workers' compensation laws cover all employees in all states.

____ **8.** Except to investigate theft, employers cannot order employees to take lie-detector tests.

____ **9.** Children fourteen and older can work in hazardous occupations.

____ **10.** Some employees can continue their group health benefits after a loss of employment.

FILL-IN QUESTIONS

(Answers at the Back of the Book)

Under the employment-at-will doctrine, _____ (either/neither) party may terminate an employment relationship at any time and for any reason _____ (unless/even if) a contract provides to the contrary. An employee who is fired in violation of a federal or state statute _____ (may/may not) bring an action for wrongful discharge. _____ (Some/No) courts have held that an implied contract exists between an employer and an employee. _____ (All/A few states) have held that all employment contracts contain an implied covenant of good faith. An employer _____ (may/may not) fire a worker for reasons that violate a public policy of the jurisdiction.

MULTIPLE-CHOICE QUESTIONS

(Answers at the Back of the Book)

____ **1.** Flash in the Pan is a fast-food restaurant. To verify Flash in the Pan's compliance with statutes governing employees' wages and hours, its personnel records should be checked against the provisions of

a. the Fair Labor Standards Act.
b. the Family and Medical Leave Act.
c. the Occupational Safety and Health Act.
d. the Worker Adjustment and Retraining Notification Act.

____ **2.** Interstate Distributors, Inc., is investigating losses due to theft. Without violating employees' rights of privacy, Interstate may

a. monitor all employee phone conversations only.
b. require employees to take lie-detector tests only.
c. monitor all employee phone conversations and require employees to take lie-detector tests.
d. none of the choices.

____ **3.** Erin, an employee of First-Stop Machine Shop, is injured. For Erin to receive *workers' compensation*, the injury must be

a. accidental and arise out of a preexisting disease or condition.
b. accidental and occur on the job or in the course of employment.
c. intentional and arise out of a preexisting disease or condition.
d. intentional and occur on the job or in the course of employment.

___ **4.** Michelle, an employee of Neverquit Company, is covered by federal overtime provisions. These rules apply only after an employee has worked more than

    a. eight hours in a day.
    b. five days in a week.
    c. forty hours in a week.
    d. 160 hours in a month.

___ **5.** Rose is an employee of Soaring Sales Company. Rose and Soaring contribute to the federal social security system under

    a. the Employee Payments Act.
    b. the Employment Retirement Income Security Act.
    c. the Federal Insurance Contributions Act.
    d. the Federal Unemployment Tax Act.

___ **6.** Digby Road Construction, Inc., sets up a pension fund for its employees. Digby's operation of the fund is regulated by

    a. the Employer Payments Act.
    b. the Employment Retirement Income Security Act.
    c. the Federal Insurance Contributions Act.
    d. the Federal Unemployment Tax Act.

___ **7.** Fruit Packaging Corporation provides health insurance for its 150 employees, including Gladys. When Gladys takes twelve weeks' leave to care for her child, she

    a. can collect "leave pay" equal to twelve weeks' of health insurance coverage.
    b. can continue her heath insurance at Fruit Packaging's expense.
    c. can continue her heath insurance at her expense.
    d. loses her heath insurance immediately on taking leave.

___ **8.** Reddy Power Corporation provides health insurance for its employees. When Reddy closes one of its offices and terminates the employees, the employees

    a. can collect "severance pay" equal to twelve weeks' of health insurance coverage.
    b. can continue their heath insurance at Reddy's expense.
    c. can continue their heath insurance at their expense.
    d. lose their heath insurance immediately on termination of employment.

___ **9.** Reba works for Silo Storage Company as an at-will employee. This employment may be terminated at any time for any reason by

    a. neither Reba nor Silo Storage.
    b. Reba only.
    c. Reba or Silo Storage.
    d. Silo Storage only.

___ **10.** Millions Mining Company is a private employer that wants to test its employees for drug use. This testing may

    a. be limited or prohibited at the sole discretion of the employer.
    b. be limited or prohibited under a state constitution, statute, or court decision.
    c. not be permitted under any circumstances.
    d. not be prohibited under any circumstances.

SHORT ESSAY QUESTIONS

1. What is the employment-at-will doctrine? What are its exceptions?

2. What protection does federal law offer from the risks of employment-related injury, death, or disease?

GAMEPOINTS

(Answers at the Back of the Book)

1.   You are playing "Brain Drain," a video game that involves a quest through the unexplored realms of the imagination, attempting to reach Level 14. It is difficult to advance from level to level because the obstacles that must be overcome and the objectives that must be attained are different, complex, and puzzling. For four consecutive weeks, you play 45, 42, 39, and 31 hours. If this play were work, and you were a nonexempt employee covered by the Fair Labor Standards Act, how many hours of overtime pay, if any, would you be entitled to? What would be the rate?

2.   In the video game, "Invasive Species," Earth is invaded by huge, insect-like aliens with superior intelligence. Your avatar Derek works for Invasion Extermination Service, Inc. Following the service's prescribed procedures, Derek sprays the invaders with "Eradicate," a chemical supplied by the service. Eradicate effectively wipes out the invaders—one at a time with a short delay, which allows for plenty of game action—but also injures your avatar. According to the principles set out in this chapter, is Derek eligible for workers' compensation? Could Derek successfully sue his employer for negligence?

Chapter 22
Employment Discrimination

WHAT THIS CHAPTER IS ABOUT

The law restricts employers and unions from discriminating against workers on the basis of race, color, religion, national origin, gender, age, or handicap. A class of persons defined by one or more of these criteria is a *protected class*. This chapter outlines these laws.

CHAPTER OUTLINE

I. TITLE VII OF THE CIVIL RIGHTS ACT OF 1964
Prohibits employment discrimination against employees, applicants, and union members on the basis of race, color, national origin, religion, and gender.

A. WHO IS SUBJECT TO TITLE VII?
Employers with fifteen or more employees, labor unions with fifteen or more members, labor unions that operate hiring halls, employment agencies, and federal, state, and local agencies.

B. THE EQUAL EMPLOYMENT OPPORTUNITY COMMISSION
(1) A victim files a claim with the Equal Employment Opportunity Commission (EEOC); (2) the EEOC investigates and seeks a voluntary settlement; (3) if no settlement is reached, the EEOC may sue the employer; (4) if the EEOC chooses not to sue, the victim may file a lawsuit.

C. INTENTIONAL AND UNINTENTIONAL DISCRIMINATION
Title VII prohibits both intentional and unintentional discrimination.

1. Disparate-Treatment Discrimination
This is intentional discrimination by an employer against an employee.

    a. *Prima Facie* Case—Plaintiff's Side of the Case
    A plaintiff must show (1) he or she is a member of a protected class, (2) he or she applied and was qualified for the job, (3) he or she was rejected by the employer, (4) the employer continued to seek applicants or filled the job with a person not in a protected class.

    b. Defense—Employer's Side of the Case
    An employer must articulate a legal reason for not hiring the plaintiff. To prevail, the plaintiff must show that the employer's reason is a pretext and that discriminatory intent motivated the decision.

2. Disparate-Impact Discrimination

    a. Types of Disparate-Impact Discrimination
    Disparate-impact discrimination results if, because of a requirement or hiring practice—

    1) an employer's work force does not reflect the percentage of members of protected classes that characterizes qualified individuals in the local labor market, or

    2) members of protected class are excluded from employer's work force at substantially higher rate than nonmembers (under EEOC's "four-fifths rule," selection rate for protected class must be at least 80 percent of rate for group with the highest rate).

b. *Prima Facie* **Case—Plaintiff's Side of the Case**
Plaintiff must show a connection between a requirement or practice and a disparity; no evidence of discriminatory intent is needed.

D. DISCRIMINATION BASED ON RACE, COLOR, AND NATIONAL ORIGIN
Employers cannot effectively discriminate against employees on the basis of race, color, national origin, or religion (absent a substantial, demonstrable relationship between the trait and the job, etc.).

1. Reverse Discrimination
Discrimination against majority individuals is reverse discrimination.

2. Potential Section 1981 Claims
This statute (42 U.S.C. Section 1981) protects against discrimination on the basis of race or ethnicity in the formation or enforcement of contracts, including employment contracts, with no limit on the amount of damages.

E. DISCRIMINATION BASED ON RELIGION
Title VII prohibits employers and unions from discriminating against persons because of their religions.

F. DISCRIMINATION BASED ON GENDER
Employers cannot discriminate against employees on the basis of gender (unless gender is essential to a job, etc.). The Pregnancy Discrimination Act of 1978 amended Title VII: employees affected by pregnancy or related conditions must be treated the same as persons not so affected but similar in ability to work.

1. Equal Pay Act
The Equal Pay Act of 1963 prohibits gender-based discrimination in wages paid for equal work when a job requires equal skill, effort, and responsibility under similar conditions.

2. 2009 Equal Pay Legislation
The Paycheck Fairness Act of 2009 prohibits gender-based discrimination in assessing an employee's education, training, or experience. Under the Lily Ledbetter Fair Pay Act of 2009, each time a person is paid discriminatory wages, benefits, or compensation, a cause of action arises and the victim has 180 days to file a complaint.

G. CONSTRUCTIVE DISCHARGE
Constructive discharge occurs when an employer causes working conditions to be so intolerable that a reasonable person in an employee's position would feel compelled to quit.

1. Proving Constructive Discharge
An employee must show that the employer caused the intolerable conditions, and knew, or had reason to know, of the intolerable conditions and failed to correct them within a reasonable time.

2. Applies to All Title VII Discrimination
An employee can seek damages for loss of income, including back pay.

H. SEXUAL HARASSMENT

1. Forms of Harassment
(1) *Quid pro quo* harassment: when promotions, etc., are doled out on the basis of sexual favors; (2) hostile-environment harassment: when an employee is subjected to offensive sexual comments, etc.

2. Harassment by Supervisors, Co-Workers, or Others

a. When an Employer May Be Liable
If anyone (employee or nonemployee) harasses an employee, and the employer knew, or should have known, and failed to take immediate corrective action, the employer may be

liable. To be liable for a supervisor's harassment, the supervisor must have taken a tangible employment action against the employee.

b. Employer's Defense
(1) Employer took "reasonable care to prevent and correct promptly any sexually harassing behavior," and (2) employee suing for harassment failed to follow employer's policies and procedures.

3. Same-Gender Harassment
Title VII protects persons who are harassed by members of the same gender.

I. ONLINE HARASSMENT
Employers may avoid liability if they take prompt remedial action. Privacy rights must be considered if the action includes electronic monitoring of employees.

J. REMEDIES UNDER TITLE VII
Reinstatement, back pay, retroactive promotions, and damages.

1. Damages
Compensatory damages are available only in cases of intentional discrimination. Punitive damages are available only if an employer acted with malice or reckless indifference

2. Limits
Total damages are limited to specific amounts against specific employers (from $50,000 against those with 100 or fewer employees to $300,000 against those with more than 500 employees).

II. DISCRIMINATION BASED ON AGE

A. AGE DISCRIMINATION IN EMPLOYMENT ACT (ADEA) OF 1967
Prohibits employment discrimination on the basis of age (including mandatory retirement), by employers with twenty or more employees, against individuals forty years of age or older. Administered by the EEOC, but private causes of action are also possible.

B. PRINCIPLES ARE SIMILAR TO TITLE VII
To establish a *prima facie* case, a plaintiff must show that he or she was (1) forty or older, (2) qualified for a position, and (3) rejected in circumstances that prove age discrimination. The employer must articulate a legal reason for the action. The plaintiff may show it is a pretext.

C. STATE EMPLOYEES NOT COVERED BY THE ADEA
Under the Eleventh Amendment to the Constitution, a state is immune from suits brought by private individuals in federal court unless the state consents to the suit. A state agency sued by a state employee for age discrimination may have the suit dismissed on this ground.

III. DISCRIMINATION BASED ON DISABILITY
Under the Americans with Disabilities Act (ADA) of 1990, an employer cannot refuse to hire a person who is qualified but disabled. Covered are all employers (except the states) with fifteen or more employees.

A. PROCEDURES AND REMEDIES UNDER THE ADA

1. Procedures
A plaintiff must show he or she (1) has a disability, (2) is otherwise qualified for a job and (3) was excluded solely because of the disability. A suit may be filed only after a claim is pursued through the EEOC (which may file a suit even if the employee agrees to arbitration).

2. Remedies
Job reinstatement, back pay, some compensatory and punitive damages (for intentional discrimination), and certain other relief. Repeat violators may be fined up to $100,000.

B. **WHAT IS A DISABILITY?**

"(1) A physical or mental impairment that substantially limits one or more of the major life activities . . . ; (2) a record of such impairment; or (3) being regarded as having such an impairment." Includes AIDS, blindness, cancer etc., but not kleptomania and others. Employers cannot consider mitigating measures (such as glasses) or medication when determining whether an individual has a disability.

C. **REASONABLE ACCOMMODATION**

For a person with a disability, an employer may have to make a reasonable accommodation (more flexible working hours, new job assignment, different training materials or procedures)—but not an accommodation that will cause *undue hardship* ("significant difficulty or expense").

1. **Job Applications and Physical Exams**

The application process must be accessible to those with disabilities. Employers cannot require a disabled person to take a preemployment physical (unless all applicants do). Disqualification must be from problems that render a person unable to perform the job.

2. **Substance Abusers**

The ADA protects addicts who have completed or are in supervised rehabilitation, and alcoholics to the extent of equal treatment.

3. **Health-Insurance Plans**

Workers with disabilities must be given the same access as other workers to employer-provided insurance plans. If a plan includes a disability-based distinction, it violates the ADA unless proved to be a business necessity.

4. **Association Discrimination**

An employer cannot take an adverse employment action based on the disability of a person with whom an applicant or employee is known to have a relationship or association (a disabled spouse, for example).

IV. DEFENSES TO EMPLOYMENT DISCRIMINATION

The first defense is to assert that the plaintiff did not prove discrimination. If discrimination is proved, an employer may attempt to justify it as—

A. **BUSINESS NECESSITY**

An employer may show that there is a legitimate connection between a job requirement that discriminates and job performance.

B. **BONA FIDE OCCUPATIONAL QUALIFICATION (BFOQ)**

Another defense applies when discrimination against a protected class is essential to a job—that is, when a particular trait is a BFOQ. Generally restricted to cases in which gender is essential. Race can never be a BFOQ.

C. **SENIORITY SYSTEMS**

An employer with a history of discrimination may have no members of protected classes or disabled workers in upper-level positions. If no present intent to discriminate is shown, and promotions, etc., are distributed according to a fair seniority system, the employer has a good defense.

D. **AFTER-ACQUIRED EVIDENCE OF EMPLOYEE MISCONDUCT**

Evidence of an employee's prior misconduct acquired after a lawsuit is filed may limit damages but is not otherwise a defense.

V. AFFIRMATIVE ACTION

An affirmative action program attempts to make up for past discrimination by giving members of protected classes preferential treatment in hiring or promotion.

A. CONSTITUTIONALITY OF AFFIRMATIVE ACTION PROGRAMS

An employment program cannot use quotas or preferences for unqualified persons. Once it succeeds, it must be changed or dropped. Some states have ended government-sponsored programs.

B. AFFIRMATIVE ACTION IN SCHOOLS

Automatic preference on the basis of a protected characteristic violates the equal protection clause.

TRUE-FALSE QUESTIONS

(Answers at the Back of the Book)

___ **1.** Once an affirmative action program has succeeded, it must be changed or dropped.

___ **2.** In a sexual harassment case, an employer cannot be held liable for the actions of an employee.

___ **3.** In a sexual harassment case, an employer cannot be held liable for the actions of a nonemployee.

___ **4.** Women affected by pregnancy must be treated for all job-related purposes the same as persons not so affected but similar in ability to work.

___ **5.** Employment discrimination against persons with a physical or mental impairment that substantially limits their everyday activities is prohibited.

___ **6.** Discrimination complaints brought under federal law must be filed with the Equal Opportunity Employment Commission.

___ **7.** If the Equal Employment Opportunity Commission decides not to investigate a claim, the victim has no other option.

___ **8.** All employers are subject to Title VII of the Civil Rights Act of 1964.

___ **9.** Disparate-treatment discrimination occurs when an employer intentionally discriminates against an employee.

___ **10.** Title VII prohibits employers and unions from discriminating against persons because of their religions.

FILL-IN QUESTIONS

(Answers at the Back of the Book)

The Equal Employment Opportunity Commission (EEOC) monitors compliance with the federal antidiscrimination laws. The EEOC _____ (can/cannot) sue organizations that violate these laws. A victim files a claim with the EEOC, which investigates and _____ _____ (must sue/may sue if a settlement between the parties is not reached). If the EEOC does not sue, the victim may sue. On proof of discrimination, a victim may be awarded _____ _____ (reinstatement and back pay/reinstatement, back pay, and retroactive promotions).

MULTIPLE-CHOICE QUESTIONS

(Answers at the Back of the Book)

_____ **1.** Dona applies to Estuary Management Corporation for an administrative assistant's job, which requires certain typing skills. Dona cannot type but tells Estuary that she is willing to learn. Estuary does not hire her, and she later sues. To successfully defend against the suit under Title VII, Estuary must show that

    a. being a member of the majority is a BFOQ.
    b. Dona was not willing to learn to type.
    c. Estuary has a valid business necessity defense.
    d. Estuary's work force reflects the same percentage of members of a protected class that characterizes qualified individuals in the local labor market.

_____ **2.** Greg and Holly work for Interstate Services, Inc. (ISI), as electrical engineers. Greg is paid more than Holly because, according to ISI, he is a man with a family to support. This is prohibited by

    a. the Age Discrimination in Employment Act of 1967.
    b. the Americans with Disabilities Act of 1990.
    c. the Equal Pay Act of 1963.
    d. none of the choices.

_____ **3.** **Based on a Sample CPA Exam Question.** Under the Age Discrimination in Employment Act of 1967, Turnover Business Corporation is prohibited from

    a. committing unintentional age discrimination.
    b. forcing an employee to retire.
    c. terminating an employee between the ages of sixty-five and seventy for cause.
    d. terminating an employee as part of a rational business decision.

_____ **4.** Neville, who is hearing impaired, applies for a position with Mold Casters Company. Neville is qualified but is refused the job and sues Mold Casters. To succeed under the Americans with Disabilities Act, Neville must show that

    a. Neville was willing to make a "reasonable accommodation" for Mold Casters.
    b. Neville would not have to accept "significant additional costs" to work for Mold Casters.
    c. Mold Casters refused to make a "reasonable accommodation" for Neville.
    d. Mold Casters would not have to accept "significant additional costs" to hire Neville.

_____ **5.** Insurance Sales, Inc., promotes employees on the basis of color. Employees with darker skin color are passed over in favor of those with lighter skin color, regardless of their race. This is prohibited by

    a. the Americans with Disabilities Act of 1990.
    b. the Equal Pay Act of 1963.
    c. Title VII of the Civil Rights Act of 1964.
    d. none of the choices.

_____ **6.** Mina is an employee of Widebody Trucking Corporation. Mina attempts to resolve a gender-based discrimination claim with Widebody, whose representative denies the claim. Mina's next best step is to

    a. ask the Equal Opportunity Employment Commission whether a claim is justified.
    b. file a lawsuit.
    c. forget about the matter.
    d. secretly sabotage company operations for revenge.

___ **7.** Curt, personnel director for Digital Products, Inc., prefers to hire Asian Americans, because "they're smarter and work harder" than other minorities. This is prohibited by

   a. the Age Discrimination in Employment Act of 1967.
   b. the Americans with Disabilities Act of 1990.
   c. Title VII of the Civil Rights Act of 1964.
   d. none of the choices.

___ **8.** Simplex Corporation terminates Tom, who sues on the basis of age discrimination. To succeed under the Age Discrimination in Employment Act, Tom must show that at the time of the discharge, he was

   a. forty or older.
   b. forty or younger.
   c. replaced with someone forty or older.
   d. replaced with someone forty or younger.

___ **9.** Heavy Equipment Company requires job applicants to pass certain physical tests. Only a few female applicants can pass the tests, but if they pass, they are hired. To successfully defend against a suit on this basis under Title VII, the employer must show that

   a. any discrimination is not intentional.
   b. being a male is a BFOQ.
   c. passing the tests is a business necessity.
   d. some men cannot pass the tests.

___ **10.** Dex and Erin work for Citycore Promotions Company. Dex is Erin's supervisor. During work, he touches her in ways that she perceives as sexually offensive. She resists the advances. He cuts her pay. Citycore is

   a. liable, because Dex's conduct constituted sexual harassment.
   b. liable, because Erin resisted Dex's advances.
   c. not liable, because Dex's conduct was not job-related.
   d. not liable, because Erin resisted Dex's advances.

SHORT ESSAY QUESTIONS

1. Compare and contrast disparate-treatment discrimination and disparate-impact discrimination, and Title VII's response to each in the context of employment.

2. What does the Americans with Disabilities Act require employers to do?

GamePoints

(Answers at the Back of the Book)

1. You are playing the video game "Discrimination!" in which a player accrues points by correctly spotting, reporting, and resolving instances of discrimination in various workplaces. In one scenario, set in a packing plant owned and operated by Savory Treats, Inc., a gourmet-food packaging and shipping firm, Tanner, the company's owner, tells Vera, its human resources director, not to hire Willis, a disabled applicant. In Tanner's words, "we don't want to make changes to accommodate this guy—it'll give the other employees ideas." Is this discrimination? Why or why not?

2. Sam works as a driver for Toxic Games Warehouse, a wholesale distributor and online retailer of video games and accessories. Over a ten-year period, Sam repeatedly applies for—and is denied—a promotion to the position of dispatcher. Sam meets the requirements for the job, which are a year's driving experience and a specific license. After one interview, Sam overhears the interviewer tell a co-worker that Sam, who is white, didn't get the job because "whites are lazy." Is this employment discrimination? Explain.

Chapter 23
Immigration and Labor Law

WHAT THIS CHAPTER IS ABOUT

This chapter reviews the federal law governing immigration and labor. With respect to labor law, the chapter covers the legal recognition of the right to form unions, the process of unionizing a company, the process of collective bargaining, and labor practices considered fair and unfair under federal law.

CHAPTER OUTLINE

I. **IMMIGRATION LAW**
   Federal law sets standards for legal immigration, including preferences for persons with certain skills, and imposes sanctions on employers who hire illegal immigrants.

   A. **THE IMMIGRATION REFORM AND CONTROL ACT (IRCA) OF 1986**
      It is illegal to hire, recruit, or refer for a fee for work in the United States a person who is not authorized to work here.

      1. **I-9 Employment Verification**
         The U.S. Citizenship and Immigration Services (CIS)—part of the U.S. Department of Homeland Security—supplies Form I-9, Employment Eligibility Verification, which an employer must complete within three days of each employee's hiring. Most legal actions are against employees who claim falsely to be eligible to work or provide false documentation. The IRCA prohibits "knowing" and "should have known" violations.

      2. **Enforcement**
         U.S. Immigration and Customs Enforcement (ICE) officers conduct random audits and act on written complaints that allege an employer's violation. A subpoena or warrant is not required. Sanctions include the discharge, detention, and deportation of illegal workers.

         a. **Administrative Actions**
            A determination of a violation is subject to administrative review at an employer's request. Defenses include good faith and substantial compliance with documentation requirements.

         b. **Criminal Actions**
            Charges include harboring an illegal immigrant and inducing illegal immigration. A private individual who claims injury as a result of illegal hiring may sue a convicted employer under the Racketeer Influenced and Corrupt Organizations (RICO) Act. Defenses to criminal charges include—

            1) Good faith reliance on reasonably genuine-appearing documents.
            2) Substantial compliance with documentation requirements
            3) A worker is an independent contractor not subject to verification requirements.

      3. **Penalties**
         These include civil fines of up to $11,000 for each unauthorized employee and criminal penalties of increased fines and imprisonment. An employer may be barred from future government contracts. The penalties are affected by the size of an employer's business, his or her cooperation with authorities, the seriousness of the violations, and previous transgressions.

201

4. Anti-Discrimination Provisions
An employer must evaluate applicants and employees, and their documents, in a fair and consistent manner. For example, greater proof cannot be asked of some individuals and not others. The federal Office of Special Counsel for Immigration Related Unfair Employment Practices can investigate and file a discrimination complaint. Private individuals may also file complaints. Standards and procedures parallel Title VII of the Civil Rights Act of 1964.

B. THE IMMIGRATION ACT
Persons who immigrate to the United States to work include those with special skills, or "extraordinary ability." To hire such individuals, an employer must petition the CIS. An immigrant employee's ability to stay in the United States and to switch jobs here is limited.

1. I-551 Alien Registration Receipts
An employer may hire a "self-authorized" noncitizen who (a) is a lawful permanent resident (as proved by an I-551 Alien Registration Receipt, or "green card") or (b) has a temporary Employment Authorization Document. To obtain a "green card" for an immigrant, an employer must show that no U.S. worker is qualified, willing, and able to take the job (which must be permanent and full-time).

2. The H-1B Visa Program
A sponsoring employer may obtain a visa for a person to work in the United States for three to six years in a "specialty occupation" that requires highly specialized knowledge and a college degree. The annual quota for this program is filled quickly each year.

3. Labor Certification
Before submitting an H-1B application, an employer must obtain a Labor Certification form from the U.S. Department of Labor. To obtain the form, the employer must agree to pay a competitive wage and attest that the hiring will not adversely affect other similarly employed workers. The form must be posted. An application may be rejected for omissions or inaccuracy.

4. H-2, O, L, and E Visas
Temporary nonimmigrant visas are also available for agricultural seasonal workers, a company's managers and executives, certain investors and entrepreneurs, and performers, athletes, and other "acclaimed" individuals.

II.   FEDERAL LABOR LAWS
All employers whose businesses involve or affect interstate commerce are subject to these laws. Agricultural workers and domestic servants are excluded.

A. NORRIS-LaGUARDIA ACT OF 1932
This law restricts federal courts' power to issue injunctions against unions engaged in peaceful strikes, picketing, and boycotts.

B. NATIONAL LABOR RELATIONS ACT (NLRA) OF 1935
The NLRA established the right of employees to bargain collectively and to strike, and—

1. Unfair Employer Practices
Prohibits interfering with union activities, discriminating against union employees, refusing to bargain with union, other practices.

2. National Labor Relations Board (NLRB)
Created to oversee union elections, prevent employers from engaging in unfair practices, investigate employers in response to employee charges of unfair labor practices, issue cease-and-desist orders.

3. Workers Protected by the NLRA
Protected employees include job applicants, including those paid by a union to unionize the employer's work force.

C. LABOR-MANAGEMENT RELATIONS ACT (LMRA) OF 1947

Prohibits unions from refusing to bargain with employers, engaging in certain types of picketing, featherbedding, and other unfair union practices. Expressly preserves union shops, but allows states to pass right-to-work laws, which make it illegal to require union membership for employment.

D. LABOR-MANAGEMENT REPORTING AND DISCLOSURE ACT (LMRDA) OF 1959

1. Union Business

Requires elections of union officers under secret ballot; prohibits ex-convicts and Communists from holding union office; makes officials accountable for union property; allows members to participate in union meetings, nominate officers, vote in proceedings.

2. Hot-Cargo Agreements

Outlaws hot-cargo agreements (or secondary boycotts, in which employers agree not to handle, use, or deal in non-union goods of other employers).

E. COVERAGE AND PROCEDURES

1. Employers and Employees

Covered are all employers whose business activity affects or involves interstate commerce. Some workers are specifically excluded. Railroad and airline employees fall under the Railway Labor Act, which resembles the National Labor Relations Act. Agricultural and domestic workers are excluded from labor laws altogether.

2. Complaint Process

An employee who believes that an employer has committed an unfair labor practice can file a form with the local NLRB office. The charge will be investigated, and there may be an administrative hearing, with an order, which may be appealed to a federal appellate court.

III. THE DECISION TO FORM OR TO SELECT A UNION

A. PRELIMINARY ORGANIZING

1. Workers Sign Authorization Cards

A majority of the relevant workers must sign authorization cards, which state that they want a certain union to represent the workforce.

2. The Employer Is Asked to Recognize the Union

If the employer refuses, unionizers must present authorization cards from at least 30 percent of the workers to the NLRB regional office with a petition for an election.

B. APPROPRIATE BARGAINING UNIT

The NLRB determines this, which requires a mutuality of interest among the workers to be represented. Mutuality of interest requires—

1. Job Similarity

Similar levels of skill, wages, benefits, working conditions.

2. Work-Site Proximity

It may be a problem if the workers are at many different sites.

3. Nonmanagement Employees

Members of management cannot be part of a union.

IV. UNION ELECTION

The NLRB supervises the election. If a majority of workers choose to be represented by a certain union, the NLRB certifies it as their representative. The employees may also call for an election to decertify a union by petitioning the NLRB with 30 percent employee support and no certification in the past year.

A. UNION ELECTION CAMPAIGN
Union representatives may campaign among workers to solicit votes.

1. Employer Limits
Employers may limit the campaign activities of union supporters (such as where on company property and when campaigning may occur).

2. Restrictions on Employer Limits
An employer may prohibit *all* solicitation during work time or in certain places but may not prohibit *only* union solicitation. Workers also have a right to a reasonable opportunity to campaign (nonworking areas on the employer's property during nonworking time).

B. MANAGEMENT ELECTION CAMPAIGN
Management may campaign against a union (or for the union's decertification). Employers may campaign on company property on company time without giving union supporters an opportunity for rebuttal.

1. No Threats
Management may not threaten its employees with reprisals if the union's elected.

2. "Laboratory Conditions"
Management may not offer special benefits for a nonunion vote, undertake certain surveillance of workers or create the impression of observing workers to identify union sympathizers, or question individual workers about their position on unionization. If the employer issued threats or engaged in other unfair labor practices, the NLRB may certify the union even if it loses the election.

V.   COLLECTIVE BARGAINING
The central legal right of a union is to engage in collective bargaining on the members' behalf. In collective bargaining, as in most business negotiations, each side uses its economic power to pressure or persuade the other side to grant concessions.

A. SUBJECTS OF BARGAINING

1. Terms and Conditions of Employment
Employers may bargain with workers over wages, hours of work, and other terms and conditions of employment—safety rules, insurance coverage, pension and other benefit plans, discipline procedures, grievance procedures, and the price of food in the company cafeteria.

2. Closing or Relocating a Plant
Employers need not bargain over economic issues within their business discretion (such as plant closure), although they may choose to do so to obtain concessions, and they must bargain over the economic consequences of such decisions. Also, if relocation does not involve a basic change in the nature of an operation, management must bargain over the decision unless—

a. The work performed at the new plant is significantly different from the work at the old plant.
b. The work performed at the old plant is to be discontinued and not moved to the new plant.
c. The move involves a change in the scope and direction of the enterprise.
d. Labor costs were not a factor in the decision, or if they were, the union could not have offered concessions that would have changed the decision to relocate.

B. GOOD FAITH BARGAINING
Parties must bargain in good faith. Refusing to do so is an unfair labor practice. The NLRB may order a party to bargain in good faith and may require one party to reimburse the other for any related litigation expenses. Examples of bad faith include—

1. Excessive delaying tactics.
2. Insistence on obviously unreasonable contract terms.

3. Making a single take-it-or-leave-it offer and refusing modifications.
4. Engaging in a campaign to undermine the union.
5. Constantly shifting positions on disputed terms.
6. Sending representatives who lack authority to commit to a contract.

VI. STRIKES AND LOCKOUTS

When bargaining reaches an impasse, the union may call a strike to pressure the employer to make concessions.

A. WHAT A STRIKE IS

In a strike, the workers refuse to work and may picket their employer. Workers then lose the right to get paid, and management loses production and possibly customers. A strike may result from unfair labor practices or economic disagreements—mostly because the union wants a better contract.

B. THE RIGHT TO STRIKE

The NLRA guarantees the right to strike, within limits. The First Amendment protects strike activities, such as picketing. Nonworkers have a right to participate. Workers can refuse to cross a picket line.

C. ILLEGAL STRIKES

Illegal strikes include violent (or threatened violent) strikes, massed picketing, strikers barring nonunion workers access to a work site, sit-down strikes, and—

1. Secondary Boycotts

Picketing cannot be directed against a secondary employer, but common situs picketing (at a site occupied by both primary and secondary employers) is permitted.

2. Hot-Cargo Agreements

Employers cannot agree with unions not to handle, use, or deal in non-union-produced goods of other employers. Consumer boycotts of primary and secondary employers are legal.

3. Wildcat Strikes

Employees cannot call a strike without the authorization of the certified union.

4. Strikes That Threaten National Health or Safety

These are not illegal, but to encourage a settlement, the president of the United States can obtain an injunction to last for eighty days, while the government works to produce a settlement.

5. Strikes That Contravene No-strike Clauses

A strike that contravenes a collective bargaining agreement's no-strike clause may be enjoined.

D. REPLACEMENT WORKERS

An employer may hire workers to replace strikers permanently and may use an employment agency to recruit them.

E. THE RIGHTS OF STRIKERS AFTER A STRIKE

1. Economic Strikes over Working Conditions

Strikers have no right to return to their jobs, but must be given preference to any vacancies and also retain their seniority rights.

2. Employer Unfair Labor Practice Strikes

Strikers must be given their jobs back.

F. LOCKOUTS

An employer can shut down to prevent employees from working, but may not use a lockout to break a union and pressure employees into decertification. There must be an economic justification for a lockout.

VII.   UNFAIR LABOR PRACTICES

A.   EMPLOYER'S UNFAIR PRACTICES

1.   Refusal to Recognize Union and Negotiate

For one year after certification, it is presumed that the union enjoys majority support; after this period, the presumption is can be rebutted. With evidence to support a good faith belief that union has no majority support, an employer can refuse to recognize the union.

2.   Interference in Union Activities

An employer may not interfere with, restrain, or coerce employees in the exercise of their rights to form a union and bargain collectively.

3.   Domination of Unions

The NLRA forbids company unions and other forms of employer domination of workers' unions.

4.   Discrimination against Union Employees

Employers cannot discriminate against union workers (in layoffs, hiring, or closing a plant).

B.   UNION'S UNFAIR PRACTICES

1.   Secondary Boycotts

2.   Discriminating against Nonunion Workers

A union cannot threaten employees with violence, use economic coercion, picket, or otherwise discriminate (or influence employers to discriminate) against workers who refuse to join a union.

3.   Demanding the Hiring of Unnecessary Workers

4.   Picketing to Coerce Unionization without Majority Support

5.   Refusing to Bargain in Good Faith with Employer

6.   Imposing Excessive Fees or Dues

A nonunion employee subject to a union shop clause who must pay dues cannot be required to contribute to causes or to lobby politicians.

VIII.   RIGHTS OF NONUNION EMPLOYEES

A.   CONCERTED ACTIVITY

This activity must be for employees' mutual aid regarding wages, hours, or terms and conditions of employment. A single employee's action may be protected if it is taken for the benefit of other employees and the employee discussed it with other approving workers.

B.   SAFETY

An employee can walk off the job if he or she has a good faith belief that working conditions are abnormally dangerous.

TRUE-FALSE QUESTIONS

(Answers at the Back of the Book)

____   **1.**   Employers can agree with unions not to handle, use, or deal in non-union-produced goods.

____   **2.**   Management serves as the representative of workers in bargaining with a union.

____   **3.**   An employer must consider all job applicants—citizen and noncitizen—in deciding whom to hire.

____ 4. Employees have no right to engage in collective bargaining through elected representatives.

____ 5. Similarity of workers' jobs is a factor in determining which workers are to be represented by a union.

____ 6. Supervisors and managers cannot be members of a union.

____ 7. An employer cannot consider union participation as a criterion for deciding which workers to hire.

____ 8. An employer can use a lockout to break a union and pressure employees into decertifying it.

____ 9. An individual who claims injury as a result of an employer's illegal hiring of noncitizens has no recourse.

____ 10. An immigrant employee's ability to stay in the United States and to switch jobs here is limited.

FILL-IN QUESTIONS

(Answers at the Back of the Book)

Peaceful strikes, picketing, and boycotts are protected under the _____ (National Labor Relations/Norris-LaGuardia) Act, which also restricts federal courts in enjoining unions engaged in peaceful strikes. Employees' rights to organize, to engage in collective bargaining through elected representatives, and to engage in concerted activities for those and other purposes were established in the _____ (National Labor Relations/Norris-LaGuardia) Act. Requiring union membership as a condition of employment is prohibited by the Labor-Management _____ (Relations/Reporting and Disclosure) Act. This act also _____ (allows/prohibits) requiring workers to join the union after a certain time on the job. This act also _____ (allows/prohibits) laws making it illegal to require union membership for continued employment.

MULTIPLE-CHOICE QUESTIONS

(Answers at the Back of the Book)

____ 1. Steel Worx, Inc., refuses to pay its workers for time spent on union activities. This violates

   a. the Labor-Management Relations Act.
   b. the National Labor Relations Act.
   c. the Norris-LaGuardia Act.
   d. no federal labor law.

____ 2. Mosul, Natomi, and Omar apply to work for Precision Engineering, Inc. These individuals' identities and eligibility to work must be verified by

   a. the employer.
   b. the individuals.
   c. the individuals' country of origin.
   d. the U.S. Citizenship and Immigration Services.

____ 3. Delta Aircraft Company, a U.S. employer, may hire Ewan, a noncitizen, if Ewan is

   a. a lawful permanent resident of the United States.
   b. an unlawful but currently employed visitor to the United States.
   c. an unlawful but only temporary and unemployed resident in the United States.
   d. all of the choices.

____ **4.** Assembly Workers of America (AWA) represents employees of Biggie Motors Company. During collective bargaining, AWA wants to negotiate changes to Biggie's health insurance plan and safety rules. Biggie can refuse to bargain over changes to

   a. the plan only.
   b. the rules only.
   c. the plan and the rules.
   d. neither the plan nor the rules.

____ **5.** Federated Union Workers (FUW) represents employees of Gold Refining Company. During collective bargaining, FUW wants to negotiate to the closure of a Gold plant and the procedure for employee grievances. Gold can refuse to negotiate over

   a. the closure only.
   b. the procedure only.
   c. the closure and the procedure.
   d. neither the closure nor the procedure.

____ **6.** The employees of Tristate Industries, Inc. (TII), designate United Machinists Union (UMU) as their bargaining representative. TII refuses to bargain with UMU and fires several workers for "choosing the wrong side." This violates

   a. the Labor-Management Relations Act.
   b. the National Labor Relations Act.
   c. the Norris-LaGuardia Act.
   d. no federal labor law.

____ **7.** During a union election campaign, E.L. Electric Company asks its employees to openly declare their views on the union, so that "everyone knows where everyone stands." This is an unfair labor practice

   a. only if it is a condition of continued employment.
   b. only if the employees do not want to do it.
   c. under any circumstances.
   d. under no circumstances.

____ **8.** Omega Oil Refining Corporation wants to hire Parfez, who has certain special skills to fill a technical position. To hire Parfez, Omega must petition

   a. CIS.
   b. H1-B.
   c. ICE.
   d. RICO.

____ **9.** During a union election campaign at Wayward Shipping Corporation, Wayward may *not*

   a. designate where and when campaigning may occur.
   b. prohibit all solicitation during work time.
   c. promise to hire more workers if the union loses the election.
   d. threaten employees with the loss of their jobs if the union wins the election.

____ **10.** National Workers Union (NWU) represents the employees of Office Supplies Company, Inc. NWU calls an economic strike, and Office hires replacement workers. After the strike, the replacement workers

   a. must be retained and the former strikers must be rehired.
   b. must be terminated and the former strikers must be rehired.
   c. must be terminated whether or not the former strikers are rehired.
   d. may be retained or terminated whether or not the former strikers are rehired.

SHORT ESSAY QUESTIONS

1. What are the four basic federal labor laws and what do they provide?

2. Which types of strikes are illegal?

GAMEPOINTS

(Answers at the Back of the Book)

1. In the video game "Malice at the Palace," your avatar works as an operative for Palace Packaged Foods, Inc., a producer and purveyor of frozen organic delights. Palace employs temporary workers by the hundreds during winter and spring holiday seasons. Occasionally, a position opens for an individual with highly specialized skills, particularly to operate and maintain the company's inventory and sales control systems. Palace's president Pearson Periwinkle asks you whether the company can hire noncitizens to fill the temporary or special skills positions. If so, Periwinkle wants to know the procedures to follow to fill them. If not, he wants to be assured that the company hires only citizens. What do you say?

2. Still playing "Malice at the Palace," your avatar is asked by Periwinkle about a unionization situation. Danica is a Palace line supervisor. Among the line workers that Danica supervises are her daughter and son-in-law. Danica's relatives and other line workers designate the Packaged Foods Workers Union as their bargaining representative. Danica is not involved. Periwinkle wants to take steps to oppose the union. What can he do to thwart the unionization of Palace's employees? Can he legally fire Danica for the actions of her relatives and threaten the others with discharge?

CUMULATIVE HYPOTHETICAL PROBLEM
FOR UNIT FIVE—INCLUDING CHAPTERS 20–23

(Answers at the Back of the Book)

Dot, Earl, Frank, Gail, Hal, Ira, Jane, Karen, Larry, and Mike work for International Sales Corporation (ISC).

_____ **1.** Dot, who works in ISC's warehouse, is injured on the job. Dot may NOT collect workers' compensation benefits if she

    a. files a civil suit against a third party based on the injury.
    b. intentionally caused her own injury.
    c. was injured as a result of a co-worker's act.
    d. worked for ISC for less than sixty days.

_____ **2.** Earl retires from ISC at the age of sixty-five. Frank retires at sixty-seven. Because of a disability, Gail, after fifteen years, is unable to continue working for ISC. Hal is discharged from ISC as part of a reduction in force. All of the following benefits are part of Social Security EXCEPT

    a. Earl's government retirement payments.
    b. Frank's Medicare payments.
    c. Gail's government disability payments.
    d. Hal's unemployment benefits.

_____ **3.** Ira works for ISC as a sales representative at a salary of $3,000 per month, plus a 10 percent commission. As ISC's agent, Ira

    a. cannot be dismissed during the six-month period without cause.
    b. cannot enforce the agency unless it is in writing and signed by Delta.
    c. is an agent coupled with an interest.
    d. must act solely in Delta's interest in matters concerning Delta's business.

____ **4.** Four employees file suits against ISC, alleging discrimination. Title VII of the Civil Rights Act of 1964 covers all of the following EXCEPT Jane's suit alleging discrimination on the basis of

a. age.
b. gender.
c. race.
d. religion.

____ **5.** Karen, an ISC manager, wants to institute a policy of mandatory retirement for all employees at age sixty-four. Larry, an ISC manager, wants to discharge Mike, who is age sixty-seven, for cause. Under federal anti-discrimination law

a. only Karen's wish can be granted.
b. only Larry's wish can be granted.
c. both Karen's and Larry's wishes can be granted.
d. none of the above.

QUESTIONS ON THE FOCUS ON ETHICS FOR UNIT FIVE— THE EMPLOYMENT ENVIRONMENT

(Answers at the Back of the Book)

____ **1.** Evon is Frasier's agent. Ethics would prevent Evon from

a. being loyal to Frasier.
b. disclosing Evon's interest in property being bought by Frasier.
c. profiting from the agency relation with Frasier's consent
d. representing Gertruda in a transaction with Frasier.

____ **2.** Harry is Irma's agent. Ethics might prescribe otherwise, but Harry's legal duties to Irma do *not* include

a. compensation.
b. cooperation.
c. loyalty.
d. reimbursement.

____ **3.** Dave works for Executive Sales Corporation. Reasons for holding Executive liable under the doctrine of *respondeat superior* for Dave's tort injuring Flo do not include the employer's

a. ability to afford Flo more effective relief.
b. ability to pay for Flo's injury.
c. control over Dave.
d. guilt or innocence.

Chapter 24
Consumer Protection

WHAT THIS CHAPTER IS ABOUT

Federal and state laws protect consumers from unfair trade practices, unsafe products, discriminatory or unreasonable credit requirements, and other problems related to consumer transactions. This chapter focuses on *federal* consumer law.

CHAPTER OUTLINE

I. DECEPTIVE ADVERTISING

The Federal Trade Commission Act of 1914 created the Federal Trade Commission (FTC) to prevent unfair and deceptive trade practices. *Deceptive advertising* is advertising that would mislead a consumer—scientifically untrue claims and misleading half-truths, for example. Puffing (vague generalities, obvious exaggeration) is not deceptive.

A. BAIT-AND-SWITCH ADVERTISING
This occurs when a seller refuses to show an advertised item, fails to have adequate quantities on hand, fails to promise to deliver within a reasonable time, or discourages employees from selling the item. The FTC has issued rules to prevent this practice.

B. ONLINE DECEPTIVE ADVERTISING
The same laws that apply to other forms of advertising apply to online ads, under FTC guidelines—

1. Ads must be truthful and no misleading.
2. Any claims in an ad must be substantiated.
3. Ads cannot be unfair (likely to cause substantial, reasonably unavoidable consumer injury not outweighed by any benefit to the consumer or competition).
4. Disclosure of qualifying or limiting information must be "clear and conspicuous." Burying this information on an internal Web page is not recommended except in certain circumstances.

C. FTC ACTIONS AGAINST DECEPTIVE ADVERTISING

1. **The Complaint Order**
An FTC action against those who are accused of deceptive advertising begins with an investigation, often after a consumer complaint. The investigation may lead to a formal complaint. If the alleged offender does not agree to settle, a hearing is held before an administrative law judge.

2. **The Cease-and-Desist Order**
A cease-and-desist order or an order that requires counteradvertising may be issued. FTC orders may be appealed, but courts generally defer to the FTC's judgment.

D. TELEMARKETING AND FAX ADVERTISING

1. **Telephone Consumer Protection Act (TCPA) of 1991**
The TCPA prohibits (1) phone solicitation using an automatic dialing system or a prerecorded voice and (2) transmission of ads via fax without the recipient's permission. The Federal

211

Communications Commission can impose fines of up to $11,000 per day for junk fax violations. Consumers can recover actual losses or $500, whichever is greater, for each violation. If a defendant willfully or knowingly violated the act, a court can award treble damages.

2. Telemarketing and Consumer Fraud and Abuse Prevention Act of 1994
This act authorized the FTC to set rules for telemarketing and bring actions against fraudulent telemarketers. The FTC's Telemarketing Sales Rule of 1995 makes it illegal to misrepresent information and requires disclosure. The FTC also set up the national Do Not Call Registry.

II. LABELING AND PACKAGING

A. FEDERAL STATUTES
Federal statutes included the Fur Products Labeling Act of 1951, the Wool Products Labeling Act of 1939, the Flammable Fabrics Act of 1953, the Comprehensive Smokeless Tobacco Health Education Act of 1986, and the Energy Policy and Conservation Act of 1975.

B. FAIR PACKAGING AND LABELING ACT OF 1966
This act requires that product labels identify (1) the product, (2) the net quantity of contents; and the size of a serving if the number of servings is stated, (3) the manufacturer, and (4) the packager or distributor. The U.S. Food and Drug Administration and the U.S. Department of Agriculture are the chief agencies that issue regulations on food labeling.

III. SALES
Federal agencies that regulate sales include the FTC and the Federal Reserve Board of Governors (Regulation Z governs credit provisions in sales contracts)..

A. COOLING-OFF LAWS
Some states' "cooling-off" laws permit a buyer to rescind a door-to-door purchase within a certain time. The FTC has a three-day period. Other state laws, including the Uniform Commercial Code's warranty sections, also apply.

B. TELEPHONE AND MAIL-ORDER SALES

1. FTC "Mail or Telephone Order Merchandise Rule" of 1993
For goods bought via phone lines or through the mail, merchants must ship orders within the time promised in their ads, notify consumers when orders cannot be shipped on time, and issue a refund within a specified time if a consumer cancels an order.

2. Postal Reorganization Act of 1970
Unsolicited merchandise sent by the mail may be retained, used, discarded, or disposed of, without obligation to the sender.

C. ONLINE SALES
The same federal and state laws that apply to other media generally protect consumers online.

IV. CREDIT PROTECTION

A. TRUTH-IN-LENDING ACT (TILA) OF 1968
The TILA, administered by the Federal Reserve Board, requires the disclosure of credit terms.

1. Who Is Subject to the TILA?
Creditors who, in the ordinary course of business, lend money or sell goods on credit to consumers, or arrange for credit for consumers, are subject to the TILA.

2. **Disclosure Requirements**

Under Regulation Z, in any transaction involving a sales contract in which payment is to be made in more than four installments, a lender must disclose all the credit terms clearly and conspicuously.

3. **Equal Credit Opportunity Act of 1974**

This act prohibits (1) denial of credit on the basis of race, religion, national origin, color, sex, marital status, age and (2) credit discrimination based on whether an individual receives certain forms of income.

4. **Credit-Card Protection**

Liability of a cardholder is $50 per card for unauthorized charges made before the issuer is notified the card is lost. An issuer cannot bill for unauthorized charges if a card was improperly issued. To withhold payment for a faulty product, a cardholder must use specific procedures. Other rules—

   a. Protect consumers from retroactive increases in interest rates on existing balances unless an account is sixty days delinquent.
   b. Require forty-five days advance notice to consumers before changing credit terms.
   c. Require monthly bills to be sent twenty-one days before their due date.
   d. Limit interest-rate increases to specific situations.
   e. Prohibit over-limit fees except in specific situations.
   f. Require the application of payments for more than the minimum amount due to the highest-interest balances (such as cash advances).
   g. Prevent computing finance charges based on the previous billing cycle.

5. **Consumer Leasing Act of 1988**

Those who lease consumer goods in the ordinary course of their business, if the goods are priced at $25,000 or less and the lease term exceeds four months, must disclose all material terms in writing.

B. **FAIR CREDIT REPORTING ACT (FCRA) OF 1970**

1. **What the FCRA Provides**

Consumer credit reporting agencies may issue credit reports only for certain purposes (extension of credit, etc.); a consumer who is denied credit, or is charged more than others would be, on the basis of a report must be notified of the fact and of the agency that issued the report, and be allowed to correct any misinformation.

2. **Consumers Can Have Inaccurate Information Deleted**

If a consumer discovers that the report contains inaccurate information, the agency must delete it within a reasonable period of time.

3. **Remedies for Violations**

A credit agency may be liable for actual damages and additional damages up to $1,000, plus attorneys' fees. Creditors and others, including insurance companies, that use credit information may also be liable.

C. **FAIR AND ACCURATE CREDIT TRANSACTIONS ACT (FACT ACT) OF 2003**

The FACT Act established a national "fraud alert" system so that consumers who suspect ID theft can place an alert on their credit files. Also—

1. **Credit-Reporting Agencies' Responsibilities**

Consumer credit-reporting agencies must provide consumers with free copies of their reports and stop reporting allegedly fraudulent information once a consumer shows that ID theft occurred.

2. Other Businesses' Responsibilities

Businesses must include shortened ("truncated") account numbers on credit card receipts and provide consumers with copies of records to help prove an account or transaction was fraudulent.

D. FAIR DEBT COLLECTION PRACTICES ACT (FDCPA) OF 1977

The FDCPA applies only to debt-collection agencies that, usually for a percentage of the amount owed, attempt to collect debts on behalf of someone else.

1. What the FDCPA Prohibits

a. Contacting the debtor at the debtor's place of employment if the employer objects.
b. Contacting the debtor during inconvenient times or at any time if an attorney represents the debtor.
c. Contacting third parties other than the debtor's parents, spouse, or financial advisor about payment unless a court agrees.
d. Using harassment, or false and misleading information.
e. Contacting the debtor any time after the debtor refuses to pay the debt, except to advise the debtor of further action to be taken.

2. Notification and Bona Fide Errors

Collection agencies must give a debtor a validation notice that states he or she has thirty days to dispute the debt and request written verification of it. Debt collectors are not liable if they can show that a violation was unintentional and the result of a "bona fide error" despite following procedures designed to avoid such errors.

3. Remedies

A debt collector may be liable for actual damages, plus additional damages not to exceed $1,000 and attorneys' fees.

E. GARNISHMENT OF WAGES

To collect a debt, a creditor may use garnishment, which involves attaching a debtor's assets that are in the possession of a third party (employer, bank). The debtor must be notified and have an opportunity to respond. The amount that may be garnished is limited.

V. CONSUMER HEALTH AND SAFETY

A. FOOD AND DRUGS

The Federal Food, Drug, and Cosmetic Act (FFDCA) of 1938 sets food standards, levels of additives, classifications of food and food ads; regulates medical devices. Drugs must be shown to be effective and safe. Enforced by the Food and Drug Administration (FDA).

B. CONSUMER PRODUCT SAFETY

The Consumer Product Safety Act of 1972 requires manufacturers to report on any products already sold or intended for sale if the products have proved to be hazardous. The act includes a scheme for the regulation of products and safety by the Consumer Product Safety Commission (CPSC). The CPSC—

1. Conducts research on product safety.
2. Maintains a clearinghouse on the risks associated with some products.
3. Sets standards for consumer products.
4. Bans the manufacture or importation and sale of products that are potentially hazardous to consumers.
5. Removes from the market any products imminently hazardous.
6. Requires manufacturers to report on any products already sold or intended for sale if the products have proved to be hazardous.
7. Administers other product safety legislation.

TRUE-FALSE QUESTIONS
(Answers at the Back of the Book)

____ 1. Advertising will be deemed deceptive if a consumer would be misled by the advertising claim.

____ 2. Labels must be accurate.

____ 3. A consumer cannot rescind a contract freely entered into.

____ 4. The TILA applies to creditors who, in the ordinary course of business, sell goods on credit to consumers.

____ 5. A consumer can include a note in his or her credit file to explain any misinformation in the file, but the misinformation cannot be deleted.

____ 6. The same laws that apply to other media generally protect consumers online.

____ 7. The Fair Debt Collection Practices Act applies to anyone who attempts to collect a debt.

____ 8. There are no federal agencies that regulate sales.

____ 9. One who leases consumer goods in the ordinary course of business does not have to disclose any material terms in writing.

____ 10. An advertiser cannot fax ads to consumers without their permission.

FILL-IN QUESTIONS
(Answers at the Back of the Book)

The Truth-in-Lending Act contains provisions regarding credit cards. One provision limits the liability of the cardholder to _____ ($50/$500) per card for unauthorized charges made _____ (after/before) the credit card issuer is notified that the card has been lost. Another provision _____ (allows/prohibits) a credit card company _____ (from billing/to bill) a consumer for any unauthorized charges _____ (unless/if) the credit card was improperly issued by the company.

MULTIPLE-CHOICE QUESTIONS
(Answers at the Back of the Book)

____ 1. Ed takes out a student loan from First National Bank. After graduation, Ed goes to work, but he does not make payments on the loan. The bank agrees with Good Collection Agency (GCA) that if GCA collects the debt, it can keep a percentage of the amount. To collect the debt, GCA can contact

a. Ed at his place of employment, even if his employer objects.
b. Ed at unusual or inconvenient times or any time if he retains an attorney.
c. Ed only to advise him of further action that GCA will take.
d. third parties, including Ed's parents, unless ordered otherwise by a court.

____   2. Tasty Treat Company advertises that its cereal, "Fiber Rich," reduces cholesterol. After an investigation and a hearing, the FTC finds no evidence to support the claim. To correct the public's impression of Fiber Rich, the most appropriate action would be

    a. a cease-and-desist order.
    b. a civil fine.
    c. a criminal fine.
    d. counteradvertising.

____   3. Snarky Bling Corporation sells consumer products. Generally, the labels must use words as they are

    a. normally used in the scientific community.
    b. ordinarily understood by consumers.
    c. reasonably approved by ABC's officers.
    d. typically explained by the marketing department.

____   4. Nick comes to Maria's home and, after a long presentation, sells her a vacuum cleaner. Maria has

    a. no right to rescind this transaction.
    b. three days to exercise any "lowest" price guaranty.
    c. three days to rescind this transaction.
    d. three days to substitute a neighbor as the customer in this transaction.

____   5. The ordinary business of Homeowner Credit Company is to lend money to consumers. Homeowner must disclose all credit terms clearly and conspicuously in

    a. all credit transactions.
    b. any credit transaction in which payments are to be made in more than four installments.
    c. any credit transaction in which payments are to be made in more than one installment.
    d. no credit transaction.

____   6. Eve borrows money to buy a car and to pay for repairs to the roof of her house. She also buys furniture in a transaction financed by the seller whom she will repay in installments. If all of the parties are subject to the Truth-in-Lending Act, Regulation Z applies to

    a. the car loan only.
    b. the home improvement loan only.
    c. the retail installment sale only.
    d. the car loan, the home improvement loan, and the retail installment sale.

____   7. Krunchies, Inc., sells snack foods. Krunchies must include on the packages

    a. no nutrition information.
    b. the identity of the product only.
    c. the identity of the product, the net quantity of the contents, and the number of servings.
    d. the net quantity of the contents and the number of servings only.

____   8. US Tobacco Corporation (USTC) sells tobacco products. On the packages of its *smokeless* tobacco products, USTC must include warnings about health hazards associated with

    a. cigarettes.
    b. smokeless products.
    c. tobacco products generally.
    d. none of the choices.

___ 9. Slick Toy Company begins marketing a new toy that is highly flammable. The Consumer Product Safety Commission may

    a. ban the toy's future manufacture and sale, and order that the toy be removed from the market.
    b. ban the toy's future manufacture and sale only.
    c. do nothing until there is an injury or damage on which to base an action.
    d. order that the toy be removed from the market only.

___ 10. Jada receives an unsolicited credit card in the mail and tosses it on her desk. Without Jada's permission, her roommate Loni uses the card to buy new clothes for $1,000. Jada is liable for

    a. $1,000.
    b. $500.
    c. $50.
    d. $0.

SHORT ESSAY QUESTIONS

1. What are some of the more common deceptive advertising techniques and the ways in which the FTC may deal with such conduct?

2. What are the primary provisions of the Truth-In-Lending Act?

GAMEPOINTS

(Answers at the Back of the Book)

1. You are an extraordinarily successful video game designer with six multi-million sellers, including "Fireball" and its sequels "Infernal Inferno" and "Flaming Skull." You visit your local Car Sales Showroom and choose a couple of rides. To pay for the vehicles and their customizing, you contact Gamesters Credit Union. In the course of the loan transaction, the Gamester's representative tells you the interest rate but not all of the lender's terms because "it would take too long." Does this comply with the law?

2. To increase the sales of your most recent video game release and profit from related merchandise, you begin your "Life Is Hot" North American tour of video game outlets and competitive venues. In your contract with Midwest Promotions, Inc., covering twenty-two dates, you demand a buffet of specific foods to be available at each location. What is the general legal standard with respect to food? Which federal agencies monitor and enforce statutes involving food?

Chapter 25
Environmental Law

WHAT THIS CHAPTER IS ABOUT

This chapter covers environmental law, which is the law that relates to environmental protection—common law actions and federal statutes and regulations.

CHAPTER OUTLINE

I. **COMMON LAW ACTIONS**

    A. **NUISANCE**
    Persons cannot use their property in a way that unreasonably interferes with others' rights to use or enjoy their own property. An injured party may be awarded damages or an injunction.

        1. **Private Nuisance**
        A private nuisance occurs when an individual suffers distinct harm separate from that affecting the general public. Some states require this for an individual plaintiff.

        2. **Public Nuisance**
        A public authority can maintain an action to stop a public nuisance.

    B. **NEGLIGENCE AND STRICT LIABILITY**
    A business that fails to use reasonable care may be liable to a party whose injury was foreseeable. Businesses that engage in ultrahazardous activities are strictly liable for whatever injuries the activities cause.

II. **FEDERAL, STATE, AND LOCAL REGULATION**

    A. **STATE AND LOCAL REGULATIONS**
    States regulate the environment through zoning or more direct regulation. City, county, and other local governments control some aspects through zoning laws, waste removal and disposal regulations, aesthetic ordinances, and so on.

    B. **FEDERAL REGULATION**

        1. **Environmental Regulatory Agencies**
        The Environmental Protection Agency (EPA) coordinates federal environmental responsibilities and administers most federal environmental policies and statutes. State and local agencies implement environmental statutes and regulations. Citizens can sue to enforce the regulations.

        2. **Environmental Impact Statements**
        The National Environmental Policy Act (NEPA) of 1969 requires all federal agencies to consider environmental factors in making significant decisions.

            a. **When an Environmental Impact Statement Must Be Prepared**
            Whenever a major federal action significantly affects the quality of the environment. An action qualifies as *major* if it involves a substantial commitment of resources (monetary or otherwise). An action is *federal* if a federal agency has the power to control it.

219

      b. What an EIS Must Analyze
      (1) The impact on the environment that the action will have, (2) any adverse effects to the environment and alternative actions that might be taken, and (3) irreversible effects the action might generate.

      c. When an Agency Decides That an EIS Is Unnecessary
      It must issue a statement supporting this conclusion.

III. AIR POLLUTION
The Clean Air Act of 1963 (and amendments) is the basis for regulation.

A. MOBILE SOURCES
Regulations governing air pollution from automobiles and other mobile sources specify standards and time schedules. For example, under the 1990 amendments to the Clean Air Act—

1. New Automobiles' Exhaust
Manufacturers had to cut emission of nitrogen oxide by 60 percent and emission of other pollutants by 35 percent. Other sets of emission controls became effective in 2004.

2. Sport Utility Vehicles and Light Trucks
These vehicles are now subject to the same standards as cars.

3. New Standards
The EPA updates these and other standards when new scientific evidence is available. In 2009, the EPA concluded that greenhouse gases, including carbon dioxide, are a public danger.

B. STATIONARY SOURCES
The primary responsibility for controlling and preventing pollution from stationary sources (such as industrial plants) rests with the states. The EPA sets air quality standards for stationary sources (such as industrial plants), and the states formulate plans to achieve them.

1. Listing of Hazardous Air Pollutants
The focus is on hazardous air pollutants (HAPs), which are likely to cause death or serious illnesses (such as cancer). The EPA lists about 200 HAPs.

2. Air Pollution Control Standards
Different standards apply to sources in clean areas and sources in polluted areas, and to existing sources and major new sources. Performance standards for major sources require the use of maximum achievable control technology (MACT), which is subject to EPA guidelines.

C. PENALTIES
Civil penalties include assessments of up to $25,000 per day, or an amount equal to a violator's economic benefits from noncompliance, plus up to $5,000 per day for other violations. Criminal penalties include fines of up to $1 million and imprisonment of up to two years. Private citizens can also sue.

IV. WATER POLLUTION

A. NAVIGABLE WATERS
The Clean Water Act of 1972 amended the Federal Water Pollution Control Act (FWPCA) of 1948 to provide—

1. Goals
The goals of the statutes are to (1) make waters safe for swimming, (2) protect fish and wildlife, and (3) eliminate the discharge of pollutants into the water.

2. Focus on Point-Source Emissions

Under a National Pollutant Discharge Elimination System (NPDES), a point source of pollution emitted into water must have a permit. Permits can be obtained from the EPA and authorized state agencies and Indian tribes, and must be reissued every five years. The NPDES includes—

a. National effluent standards set by the EPA for each industry.
b. Water-quality standards set by the states under EPA supervision.
c. A discharge-permit program that sets water-quality standards to limit pollution.
d. Provisions for toxic chemicals and oil spills.
e. Construction grants and loans for publicly owned treatment works (chiefly sewage plants).

3. Standards for Equipment

Regulations specify the use of the best available control technology (BACT) for new sources. Existing sources must first install the best practical control technology (BPCT).

4. Wetlands

Wetlands include "those areas that are inundated or saturated by surface or ground water at a frequency and duration sufficient to support, and that under normal circumstances do support, a prevalence off vegetation typically adapted for life in saturated soil conditions."

5. Violations, Penalties, and Remedies

Lying about a discharge is more serious than admitting to an improper discharge. Civil penalties range from $10,000 (up to $25,000 per violation) to $25,000 per day. Criminal penalties (for intentional violations only) include substantial fines and imprisonment. Injunctions, damages, and clean-up costs can be imposed. And citizens can sue.

B. DRINKING WATER

The Safe Drinking Water Act of 1974 requires the EPA to set maximum levels for pollutants in public water systems. Operators must come as close to these as possible using the best available technology. Suppliers must inform the public of the source of the water, the level of contaminants, and possible health concerns.

C. OCEAN DUMPING

The Marine Protection, Research, and Sanctuaries Act of 1972—

1. Radiological Waste and Other Materials

Dumping of radiological, chemical, and biological warfare agents, and high-level radioactive waste is prohibited. Transporting and dumping other materials requires a permit.

2. Penalties

Civil penalties include assessments of not more than $50,000 or revocation or suspension of a permit. Criminal penalties include fines of up to $50,000, imprisonment for not more than a year, or both. Injunctions can be imposed.

D. OIL POLLUTION

The Oil Pollution Act of 1990 provides that any oil facility, shipper, vessel owner, or vessel operator that discharges oil may be liable for clean-up costs, and damages for harm to natural resources, private property, and local economies. Fines of $2 million to $350 million are possible.

V. TOXIC CHEMICALS

A. PESTICIDES AND HERBICIDES

1. Federal Insecticide, Fungicide, and Rodenticide Act (FIFRA) of 1947

a. Registration, Certification, and Use
Products must be (1) registered before they can be sold, (2) certified and used only for approved applications, and (3) used in limited quantities when applied to food crops.

b. Labels
Labels must not be false or misleading. A product cannot be sold with a destroyed or defaced label.

c. Penalties
For producers: suspension or cancellation of registration, up to a $50,000 fine, imprisonment up to one year. For commercial dealers: up to a $25,000 fine, imprisonment up to one year. For farmers and other private users: a $1,000 fine, imprisonment up to thirty days.

2. Acceptable Risks
To remain on the market, a product must have no more than a one-in-a-million risk to people of cancer from exposure, which includes eating food with pesticide residue.

B. TOXIC SUBSTANCES
Under the Toxic Substances Control Act of 1976, for substances that potentially pose an imminent hazard or an unreasonable risk of injury to health or the environment, the EPA may require special labeling, set production quotas, or limit or prohibit the use of a substance.

VI. HAZARDOUS WASTES

A. RESOURCE CONSERVATION AND RECOVERY ACT (RCRA) OF 1976
Under the RCRA, the EPA determines which forms of solid waste are hazardous, and sets requirements for disposal, storage, and treatment. Penalties include up to $25,000 (civil) per violation, $50,000 (criminal) per day, imprisonment up to two years (may be doubled for repeaters).

B. SUPERFUND
The Comprehensive Environmental Response, Compensation, and Liability Act (CERCLA) of 1980 regulates the clean-up of leaking hazardous waste disposal sites.

1. Potentially Responsible Parties
If a release or a threatened release occurs, the EPA can clean up a site and recover the cost from (1) the person who generated the wastes disposed of at the site, (2) the person who transported the wastes to the site, (3) the person who owned or operated the site at the time of the disposal, or (4) the current owner or operator.

2. Joint and Several Liability
One party can be charged with the entire cost (which that party may recover in a contribution action against others).

3. Minimizing Liability
Businesses that conduct self-audits and promptly detect, disclose, and correct wrongdoing are subject to lighter penalties. There may be no fines for small companies that correct violations within 180 days (360 days if pollution-prevention techniques are involved).

4. Defenses to Liability
An innocent property owner may avoid liability by showing the lack of a contractual or employment relation to the party who released the hazardous substance. In effect, this requires a buyer to investigate possible hazards at the time property is bought.

TRUE-FALSE QUESTIONS

(Answers at the Back of the Book)

_____ 1. No common law doctrines apply against polluters today.

_____ 2. Local governments can control some aspects of the environment through zoning laws.

_____ 3. Under federal environmental laws, there is a single standard for all polluters and all pollutants.

_____ 4. The Toxic Substances Control Act of 1976 regulates clean-ups of leaking hazardous waste disposal sites.

_____ 5. The Environmental Protection Agency (EPA) can clean up a release of hazardous waste at a hazardous waste disposal site and recover the entire cost from the site's owner or operator.

_____ 6. States may restrict discharge of chemicals into the water or air.

_____ 7. A party who violates the Clean Air Act may realize economic benefits from the noncompliance.

_____ 8. The Environmental Protection Agency sets limits on discharges of pollutants into water.

_____ 9. A party who only transports hazardous waste to a disposal site cannot be held liable for any costs to clean up the site.

_____ 10. The Environmental Protection Agency sets maximum levels for noise.

FILL-IN QUESTIONS

(Answers at the Back of the Book)

The National Environmental Policy Act requires _____ (federal/state and local) agencies to prepare environmental impact statements (EIS) when major _____ (federal/state and local) actions significantly affect the quality of the environment. An EIS analyzes (1) the _____ (environmental impact that an action will have/environment's impact on a project), (2) any adverse effects to the _____ (environment/project) and alternative courses of action, and (3) irreversible effects that _____ (an action might cause to the environment/the environment might cause to the project). If an agency decides that an EIS is unnecessary, it must issue a statement announcing that decision _____ (and reasons/but it need not provide reasons) supporting the conclusion.

MULTIPLE-CHOICE QUESTIONS

(Answers at the Back of the Book)

_____ 1. The U.S. Department of the Interior's approval of coal mining operations in several eastern states requires an environmental impact statement

   a. because it affects the quality of the environment, is "federal," and is "major."
   b. only because it affects the quality of the environment.
   c. only because it is "federal."
   d. only because it is "major."

_____ **2.** Red Glow Power Plant burns fossil fuels. Under the Clean Air Act and EPA regulations, as a major new source of possible pollution, to reduce emissions the plant must use

    a. the best available technology (BAT).
    b. the lowest common denominator (LCD).
    c. the maximum achievable control technology (MACT).
    d. the minimum allowable technology (MAT).

_____ **3.** National Motors Corporation (NMC) makes sport utility vehicles (SUVs). Under the Clean Air Act, NMC is required to makes its SUVs comply with standards that, with respect to automobile exhaust emissions, are

    a. different but neither more nor less strict.
    b. less strict.
    c. more strict.
    d. the same.

_____ **4.** Mills Industries, Inc., fails to obtain a permit before discharging waste into navigable waters. Under the Clean Water Act, Eagle can be required

    a. only to clean up the pollution.
    b. only to pay for the cost of cleaning up the pollution.
    c. to clean up the pollution or pay for the cost of doing so.
    d. to do nothing.

_____ **5.** Petro, Inc., ships unlabeled containers of hazardous waste to off-site facilities for disposal. If the containers later leak, Petro could be found to have violated

    a. neither the Comprehensive Environmental Response, Compensation, and Liability Act (CERCLA) nor the Resource Conservation and Recovery Act (RCRA).
    b. the CERCLA and the RCRA.
    c. the CERCLA only.
    d. the RCRA only.

_____ **6.** HazMat Company operates a hazardous waste storage facility. If HazMat buries unlabeled containers without determining their contents and the containers leak, HazMat could be found to have violated

    a. neither the Comprehensive Environmental Response, Compensation, and Liability Act (CERCLA) nor the Resource Conservation and Recovery Act (RCRA).
    b. the CERCLA and the RCRA.
    c. the CERCLA only.
    d. the RCRA only.

_____ **7.** The U.S. Department of the Interior approves minor landscaping around a federal courthouse in St. Louis. This does *not* require an environmental impact statement

    a. only because it does not affect the quality of the environment.
    b. only because it is not "major."
    c. only because it is not "federal."
    d. because it does not affect the quality of the environment, is not "major," and is not "federal."

_____ **8.** Evolve Industries' factories emit toxic air pollutants. Under the Clean Air Act and EPA regulations, Evolve is required to

    a. eliminate all air polluting emissions.
    b. install emission control equipment on its products.
    c. reduce emissions by installing the maximum achievable control technology.
    d. remove all pollutants from its factories.

___ **9.** Suburban Development Company (SDC) owns wetlands that it wants to fill in and develop as a site for homes. Under the Clean Water Act, before filling and dredging, SDC must obtain a permit from

   a. no one.
   b. the Army Corps of Engineers.
   c. the EPA.
   d. the U.S. Department of the Navy.

___ **10.** Nimby Company owns a hazardous waste disposal site that it sells to Omega Properties, Inc. Later, the EPA discovers a leak at the site and cleans it up. The EPA can recover the cost from

   a. Nimby only.
   b. Nimby or Omega.
   c. neither Nimby nor Omega.
   d. Omega only.

SHORT ESSAY QUESTIONS

1. What does the National Environmental Policy Act require?

2. What federal laws regulate toxic chemicals?

GAMEPOINTS

(Answers at the Back of the Book)

1. In the video game "eMission Impossible," your avatar's name is "Felps" and your objective—should you decide to accept it—is to expose Sludge, your nemesis, to the punishment that can be meted out with the Sword of Clean Sweep. Your avatar sails through a galaxy of pollutants before landing on the planet Toxin. There, on the shore of a bay that empties into the vast Toxin Sea, waste is spewing into the water from a variety of sources—a trash removal outfit, a radioactive materials storage unit, a military base, and an oil refinery. Which laws discussed in this chapter apply to this dumping? What are the penalties?

2. In the play of "eMission Impossible," Felps accuses Sludge—the odious reprobate—of leaking hazardous waste from Toxin into the vastness of space. Sludge doesn't deny a role, but claims that Toxin is no longer his. Felps can draw the Sword of Clean Sweep if you can successfully argue, under the principles set out in this chapter, that Sludge is liable. What do you say?

Chapter 26
Real Property and Land-Use Control

WHAT THIS CHAPTER IS ABOUT

This chapter covers ownership rights in real property, including the nature of those rights and their transfer. The chapter also outlines the right of the government to take private land for public use, zoning laws, and other restrictions on ownership.

CHAPTER OUTLINE

I. THE NATURE OF REAL PROPERTY

Real property consists of land and the buildings, plants, and trees on it.

A. LAND AND STRUCTURES

Includes the soil on the surface of the earth, natural products or artificial structures attached to it, the water on or under it, and the air space above.

B. AIRSPACE AND SUBSURFACE RIGHTS

Limitations on air rights or subsurface rights normally have to be indicated on the deed transferring title at the time of purchase.

1. Airspace Rights

Flights over private land do not normally violate the owners' rights.

2. Subsurface Rights

Ownership of the surface can be separated from ownership of the subsurface. In excavating, if a subsurface owner causes the land to subside, he or she may be liable to the owner of the surface.

C. PLANT LIFE AND VEGETATION

A sale of land with growing crops on it includes the crops, unless otherwise agreed. When crops are sold alone, they are personal property.

II. OWNERSHIP AND OTHER INTERESTS IN REAL PROPERTY

A. OWNERSHIP IN FEE SIMPLE

A *fee simple absolute* owner has the most rights possible—to give away the property, sell it, transfer it by will, use it for any purpose, and possess it to the exclusion of all the world—potentially forever.

B. LIFE ESTATES

A life estate lasts for the life of a specified individual ("to A for his life"). A life tenant can use the land (but not commit waste), mortgage the life estate, and create liens, easements, and leases (but not longer than the life defining the estate).

C. CONCURRENT OWNERSHIP

Persons who share ownership rights simultaneously are concurrent owners.

227

1. Tenancy in Common

A tenancy in common exists when each of two or more persons owns an *undivided* interest (each has rights in the whole—if each had rights in specific items, the interests would be *divided*). On death, a tenant's interest passes to his or her heirs. Most states presume that a co-tenancy is a tenancy in common unless there is a clear intention to establish a joint tenancy.

2. Joint Tenancy

This occurs when each of two or more persons owns an undivided interest in the property; a deceased joint tenant's interest passes to the surviving joint tenant or tenants. A joint tenancy can be terminated before a joint tenant's death by gift, by sale, or by partition (divided into equal parts).

3. Tenancy by the Entirety

A transfer of real property to a husband and wife can create a tenancy by the entirety; neither spouse can transfer separately his or her interest during his or her life. In some states, this tenancy has been abolished. A divorce, a spouse's death, or mutual agreement will end this tenancy.

4. Community Property

Here, each spouse owns an undivided half interest in property that either spouse acquired during the marriage (except property acquired by gift or inheritance). Recognized in only some states, on divorce the property is divided equally in a few states and at a court's discretion in others.

D. LEASEHOLD ESTATES

A leasehold estate is created when an owner or landlord conveys the right to possess and use property to a tenant for a certain period of time.

1. Fixed-Term Tenancy or Tenancy for Years

This is created by contract (which can sometimes be oral) by which property is leased for a specific period (a month, a year, a period of years). At the end of the period, the lease ends (without notice). If the tenant dies during the lease, the lease interest passes to the tenant's heirs.

2. Periodic Tenancy

A periodic tenancy is created by a lease that specifies the payment of rent at certain intervals and it automatically renews unless it is terminated. It can arise if a landlord allows a tenant for years to hold over. Terminates, at common law, on one period's notice.

3. Tenancy at Will

This tenancy can be terminated by either party without notice ("at will"). It exists, for example, when a tenant for years retains possession after termination with the landlord's consent before payment of the next rent (when it becomes a periodic tenancy). It lasts as long as the landlord and tenant agree, but terminates on the death of either party.

4. Tenancy at Sufferance

A tenancy at sufferance is a possession of land without right (without the owner's permission).

E. NONPOSSESSORY INTERESTS

1. Easements and Profits

Easement: the right of a person to make limited use of another person's land without taking anything from the property. *Profit*: the right to go onto another's land and take away a part or product of the land.

a. Easement or Profit Appurtenant

This arises when a landowner has a right to go onto (or remove things from) an adjacent owner's land.

    b. Easement or Profit in Gross
    This exists when a right to use or take things from another's land does not depend on owning the adjacent property.

    c. Creation of an Easement or Profit
    An easement or profit can be created by deed, will, contract, implication, necessity, or prescription.

    d. Termination of an Easement or Profit
    An easement of profit terminates when deeded back to owner of the land burdened, its owner becomes owner of the land burdened, contract terminates, or it is abandoned with the intent to relinquish the right to it.

  2. Licenses
  This is the revocable right of a person to come onto another person's land.

III. TRANSFER OF OWNERSHIP

A. LISTING AGREEMENTS
Under a listing agreement, a real estate seller may employ a real estate agent to find a buyer. This agreement can specify its duration and other terms, including the agent's commission. The agreement may be *exclusive* (only the designated agent can sell) or *open* (any agent can sell).

B. REAL ESTATE SALES CONTRACTS
The steps in a sale of real estate include the formation of a contract, a title search, financing (which may include a *mortgage*), a property inspection, and a closing.

  1. Contingencies
  A contract may be made contingent on the buyer obtaining financing at or below a certain rate of interest, or selling other property, or obtaining a survey and title insurance. A contract may be contingent on the property passing an inspection for defects and insect infestation.

  2. Closing Date and Escrow
  The buyer may deposit funds with, and the seller may give a deed to, an escrow agent to transfer when the conditions of sale are met.

  3. Implied Warranties in the Sales of New Homes
  In a few states, a seller makes no warranties (unless the deed or contract specifies otherwise)—a buyer takes the property "as is." In most states, a seller of a new house impliedly warrants that it is fit for human habitation (in reasonable working order and of reasonably sound construction). In a few states, a later buyer can recover from the original builder under this warranty.

  4. Seller's Duty to Disclose Hidden Defects
  In most states, sellers must disclose any known defect that materially affects the value of the property and that the buyer could not reasonably discover.

C. DEEDS
Possession and title to land can be passed by deed without consideration.

  1. Requirements
  (1) Names of the grantor and grantee, (2) words evidencing an intent to convey, (3) legally sufficient description of the land, (4) grantor's (and usually the spouse's) signature, and (5) delivery.

  2. Warranty Deed
  This provides the most protection against defects of title—covenants that the grantor has title to, and the power to convey, the property; that the buyer will not be disturbed in his or her

possession of the land; and that transfer is made without unknown adverse claims of third parties.

3. Special Warranty Deed
This warrants only that the grantor held good title during his or her ownership of the property, not that there were no title defects when others owned it. If all liens and encumbrances are disclosed, the seller is not liable if a third person interferes with the buyer's ownership.

4. Quitclaim Deed
This warrants less than any other deed. It conveys to the grantee only the interest the grantor had.

5. Grant Deed
By statute, this may impliedly warrant that the grantor owns the property and has not encumbered it or conveyed it to another.

6. Sheriff's Deed
This gives ownership rights to a buyer at a sheriff's sale.

D. RECORDING STATUTES
Recording statutes require transfers to be recorded in public records (generally in the county in which the property is located) to give notice to the public that a certain person is the owner. Many states require the grantor's signature and two witnesses' signatures.

1. Marketable Title
A grantor must transfer title that is free from undisclosed encumbrances and defects.

2. Title Search
This is an examination of the title records for all transactions concerning a specific parcel of real property to discover its true owner and other interested parties.

3. Methods of Ensuring Good Title
These include hiring an attorney to provide an opinion based on a reading of an abstract of title; holding a court hearing in those states that use the Torrens system of title registration; and (most commonly) obtaining title insurance, which insures the grantee against losses due to title defects.

E. ADVERSE POSSESSION
A person who possesses another's property acquires title good against the original owner if the possession is (1) actual and exclusive; (2) open, visible, and notorious; (3) continuous and peaceable for a statutorily required period of time; and (4) hostile, as against the whole world.

IV. LIMITATIONS ON THE RIGHTS OF PROPERTY OWNERS

A. EMINENT DOMAIN
The government can take private property for public use (most states limit taking of private property and giving it to private developers). To obtain title, a condemnation proceeding is brought. The U.S. Constitution's Fifth Amendment requires that just compensation be paid for a taking; thus, in a separate proceeding a court determines the land's fair value (usually market value) to pay the owner.

B. RESTRICTIVE COVENANTS
A restrictive covenant is a private restriction on the use of land. It runs with the land if the original parties and their successors are entitled to its benefit or burdened with its obligation. It must be in writing and subsequent owners of the property must know of it.

C. INVERSE CONDEMNATION
Inverse condemnation occurs when a government takes private property without paying for it. This may be accomplished by use or occupation of the land, or through the imposition of regulations that cause land to lose its value. The former owner must sue to obtain compensation.

V.   Land-Use Control and Zoning

Most states control land use through planning boards and zoning authorities at a city or county level. The federal government influences regulation through the allocation of federal funds. Zoning laws control development within a municipality by regulating the use of property in different zones.

A. POLICE POWER

Zoning is a constitutional use of a municipality's police power as long as it is rationally related to the community's health, safety, or welfare.

1. Subdivision Regulations

Subdivision regulations are different from zoning ordinances, although they may be administered by the same local agencies.

2. Growth-Management Ordinances

A growth-management ordinance may prohibit the issuance of residential building permits for a specific period of time, until the occurrence of a specific event (such as a decline in the total number of residents), or on the basis of the availability of necessary public services.

B. PURPOSE AND SCOPE OF ZONING LAWS

Zoning laws encourage sustainable and organized development, and control growth. Among other things, zoning ordinances classify land by permissible use as part of a comprehensive plan.

1. Permissible Uses of Land

Generally, municipalities divide land into districts for present and future uses. The districts may be divided into subdistricts. Types of permissible uses are—

a. *Residential.* Here, buildings are constructed for human habitation.

b. *Commercial.* This land is designated for business or government activities—stores, offices, hotels, theaters, sports stadiums, and courthouses, for example.

c. *Industrial.* This category includes manufacturing, shipping, and transportation. Because of the potential for these uses to interfere with others' enjoyment of their property, these areas are often farther from residential and commercial districts.

d. *Conservation.* These districts are dedicated to soil and water conservation efforts.

2. Other Zoning Restrictions

Ordinances may dictate details such as the distance a building must be from a property line, visual appearance (for example, height and width), and the location and operation of certain businesses to regulate traffic and for other purposes.

C. ZONING LAW EXCEPTIONS AND SPECIAL INCENTIVES

1. Variances

A variance allows an exception to zoning rules. But the need for a variance cannot be self-created (for example, a party cannot buy property for a purpose that is not permitted and argue that a variance is needed to use the property). To obtain a variance, there must be—

a. *Notice.* Neighbors who might object must be notified.

b. *Public hearing.* The party seeking the variance must show that it is necessary for reasonable development, it is the least intrusive option, and the essential character of the neighborhood will not change.

c. *Decision.* A hearing examiner determines whether the variance will be granted.

2. Special-Use Permits

A special-use, or conditional-use, permit allows an owner to use property for a certain purpose only in compliance with specific requirements (a business that conforms to the style of a neighborhood in a residential district, for example).

3. Special Incentives
Special incentives (tax credits or lower tax rates) can encourage certain uses (new businesses or preservation of historical homes) or support environmental goals (energy efficiency).

TRUE-FALSE QUESTIONS

(Answers at the Back of the Book)

_____ 1. A fee simple absolute is potentially infinite in duration and can be disposed of by deed or by will.

_____ 2. The owner of a life estate has the same rights as a fee simple owner.

_____ 3. An easement allows a person to use land and take something from it, but a profit allows a person only to use land.

_____ 4. Deeds offer different degrees of protection against defects of title.

_____ 5. The government can take private property for _private_ uses only.

_____ 6. A periodic tenancy is a tenancy for a specified period of time, such as a month, a year, or a period of years.

_____ 7. In most states, the seller of a new house impliedly warrants that it will be fit for human habitation.

_____ 8. The government can take private property for _public_ use without just compensation.

_____ 9. To obtain a variance, a landowner must show that his or her alternative use of the land would substantially alter its essential character.

_____ 10. Real property consists of, in part, land and the buildings on it.

FILL-IN QUESTIONS

(Answers at the Back of the Book)

The deed that provides the most protection against defects of title is the _____ (warranty/special warranty/quitclaim) deed. Among other things, it covenants that the transfer is made without any unknown adverse claims of third parties. The deed that warrants only that the grantor has done nothing to lessen the value of the property is the _____ (warranty/special warranty/quitclaim) deed. Under this deed, the seller may not be liable if a third person interferes with the buyer's ownership. The deed that warrants less than any other deed is the _____ (warranty/special warranty/quitclaim) deed. This deed conveys to the grantee only whatever interest the grantor had.

MULTIPLE-CHOICE QUESTIONS

(Answers at the Back of the Book)

_____ 1. Ezmé owns two hundred acres next to Floyd's lumber mill. Ezmé sells to Floyd the privilege of removing the timber from her land. This privilege is

    a. a fee simple.
    b. a license.
    c. an easement.
    d. a profit.

___ **2.** To acquire the ownership of a strip of waterfront property by adverse possession, Glenn must occupy the property exclusively, continuously, and peaceably for a specified period of time

    a. in an open, hostile, and adverse manner.
    b. until the owner files a suit.
    c. without the owner's knowledge.
    d. with the state's permission.

___ **3.** Eligio owns an apartment building in fee simple. Eligio can

    a. give the building away only.
    b. give the building away, sell it, or transfer it by will.
    c. not give the building away, sell it, or transfer it by will.
    d. sell the building or transfer it by a will only.

___ **4.** Urban City wants to acquire undeveloped land within the city limits to convert into a public park. Urban City brings a judicial proceeding to obtain title to the land. This is

    a. adverse possession.
    b. an easement.
    c. constructive eviction.
    d. the power of eminent domain.

___ **5.** Samira Entertainment Company sells an office building to Tivoli Restaurants, Inc. To be valid, the deed that conveys the property must include

    a. a description of the property.
    b. a due date for the payment of the price.
    c. a requirement that the seller perform structural repairs to the building.
    d. a requirement that the buyer carry liability insurance.

___ **6.** Dayton owns a half-acre of land fronting Elsinore Lake. Fritz owns the property behind Dayton's land. No road runs to Dayton's land, but Fritz's driveway runs between a road and Dayton's property, so Dayton uses Fritz's driveway. The right-of-way that Dayton has across Fritz's property is

    a. a tenancy in common.
    b. a license.
    c. an easement.
    d. a profit.

___ **7.** Landlock Corporation wants to convert a warehouse near Metro City into a shopping mall and to construct an apartment tower on adjacent land. Local policy concerning growth, and building requirements and restrictions can be found in Metro City's

    a. warranty deeds.
    b. restrictive covenants.
    c. area and development plans, and zoning ordinances.
    d. none of the choices.

___ **8.** Oak Grove, Inc., wants to develop a suburban tract, subdividing the land to build single-family homes. Formation of the subdivision and such public facilities as streets and schools are responsibilities of

    a. the banks and other institutions that will provide the financing for the construction and sales.
    b. the families and other parties who will purchase the homes.
    c. Oak Grove and the local agency that oversees the zoning process.
    d. none of the choices.

___   9.   Raze & Raise Associates buys forty acres of land to build a corporate complex. After construction begins, the county zones the surrounding, undeveloped area for a nature preserve, in which it includes 75 percent of Raze & Raise's land. The county owes Raze & Raise

   a.   just compensation.
   b.   land of equivalent value.
   c.   private use of the preserve.
   d.   nothing.

___   10.   Wizard Games, LLC, wants to convert a residential duplex into a small office building. The duplex is in an area zoned for residential use only. Wizard can be granted a variance if

   a.   Wizard would realize a higher return on the office building than on the duplex.
   b.   all property owners within the zone agree that an office building is acceptable.
   c.   granting a variance will not substantially alter the character of the area.
   d.   no one objects before Wizard begins the conversion.

SHORT ESSAY QUESTIONS

1.   What are the principal features of the four forms of concurrent property ownership (tenancy in common, joint tenancy, tenancy by the entirety and community property)?

2.   Describe the power of eminent domain and the process by which private property is condemned for a public purpose.

GAMEPOINTS

(Answers at the Back of the Book)

1.   The video game "Storm" features different sports played in the midst of natural disasters—skiing in a blizzard, running a marathon under the belch and plume of an erupting volcano, and so on. In one segment, a tornado fells a forest of trees. Your goal is to quickly make the timber into lumber and build a beach house before a tsunami comes ashore and converts the structure into floating debris. How would you describe the property aspect of the wood in this segment?

2.   In the video game "Alphabetrix," your character follows letters of the alphabet through imaginary landscapes to solve puzzles, untangle mysteries, and spell uncommon words. Distracted by the play of the game, you forget about a pending transfer of a certain parcel of your real property. At the last minute, you hastily write the sales price on the deed and deliver it to the buyer, expecting that it will not effectively transfer title until she adds the source of funds for the purchase and signs it. Of these last-minute acts, which is actually needed to make the deed valid?

Chapter 27
Antitrust and Monopoly

WHAT THIS CHAPTER IS ABOUT

This chapter outlines the background, exemptions, and enforcement of the major antitrust statutes—the Sherman Act, the Clayton Act, and the Federal Trade Commission Act. Monopoly is covered in some detail. Keep in mind that the basis of the antitrust laws is a desire to foster competition (to result in lower prices and so on).

CHAPTER OUTLINE

I.   MARKET POWER
Market power is the extent to which a firm can ignore competitors in setting its prices or can in some way limit competition.

II.   THE COMMON LAW AND THE RESTRAINT OF TRADE
Restraints of trade include agreements between suppliers in a market to limit output. Agreements between business firms that reduce competition are against public policy (except covenants-not-to-compete included in a sale of a business).

III. THE ORIGINS OF FEDERAL ANTITRUST LEGISLATION
When monopolies increased in the late nineteenth century, Congress felt that the common law (under which an agreement to limit competition is unenforceable but cannot be challenged by one who is not a party to it) was not sufficient to protect against anticompetitive conduct.

IV.   OVERVIEW OF THE MAJOR FEDERAL ANTITRUST LAWS
These laws seek to promote competitive business and limit the anticompetitive use of market power.

A. SHERMAN ACT OF 1890
The Sherman Act applies to restraints that substantially affect interstate commerce. It also covers activities by U.S. nationals abroad that have an effect on U.S. foreign commerce. The act prohibits—

1. **Restraints of Trade [Section 1]**
   Requires two or more persons; focus is on agreements (written or oral) that are restrictive (see Chapter 28).

2. **Monopolies [Section 2]**
   Applies to individuals and to several people; concerns the structure of a monopoly in the marketplace; focus is on the misuse of monopoly power (see below).

B. CLAYTON ACT OF 1914
Aimed at practices not covered by the Sherman Act. Violations are subject to civil, not criminal, penalties. Conduct is illegal if it substantially tends to lessen competition or create monopoly power—

235

1. **Price Discrimination [Section 2]**
   This occurs when a seller charges different prices to competitive buyers for identical goods (see Chapter 28).

   a. **Required Elements**
      (1) The seller must be engaged in interstate commerce, (2) the goods must be of like grade or quality, (3) the goods must have been sold to two or more buyers, and (4) the effect of the price discrimination must be to substantially lessen competition or create a competitive injury.

   b. **Defenses**
      (1) A buyer's purchases saved the seller production and sales costs, (2) a lower price was charged temporarily and in good faith to meet another seller's equally low price to the buyer's competitor, or (3) changing conditions affected the market for or marketability of the goods.

2. **Exclusionary Practices [Section 3]**
   These include exclusive-dealing contracts and tying arrangements (see Chapter 28).

3. **Corporate Mergers [Section 7]**
   A person or firm cannot hold stock or assets in another firm if the effect may be to substantially lessen competition (see Chapter 28).

4. **Interlocking Directorates [Section 8]**
   No person may be a director in two or more corporations at the same time if either firm has capital, surplus, or undivided profits of more than a certain amount or if a firm's competitive sales are more than a certain amount. (The limits are updated annually.)

C. **FEDERAL TRADE COMMISSION ACT OF 1914**
   Section 5 condemns all forms of anticompetitive behavior not covered by other federal antitrust laws.

V. ENFORCEMENT AND EXEMPTIONS

A. **U.S. DEPARTMENT OF JUSTICE (DOJ)**
   The DOJ prosecutes violations of the Sherman Act as criminal or civil violations. Violations of the Clayton Act are not crimes; the DOJ can enforce it only through civil proceedings. Remedies include divestiture and dissolution.

B. **FEDERAL TRADE COMMISSION (FTC)**
   The FTC enforces the Clayton Act; has the sole authority to enforce the Federal Trade Commission Act of 1914 (Section 5 condemns all forms of anticompetitive behavior that are not covered by other federal antitrust laws); issues administrative orders; can seek court sanctions.

C. **PRIVATE PARTIES**

1. **Treble Damages and Attorneys' Fees**
   Private parties can sue for treble damages and attorneys' fees under the Clayton Act if they are injured by a violation of any federal antitrust law (except the FTC Act).

2. **Injunctions**
   Private parties may seek an injunction to prevent an antitrust violation if it will injure business activities protected by the antitrust laws.

D. **EXEMPTIONS FROM ANTITRUST LAWS**

1. **Labor Activities**
   A labor union can lose its exemption if it combines with a non-labor group.

2. **Agricultural Associations and Fisheries**
   Except exclusionary practices or restraints of trade against competitors.

3. Insurance Companies
Exempt in most cases when state regulation exists.

4. Foreign Trade
U.S. exporters may cooperate to compete with similar foreign associations (if it does not restrain trade in the United States or injure other U.S. exporters).

5. Professional Baseball
Players may sue team owners for anticompetitive practices. Other professional sports are not exempt.

6. Oil Marketing
States set quotas on oil to be marketed in interstate commerce.

7. Cooperative Research and Production
Cooperative research among small business firms is exempt.

8. Joint Efforts to Obtain Legislative or Executive Action
Joint efforts by businesspersons to obtain executive or legislative action are exempt (*Noerr-Pennington* doctrine). Exception: an action is not protected if "no reasonable [person] could reasonably expect success on the merits" and it is an attempt to make anticompetitive use of government processes.

9. Other Exemptions
a. Activities approved by the president in furtherance of defense.
b. State actions, when the state policy is clearly articulated and the policy is actively supervised by the state.
c. Activities of regulated industries when federal commissions, boards, or agencies have primary regulatory authority.

VI.   U.S. ANTITRUST LAWS IN THE GLOBAL CONTEXT

A. THE EXTRATERRITORIAL APPLICATION OF U.S. ANTITRUST LAWS
For U.S. courts to exercise jurisdiction over a foreign entity under U.S. antitrust laws, a violation must (1) have a substantial effect on U.S. commerce or (2) constitute a *per se* violation. Foreign governments and persons can also sue U.S. firms and persons for antitrust violations.

B. THE APPLICATION OF FOREIGN ANTITRUST LAWS
Foreign antitrust laws may apply to U.S. firms in some cases. The European Union's antitrust provisions are stricter in some ways than U.S. antitrust laws.

VIII. MONOPOLIES
A monopoly may violate Section 2 of the Sherman Act.

A. MONOPOLIZATION
This offense has two elements: (1) the possession of monopoly power in the relevant market and (2) the willful acquisition or maintenance of that power.

1. Monopoly Power
Monopoly power is sufficient market power to control prices and exclude competition.

a. Market-Share Test
A firm has monopoly power if it has a dominant share of the relevant market and there are significant barriers for new competition entering the market.

b. The Relevant Market Has Two Elements—

1) Relevant Product Market
This includes all products with identical attributes and those that are reasonably interchangeable (acceptable substitutes for each other).

2) Relevant Geographical Market
If competitors sell in only a limited area, the geographical market is limited to that area.

2. Intent Requirement
If a firm has market power as a result of a purposeful act to acquire or maintain that power through anticompetitive means, it is a violation. Intent may be inferred from evidence that the firm had monopoly power and engaged in anticompetitive behavior.

3. Unilateral Refusals to Deal
A firm is free to deal, or not, unilaterally, with whomever it wishes unless it has or is likely to acquire monopoly power and the refusal is likely to have an anticompetitive effect.

B. ATTEMPTS TO MONOPOLIZE
Any action (such as predatory pricing or bidding) challenged as an attempt to monopolize (1) must be intended to exclude competitors and garner monopoly power and (2) must have a dangerous probability of success.

TRUE-FALSE QUESTIONS
(Answers at the Back of the Book)

____ **1.** Monopoly power is market power sufficient to control prices and exclude competition.

____ **2.** A relevant product market includes products that are reasonably acceptable substitutes.

____ **3.** Market power is the extent to which a firm can exclude competition.

____ **4.** Antitrust law is intended to eliminate competition in business markets.

____ **5.** A firm that can ignore its competitors in setting a price for its product has no market power.

____ **6.** A determining factor as to whether a firm is a monopoly is its size in terms of the relevant market.

____ **7.** An unsuccessful attempt to monopolize is not a violation of antitrust law.

____ **8.** No person can be a director in two or more corporations at the same time.

____ **9.** A business firm can be dissolved for an antitrust violation.

____ **10.** A private party who has been injured by an antitrust violation cannot sue for damages.

FILL-IN QUESTIONS
(Answers at the Back of the Book)

_____ (Monopoly power/A restraint of trade) is any agreement that has the effect of reducing competition in the marketplace. _____ (Monopoly power/ Restraint of trade) is an extreme amount of market power. A firm that can raise its prices somewhat without too much concern for its competitors' response has some degree of market power. Determining whether such power is sufficient to call it _____ (monopoly power/ a restraint of trade) is one of the most difficult tasks in antitrust law.

MULTIPLE-CHOICE QUESTIONS

(Answers at the Back of the Book)

____ 1. Wassup, Inc., controls 80 percent of the market for communications equipment in the southeastern United States. To show that Wassup is monopolizing that market in violation of the Sherman Act requires proof of Wassup's

   a. possession of monopoly power in the relevant market *and* its willful acquisition or maintenance.
   b. possession of monopoly power in the relevant market only.
   c. willful acquisition or maintenance of monopoly power only.
   d. none of the choices.

____ 2. A group of foreign manufacturers organize to control the price for DVD players in the United States. Vivid View Inc., a U.S. firm, joins the group. If their actions have a substantial effect on U.S. commerce, a suit for violations of U.S. antitrust laws may be brought against

   a. neither Vivid View nor the foreign manufacturers.
   b. only the foreign manufacturers.
   c. only Vivid View.
   d. Vivid View and the foreign manufacturers.

____ 3. Redd Company, Whyte Corporation, and Bloo, Inc., are the only suppliers in a certain market. They agree to limit their output so that prices will increase. This agreement is

   a. a legitimate exercise of market power.
   b. an economically efficient contract.
   c. a restraint of trade.
   d. a socially beneficial joint venture.

____ 4. Carbo Soft Drink Company begins to sell its products at prices substantially below cost. This is *not* an antitrust violation if Carbo Soft Drink is trying to

   a. drive competitors from the market.
   b. engage in anticompetitive activity.
   c. gain access to the market.
   d. obtain monopoly profits.

____ 5. Giganto Office Equipment, Inc., sells its products throughout the United States. For the purpose of determining its market share, the relevant market consists of

   a. the geographical market and the product market.
   b. the geographical market only.
   c. the product market only.
   d. the share of the market into which the seller first sought entry.

____ 6. Price Data Corporation and Consumer Marketing, Inc., are competitors. They form a joint venture to research, develop, and produce new software for a particular line of research and reporting. This joint venture is

   a. a violation of the Sherman Act.
   b. exempt from the antitrust laws.
   c. subject to continuing review by the appropriate federal agency.
   d. subject to the consideration under the Clayton Act.

____   7. Golden Goose, Inc., has a 90-percent share of its market in the United States. This is an unlawful monopoly if Golden Goose acquired its market share through

   a. anticompetitive conduct.
   b. business acumen.
   c. historical circumstances.
   d. any of the choices.

____   8. Fruits & Vegetables, Inc., sells produce, charging different prices to Green Grocery and Hasty Market for the same goods, with the ultimate effect of substantially reducing competition. This is

   a. attempted monopolization.
   b. monopolization.
   c. not an antitrust violation.
   d. price discrimination.

____   9. The Clayton Act and the Sherman Act can be enforced through civil proceedings by

   a. private parties only.
   b. the Federal Trade Commission only.
   c. the Federal Trade Commission, the U.S. Department of Justice, and private parties.
   d. the U.S. Department of Justice only.

____   10. United Company uses its market power to impose tying arrangements on its customers. Civil sanctions may be sought against United by

   a. the Federal Trade Commission only.
   b. the Federal Trade Commission, the U.S. Department of Justice, and United's customers.
   c. the U.S. Department of Justice only.
   d. United's customers only.

SHORT ESSAY QUESTIONS

1. What is price discrimination as prohibited by the Clayton Act?

2. Under what circumstances can a private party sue to enforce antitrust laws?

GAMEPOINTS

(Answers at the Back of the Book)

1.   You and three of your friends form Gamies, Inc., to develop a series of video games that do not require players to hold controllers or other devices—as players move, their avatars and other on-screen elements react. Also, for the first time, your games incorporate lasers into the play. Gamies earns profits that reflect the wide appeal of the games and that eclipse those of other game makers and sellers. For a time, Gamies is the only seller in the video-laser game market. Does that mean that your firm has a monopoly? Explain.

2.   Over a period of a couple of years, Super Joystick, Inc., acquires the power to affect the market price of its products, which consist of popular video game titles. Enticed by the prospect of greater profits, Super Joystick begins to refuse to do business with those who do not contract with the company exclusively. Some retail firms fearfully agree to the deal, at least as long as Super Joystick's games are at the top of the sales charts. Prices for Super Joystick's products rise and its competitors' shares of the market drop. Is this a violation of antitrust laws? If so, why?

Chapter 28
Antitrust and Restraints of Trade

WHAT THIS CHAPTER IS ABOUT

This chapter outlines the aspect of antitrust at which most of the statutes have been directed: anticompetitive agreements between rival firms to fix prices, restrict output, divide markets, exclude other competitors, or otherwise limit competition. The focus of this chapter is on concerted behavior.

CHAPTER OUTLINE

I. RESTRAINT OF TRADE: AN OVERVIEW

A. *PER SE* VIOLATIONS
Agreements that are blatantly anticompetitive are illegal *per se*.

B. THE RULE OF REASON
If an agreement is not a *per se* violation, it is subject to the rule of reason, under which a court considers the purpose of an agreement, the power of the parties, the effect of the action on trade, and in some cases, whether there are less restrictive alternatives to achieve the same goals. If the competitive benefits outweigh the anticompetitive effects, the agreement is held lawful.

II. HORIZONTAL RESTRAINTS
These are agreements that restrain competition between rivals in the same market.

A. PRICE FIXING
Any agreement among competitors to fix prices is a *per se* violation.

B. GROUP BOYCOTTS
An agreement by two or more sellers to refuse to deal with a particular person or firm is a *per se* violation if it is intended to eliminate competition or prevent entry into a given market.

C. HORIZONTAL MARKET DIVISION
An agreement between competitors to divide up territories or customers is a *per se* violation.

D. TRADE ASSOCIATIONS
These are businesses within the same industry or profession organized to pursue common interests (exchange information, set industry standards, etc.). In a concentrated industry (in which a single firm or a small number of firms control a large percentage of market sales), a trade association may facilitate anticompetitive acts. The rule of reason is applied to trade association actions.

III. VERTICAL RESTRAINTS
A restraint of trade that results from an agreement between firms at different levels in the manufacturing and distribution process. (Backward integration moves down the chain of production toward a supplier; forward integration moves up toward the consumer market.)

A. TERRITORIAL OR CUSTOMER RESTRICTIONS
This is an agreement between a manufacturer and a distributor or retailer to restrict sales to certain area or customers. These agreements are judged under the rule of reason.

241

B. RESALE PRICE MAINTENANCE AGREEMENT
In a resale price maintenance agreement between a manufacturer and a distributor or retailer, the manufacturer specifies the retail prices of its products. This is subject to the rule of reason.

C. REFUSALS TO DEAL
A firm is free to deal, or not, unilaterally, with whomever it wishes.

D. PRICE DISCRIMINATION
This can occur when a seller charges different prices to competitive buyers for identical goods or offers different delivery terms or other conditions.

1. Elements
(1) The seller must be engaged in interstate commerce, (2) the effect of the price discrimination must be to substantially lessen competition or create a competitive injury, and (3) a seller's pricing policies must include a reasonable prospect of the seller's recouping its losses.

2. Exceptions
A seller may charge a lower price temporarily and in good faith to meet another seller's equally low price to a buyer's competitor. Courts may weigh differences in production, transportation, or other costs, or changes in market conditions to determine whether there is a violation.

3. Not an Exception
Customer preferences (for one size of container over another or one brand over another) can influence pricing decisions (customers might be willing to pay a higher price for the same goods), but the United States Supreme Court has held that is not a relevant factor.

E. EXCLUSIONARY PRACTICES

1. Exclusive-Dealing Contracts
This is a contract under which a seller forbids the buyer to buy products from the seller's competitors. It is prohibited if the effect is "to substantially lessen competition or tend to create a monopoly."

2. Tying Arrangements
This occurs when a seller conditions the sale of a product on the buyer's agreement to buy another product produced or distributed by the same seller. Legality depends on the agreement's purpose and its likely effect on competition in the relevant markets.

F. MERGERS
A person or firm cannot hold stock or assets in another firm if the effect may be to substantially lessen competition.

1. Horizontal Mergers
These are mergers between firms competing with each other in the same market. If a merger creates an entity with a resulting significant market share, it may be presumed illegal.

a. Factors
These include—

1) The degree of concentration in the relevant market.
2) The ease of entry into the relevant market.
3) Economic efficiency.
4) The financial condition of the merging firms.
5) The nature and prices of the products.

b. Market Concentration—FTC/DOJ Guidelines
The Herfindahl-Hirschman Index (HHI) is computed by adding the squares of each of the percentage market shares of firms in the relevant market.

1) **Pre-merger HHI Between 1,000 and 1,800**
   The industry is moderately concentrated, and the merger will be challenged only if it increases the HHI by 100 points or more.

2) **Pre-merger HHI Greater than 1,800**
   The market is highly concentrated; if a merger produces an increase in the HHI between 50 and 100 points, it raises concerns; if more than 100 points, it is likely to enhance market power.

2. **Vertical Mergers**
   This occurs when a company at one stage of production acquires a company at a higher or lower stage of production. Legality depends on market concentration, barriers to entry into that market, and the parties' intent.

3. **Conglomerate Mergers**

   a. **Market-Extension Merger**
      This is when a firm seeks to sell its product in a new market by merging with a firm already established in that market.

   b. **Product-Extension Merger**
      This is when a firm seeks to add a closely related product to its existing line by merging with a firm already producing that product.

   c. **Diversification Merger**
      This is when a firm merges with another firm that offers a product or service wholly unrelated to the first firm's existing activities.

TRUE-FALSE QUESTIONS

(Answers at the Back of the Book)

1. A horizontal restraint results from an agreement between firms at different levels in the manufacturing and distribution process.

2. An agreement that restrains competition between rivals in the same market is a vertical restraint.

3. An exclusive dealing contract is a contract under which competitors agree to divide up customers.

4. Price discrimination occurs when a seller forbids a buyer to buy from the seller's competitors.

5. A horizontal merger results when a company at one stage of production acquires another company at a higher or lower stage in the chain of production and distribution.

6. A merger between firms that compete with each other in the same market is a vertical merger.

7. An agreement that is inherently anticompetitive is illegal *per se*.

8. An agreement between competitors to fix prices is a *per se* violation.

9. A *per se* violation of the Sherman Act is analyzed under the rule of reason.

10. Any agreement among competitors to divide up customers is a *per se* violation of the Sherman Act.

FILL-IN QUESTIONS

(Answers at the Back of the Book)

1. Prices may be controlled by an agreement among competitors to divide their market, or a _____ (horizontal/vertical) market division. A relationship between firms at the same level of operations is a _____ (horizontal/vertical) relationship. The division _____ (may/must) be geographical _____ (and/or) by class of customer. Such market divisions are considered *per se* violations of the Sherman Act.

2. Another set of restraints involves those imposed by a seller on a buyer, or vice versa, in what is termed a _____ (horizontal/vertical) relationship. A relationship between firms that encompasses an entire chain of production is a _____ (horizontal/vertical) relationship. A single firm that carries out two or more of the different functional phases in the chain is a _____ (horizontally/vertically) integrated firm. Marketing decisions within such a firm are not subject to attack under the Sherman Act.

MULTIPLE-CHOICE QUESTIONS

(Answers at the Back of the Book)

____ **1.** Natural Gas Association (NGA) is a group of independent mining companies. Demand for natural gas falls. The price drops. Natural Gas Distributors Association, a group of distributing companies, agrees to buy NGA's gas and sell it according to a schedule that will increase the price. This agreement is

    a. a *per se* violation of the Sherman Act.
    b. exempt from the antitrust laws.
    c. not subject to scrutiny under the antitrust laws.
    d. subject to evaluation under the rule of reason.

____ **2.** Tech, Inc., sells its brand-name computer equipment directly to its franchised retailers. Depending on how existing franchisees do, Tech may limit the number of franchisees in a given area to reduce intrabrand competition. Tech's restrictions on the number of dealers is

    a. a *per se* violation of the Sherman Act.
    b. exempt from the antitrust laws.
    c. subject to continuing review by the appropriate federal agency.
    d. subject to the rule of reason.

____ **3.** Platinum Corporation is charged with a violation of antitrust law that requires evaluation under the rule of reason. The court will consider

    a. only the effect of the conduct on trade.
    b. only the power of the parties to accomplish what they intend.
    c. only the purpose of the conduct.
    d. the effect of the conduct, the power of the parties, and the purpose of the conduct.

____ **4.** Handy Tools, Inc., charges Jake's Valu Tools Store five cents per item and Kitchener's Home Store ten cents per item for the same product. The two stores are competitors. If this substantially lessens competition, it constitutes

    a. a legitimate business practice.
    b. a market division.
    c. an exclusionary practice.
    d. price discrimination.

_____ **5.** Rally, Inc., and Sport Corporation are competitors. They merge, after which Sport is the surviving firm. To assess whether the merger is in violation of the Clayton Act requires a determination of the percentage of the firms' market share. Determining market share requires consideration of

   a. Sport's financial condition only.
   b. the nature and prices of Rally's products only.
   c. the ease of all competitors' entry into the relevant market only.
   d. the financial condition of both firms, the nature and prices of their products, and the ease of competitors' entry into the relevant market.

_____ **6.** Office Systems, Inc., sells computerized business systems under contracts that prohibit Office's buyers from purchasing supplemental or separate systems from Office's competitors. These contracts are

   a. a *per se* violation of the Sherman Act.
   b. exempt from the antitrust laws.
   c. not subject to scrutiny under the antitrust laws.
   d. subject to evaluation under the rule of reason.

_____ **7.** Medico Pharma Company is charged with violating antitrust law, subject to evaluation under the rule of reason. Medico's conduct is unlawful

   a. if the anticompetitive harm outweighs the competitive benefits.
   b. if the competitive benefits outweigh the anticompetitive harm.
   c. if the conduct is blatantly anticompetitive.
   d. only if it does not qualify for an exemption.

_____ **8.** Richer Resources, Inc., and Sellers Supply Corporation are competitors. They merge, and after the merger, Richer Resources is the surviving firm. To assess whether this is in violation of the Clayton Act requires a look at

   a. concentration.
   b. discrimination.
   c. division.
   d. power.

_____ **9.** Cable, Inc., manufactures DVD players and sells them to ElectriCity and other retailers. ElectriCity agrees with Cable to sell the players at a certain price. This agreement is

   a. a *per se* violation of the Sherman Act.
   b. exempt from the antitrust laws.
   c. not subject to scrutiny under the antitrust laws.
   d. subject to evaluation under the rule of reason.

_____ **10.** Interstate Sales, Inc. (ISI), is charged with violating antitrust law. ISI's conduct is a *per se* violation

   a. if the anticompetitive harm outweighs the competitive benefits.
   b. if the competitive benefits outweigh the anticompetitive harm.
   c. if the conduct is blatantly anticompetitive.
   d. only if it does not qualify for an exemption.

SHORT ESSAY QUESTIONS

1. How does Section 1 of the Sherman Act deal horizontal restraints?

2. How does the Clayton Act deal with exclusionary practices?

GAMEPOINTS

(Answers at the Back of the Book)

1. You go to Games Galore Store to buy a copy of the latest installment in the "Furious Finale" video game series. It is available only at the manufacturer's price, which is the same price at all local outlets, and not otherwise available. Previous installments were nearly half the price and could be bought directly from the maker, who has agreed with the merchants that it will not compete in their market if they sell at the "suggested" price. Is this legal? Explain.

2. At Games Galore, you ask for a copy of Apoplexy Inc.'s popular "Black Op" game. The clerk tries to interest you in buying a copy of Apoplexy's "Carousel" too. But the games are very different. "Carousel" is unpopular, and its play is poor. The clerk says that Apoplexy requires the store to buy a copy of "Carousel" with each copy of "Black Op." Which of the actions identified in this chapter does this arrangement appear to be? What factors would a court consider to decide whether this deal violates antitrust law?

Chapter 29
Investor Protection and Corporate Governance

WHAT THIS CHAPTER IS ABOUT

The general purpose of securities laws is to provide sufficient, accurate information to investors to enable them to make informed buying and selling decisions about securities. This chapter provides an outline of federal securities laws. This chapter also discusses issues of corporate governance.

CHAPTER OUTLINE

I. THE SECURITIES AND EXCHANGE COMMISSION (SEC)

The SEC administers the federal securities laws and regulates the sale and purchase of securities.

A. THE SEC'S MAJOR RESPONSIBILITIES

1. Interpret federal securities laws and investigate violations.
2. Issue new rules and amend existing rules.
3. Oversee the inspection of securities firms, brokers, investment advisers, and ratings agencies.
4. Oversee private regulatory organizations in the securities, accounting, and auditing fields.
5. Coordinate U.S. securities regulation with federal, state, and foreign authorities.

B. UPDATING THE REGULATORY PROCESS

The SEC requires companies to file certain information electronically so that it may be made available online in the SEC's EDGAR (Electronic Data Gathering, Analysis, and Retrieval) database.

C. THE SEC'S EXPANDING REGULATORY POWERS

The SEC's powers include the power to seek sanctions against those who violate foreign securities laws; to suspend trading if prices rise and fall in short periods of time; to exempt persons, securities, and transactions from securities law requirements; and to require more corporate disclosure.

II. THE SECURITIES ACT OF 1933

Requires all essential information concerning the issuance (sales) of new securities to be disclosed to investors.

A. WHAT IS A SECURITY?

1. **A Security Is an Investment**
Examples: stocks, bonds, stock options, and investment contracts in condominiums, franchises, limited partnerships, and oil or gas or other mineral rights.

2. **Courts' Interpretation of the Securities Act**
A security exists in any transaction in which a person (1) invests (2) in a common enterprise (3) reasonably expecting profits (4) derived *primarily* or *substantially* from others' managerial or entrepreneurial efforts.

247

B. REGISTRATION STATEMENT

Before offering securities for sale, issuing corporations must (1) file a registration statement with the Securities and Exchange Commission (SEC) and (2) provide investors with a prospectus that describes the security being sold, the issuing corporation, and the investment or risk.

1. Contents of the Registration Statement

The statement must be in plain English, must be filed electronically, and must describe—

a. The security being offered and its relationship to the registrant's other securities.
b. The registrant's properties and business, including a financial statement certified by an independent public accountant.
c. The registrant's management; its compensation and other benefits, including pensions and stock options, and any interests of directors or officers in material transactions with the corporation.
d. How the registrant intends to use the proceeds of the sale.
e. Pending lawsuits.

2. Registration Process

Securities cannot be sold or advertised until after the SEC reviews the registration statement for completeness (unless it was issued by a well-known seasoned investor).

a. Waiting Period

After a statement is filed, there is a waiting period of at least twenty days. During this time, only certain types of offers—and no sales—are allowed. A preliminary (red herring) prospectus may be issued, often without stating a price. A free-writing prospectus (any type of offer that describes the issuer or the security) tells investors to obtain a prospectus at the SEC's Web site.

b. Posteffective Period

An issuer can now offer and sell the securities without restrictions (except that investors who were given a preliminary or free-writing prospectus must be given a final prospectus).

c. Restrictions Relaxed for Well-Known Seasoned Issuers

A well-known seasoned issuer is a firm that has issued at least $1 billion in securities in the previous three years or has at least $700 million of value of outstanding stock in the public's hands. This issuer can offer securities for sale without waiting for SEC review and approval of the registration statement.

C. EXEMPT SECURITIES

Securities that can be sold (and resold) without being registered include—

1. Government-issued securities.
2. Bank and financial institution securities.
3. Short-term notes and drafts (maturity does not exceed nine months.)
4. Securities of nonprofit, educational, and charitable organizations.
5. Securities issued by common carriers (trucking companies and railroads).
6. Any insurance, endowment, or annuity contract issued by a state-regulated insurance company.
7. Securities issued in a corporate reorganization in which one security is exchanged for another or in a bankruptcy proceeding.
8. Securities issued in stock dividends and stock splits.

D. EXEMPT TRANSACTIONS

Securities that can be sold without being registered include those sold in the following transactions.

1. **Regulation A Offerings**

   An issuer's offer of up to $5 million in securities in any twelve-month period is exempt. The issuer must file with the SEC a notice of the issue and an offering circular (also provided to investors before the sale) but this is a simpler and less expensive process than full registration. A company can "test the waters" (determine potential interest) before preparing the circular.

2. **Regulation D Offerings**

   Private, noninvestment company offers may be exempt. (A *noninvestment company* is a firm that is not engaged primarily in the business of investing or trading in securities.)

   a. **Offerings Up to $1 Million**

      Private, noninvestment company offerings up to $1 million in a twelve-month period are exempt [Rule 504]. This is the exemption used by most small businesses.

   b. **Offerings Up to $5 Million**

      Private, noninvestment company offerings up to $5 million in a twelve-month period if (1) no general solicitation or advertising is used; (2) the SEC is notified of the sales; (3) precaution is taken against nonexempt, unregistered resales; and (4) there are no more than thirty-five unaccredited investors. If the sale involves any unaccredited investors, all investors must be given material information about the company, its business, and the securities. The buyer cannot sell the securities for at least a year [Rule 505].

   c. **Offerings in Unlimited Amounts**

      Nonpublic and not generally advertised offerings in unlimited amounts are subject to essentially the same requirements as Rule 505, except (1) there is no limit on the amount of the offering and (2) the issuer must believe that each unaccredited investor has sufficient knowledge or experience to evaluate the investment [Rule 506].

3. **Resales and Safe Harbor Rules**

   Most securities can be resold without registration. Resales of small offerings [Rule 505] and private offerings [Rule 506] are exempt from registration under the following rules.

   a. **Rule 144**

      There must be adequate public information about the issuer, the securities must be sold in limited amounts in unsolicited brokers' transactions, the SEC must be notified of the resale, and—

      1) **The Securities Must Have Been Owned for at Least Six Months**

         If the issuer is subject to the 1934 act's reporting requirements.

      2) **The Securities Must Have Been Owned for at Least One Year**

         If the issuer is *not* subject to the 1934 act's reporting requirements.

   b. **Rule 144A**

      The securities, on issue, must not have been of the same class as securities listed on a national securities exchange or a U.S. automated interdealer quotation system. The securities are sold only to an institutional investor. The seller on resale must take steps to tell the buyer they are exempt.

E. **VIOLATIONS OF THE 1933 ACT**

   If registration statement or prospectus contains material false statements or omissions, liable parties include anyone who signed the statement.

1. **Penalties**

   Fines up to $10,000; imprisonment up to five years; injunction against selling securities; order to refund profits; damages in civil suits.

2. **Defenses**

Statement or omission was not material; plaintiff knew of misrepresentation and bought stock anyway; Most important is the *due diligence* defense, under which any defendant, except the issuer, can assert that he or she reasonably believed at the time of the registration statement the information was true and there were no material omissions.

III. THE SECURITIES EXCHANGE ACT OF 1934

This act regulates the markets in which securities are traded by requiring continuous periodic disclosure by Section 12 companies (corporations with securities on the exchanges and firms with assets in excess of $10 million and five hundred or more shareholders).

A. INSIDER TRADING—SECTION 10(b) AND SEC RULE 10b-5

Section 10(b) proscribes the use of "any manipulative or deceptive device or contrivance in contravention of such rules and regulations as the [SEC] may prescribe." SEC Rule 10b-5 prohibits the commission of fraud in connection with the purchase or sale of any security (registered or unregistered) when the requisites of federal jurisdiction are met. States have securities laws that may apply if federal law does not.

1. **What Triggers Liability**

Any material omission or misrepresentation of material facts in connection with the purchase or sale of a security can trigger liability. Fraud includes the failure to disclose inside information.

2. **What Does Not Trigger Liability**

Under the Private Securities Litigation Reform Act of 1995, financial forecasts and other forward-looking statements do not trigger liability if they include "meaningful cautionary statements identifying factors that could cause actual results to differ materially."

3. **Who Can Be Liable**

Those who take advantage of inside information when they know that it is unavailable to the person with whom they are dealing can be liable.

   a. **Insiders**

   Officers, directors, majority shareholders, and persons having access to or receiving information of a nonpublic nature on which trading is based (accountants, attorneys).

   b. **Outsiders**

   1) **Tipper/Tippee Theory**

   One who acquires inside information as a result of an insider's breach of fiduciary duty to the firm whose shares are traded can be liable, if (1) there is a breach of duty not to disclose the information, (2) the disclosure is for personal benefit, and (3) the tippee knows or should know of the breach and benefits from it.

   2) **Misappropriation Theory**

   One who wrongfully misappropriates inside information and trades on it to his or her gain can be liable, if a duty to the lawful possessor of the information was breached and harm to another results. Liability is based on a fiduciary's deception of those who entrusted him or her with access to confidential information.

B. INSIDER REPORTING AND TRADING—SECTION 16(b)

Officers, directors, and shareholders owning 10 percent of the securities registered under Section 12 are required to file reports with the SEC concerning their ownership and trading of the securities.

1. **Corporation Is Entitled to All Profits**

A firm can recapture *all* profits realized by an insider on *any* purchase and sale or sale and purchase of its stock in any six-month period.

2. **Applicability of Section 16(b)**
Section 16(b) applies to stock, warrants, options, and securities convertible into stock.

C. **REGULATION OF PROXY STATEMENTS**
Section 14(a) regulates the solicitation of proxies from shareholders of Section 12 companies. Whoever solicits a proxy must disclose, in the proxy statement, all of the pertinent facts.

D. **VIOLATIONS OF THE 1934 ACT**
Violations of Section 10(b) and Rule 10b-5 include insider trading (a crime). Section 10(b) and Rule 10b-5 require proof of *scienter* (intent to defraud or knowledge of misconduct). Violations of Section 16(b) include sales by insiders of stock acquired less than six months before.

1. **Criminal Penalties**
Maximum jail term is twenty-five years; fines up to $5 million for individuals and $2.5 million for partnerships and corporations. The standard of proof is beyond a reasonable doubt.

2. **Civil Sanctions**

a. **The SEC**
The SEC can bring suit in federal court against anyone violating or aiding in a violation of the 1934 act or SEC rules. Penalties include triple the profits gained or loss avoided by the guilty party.

b. **Private Parties**
A corporation can sue under Section 16(b) to recover short-swing profits. A private party can sue under Section 10(b) and Rule 10b-5 to rescind a contract to buy or sell securities or to obtain damages to the extent of a violator's illegal profits. Those found liable have a right of contribution.

IV. STATE SECURITIES LAWS

A. **REQUIREMENTS**
All states regulate the offer and sale of securities within individual state borders. Exemptions from federal law are not exemptions from state laws, which have their own exemptions. Disclosure requirements and antifraud regulations are often patterned on federal provisions.

B. **CONCURRENT REGULATION**
Under the National Market Securities Improvement Act of 1996, the SEC regulates most national securities activities. The Uniform Securities Act, issued by the National Conference of Commissioners on Uniform State Laws and adopted in seventeen states, is designed to coordinate state and federal securities regulation and enforcement efforts.

V. CORPORATE GOVERNANCE

Corporate governance is the system by which corporations are governed and controlled, according to the Organization of Economic Cooperation and Development. Effective governance requires more than compliance with the law. Because corporate ownership is separated from corporate control, conflicts of interest can arise.

A. **ATTEMPTS AT ALIGNING THE INTERESTS OF OFFICERS WITH SHAREHOLDERS**
Providing stock options to align the financial interests of shareholders and officers has proved to be an imperfect control device. Officers have manipulated circumstances to artificially inflate stock prices to keep the value of options high, or the options have been "repriced" to avoid losses when stock prices dropped.

B. **THE GOAL IS TO PROMOTE ACCOUNTABILITY**
Corporate oversight involves (1) the audited reporting of corporate financial progress so that managers can be evaluated and (2) legal protection for shareholders.

C. GOVERNANCE AND CORPORATE LAW

Under the law, a corporation must have a board of directors elected by the shareholders. Thus, the key element of corporate structure is the board, which makes important decisions about the firm.

1. The Board of Directors

Directors, who must operate for the shareholders' benefit, are responsible for monitoring officers and can be sued for failing to do their jobs effectively.

2. The Compensation Committee

This committee determines the amount of compensation to be paid to the officers and is responsible for assessing those officers' performance.

D. THE SARBANES=OXLEY ACT OF 2002

This act imposes strict disclosure requirements and harsh penalties for violations of securities laws.

1. Reporting on Effectiveness of Internal Controls

An independent audit of management's assessment of internal controls must be filed with the SEC. Public companies with a market capitalization of less than $75 million are exempt.

2. Other Provisions

Certain reports must be filed with the SEC earlier than under previous law. Other provisions create new private civil actions and expand the SEC's remedies.

3. Internal Controls and Accountability

The act introduces federal corporate governance requirements for public companies' boards and auditors to monitor company officers and ensure that corporate financial reports filed with the SEC are accurate and timely.

4. Certification and Monitoring

Chief executive officers and chief financial officers must certify that these documents are accurate and complete. These officers are directly accountable for the accuracy of the reports, and may be subject to civil and criminal penalties for violations.

VI.   ONLINE SECURITIES FRAUD

A. INVESTMENT SCAMS

There are infinite variations of investment scams, but most promise spectacular returns for small investments. Many are pyramid ("Ponzi") schemes, in which initial "investors" are paid with funds provided by later participants. Scams may be propagated via spam, fraudulent Web pages, online newsletters and bulletin boards, chat rooms, blogs, and tweets.

B. ONLINE INVESTMENT NEWSLETTERS AND FORUMS

To inflate the price of a stock and profit from its sale, its holders may pay others to tout the stock online. Potential investors may be duped if the identities of those who pay for this service are not disclosed when the law requires it. The same tactic may be employed in other online venues such as forums, using any number of aliases to falsify interest in the stock.

C. PONZI SCHEMES

These schemes often claim to consist of risk-free or low-risk investments. They sometimes fool U.S. residents into investing in offshore companies.

TRUE-FALSE QUESTIONS

(Answers at the Back of the Book)

____ 1. A security that does not qualify for an exemption must be registered before it is offered to the public.

_____ 2. Before a security can be sold to the public, prospective investors must be provided with a prospectus.

_____ 3. Stock splits are generally exempt from the registration requirements of the Securities Act of 1933.

_____ 4. Sales of securities may not occur until twenty days after registration.

_____ 5. Private offerings of securities in unlimited amounts that are not generally solicited or advertised must be registered before they can be sold.

_____ 6. A proxy statement must fully and accurately disclose all of the facts that are pertinent to the matter on which shareholders are being asked to vote.

_____ 7. All states have disclosure requirements and antifraud provisions that cover securities.

_____ 8. *Scienter* is not a requirement for liability under Section 10(b) of the Securities Exchange Act of 1934.

_____ 9. No one who receives inside information as a result of another's breach of his or her fiduciary duty can be liable under SEC Rule 10b-5.

_____ 10. No security can be resold without registration.

FILL-IN QUESTIONS

(Answers at the Back of the Book)

The SEC can award "bounty" payments to persons providing information leading to the _____ (conviction/prosecution) of insider-trading violations. Civil penalties include _____ (double/triple) the profits gained or the loss avoided. Criminal penalties include maximum jail terms of _____ (ten/ twenty-five) years. Violators _____ (may/may not) also be subject to multi-million-dollar fines.

MULTIPLE-CHOICE QUESTIONS

(Answers at the Back of the Book)

_____ 1. Frank, an officer of Gyra Gizmo, Inc., learns that Gyra has developed a new source of energy. Frank tells Huey, an outsider. They each buy Gyra stock. When the development is announced, the stock price increases, and they each immediately sell their stock. Subject to liability for insider trading

a. are Frank and Huey.
b. is Frank only.
c. is Huey only
d. is Gyra, but neither Frank nor Huey.

_____ 2. Centro Associates sells securities. The definition of a security does *not* include, as an element,

a. an investment.
b. a common enterprise.
c. a reasonable expectation of profits.
d. profits derived entirely from the efforts of the investor.

____ 3. Elmo, a director of Far East Development Company, learns that a Far East engineer has developed a new, improved product. Over the next six months, Elmo buys and sells Far East stock for a profit. Of Elmo's profit, Far East may recapture

a. all.
b. half.
c. 10 percent.
d. none.

____ 4. Superior, Inc., is a private, noninvestment company. In one year, Superior advertises a $300,000 offering. Concerning registration, this offering is

a. exempt because of the low amount of the issue.
b. exempt because it was advertised.
c. exempt because the issuer is a private company.
d. not exempt.

____ 5. Huron, Inc., makes a $6 million private offering to twenty accredited investors and less than thirty unaccredited investors. Huron advertises the offering and believes that the unaccredited investors are sophisticated enough to evaluate the investment. Huron gives material information about itself, its business, and the securities to all investors. Concerning registration, this offering is

a. exempt because of the low amount of the issue.
b. exempt because it was advertised.
c. exempt because the issuer believed that the unaccredited investors were sophisticated enough to evaluate the investment.
d. not exempt.

____ 6. Ontario, Inc., in one year, advertises two $2.25 million offerings. Buying the stock are twelve accredited investors. Concerning registration, this offering is

a. exempt because of the low amount of the issue.
b. exempt because it was advertised.
c. exempt because only accredited investors bought stock.
d. not exempt.

____ 7. Natural Soy, Inc., wants to make an offering of securities to the public. The offer is not exempt from registration. Before Natural Soy sells these securities, it must provide *investors* with

a. a marketing and management plan.
b. a prospectus.
c. a registration statement.
d. samples of its products.

____ 8. Great Lakes Company is a private, noninvestment company. Last year, as part of a $250,000 advertised offering, Great Lakes sold stock to Jon, a private investor. Jon would now like to sell the shares. Concerning registration, this resale is

a. exempt because of the low amount of the original issue.
b. exempt because the offering was advertised.
c. exempt because all resales are exempt.
d. not exempt.

___ 9. Fat City Games, Inc.'s registration statement must include

   a. a description of the accounting firm that audits Fat City.
   b. a description of the security being offered for sale.
   c. a financial forecast for Fat City's next five years.
   d. a marketing and management plan to ensure Fat City's success.

___ 10. **Based a Sample CPA Question.** Under the Securities Exchange Act of 1934, the Securities and Exchange Commission is responsible for all of the following activities EXCEPT

   a. investigating securities fraud.
   b. prosecuting criminal violations of federal securities laws.
   c. regulating the activities of securities brokers.
   d. requiring disclosure of facts concerning offerings of securities listed on national securities exchanges.

SHORT ESSAY QUESTIONS

1. What is the process by which a company sells securities to the public?

2. How is insider trading regulated by Section 10(b), SEC Rule 10b-5, and Section 16(b)?

GAMEPOINTS

(Answers at the Back of the Book)

1. The video game "High End High" is set in the world of finance. Your avatar has the opportunity to invest in a variety of enterprises in different scenarios, mostly involving exotic or cutting edge products or services. In the game, NanoGene, Inc., advertises online that it will make a $4.5 million offering of stock on within thirty days. The firm makes the offer and less than a week after the first sale notifies the Securities and Exchange Commission (SEC). All buyers—including you and fifty-two other unaccredited investors, as well as more sophisticated individuals and institutions—are given material information about the company, its business, its possible future, and its stock. You invest heavily in NanoGene, and the offering, which the firm does not register, is sold out within six months. Did you invest in a company that will soon be leveled with sanctions by the SEC? Discuss.

2. Still playing "High End High," which you can lose only by losing everything, you decide that, unlike your precipitous invest mention NanoGene, you will now act only on "material information." What information do you think meets this qualification?

CUMULATIVE HYPOTHETICAL PROBLEM FOR UNIT SIX—INCLUDING CHAPTERS 24–29

(Answers at the Back of the Book)

Corrosive Chemical Corporation makes and sells chemical products to industrial customers and individual consumers.

___ 1. Corrosive advertises its products with slogans that consist of vague generalities. Because of this advertising, the Federal Trade Commission may

   a. issue a cease-and-desist order only.
   b. require counteradvertising only.
   c. issue a cease-and-desist order or require counteradvertising.
   d. neither issue a cease-and-desist order nor require counteradvertising.

_____ **2.** To determine whether Corrosive is violating regulations issued by the Environmental Protection Agency (EPA), the EPA may *not*

    a. arbitrarily order Corrosive to shut its manufacturing site down.
    b. conduct an on-site inspection of Corrosive's manufacturing site.
    c. obtain a search warrant to search Corrosive's premises for a specific item.
    d. test Corrosive's products on its manufacturing site.

_____ **3.** Corrosive's manufacturing process generates hazardous waste that is transported to Dump-It Company's disposal site by Toxic Trucking, Inc. If the EPA cleans up Dump-It's site, liability for the cost may be assessed against

    a. Corrosive, Dump-It, or Toxic.
    b. Corrosive or Dump-It only.
    c. Corrosive or Toxic only.
    d. Dump-It or Toxic only.

_____ **4.** Corrosive charges Resource Refining, Inc., less per item than Corrosive charges Standard Industrial Corporation for the same product. The two buyers are competitors. This pricing difference violates antitrust law

    a. if both buyers' customers pay the same price for the buyers' products.
    b. if Resource and Standard know what each other pays.
    c. if the pricing substantially lessens competition.
    d. under no circumstances.

_____ **5.** The Corrosive board of directors decides to issue additional stock in the firm. The registration statement must include

    a. a copy of the corporation's most recent proxy statement.
    b. the names of prospective accredited investors.
    c. the names of the current shareholders.
    d. the principal purposes for which the proceeds from the offering will be used.

QUESTIONS ON THE FOCUS ON ETHICS FOR UNIT SIX— THE REGULATORY ENVIRONMENT

(Answers at the Back of the Book)

_____ **1.** The U.S. Fish and Wildlife Service (FWS) prohibits Victor from harvesting the timber on fifty acres of his land until it is clear that the timber is not a habitat for an endangered species. Victor files a suit against the FWS. The court is most likely to hold that this is

    a. a compensatory "taking."
    b. a "taking" but not compensatory.
    c. compensatory but not a "taking."
    d. not a compensatory "taking."

_____ **2.** Among other global enterprises, Yang Ltd. in China, Rio de Angel S.A. in South America, and Clear Creek Corporation in the United States emit pollutants in to the air and water. The chief difficulty in applying a single standard to each of these polluters is that pollutants

    a. are not persons or entities.
    b. are too costly to clean up in proportion to the benefit gained.
    c. do not stop at a nation's borders.
    d. increase in output the more economic growth a nation experiences.

___ **3.** Pristine Property Company buys forty acres of land to build a corporate complex. After construction begins, the county zones the surrounding, undeveloped area for a nature preserve, in which it includes 75 percent of Pristine's land. The county owes Pristine

a. just compensation.
b. land of equivalent value.
c. private use of the preserve.
d. nothing.

Answers

Chapter 1

True-False Questions

1. T
2. F. Legal positivists believe that there can be no higher law that a nation's positive law (the law created by a particular society at a particular point in time). The belief that law should reflect universal moral and ethical principles that are part of human nature is part of the natural law tradition.
3. T
4. T
5. T
6. F. With respect to federal statutes, the U.S. Constitution is the supreme law of the land. A federal statute the conflicts with the U.S. Constitution may be struck as unconstitutional.
7. F. The National Conference of Commissioners on Uniform State Laws drafted the Uniform Commercial Code (and other uniform laws and model codes) and proposed it for adoption by the states.
8. F. This is the definition of civil law. Criminal law relates to wrongs against society as a whole and for which society has established sanctions.
9. T
10. F. A citation may contain the names of the parties, the year in which the case was decided, and the volume and page numbers of a reporter in which the opinion may be found, but it does not include the name of the judge who decided the case.

Fill-in Questions

with similar facts; precedent; permits a predictable

Multiple-Choice Questions

1. D. Legal positivists believe that there can be no higher law than the written law of a given society at a particular time. They do not believe in "natural rights."
2. B. The use of precedent—the doctrine of *stare decisis*—permits a predictable, relatively quick, and fair resolution of cases. Under this doctrine, a court must adhere to principles of law established by higher courts.
3. D. The doctrine of *stare decisis* attempts to harmonize the results in cases with similar facts. When the facts are sufficiently similar, the same rule is applied. Cases with identical facts could serve as binding authority, but it is more practical

A-1

to expect to find cases with facts that are not identical but similar—as similar as possible.

4. A. An order to do or refrain from a certain act is an injunction. An order to perform as promised is a decree for specific performance. These remedies, as well as rescission, are equitable remedies. An award of damages is a remedy at law.

5. B. Equity and law provide different remedies, and at one time, most courts could grant only one type. Today, most states do not maintain separate courts of law and equity, and a judge may grant either or both forms of relief. Equitable relief is generally granted, however, only if damages (the legal remedy) is inadequate.

6. C. The U.S. Constitution is the supreme law of the land. Any state or federal law or court decision in conflict with the Constitution is unenforceable and will be struck. Similarly, provisions in a state constitution take precedence over the state's statutes, rules, and court decisions.

7. B. In establishing case law, or common law, the courts interpret and apply state and federal constitutions, rules, and statutes. Case law applies in areas that statutes or rules do not cover. Federal law applies to all states, and preempts state law in many areas.

8. A. Law that defines, describes, regulates, or creates rights or duties is substantive law. Law that establishes methods for enforcing rights established by substantive law is procedural law. Criminal law governs wrongs committed against society for which society demands redress.

9. B. In reasoning by analogy, a judge compares the facts in one case to the facts in another case and to the extent that the facts are similar, applies the same legal principle. If the facts can be distinguished, different legal rules may apply. In either case, a judge will ordinarily state his or her reasons for applying a certain principle and arriving at a certain conclusion.

10. C. A concurring opinion makes or emphasizes a point different from those made or emphasized in the majority's opinion. An opinion written for the entire court is a unanimous opinion. An opinion that outlines only the majority's views is a majority opinion. A separate opinion that does not agree with the majority's decision is a dissenting opinion.

GamePoints

1. A breach of contract falls, of course, in the area of the law of contracts. Contract law is a part of civil law, in contrast to criminal law. Civil law spells out duties that exist between persons. The remedies available for a breach of contract include money damages, which is the usual remedy at law. If this

remedy is unavailable or inadequate, the breaching party might be ordered to perform as promised. Or the contract might be cancelled and the parties returned to the positions they held before the contract's formation.

2. Sources of law that might afford an opportunity for relief for a breach of contract or warranty, as this problem poses, include statutory law. In particular, the Uniform Commercial Code, which provides a uniform, yet flexible, set of rules governing commercial transactions, is most likely to be brought to bear on this issue. Administrative law is also a possibility, because regulations may affect every aspect of a business operation, including the way a firm makes and sells its products.

Chapter 2

True-False Questions

1. T
2. T
3. F. The decisions of a state's highest court on all questions of state law are final. The United States Supreme Court can overrule only those state court decisions that involve questions of federal law.
4. T
5. F. Pleadings inform each party of the other's claims and specify the issues. Pleadings consist of a complaint and an answer, not a motion to dismiss.
6. F. In ruling on a motion for summary judgment, a court can consider evidence outside the pleadings, such as answers to interrogatories.
7. T
8. T
9. F. A losing party may appeal an adverse judgment to a higher court, but the party in whose favor the judgment was issued may also appeal if, for example, he or she is awarded less than sought in the suit.
10. T

Fill-in Questions

trial; reviewing; factual issues; the law to the facts; of law but not of fact

Multiple-Choice Questions

1. A. On a "sliding scale" test, a court's exercise of personal jurisdiction depends on the amount of business that an individual or firm transacts over the Internet. Jurisdiction is most likely proper when there is substantial business, most likely improper

when a Web site is no more than an ad, and may or may not be appropriate when there is some interactivity. "Any" interactivity with "any resident" of a state would likely not be enough, however.

2. A. As noted above, a corporation is subject to the jurisdiction of the courts in any state in which it is incorporated, in which it has its main office, or in which it does business. The court may be able to exercise personal jurisdiction or in rem jurisdiction, or the court may reach a defendant corporation with a long arm statute. In the right circumstances, this firm might also be involved in a suit in a federal court, if the requirements for federal jurisdiction are met: a federal question is involved, or there is diversity of citizenship and the amount in controversy is $75,000 or more.

3. D. An appeals court examines the record of a case, looking mostly at questions of law for errors by the court below. If it determines that a retrial is necessary, the case is sent back to the lower court. For this reason, an appellant's best ground for an appeal focuses on the law that applied to the issues in the case, not questions concerning the credibility of the evidence or other findings of fact.

4. D. The United States Supreme Court is not required to hear any case. The Court has jurisdiction over any case decided by any of the federal courts of appeals and appellate authority over cases decided by the states' highest courts if the latter involve questions of federal law. But the Court's exercise of its jurisdiction is discretionary, not mandatory.

5. C. In the suit in this question, the court can exercise in rem jurisdiction. A court can exercise jurisdiction over property located within its boundaries. A corporation is also subject to the jurisdiction of the courts in any state in which it is incorporated, in which it has its main office, or in which it does business.

6. A. Every state has at least one court of appeals, which may be an intermediate appellate court or the state's highest court. If a federal or constitutional issue is involved, the case may ultimately be appealed to the United States Supreme Court.

7. A. An important part of the discovery process is a deposition, which is sworn testimony. Interrogatories are a series of written questions for which written answers are prepared and signed under oath by the plaintiff or defendant. A pretrial conference involves the plaintiff, the defendant, their attorneys, and judge.

8. D. After a plaintiff calls and questions the first witness on direct examination, the defendant questions the witness on cross-examination. The plaintiff may then question the witness again (redirect examination), and the defendant may follow (re-

cross-examination). Then the plaintiff's other witnesses are called, and the defendant presents his or her case.

9. C. After a verdict, the losing party can move for a new trial or for a judgment notwithstanding the verdict. If these motions are denied, he or she can appeal.

10. C. For obvious reasons, a losing party may wish to appeal a judgment. A winning party has the same right to appeal if he or she is dissatisfied with the relief granted.

GamePoints

1. You could file a suit against your opponent in this problem in a trial court of general jurisdiction in either the state of your residence or the state of the defendant's home. Because there appears to be diversity of citizenship in the situation set out here, and the amount in controversy could conceivably exceed the jurisdictional amount, a suit might alternatively be filed in a federal district court, which is the equivalent of a state trial court of general jurisdiction.

2. Even if you meet the requirements for the United States Supreme Court to exercise jurisdiction in your case—there is a federal question at issue, or a federal court of appeals has reviewed your case, or both—the Supreme Court can still refuse to hear your appeal. There is no absolute right of appeal to the nation's highest Court. A party may ask the Court to issue a writ of *certiorari* (this is an order to a lower court to send the Court the record of the case for review), but the Court may deny the request.

Chapter 3

True-False Questions

1. F. Most lawsuits—as many as 95 percent—are dismissed or settled before they go to trial. Courts encourage alternative dispute resolution (ADR) and sometimes order parties to submit to ADR, particularly mediation, before allowing their suits to come to trial.

2. F. In mediation, a mediator assists the parties in reaching an agreement, but not by deciding the dispute. The mediator emphasizes points of agreement, helps the parties evaluate their positions, and proposes solutions.

3. F. If an arbitration agreement covers the subject matter of a dispute, a party to the agreement can be compelled to arbitrate the dispute. A court would order the arbitration without ruling on the basic controversy.

4.   F. The jury verdict after a summary jury trial (SJT) is not binding. SJT is a form of alternative dispute resolution in which the parties' attorneys present their cases to a jury, but no witnesses are called, and the verdict is advisory only.

5.   F. Negotiation typically does not involve a third party. The major difference between negotiation and mediation is that mediation does involve the presence of a third party—a mediator—who assists the parties in reaching an agreement and who often suggests solutions towards that end.

6.   T

7.   F. In court-annexed arbitration, either party may reject an award, and the case will go to trial, with the court reconsidering all evidence and legal questions as though no arbitration occurred.

8.   F. The goal of *mediation* is to come to a resolution that benefits both sides in a dispute. This is one of the advantages of mediation and has contributed to its increasing popularity as a form of dispute resolution.

9.   T

10.   T

Fill-in Questions

Negotiation; Mediation; a mediator; Arbitration; an arbitrator

Multiple-Choice Questions

1.   D. Negotiation is an informal means of dispute resolution. Generally, unlike mediation and arbitration, no third party is involved in resolving the dispute. In those two forms, a third party may render a binding or nonbinding decision. Arbitration is a more formal process than mediation or negotiation. Litigation involves a third party—a judge—who renders a legally binding decision.

2.   B. In a summary jury trial, the jury's verdict is not binding, as it would otherwise be in a court trial. In a mini-trial, the attorneys argue a case and a third party renders an opinion, but the opinion discusses how a court would decide the dispute. Early neutral case negotiation is what its name suggests, involving a third party who evaluates the disputing parties' positions.

3.   C. Online dispute resolution (ODR) is a new type of alternative dispute resolution. Most ODR forums resolve disputers informally and come to nonbonding resolutions. Any party to a dispute being considered in ODR may discontinue the process and appeal to a court at any time.

4.   D. Neither the amount involved nor the parties' satisfaction is relevant. An arbitrator's award will be set aside if it violates pubic policy. Other grounds on which an award may be set aside arise from the arbitrator's conduct—for example, if his or her bad faith substantially prejudices the rights of one of the parties, or if he or she decides issues that the parties did not agree to submit to arbitration.

5.   D. In mediation, no sanction can be imposed that the parties have not agreed to. Also, in mediation the neutral third party (the mediator) does not decide the controversy, and there is no deadline to resolving the dispute. The goal of mediation is to come to a resolution that benefits both parties.

6.   A. A mini-trial is not a public proceeding held in a court. It is a private proceeding in which attorneys briefly argue each party's case. A third party indicates how a court would likely decide the issue.

7.   A. A summary jury trial can look like a regular jury trial. The basic difference between a traditional trial and a summary jury trial is that in the latter the verdict is advisory only. It is required that after the verdict in a summary jury trial, the parties attempt to negotiate a resolution of their dispute.

8.   D. There are certain disputes that, in most states, are not submitted to arbitration by the courts. In most states, court-annexed arbitration is available only when a dispute does *not* involve title to real estate. Similarly, court-annexed arbitration is usually available only if a court's equity powers are *not* involved. Also, such a proceeding may be compelled only if one of the parties has demanded a jury trial.

9.   C. Many parties prefer arbitration over litigation. The advantages of arbitration include lower cost than traditional litigation, the speed with which a dispute can be resolved compared to litigation, and the possibility of less formal rules and less rigid proceedings than court trials.

10.   D. Mediation is becoming the most popular form of ADR, with participants reporting high rates of satisfaction with the results. The advantages of mediation include lower cost than either arbitration or traditional litigation, the speed with which a dispute can be resolved compared to arbitration or litigation, and resolutions that benefit both sides to a dispute.

GamePoints

1.   The bases on which any award might be set aside include the arbitrator's (1) corruption, fraud, or other "undue means;" (2) bias; and (3) acts that substantially prejudice the rights of the one of the parties. These are not simple mistakes in judgment, but show bad faith on the part of the arbitrator.

They affect the integrity of the process and the honesty and impartiality of the arbitrator. A bribe—Garvey's offer to split the proceeds of an award with the arbitrator—constitutes "undue means." Letting only one side—Garvey—argue his case is clearly bias. A meeting between the arbitrator and one party outside the presence of the other party likewise taints the arbitration process by affecting its integrity. This can substantially prejudice the rights of the party who is not present. Thus, there are several grounds on which to base a request to a court that this award be set aside.

2. The fundamental difference between *voluntary* arbitration and *court-annexed* arbitration is the finality and reviewability of the award. With voluntary arbitration, submission of the dispute is voluntary, but in a case of binding arbitration compliance with the decision of the arbitrator can be mandatory. With court-annexed arbitration, submission of the dispute is mandatory, but compliance with the award is voluntary.

Thus, with court-annexed arbitration, either party—Hildebrand or you—may reject the award for any reason. If either of you rejects the award, the case proceeds to trial, and the court reconsiders the evidence and questions of law as if there had been no arbitration. This protects both of you from being denied your "day in court." The party who rejects the award may be required to pay court costs and fees if he does not improve his position by going to court. If either of you fails to appear at, or to participate in, the court-ordered arbitration proceeding, you will be considered to have waived the right to reject the award.

Chapter 4

True-False Questions

1. T
2. T
3. T
4. F. According to utilitarianism, it is the consequences of an act that determine how ethical the act is. Applying this theory requires determining who will be affected by an act, assessing the positive and negatives effects of alternatives, and choosing the alternative that will provide the greatest benefit for the most people. Utilitarianism is premised on acting so as to do the greatest good for the greatest number of people. An act that affects a minority negatively may still be morally acceptable.
5. T

6. F. In situations involving ethical decisions, a balance must sometimes be struck between equally good or equally poor courses of action. The choice is often between equally good alternatives—benefiting shareholders versus benefiting employees, for example—and sometimes one group may be adversely affected. (The legality of a particular action may also be unclear.)
7. T
8. F. Simply obeying the law will not meet all ethical obligations. The law does not cover all ethical requirements. An act may be unethical but not illegal. In fact, compliance with the law is at best a moral minimum. Furthermore, there is an ethical aspect to almost every decision that a business firm makes.
9. T
10. F. Bribery is also a legal issue, regulated in the United States by the Foreign Corrupt Practices Act. Internationally, a treaty signed by the members of the Organization for Economic Cooperation and Development makes bribery of public officials a serious crime. Each member nation is expected to enact legislation implementing the treaty.

Fill-in Questions

Religious standards; Kantian ethics; the principle of rights

Multiple-Choice Questions

1. C. Business ethics focus on the application of moral principles in a business context. Different standards are not required. Business ethics is a subset of ethics that relates specifically to what constitutes right and wrong in situations that arise in business.
2. B. Traditionally, ethical reasoning relating to business has been characterized by two fundamental approaches—duty-based ethics and utilitarianism, or outcome-based ethics. Duty-based ethics derive from religious sources or philosophical principles. These standards may be absolute, which means that an act may not be undertaken, whatever the consequences.
3. A. Under religious ethical standards, it is the nature of an act that determines how ethical the act is, not its consequences. This is considered an *absolute* standard. But this standard is tempered by an element of compassion (the "Golden Rule").
4. A. In contrast to duty-based ethics, outcome-based ethics (utilitarianism) involves a consideration of the consequences of an action. Utilitarianism is premised on acting so as to do the greatest good for the greatest number of people.

5. C. Utilitarianism requires determining who will be affected by an action, assessing the positive and negatives effects of alternatives, and choosing the alternative that will provide the greatest benefit for the most people. This approach has been criticized as tending to reduce the welfare of human beings to plus and minus signs on a cost-benefit worksheet.

6. A. A corporation, for example, as an employer, commonly faces ethical problems that involve conflicts among itself, its employees, its customers, its suppliers, its shareholders, its community, or other groups. Increasing wages, for instance, may benefit the employees and the community, but reduce profits and the ability of the employer to give pay increases in the future, as well as decreasing dividends to shareholders. To be considered socially responsible, when making a decision, a business firm must take into account the interests of all of these groups, as well as society as a whole.

7. B. Striking a balance between what is profitable and what is legal and ethical can be difficult. A failure to act legally or ethically can result in a reduction in profits, but a failure to act in the profitable interest of the firm can also cause profits to suffer. In any profession, however, there is a responsibility, both legal and ethical, not to misrepresent material facts, even at the expense of some profits. This is a clear ethical standard in the legal profession and in the accounting profession. This question and answer are based on a question that was included in the CPA exam in November 1994.

8. A. In part because it is impossible to be entirely aware of what the law requires and prohibits, the best course for a business firm is to act responsibly and in good faith. This course may provide the best defense if a transgression is discovered. Striking a balance between what is profitable and what is legal and ethical can be difficult, however. A failure to act legally or ethically can result in a reduction in profits, but a failure to act in the profitable interest of the firm can also cause profits to suffer. *Optimum* profits are the maximum profits that a firm can realize while staying within legal and ethical limits.

9. D. The principle of rights theory of ethics follows the belief that persons have fundamental rights. This belief is implied by duty-based ethical standards and Kantian ethics. The rights are implied by the duty that forms the basis for the standard (for example, the duty not to kill implies that persons have a right to live), or by the personal dignity implicit in the Kantian belief about the fundamental nature of human beings. Not to respect these rights would, under the principle of rights theory, be morally wrong.

10. A. The Foreign Corrupt Practices Act prohibits any U.S. firm from bribing foreign officials to influence official acts to provide the firm with business opportunities. Such payments are allowed, however, if they would be lawful in the foreign country. Thus, to avoid violating the law, the firm in this problem should determine whether such payments are legal in the minister's country.

GamePoints

1. Ethics is the study of what constitutes right and wrong behavior, focusing on morality and the way in which moral principles are derived or the way in which such principles apply to conduct in daily life. Sometimes the issues that arise concern fairness, justice, and "the right thing to do." In the context of this problem, to address these questions, it might be considered what is at stake. If there is a competition with other players or some other situation in which consulting outside sources is questionable, then it is unethical to review the Web sites. If, however, you are playing alone, and you have made your best attempt to advance, it may not be unethical to seek help.

2. The ethics in this situation relate to fairness, justice, "the right thing to do," and personal honesty and integrity. Intentionally lying to a vendor about the condition of goods sold is untruthful, illegal, and unethical. It is a breach of a duty of good faith, without which the social and economic dealings among us all could not continue. To further lie to others about the same issue would compound the breach. None of the approaches to ethical reasoning described in this chapter would support any of the acts set out in the problem.

Cumulative Hypothetical Problem for Unit One—Including Chapters 1–4

1. A. Mediation involves the a third party, a mediator. The mediator does not decide the dispute but only assists the parties to resolve it themselves. Although the mediator does not render a legally binding decision, any agreement the parties reach may be legally binding.

2. D. These state and federal courts would all have jurisdiction over the defendant. The customer's state could exercise jurisdiction over the firm through its long arm statute. The firm's state would have jurisdiction over it as a resident. A federal court could hear the case under its diversity jurisdiction: the parties are residents of different states and the amount in controversy is at least $75,000.

3. A. Damages, or money damages, is a remedy at law. Remedies in equity include injunctions, specific performance, and rescission. The distinction arose because the law courts in England could not always grant suitable remedies, and so equity courts were created to grant other types of relief. The U.S. legal system derives from the English system.

4. C. The power of judicial review is the power of any state or federal court to review a statute and declare it unconstitutional. Courts can also review the actions of the executive branch, which includes administrative agencies, to determine their constitutionality. A statute or rule that is declared unconstitutional is void. The power of judicial review is not expressly stated in the Constitution but is implied.

5. D. Ethics is the study of what constitutes right or wrong behavior. It focuses on the application of moral principles to conduct. In a business context, ethics involves the application of moral principles to business conduct.

Questions on the Focus on Ethics for Unit One—Ethics and the Foundations

1. D. Ethics is the study of what constitutes right or wrong behavior. It focuses on the application of moral principles to conduct. In a business context, ethics involves the application of moral principles to business conduct. Legal liability is a separate question and may, or may not, indicate unethical behavior. Profitability is also a separate issue. A reference to the "moral minimum" in the context of ethics refers to compliance with the law as the least a corporation can do to perform ethically.

2. A. If a business firm does not conduct its operations ethically, its goodwill, reputation, and future profits likely suffer. A firm that shows a commitment to ethical behavior often receives benefits greater than any advantages it may have sacrificed to do "what's right." A firm that is perceived as ethical may also attract investors.

3. C. Because of the many stakeholders to whom a business may owe a duty, there are circumstances in which a firm could act socially irresponsible in maintaining a position for its "rightness," particularly if it could be interpreted as "weak." Shareholders are owed a return on their investments, employees are owed jobs and payment for their work, communities need vibrant economies, and so on. None of this would be possible if the business at the core did not make a profit. Of course, there should be at least some basis in truth or rightness for a legal position, or it will ultimately be a losing argu-

ment. In that situation, the firm could not meet its obligations.

Chapter 5

True-False Questions

1. F. A federal form of government is one in which separate states form a union and divide sovereign power between themselves and a central authority. The United States has a federal form of government.

2. F. The president does not have this power. Under the doctrine of judicial review, however, the courts can hold acts of Congress and of the executive branch unconstitutional.

3. T

4. T

5. F. Under the supremacy clause, when there is a direct conflict between a federal law and a state law, the federal law takes precedence over the state law, and the state law is rendered invalid.

6. T

7. F. The protections in the Bill of Rights limit the power of the federal government. Most of these protections also apply to the states through the due process clause of the Fourteenth Amendment.

8. F. Commercial speech (advertising) can be restricted as long as the restriction (1) seeks to implement a substantial government interest, (2) directly advances that interest, and (3) goes no further than necessary to accomplish its objective.

9. F. Due process relates to the limits that the law places on the liberty of *everyone*. Equal protection relates to the limits that the law places on only *some people*.

10. T

Fill-in Questions

states; states; state

Multiple-Choice Questions

1. D. Under Articles I, II, and III of the U.S. Constitution, the legislative branch makes the law, the judicial branch interprets the law, and the executive branch enforces the law. There is no separate "administrative branch."

2. A. Under the commerce clause, Congress has the power to regulate every commercial enterprise in the United States. Recently, the United States Supreme Court has struck down federal laws, to limit this power somewhat, in areas that have

"nothing to do with commerce," including non-economic, criminal conduct.

3. A. State statutes that impinge on interstate commerce are not always struck down, nor are they always upheld. A court will balance a state's interest in regulating a certain matter against the burden that the statute places on interstate commerce. If the statute does not substantially interfere, it will not be held in violation of the commerce clause.

4. A. The First Amendment provides corporations and other business entities with significant protection of their political speech. As another example, a law that forbids a corporation from using inserts in its bills to its customers to express its views on controversial issues would also violate the First Amendment.

5. B. Commercial speech does not have as much protection under the First Amendment as noncommercial speech. Commercial speech that is misleading may be restricted, however, if the restriction (1) seeks to advance a substantial government interest, (2) directly advances that interest, and (3) goes no further than necessary.

6. B. Aspects of the Fifth and Fourteenth Amendments that cover procedural due process concern the procedures used to make any government decision to take life, liberty, or property. These procedures must be fair, which generally mean that they give an opportunity to object.

7. C. Substantive due process focuses on the content (substance) of a law under the Fifth and Fourteenth Amendments. Depending on which rights a law regulates, it must either promote a compelling or overriding government interest or be rationally related to a legitimate governmental end.

8. A. Equal protection means that the government must treat similarly situated individuals in a similar manner. The equal protection clause of the Fourteenth Amendment applies to state and local governments, and the due process clause of the Fifth Amendment guarantees equal protection by the federal government. Generally, a law regulating an economic matter is considered valid if there is a "rational basis" on which the law relates to a legitimate government interest.

9. D. A federal law takes precedence over a state law on the same subject. Also under the supremacy clause, if Congress chooses to act exclusively in an area in which the states have concurrent power, Congress is said to preempt the area.

10. A. Dissemination of obscene materials is a crime. Speech that harms the good reputation of another, or defamatory speech, is not protected under the First Amendment. "Fighting words," which are words that are likely to incite others to respond with violence, are not constitutionally protected.

Other unprotected speech includes other speech that violates criminal laws, such as threats.

GamePoints

1. The First Amendment to the U.S. Constitution guarantees the freedom of speech. The courts interpret this amendment to give substantial protection to commercial speech, including advertising. But this protection is not as extensive as that given to noncommercial speech. Even if commercial speech is not related to illegal activities nor misleading, it may be restricted if a state has a substantial interest that cannot be achieved by less restrictive means. In this problem, the state has a substantial interest in consumers not being misled. This consideration affects what can be said in any product's ads.

2. State governments have the authority to regulate affairs within their borders, in part under the Tenth Amendment, which reserves all powers to the states not delegated to the national government. This authority is known as the states' police power, and under it, the states regulate private activities to protect or promote the public order, health, safety, morals, and general welfare. If these state regulations conflict with federal law, however, they are rendered invalid under the Constitution's supremacy clause.

Chapter 6

True-False Questions

1. T
2. T
3. T
4. F. Agencies formulate and issue their rules under the authority of Congress. These rules are as legally binding as the laws enacted by Congress. It is for this reason, in part, that rulemaking procedures generally include opportunities for public comment, that the rules are subject to review by the courts, and that agencies are subject to other controls by the three branches of government.
5. F. Appeal is not mandatory, and if there is no appeal, the initial order becomes final. Either side may appeal the determination in an agency adjudication, however, to the commission that oversees the agency or ultimately to a federal court.
6. F. Congress can influence agency policy in several ways. These include that Congress can create or abolish an agency, or influence policy by the appropriation of funds for certain purposes. Congress can also revise the functions of an agency.

7.   T
8.   T
9.   T
10.   F. In most circumstances, a warrant is required for a search or the agency will be held to have violated the Fourth Amendment. Warrants are not required, however, to conduct searches in businesses in highly regulated industries, in certain hazardous operations, and in emergencies.

Fill-in Questions

Federal Register; anyone; must; *Federal Register*

Multiple-Choice Questions

1.   A. Agency powers include functions associated with the legislature (rulemaking), executive branch (investigation), and courts (adjudication). Under Article I of the U.S. Constitution and the delegation doctrine, Congress has the power to establish administrative agencies and delegate any or all of these powers to those agencies.
2.   C. Agencies may obtain information through subpoenas or searches. A subpoena may compel the appearance of a witness (a subpoena *ad testificandum*) or the provision of certain documents and records (a subpoena *duces tecum*). In some cases, particularly searches of businesses involved in a highly regulated industry, searches may be conducted without warrants.
3.   D. Procedures vary widely among agencies, even within agencies. But under the Administrative Procedure Act, rulemaking typically includes these steps: notice, opportunity for comment, and publication in the *Federal Register* of a final draft of the rule. The notice-and-comment period opens a proposed rule to public comment. The period must be at least thirty days, and it s often longer.
4.   C. An agency has the authority to issue subpoenas. There are limits on agency demands for information, however. An investigation must have a legitimate purpose. The information that is sought must be relevant. The party from whom the information is sought must not be unduly burdened by the request. And the demand must be specific.
5.   A. This is the "arbitrary and capricious" test under which acts committed willfully, unreasonable, and without considering the facts can be overturned. (The other choices are not legitimate grounds for judicial review.) A court may also consider whether the agency has exceeded its authority or violated any constitutional provisions. Depending on the circumstances, when a court reviews an act of an administrative agency, the court may also determine whether the agency has properly interpreted laws applicable to the action under review, acted in accord with procedural requirements, or reached conclusions that are not supported by substantial evidence.
6.   B. The Government-in-the-Sunshine Act requires "every portion of every meeting of an agency" that is headed by a "collegial body" to be open to "public observation." The Freedom of Information Act requires the federal government to disclose certain records to persons on request, with some exceptions. The Regulatory Flexibility Act requires, among other things, analyses of new regulations in certain circumstances. The Small Business Regulatory Enforcement Fairness Act covers several matters important to businesses, including the federal courts' authority to enforce the Regulatory Flexibility Act, but it does not cover the opening of agency meetings to the public.
7.   C. The Administrative Procedure Act provides for court review of most agency actions, but first a party must exhaust all other means of resolving a controversy with an agency. (Also, under the ripeness doctrine, the agency action must be ripe for review: the action must be reviewable—which agency actions presumably are—the party must have standing, and an actual controversy must be at issue.)
8.   D. The president's veto is a method by which the authority of an agency can be checked or curtailed. The limits listed in the other responses in this question are choices available to Congress to limit the authority of administrative agencies.
9.   B. After an agency publishes notice of a proposed rule, any interested parties can express their views in writing, or orally if a hearing is held. The agency must respond to all significant comments by modifying the final rule or explaining, in the statement accompanying the final rule, why it did not modify the rule in response to the comments.
10.   B. An administrative law judge (ALJ) presides over hearings when cases are brought to the agency. Like other judges, an ALJ has the power to administer oaths, take testimony, rule on questions of evidence, and make determinations of fact. It is important to note that an ALJ works for the agency but must not be biased in the agency's favor. There are provisions in the Administrative Procedure Act to prevent the bias, and to otherwise promote the fairness, of the ALJs, for example by prohibiting ex parte comments to the ALJ from any party to the proceeding.

GamePoints

1.   The Occupational Health and Safety Administration (OSHA) establishes standards that protect

employees from exposure to workplace hazards and ensure a safe working environment. OSHA is a federal agency so the employer must be engaged in interstate commerce or an activity affecting interstate commerce. An on-site inspection of a workplace by an OSHA inspector does not need to be conducted after working hours and the employer does not need to be given advance notice of the visit. If an employee requests an inspection, the inspector has probable cause to obtain a warrant. If the employer agrees to an inspection, no warrant is needed. Assuming the warehouse in this problem is a workplace and subject to federal rules, the only objection of the employer that might be valid is the insistence on a warrant.

2. You could respond by filing an answer to the allegation. The case will be heard in a trial-like setting before an administrative law judge. Hearing procedures differ among different agencies. The procedure may be informal (sitting around a table in a conference room, for example) or more formal. The latter resembles a trial, with discovery, the presentation of witness testimony and physical evidence, and such steps as cross-examination. After the hearing, the judge makes a decision and issues an order. If necessary, you will than have an opportunity to appeal to the body that runs the agency or a court.

Chapter 7

True-False Questions

1. T
2. F. Felonies are crimes punishable by imprisonment of a year or more (in a state or federal prison). Crimes punishable by imprisonment for lesser periods (in a local facility) are classified as misdemeanors.
3. F. These are elements of the crime of robbery. (Robbery also involves the use of force or fear.) Burglary requires breaking and entering a building with the intent to commit a crime. (At one time, burglary was defined to cover only breaking and entering the dwelling of another at night to commit a crime.)
4. F. This is an element of larceny. The crime of embezzlement occurs when a person entrusted with another's property fraudulently appropriates it. Also, unlike robbery, embezzlement does not require the use of force or fear.
5. T
6. F. The crime of bribery occurs when a bribe is offered. Accepting a bribe is a separate crime. In either case, the recipient does not need to perform

the act for which the bribe is offered for the crime to exist. Note, too, that a bribe can consist of something other then money.
7. F. The recipient of the goods only needs to know that the goods are stolen. The recipient does not need to know the identity of the thief or of the true owner to commit this crime. Thus, not knowing these individuals' identities is not a defense.
8. T
9. T
10. F. A business takes a risk that by electronically storing its customers' credit card numbers, or any personal information, the data may be vulnerable to theft. Cyber thieves have developed ingenuous methods for infiltrating computer networks and "stealing" this information, often without a business realizing that its system has been compromised, unlike the scene of physical break-in. The financial burden imposed by the theft and subsequent use of the data is normally borne by the business, particularly as most credit-card issuers require it.

Fill-in Questions

unreasonable; probable; due process of law; jeopardy; trial; trial by; witnesses; bail and fines

Multiple-Choice Questions

1. C. The elements of most crimes include the performance of a prohibited act and a specified state of mind or intent on the part of the actor.
2. C. Fraudulently making or altering a writing in a way that changes another's legal rights is forgery. Forgery also includes changing trademarks, counterfeiting, falsifying public documents, and altering other legal documents.
3. B. Embezzlement involves the fraudulent appropriation of another's property, including money, by a person entrusted with it. Unlike larceny, embezzlement does not require that property be taken from its owner. Unlike burglary, embezzlement does not involve breaking and entering. Unlike forgery, embezzlement does not require the making or altering of a writing. Unlike robbery, embezzlement does not involve force or fear.
4. A. This is online auction fraud. Fraud is a misrepresentation knowingly made with the intent to deceive another and on which a reasonable person relies to his or her detriment. Fraud can occur online through an auction Web site when a buyer pays for an auctioned item but does not receive it, as in this question, or receives something worth less than the promised article. In either case, it can be difficult to pinpoint a fraudulent seller, who may assume multiple identities.

5. B. This is *phishing*, a form of identity theft. In circumstances such as those set out in this question, once an unsuspecting individual responds to the request by entering the credit-card or other personal information, the phisher can use it to pose as that person or to steal the funds in the person's bank or other account. The crime may begin with a link in a fraudulent e-mail message or a URL provided in an e-mail note. The message or note may ask that the information be submitted to a certain e-mail address or via a Web site that is genuine in appearance but nonetheless false. *Vishing* is a form of phishing involves voice communication—an e-mail requesting a phone call, for example, to relate a bank account number.

6. B. The perpetrator in this set of facts is a *hacker*—someone who uses one computer to break into another. A *Trojan horse* is software, an application, or a program that appears to be legitimate but allows someone to gain unauthorized access to a computer. As with other forms of software, a Trojan horse fits the definition of *malware*, which includes any application or program that is harmful to a computer or its user. A *firewall* is hardware or software designed to prevent unauthorized access.

7. B. In considering the defense of entrapment, the important question is whether a person who committed a crime was pressured by the police to do so. Entrapment occurs when a government agent suggests that a crime be committed and pressure an individual, who is not predisposed to its commitment, to do it.

8. C. A person in police custody who is to be interrogated must be informed that he or she has the right to remain silent; anything said can and will be used against him or her in court; and he or she has the right to consult with an attorney. The person also must be told that if he or she is indigent, a lawyer will be appointed. These rights may be waived if the waiver is knowing and voluntary.

9. C. If, for example, a confession is obtained after an illegal arrest, the confession is normally excluded. Under the exclusionary rule, all evidence obtained in violation of the constitutional rights spelled out in the Fourth, Fifth, and Sixth Amendments normally is excluded, as well as all evidence derived from the illegally obtained evidence. The purpose of the rule is to deter police misconduct.

10. B. A formal charge issued by a grand jury is an indictment. A charge issued by a magistrate is called an information. In either case, there must be sufficient evidence to justify bringing a suspect to trial. The arraignment occurs when the suspect is brought before the trial court, informed of the charges, and asked to enter a plea.

GamePoints

1. The perpetrator in this set of facts—the yeti—appears to have committed several violent crimes. These include the murder of your climbing companion and assault, with a likely impending battery and the attempted murder, of your avatar. These crimes are classified by degree, which depends on the circumstances surrounding the acts. The intent of the perpetrator, whether a weapon was used, and sometimes the level of pain and suffering of the victim, are potential factors.

2. The Internet has expanded opportunities for identity theft and related crimes by providing easy access to private data. This data can be accessed illegally through a number of clandestine methods from virtually anywhere in the world. For example, through an online connection, a hacker might have invaded your computer without your knowledge to install undetected software. This application could have transmitted a copy of your keystrokes to the hacker's computer. The hacker might then have interpreted these strokes to reveal your personal and financial data. This information can be used to impersonate you and thereby spend money as you.

Chapter 8

True-False Questions

1. F. According to the principle of comity, however, a nation will give effect to the laws of another nation if those laws are consistent with the law and public policy of the accommodating nation.
2. F. The act of state doctrine tends to immunize foreign nations from the jurisdiction of U.S. courts—that is, foreign nations are often exempt from U.S. jurisdiction under this doctrine.
3. F. As with the act of state doctrine, the doctrine of sovereign immunity tends to immunize foreign nations from the jurisdiction of U.S. courts
4. F. The Foreign Sovereign Immunities Act sets forth the major exceptions to the immunity of foreign nations to U.S. jurisdiction.
5. T
6. F. U.S. courts can exercise jurisdiction over a foreign entity under U.S. antitrust laws when a violation has a substantial effect on U.S. commerce or is a *per se* violation of those laws.
7. F. Legal systems in all nations can be generally divided into *common* law and civil law systems.
8. T
9. T
10. T

Fill-in Questions

An expropriation; A confiscation; an expropriation; a confiscation

Multiple-Choice Questions

1. C. The U.S. Congress cannot tax exports, but it may establish export quotas. In particular, under the Export Administration Act of 1979, restrictions can be imposed on the export of technologically advanced products.

2. C. Under certain conditions, the doctrine of sovereign immunity prohibits U.S. courts from exercising jurisdiction over foreign nations. Under the Foreign Sovereign Immunities Act, a foreign state is not immune when the action is based on a commercial activity carried on in the United States by the foreign state.

3. A. Under the act of state doctrine, the judicial branch of one country will not examine the validity of public acts committed by a recognized foreign government within its own territory. The awarding of a government contract under the circumstances described in the problem meets this criterion.

4. C. U.S. courts give effect to the judicial decrees of another country under the principle of comity, if those decrees are consistent with the laws and public policies of the United States.

5. D. Unlike exports, imports can be taxed. A tax on an import is a tariff (generally set as a percent of the value). Imports can also be subject to quotas, which limit how much can be imported.

6. B. Although increasingly influenced by codified (statutory) law and in some observers' opinions overwhelmed with administrative rules and regulations, common law legal systems are based on judicial decisions and precedent. Despite this general frame of reference, common law courts in different nations have developed different principles.

7. C. Civil law systems are based on codified (statutory) law. Administrative rules and regulations and judicial decisions are, of course, part of the operation of a civil law system. In a civil law system, courts are permitted to interpret the statutes that make up the code and to apply the rules, but unlike a common law system, in which judicial precedent plays a significant role, the courts in a civil law system are not expected to develop their own body of law.

8. A. Generally observed legal principles of international law are violated by a confiscation. Expropriation, which is a taking of property for a proper public purpose and with the payment of just compensation, does not violate these principles.

9. B. The Civil Rights Act of 1964, and other U.S. discrimination laws, apply to U.S. firms employing U.S. citizens outside (and inside) the United States. U.S. employers everywhere must abide by U.S. employment discrimination laws, so long as those laws do not violate the laws of the countries in which their workplaces are located. But those laws protect only U.S. citizens, not citizens of foreign countries.

10. A. A distribution agreement in this context is a contract between a seller and a distributor to distribute the seller's products in the distributor's country. Such an agreement sets out the terms and conditions of the distributorship—price, currency of payment, availability of supplies, method of payment, and so on.

GamePoints

1. The doctrine of sovereign immunity protects foreign nations from review of the legal consequences of their actions in U.S. courts. But there are exceptions set forth in the Foreign Sovereign Immunities Act. A foreign state, or the instrumentality of a foreign state, is not immune when an action is based on a commercial activity carried on in the United States by the foreign state or having a distinct effect in the United States. In the problem, if the firm that reneges on its promise to your avatar is an arm of a foreign state, it is not likely immune from the jurisdiction of U.S. courts because of the effect of its commercial activity. If the firm is not part of a foreign nation, it has no claim to immunity under these principles.

2. Probably not. The government would likely assert the act of state doctrine in any suit that you might file in a U.S. court. Under this doctrine, the judicial branch of one country will not review the validity of public acts by a foreign government within its own borders. Thus, when a government seizes a privately owned business or privately owned goods, the act of state doctrine may prevent any recovery in a U.S. court. Further, together, the act of state doctrine and the doctrine of sovereign immunity tend to immunize foreign nations from the jurisdiction of U.S. courts so that, in general, U.S. firms or individuals who own property overseas have little U.S. legal protection against government actions in the countries in which they operate.

Cumulative Hypothetical Problem for Unit Two—Including Chapters 5–8

1. B. A business firm may be subject to regulations issued by federal and state administrative agencies. The firm is no less subject to those regulations if they are conflicting or if the firm does not know of the regulations. Federal agencies include the Federal Trade Commission, the Environmental Protection Agency, and the U.S. Department of Justice, all of which have counterparts at the state level in most states. A business firm is also subject to local regulations at the county and city levels.

2. B. A corporation can be compelled to produce its business records, even when those records incriminate its officers or other persons affiliated with the corporation. A partnership is subject to the same requirement. Only individuals can refuse, under the Fifth Amendment to the U.S. Constitution, to provide incriminating testimony, including business records.

3. A. A corporation can be held liable for the crimes of its employees, officers, or directors. Imprisonment is not possible, in a practical sense, as a punishment for a corporation. A business firm can be fined or denied certain privileges, however.

4. C. If a law affects only some persons (for example, when only some persons are prohibited from doing something), it may raise an equal protection issue. If all persons are affected, there may be a question of substantive due process. Under the Fifth Amendment, the federal government must treat all similarly situated persons in a similar manner.

5. C. Under the principle of comity, one nation defers and gives effect to the laws and judicial decrees of another nation. The application of this principle is founded on courtesy and respect. The principle is most likely to be applied as long as the laws and decrees of the imposing nation are consistent with the law and public policy of the accommodating nation.

Questions on the Focus on Ethics for Unit Two—The Public and International Environment

1. B. A business is not protected by the freedom of speech in the buying and selling of personal information, but tailoring that data and its sales to the censorship requirements of a political regime may arguably cooperate in the suppression of free speech, at least from an ethical perspective. A possible defense is that most, if not all, nations limit what information is available to its citizens. To follow such rules is only to obey the law of the nation and culture n which a firm does business. (The collection, buying, and selling of consumers' personal information may also violate the individuals' privacy rights. A business should formulate a privacy policy and inform those whose data the firm collects.)

2. C. The First Amendment's free speech protections extend to corporations. That is not the issue in this case. The question is whether the state's action violates this protection. When speech is political in nature, by an almost universal consensus, the First Amendment protects it. Speech may concern a purely economic matter, and a corporate view on that matter may be relevant, but that speech does not warrant as much protection. Whether a corporation should use its marketing, management, and technology skills in the political arena is perhaps an ethical question, but it is not necessarily a legal concern.

3. D. The standards for conducting regulatory searches are different from those for ordinary police searches. Proof, or even suspicion, of a regulatory violation is not necessary. Business premises may be searched simply to determine whether a violation is occurring. An industry does not need to be subject to extensive regulation for its members' premises to be searched (though if it is, a search warrant is not required). An agency is limited in obtaining private information for regulatory purposes, however, which means that this goal is not a requirement for a regulatory inspection.

Chapter 9

True-False Questions

1. F. All contracts involve promises, but all promises do not establish contracts. (A contract is an agreement that can be enforced in court.) Contract law reflects which promises society believes should be legally enforced, and assures parties to private contracts that the agreements they make will be enforceable.

2. T

3. F. A covenant not to compete may be upheld if the length of time and the size of the geographic area in which the party agrees not to compete are reasonable. A court may in fact reform these terms to make them reasonable and then enforce them as reformed.

4. F. One of the elements for a valid offer is that the terms be definite enough to be enforced by a court. This is so a court can determine if a breach had occurred and, if so, what the appropriate remedy would be. The term "a fair share" is too indefinite to constitute an enforceable term. An offer that invites, and receives, a specifically worded acceptance can create sufficiently definite terms.

5. T

6. T

7.   T

8.   T

9.   F. The Statute of Frauds requires that contracts for all transfers of interests in land be in writing to be enforceable. Included are sales, mortgages, leases, and other transfers. Other contracts that must be in writing to be enforceable under the Statute of Frauds include contracts that cannot be performed within one year of formation, collateral promises, promises made in consideration of marriage, and contracts for sale of goods priced at $500 or more.

10. T

Fill-in Questions

objective; objective; did; circumstances surrounding; in a particular transaction

Multiple-Choice Questions

1.   D. To constitute consideration, the value of whatever is exchanged for the promise must be legally sufficient. Its economic value (its "adequacy") is rarely the basis for a court's refusal to enforce a contract.

2.   B. According to the objective theory of contracts, a party's intent to enter into a contract is judged by outward, objective facts as a reasonable person would interpret them, rather than by the party's own subjective intentions. A reasonable person in the position of a party receiving an offer can know what is in the offer only from what is offered. A court might consider the circumstances surrounding a transaction, and the statements of the parties and the way they acted when they made their contract.

3.   A. In considering an implied-in-fact contract, a court looks at the parties' actions leading up to what happened. If, for example, a plaintiff furnished services, expecting to be paid, which the defendant should have known, and the defendant had a chance to reject the services and did not, the court would hold that the parties had an enforceable implied-in-fact contract.

4.   D. To disaffirm a contract, a minor must return whatever he or she received under it. In a state in which there is also an obligation to return the other party to the position he or she was in before the contract, the minor must also pay for any damage to the goods.

5.   C. Generally, a unilateral mistake—a mistake on the part of only one of the parties—does not give the mistaken party any right to relief. There are two exceptions. One of the exceptions is that the rule does not apply if the other party knew or should have known that a mistake was made.

6.   A. Consideration must be bargained for. Performance or a promise is bargained for if, as in this problem, the promisor seeks it in exchange for his or her promise and the promisee gives it in exchange for that promise.

7.   B. In general, ads (which include catalogs, price lists, and circulars, or flyers) are treated as invitations to negotiate, not offers or contracts.

8.   B. This statement makes a second offer without rejecting the first offer. An offeree may make an offer without rejecting the original offer, in which case two offers exist, each capable of acceptance.

9.   A. Under the Statute of Frauds, a contract for the sale of an interest in land must be in writing to be enforceable. A party to an oral contract involving an interest in land cannot force the other party to buy or sell the property. There is an exception to this rule. If a buyer pays part of the price, takes possession, and makes permanent improvements, and the parties cannot be returned to their pre-contract status quo, a court may grant specific performance of an oral contract for the transfer of an interest in land.

10. D. A contract with an unlicensed individual may be enforceable depending on the nature of the applicable licensing statute. If the statute bars the enforcement of such contracts, of course they are not enforceable. They are also not enforceable if the statute's purpose is to protect the public from unlicensed practitioners. Otherwise, if the statute is intended only to raise revenue, such contracts may be enforceable.

RockOn

1.   This situation describes a unilateral contract (a contract that includes the exchange of a promise for an act). The notice is the promise, and the musician's performance is the act that completes the contract. Note that the musician was not obligated to perform. If you had hired him to perform, and he had agreed, the contract would have been bilateral. At any rate, because the musician complied with the conditions of the promise, you are bound to perform as promised—that is, to pay.

2.   In the situation set out in this question, you do not have to pay the performer. There is no indication that you offered or promised to pay. All that you offered was stage time, which the performer received. As in the previous problem, the musician was not obligated to perform, so there was no contract on this basis.

Chapter 10

True-False Questions

1. T

2. F. A material breach of contract (which occurs when performance is not at least substantial) excuses the nonbreaching party from performance of his or her contractual duties and gives the party a cause of action to sue for damages caused by the breach. A *minor* breach of contract does not excuse the nonbreaching party's duty to perform, however, although it may affect the extent of his or her performance and, like any contract breach, allows the nonbreaching party to sue for damages.

3. F. An executory contract can be rescinded. If it is executory on both sides, it can be rescinded solely by agreement. In any case, the parties must make a new agreement, and this agreement must qualify as a contract. (The parties' promises not to perform are consideration for the new contract.)

4. T

5. T

6. T

7. F. Liquidated damages are certain amounts of money estimated in advance of, and payable on, a breach of contract. *Liquidated* means determined, settled, or fixed.

8. T

9. T

10. F. Damages is the usual on breach of contracts for sales of goods. To obtain specific performance, damages must *not* be an adequate remedy. If goods are unique, or a contract involves a sale of land, damages would not adequately compensate an innocent party for a breach of contract, so specific performance is available.

Fill-in Questions

the contract price and the market price; specific performance; the contract price and the market price

Multiple-Choice Questions

1. D. Accord and satisfaction, agreement, and operation of law are valid bases on which contracts are discharged, but most contracts are discharged by the parties' doing what they promised to do. A contract is fully discharged by performance when the contracting parties have fully performed what they agreed to do (exchange services for payment, for example).

2. D. Contracts that have not been fully performed on either side can be rescinded. The parties must make another agreement (which must satisfy the legal requirements for a contract). The parties' promises not to perform are consideration for the new agreement. A contract that has been fully performed on one side can be rescinded only if the party who has performed receives additional consideration to call off the deal.

3. B. This contract would thus be discharged by objective impossibility of performance. On this basis, a contract may be discharged if, for example, after it is made, performance becomes objectively impossible because of a change in the law that renders that performance illegal. This is also the result if one of the parties dies or becomes incapacitated, or the subject matter of the contract is destroyed.

4. A. A breach of contract entitles the nonbreaching party to damages, but only a material breach discharges the nonbreaching party from his or her duty to perform under the contract. In this problem, the builder has a claim for the amount due on the contract, but the buyer is entitled to have set off the difference in the value of the building as constructed (that is, to subtract the expense to finish the construction).

5. C. A novation substitutes a new party for an original party, by agreement of all the parties. The requirements are a previous valid obligation, an agreement of all the parties to a new contract, extinguishment of the old obligation, and a new contract (which must meet the requirements for a valid contract, including consideration).

6. C. A breach of contract by failing to perform entitles the nonbreaching party to rescind the contract, and the parties must make restitution by returning whatever benefit they conferred on each other, particularly when the breaching party would otherwise be unjustly enriched.

7. C. Under a contract for a sale of goods, the usual measure of compensatory damages is the difference between the contract price and the market price, plus incidental damages. On a seller's breach, the measure includes the difference between what the seller would have been owed if he or she had performed and what the buyer paid elsewhere for the goods.

8. B. On the seller's breach of a contract, the buyer is entitled to be compensated for the loss of the bargain. Here, the buyer will receive what was contracted for, but it will be late. When, as in this problem, a seller knew that the buyer would lose business if the goods were not delivered on time, the loss of the bargain is the consequential damages (the amount lost as a foreseeable consequence of the breach).

9. C. Specific performance is an award of the act promised in a contract. This remedy is granted when the legal remedy (damages) is inadequate. Damages are generally inadequate for a buyer on the breach of a contract for a sale of land, because every piece of land is considered unique. If specific performance is not available, however, as when the land cannot be sold by the contracting seller, damages are possible, and their measure is the benefit of the buyer's bargain (the difference between the contract price and the market price of the land at the time of the breach).

10. D. If the clause is determined to be a penalty clause, it will be unenforceable. To determine whether a clause is a liquidated damages clause or a penalty clause, consider first whether, when the contract was made, damages would clearly be difficult to estimate in the event of a breach. Second, consider whether the amount set as damages is a reasonable estimate. Two "yeses" mean the clause is enforceable. One "no" means the provision is an unenforceable penalty.

Issue Spotters

1. No. The builder has substantially performed its duties under the contract. Assuming this performance was in good faith, the builder could thus successfully sue for the value of the work performed. For the sake of justice and fairness, the buyer will be held to the duty to pay, less damages for the deviation from the contract deadline.

2. No. To recover damages that flow from the consequences of a breach but that are caused by circumstances beyond the contract (consequential damages), the breaching party must know, or have reason to know, that special circumstances will cause the nonbreaching party to suffer the additional loss. That was not the circumstance in this problem.

3. This clause is known as an exculpatory clause. In many cases, such clauses are not enforced, but to be effective in any case, all contracting parties must have consented to it. A clause excluding liability for negligence may be enforced if the contract was made by parties in roughly equal bargaining positions, as two large corporations would be.

RockOn

1. A party who in good faith performs substantially all of the terms of a contract can enforce the contract against the other party under the doctrine of substantial performance. To qualify as substantial, the performance must not vary greatly from the performance promised in the contract. It must create substantially the same benefits. If the defect in performance can easily be compensated for by an

award of damages, the contract will likely be held to have been substantially performed. The measure of damages is the cost to bring the object of the contract into compliance. If that cost is unreasonable, the measure is the difference in value between the performance that was rendered and complete performance. In this problem, the failure to deliver a working voice-recognition (VR) system is a breach of the contract. Assuming that the breaching party acted in good faith and the system otherwise performs as promised, it could be argued that the contract was substantially performed. If a VR system can be acquired elsewhere for a reasonable cost, this could be the measure of the nonbreaching party's damages. If a VR system cannot be had, the measure would instead reflect the difference in value between the system that was promised and the one that was delivered. Joystick would owe Out of the Box the contract price minus this amount.

2. The amount of your recovery for the promoter's breach of its contract with you would most likely include $4,250 in compensatory damages. This is the difference between the value of the breaching party's promised performance under your contract (that is, the $8,000 that the promoter would have paid you) and the value of its actual performance ($0), reduced by the amount of the loss that you avoided (the $4,250 that your band earned performing in a different venue on the contract date). You might also recover incidental damages—any amount that you spent to find the other job.

Chapter 11

True-False Questions

1. T

2. F. If a transaction involves only a service, the common law usually applies (one exception is the serving of food or drink, which is governed by the UCC). When goods and services are combined, courts have disagreed over whether a particular transaction involves a sale of goods or a rendering of service. Usually, a court will apply the law that applies to whichever feature is dominant. Article 2 does not cover sales of real estate, although sales of goods associated with real estate, including crops, may be covered. A contract for a sale of minerals, for example, is considered a contract for a sale of goods if the severance is to be made by the seller.

3. T

4. T

5. F. Under the UCC, a sales contract will be enforceable, and it will not fail for indefiniteness even if one or more terms are left open, as long as the parties intended to make a contract and there is a reasonably certain basis for the court to grant an appropriate remedy. If the price term is left open, for example, and the parties cannot later agree on a price, a court will set the price according to what is reasonable at the time for delivery. If one of the parties is to set the price, it must be set in good faith. If it is not fixed, the other party can set the price or treat the contract as canceled. A contract that does not indicate a quantity of goods may not be enforceable, however.

6. F. If the parties do not agree otherwise, the buyer or lessee must pay for the goods at the time and place of their receipt (subject, in most cases, to the buyer or lessee's right to inspect). When a sale is on credit, a buyer must pay according to credit terms, not when the goods are received. Credit terms may provide for payment within thirty days, for example. A credit period usually begins on the date of shipment.

7. T
8. T
9. T
10. F. Courts usually do enforce click-on agreements. The reasoning is that the click-on terms constitute an offer, proposed by a seller and accepted by a buyer after the buyer had an opportunity to review the terms by an act of active consent (unlike a situation involving browse-wrap terms, which sellers argue are binding without the buyer's active consent).

Fill-in Questions

F.O.B.; F.O.B.; F.O.B.; F.A.S.

Multiple-Choice Questions

1. A. If, before the time of performance, a party to a contract informs the other party that he or she will not perform, the nonbreaching party can treat the repudiation as a final breach and seek a remedy or wait, for a commercially reasonable time, hoping that the breaching party will decide to honor the contract. In either case, the nonbreaching party can suspend his or her performance.

2. C. In a transaction between merchants, additional terms in the acceptance of an offer become part of a contract unless they fall under one of three exceptions. One exception is the other merchant's objection to the terms within a reasonable time. Another exception exists if the first merchant's form expressly required acceptance of its terms. The

third exception occurs when the additional terms materially alter the original contract.

3. B. Under a shipment contract, risk passes when the seller puts the goods into a carrier's possession. Under a destination contract, risk passes when the seller tenders delivery to the buyer.

4. C. Under a destination contract, the risk of loss passes when the seller tenders delivery at the specified destination. This agreement—"F.O.B. Omni" (the buyer)—is a shipment contract under which the seller was required to deliver the goods to the buyer. Thus, the destination was the buyer's location, and the goods were lost before they reached that destination. The loss was the seller's. (Of course, the seller will most likely have insurance to cover the loss.) Also, note that "F.O.B." indicates the seller bears the cost of the transport to the specified destination.

5. B. Under a shipment contract, if the contracting parties do not specify a time for title to pass, then it passes on delivery of the goods to the carrier. Title—the formal right of ownership of property—can be significant because, under the UCC, a sale occurs when title passes from a seller to a buyer for a price.

6. B. A buyer (or lessee) can sue for damages when a seller (or lessor) repudiates the contract or fails to deliver the goods, or when the buyer has rightfully rejected or revoked acceptance of the goods. The place for determining the price is the place at which the seller was to deliver the goods. The buyer may also recover incidental and consequential damages, less expenses saved due to the breach.

7. B. Depending on the circumstances, when a seller or lessor delivers nonconforming goods, the buyer or lessee can reject the part of the goods that does not conform (and rescind the contract or obtain cover). The buyer or lessee may instead revoke acceptance, or he or she may recover damages, for accepted goods. Under the circumstances in this problem, the buyer's best course is to attempt to obtain substitute goods for those that were due under the contract. When a buyer is forced to obtain cover, the buyer can recover from the seller the difference between the cost of the cover and the contract price, plus incidental and consequential damages, less whatever expenses (such as delivery costs) were saved as a result of the seller's breach.

8. C. When goods are to be picked up by a buyer, if a seller is a merchant, the risk of loss does not pass to the buyer until the buyer takes possession of the goods (unless the parties agree otherwise). The goods were tendered before the theft, but the buyer did not take possession.

9. C. An implied warranty of merchantability arises in every sale of goods by a merchant who deals in goods of the kind. It makes no difference whether the merchant knew of or could have discovered a defect that makes a product unsafe. The warranty is that the goods are "reasonably fit for the ordinary purposes for which such goods are used." The efficiency and the quality of their manufacture, and the manufacturer's compliance with government regulations, are not factors that directly influence this determination. (The phrase "as is," or similar language, will generally disclaim most implied warranties. A specific disclaimer of the implied warranty of merchantability must mention *merchantability*.)

9. A. This phrase, or similar language, will generally disclaim most implied warranties. To specifically disclaim an implied warranty of fitness for a particular purpose, a writing must be conspicuous, but the word *fitness* does not have to be used. A specific disclaimer of the implied warranty of merchantability must mention *merchantability*. Note that warranties of title can be disclaimed only by specific language (for example, a seller states that it is transferring only such rights as it has in the goods), or by circumstances that indicate no warranties of title are made.

10. C. A binding contract can be created by clicking on, for example, an "I agree" button if an opportunity is provided to read the terms before the button is clicked. It does not make a difference whether the party clicking on the button actually reads the terms. But if the terms are not revealed until *after* an agreement is made, it is unlikely that they would be considered part of the deal. Here, the problem states that the button referred to the terms, meaning the buyer knew, or should have known, what was being agreed to, even though she did not read them.

Starbucks Coffee Co. International Sales Contract Applications

1. B. As stated in the "Breach or Default of Contract" clause on the second page, this contract is subject to Article 2 of the UCC. If the parties to a sales contract do not express some of the terms in writing, including the price term, the contract is still enforceable. A sales contract that must be in writing is only enforceable, however, to the extent of the quantity stated in writing. If these parties did not state the amount of product ordered, the contract may not be enforced because if a quantity term were left out, a court would have no basis for determining a remedy.

2. B. When a seller, as a party to a sales contract, states or otherwise expresses what the goods will be, then the goods must be that. The goods must at least conform to the seller's description of them, wherever that descriptions is, whether in the contract, in promotional materials, on labels, by salespersons, by comparison to a sample, etc. A seller's subjective belief is not the standard. The buyer's subjective belief may be the standard if the contract specifies that the goods must personally satisfy the buyer.

3. C. This clause states the terms for payment under this sales contract and indicates that the buyer has two days after the day of tender in which to pay for the goods or will be considered in breach. The "BREACH OR DEFAULT OF CONTRACT" clause sets out what happens "if either party hereto fails to perform." These are all incentives for the buyer to pay on time.

4. A. This clause allows the buyer to reject nonconforming product, although this is limited to a specific number of days. (Note that the buyer' right to reject does not need to be stated in a contract for the buyer to have that right.) This clause details the procedures that the parties may follow if the product does not meet its description. These are incentives for the seller to deliver conforming goods.

5. D. This is a destination contract, as indicated by the "ARRIVAL," "DELIVERY," "INSURANCE," and "FREIGHT" clauses. This means that the seller bears the risk of loss until the coffee is delivered to its destination (a "Bonded Public Warehouse" in Laredo, Texas).

RockOn

1. Yes, the seller is in breach of the contract in this problem. The seller did not comply with the perfect tender rule, which requires that goods and their tender not fail in any respect to conform to the contract. The note of accommodation has no bearing on this issue. And because the seller sent the nonconforming goods on the last day to ship the order, there is no time to cure the breach. In this situation, the buyer has the right the reject the goods. Of course, the buyer also has the right to accept the goods, which might be an option in this set of facts.

2. Here, you can recover the contract price plus incidental damages, which consist of the storage costs—a total of $256,000. This is the remedy when a buyer breaches a contract by refusing to accept conforming, specially manufactured goods and the seller is unable to resell them.

Chapter 12

True-False Questions

1. T

2. F. A reasonable apprehension or fear of *immediate* harmful or offensive contact is an assault.

3. T

4. F. Puffery is seller's talk—the seller's *opinion* that his or her goods are, for example, the "best." For fraud to occur, there must be a misrepresentation of a *fact*.

5. T

6. F. To establish negligence, the courts apply a *reasonable person* standard to determine whether certain conduct resulted in a breach of a duty of care.

7. F. If a party who initiates a suit does so out of malice—and without probable cause—that party may have committed malicious prosecution. But a person who files a suit based on a legally just and proper reason, even with malice, does not commit this tort. Also, to succeed, in some states, a plaintiff must show damages other than the normal cost of litigation.

8. F. This is not misconduct, in terms of a wrongful interference tort. Bona fide competitive behavior is permissible, whether or not it results in the breaking of a contract or other business relation. In fact, it is a defense to charges of wrongful interference.

9. T

10. F. One of the elements required to establish negligence is an injury, Of course, there must be a connection between the wrongful act and the injury, The breach of the duty of care must cause the injury— "but for" the wrongful act, the injury would not have occurred.

Fill-in Questions

1. negligence;

2. assumption of risk

3. comparative

Multiple-Choice Questions

1. A. To satisfy the elements of a negligence cause of action, a breach of a duty of care must cause the harm. If an injury would not have occurred without the breach, there is causation in fact. Causation in fact can usually be determined by the but-for test: but for the wrongful act, the injury would not have occurred.

2. D. This is a third party's use of predatory methods to end a business relationship between others. Individuals are permitted to interfere unreasonably with others' business to gain a share of the market. Appropriation is the use of another's name or likeness for gain, without permission. Assault concerns the apprehension or fear of immediate harmful or offensive physical contact. Conversion is a tort involving property.

3. B. An individual with knowledge, skill, or intelligence superior to that of an ordinary person has a higher standard of care than the ordinary person—that which is reasonable in light of those capabilities. Thus, a professional's duty is consistent with what is reasonable for that professional.

4. B. The basis of the tort of defamation is publication of a statement that holds an individual up to contempt, ridicule, or hatred. Publication means that statements are made to or within the hearing of persons other than the defamed party, or that a third party reads the statements. A secretary reading a letter, for example, meets this requirement. But the statements do not have to be read or heard by a specific third party. (Whether someone is a public figure is important only because a public figure cannot recover damages for defamation without proof of actual malice.)

5. A. In most states, the defense of comparative negligence can reduce the amount of a tortfeasor's liability if the injured person failed to exercise reasonable care. Although some states allow a plaintiff to recover even if his or her fault was greater than the defendant's, in many states, a plaintiff gets nothing if he or she was more than 50 percent at fault.

6. D. Trespass to personal property is intentional physical contact with another's personal property that causes damage. Sending spam through an Internet service provider (ISP) is intentional contact with the ISP's computer systems. A negative impact on the value of the ISP's equipment, by using its processing power to transmit e-mail, constitutes damage (the resources are not available for the ISP's customers). Also, service cancellations harm an ISP's business reputation and goodwill.

7. B. Trespass to land occurs when a person, without permission, enters onto another's land, or remains on the land. An owner does not need to be aware of an act before it can constitute trespass, and harm to the land is not required. A trespasser may have a complete defense, however, if he or she enters onto the land to help someone in danger.

8. C. An individual who is defending his or her life or physical wellbeing can, in self-defense, use whatever force is reasonably necessary to prevent harmful contact. A person can also act in a reasonable manner to defend others who are in danger. Individuals may use reasonable force to defend property, but not force that is likely to cause death or great bodily injury. Of course, force cannot be used once the danger has passed.

9. B. To constitute fraud, a statement of fact must be involved. Reliance on an opinion is not justified unless the person making the statement has superior knowledge of the subject matter. Puffery, or seller's talk, (for example, "this is the best product!") is too subjective.

10. B. The standard of a business that invites persons onto its premises is a duty to exercise reasonable care. Whether conduct is unreasonable depends on a number of factors, including how easily the injury could have been guarded against. A landowner has a duty to discover and remove hidden dangers, but obvious dangers do not need warnings.

GamePoints

1. The most likely tort that your opponent committed is assault. This is any intentional and unexcused threat of immediate harmful or offensive contact. In the circumstances described in this problem, your opponent most likely caused you to feel reasonably apprehensive of harmful contact. One arguable issue might be whether any harm was imminent based on Tom's statement "if I lose one more time," implying that the game must be played before any harm occurs. But his snatching the game control from your hands—an act that might constitute battery, conversion, or trespass to personal property—and raising it in a threatening manner likely offsets this interpretation.

2. To recover on the basis of negligence, the injured party—Twyla—must show that the cruiser's owner—the Prince of Peril—owed her, as the plaintiff, a duty of care, that the Prince breached that duty, that the plaintiff was injured, and that the breach caused the injury. In this game situation, the Prince's act (leaving the cruiser running while he leaped from it) most likely breached the duty of reasonable care. The earth shook. The silo collapsed. Its falling on Twyla was the direct cause of her injury, not her own negligence. Thus, liability turns on whether the plaintiff can connect the breach of duty to the injury. This involves the test of proximate cause—the question of foreseeability. The consequences to the injured party must have been a foreseeable result of the defendant's carelessness.

Chapter 13

True-False Questions

1. T

2. F. A defendant may be liable for the result of his or her act regardless of intent—that is part of the basis of the doctrine of strict liability. Similarly, it usually does not matter whether the defendant exercised reasonable care. Strict liability is liability without regard to fault or intent.

3. F. In an action based on strict liability, a plaintiff does not have to prove that there was a failure to exercise due care. That distinguishes an action based on strict liability from an action based on negligence, which requires proof of a lack of due care.

4. F. The theory of strict liability also applies in some cases involving product liability. The basis for imposing strict liability to any activity is the creation of an extraordinary risk.

5. F. An action based on negligence does not require privity of contract. At one time, there was a requirement of privity in product liability actions based on negligence, but this requirement began to be eliminated decades ago. Privity of contract is also not a requirement to bring a suit based on strict product liability.

6. F. In an action based on strict liability, a plaintiff does not have to prove that there was a failure to exercise due care. That distinguishes an action based on strict liability from an action based on negligence, which requires proof of a lack of due care. A plaintiff must show, however, that (1) a product was defective, (2) the defendant was in the business of distributing the product, (3) the product was unreasonably dangerous due to the defect, (4) the plaintiff suffered harm, (5) the defect was the proximate cause of the harm, and (6) the goods were not substantially changed from the time they were sold.

7. T

8. F. Product liability may be imposed for defects in the design or construction of products that cause injuries, but it may also be imposed for a failure to include a reasonable warning.

9. F. There is no duty to warn about such risks. Warnings about such risks do not add to the safety of products and could make other warnings seem less significant. In fact, a plaintiff's action in the face of such a risk can be raised as a defense in a product liability suit.

10. T

Fill-in Questions

1. negligence;
2. assumption of risk
3. comparative

Multiple-Choice Questions

1. A. Assumption of risk is a defense in an action based on product liability if the plaintiff knew and appreciated the risk created by the defect and voluntarily undertook the risk, even though it was unreasonable to do so.

2. A. A manufacturer may be held liable if its product is unsafe as a result of negligence in the manufacture or if the design makes it unreasonably dangerous for the use for which it is made. A manufacturer also has a duty to warn and to anticipate reasonably foreseeable misuses. An injury must not have been due to a change in the product after it was sold, but there is no requirement of privity. There is no liability, however, with respect to injuries caused by commonly known dangers, even if the manufacturer does not warn against them.

3. D. In a product liability action based on strict liability, the plaintiff does not need to prove that anyone was at fault. Privity of contract is also not an element of an action in strict liability. A plaintiff does have to show, however, in a suit against a seller, that the seller was a merchant engaged in the business of selling the product on which the suit is based. Note that recovery is possible against sellers who are processors, assemblers, packagers, bottlers, wholesalers, distributors, retailers, or lessors, as well as against manufacturers.

4. C. These choices concern the defective condition of a product that causes harm to a plaintiff. A product may be unreasonably dangerous due to a flaw in the manufacturing process, a design defect, or an inadequate warning.

5. C. All courts extend the doctrine of strict liability to injured bystanders. A defendant does not have to prove that the manufacturer or seller failed to use due care, nor is there a requirement of privity (or "intent" with regard to entering into privity). The defense of assumption of risk does not apply, because one cannot assume a risk that one does not know about.

6. B. If a manufacturer fails to use due care to make a product safe, the manufacturer may be liable for product liability based on negligence. This care must be used in designing the product, selecting the materials, producing the product, inspecting and testing any components, assembling the product, and placing warnings on the product.

7. B. If the plaintiff can prove these elements (material fact, misrepresentation, reliance, and injury), liability could be based on the circumstance that the manufacturer, when it sold its product, misrepresented the character of the product.

8. A. Strict liability is liability without fault. This is imposed on dangerous activities when they (1) involve potentially serious harm to persons or property, (2) involve a high degree of risk that cannot be completely guarded against by the exercise of reasonable care, and (3) are activities not commonly performed in the area. The other choices represent irrelevant factors.

9. C. Strict liability is applied to abnormally dangerous activities because of their extreme risk. An abnormally dangerous activity is, among other things, an activity not commonly performed in an area in which an injury or damage occurs as a result of the activity.

10. D. The theory of strict liability is a doctrine that is applied to certain activities regardless of fault. This is in part when the activities, like demolition, involve a high degree of risk that cannot be completely guarded against by the exercise of reasonable care.

RockOn

1. You are more likely to prevail on these arguments than Zot! The manufacturer has most likely committed negligence. The elements are (1) a duty of care, (2) a breach of the duty, and (3) the breach's causation of (4) an injury. In this problem, Zot! has a duty to exercise a reasonable amount of care in the manufacture of its equipment. Omitting an inexpensive resistor—whether through carelessness, oversight, poor design, or to cut costs—is likely *not* an exercise of reasonable care. This breach may cause power surges, including the one that killed your lead singer.

Privity of contract is not required to maintain a product liability action grounded in negligence. Thus, this defense fails. As for assumption of risk, a party who voluntarily enters into a situation knowing the risk involved cannot recover if he or she suffers an injury as a consequence. The requirements are knowledge of the risk and a voluntary assumption of it. Here, it is not likely that the singer knew of the risk of the surge due to the missing resistor. Thus, there is no basis for this defense.

2. Yes, you can recover damages without proof of negligence. An injured plaintiff—you, in this case—can sue a seller on a theory of strict product liability if the plaintiff can show that a good was sold in a defective or unreasonably dangerous condition and caused the injuries complained of. The plaintiff does not need to prove fault, wrongdoing, or a breach of due care by the defendant.

Chapter 14

True-False Questions

1. T
2. F. A copyright is granted automatically when a qualifying work is created, although a work can be registered with the U.S. Copyright Office.
3. T
4. T
5. F. Anything that makes an individual company unique and would have value to a competitor is a trade secret. This includes a list of customers, a formula for a chemical compound, and other confidential data.
6. F. Trade names cannot be registered with the federal government. They are protected, however, under the common law (when used as trademarks or service marks) by the same principles that protect trademarks.
7. F. A copy does not have to be the same as an original to constitute copyright infringement. A copyright is infringed if a substantial part of a work is copied without the copyright holder's permission.
8. F. A trademark may be infringed by an intentional or unintentional use of a mark in its entirety, or a copy of the mark to a substantial degree. In other words, a mark can be infringed if its use is intended or not, and whether the copy is identical or similar. Also, the owner of the mark and its unauthorized user need not be in direct competition.
9. T
10. F. Proof of a likelihood of confusion is not required in a trademark dilution action. The products involved do not even have to be similar. Proof of likely confusion is required in a suit for trademark infringement, however.

Fill-in Questions

70; 95; 120; 70

Multiple-Choice Questions

1. B. A firm that makes, uses, or sells another's patented design, product, or process without the owner's permission commits patent infringement. It is not required that an invention be copied in its entirety. Also, the object that is copied does not need to be trademarked or copyrighted, in addition to being patented.
2. A. The user of a trademark can register it with the U.S. Patent and Trademark Office, but registration is not necessary to obtain protection from trademark infringement. A trademark receives protection to the degree that it is distinctive. A fanciful symbol is the most distinctive mark.
3. D. This is not copyright infringement because no copyright is involved. This is not cybersquatting because no one is offering to sell a domain name to a trademark owner. (It is also unlikely that this violates the Anticybersquatting Consumer Protection Act because there is no indication of "bad faith intent.") Trademark dilution occurs when a trademark is used, without the owner's without permission, in a way that diminishes the distinctive quality of the mark. That has not happened here.
4. A. Copyright protects a specific list of creative works, including literary works, musical works, sound recordings, and pictorial, graphic, and sculptural works. Although there are exceptions for "fair use," a work need not be copied in its entirety to be infringed. Also, to make a case for infringement, proof of consumers' confusion is not required, and the owner and unauthorized user need not be direct competitors.
5. D. Business processes and information that cannot be patented, copyrighted, or trademarked are protected against appropriation as trade secrets. These processes and information include production techniques, as well as a product's idea and its expression.
6. C. Trademark law protects a distinctive symbol that its owner stamps, prints, or otherwise affixes to goods to distinguish them from the goods of others. Use of this mark by another party without the owner's permission is trademark infringement.
7. B. A certification mark certifies the region, materials, method of manufacture, quality, or accuracy of goods or services. A collective mark is a certification mark used by members of a cooperative, association, or other organization (a union, in this problem). A service mark distinguishes the services of one person or company from those of another. A trade name indicates all or part of a business's name.
8. B. Ten years is the period for later renewals of a trademark's registration. The life of a creator plus seventy years is a period for copyright protection. No intellectual work is protected forever, at least not without renewal. To obtain a patent, an applicant must satisfy the U.S. Patent and Trademark Office that the invention or design is genuine, novel, useful, and not obvious in light of contemporary technology. A patent is granted to the first person to create whatever is to be patented, rather than the first person to file for a patent.
9. D. The Berne Convention provides some copyright protection, but its coverage and enforcement was not as complete or as universal as that of the TRIPS (Trade-Related Aspects of Intellectual Prop-

erty Rights) Agreement. The Paris Convention allows parties in one signatory country to file for patent and trademark protection in other signatory countries. The Madrid Protocol concerns trademarks.

10. A. Publishers cannot put the contents of their periodicals into online databases and other electronic resources, including CD-ROMs, without securing the permission of the writers whose contributions are included.

GamePoints

1. Different attributes of your game device are protected under different categories of intellectual property law. The name of the product could be protected as a trademark once it is either registered or used in commerce. It might be argued that the name is not sufficiently fanciful or distinctive, but this argument could be countered by pointing out that "The Gem" is not a jewel. The device might obtain patent protection if the conditions for the grant of a patent are met—that the device's invention, discovery, or design is genuine, novel, useful, and not obvious in light of current technology. The software that drives the game might be protected under copyright law. Various other aspects of the production and selling of this product could be protected against appropriation by competitors as trade secrets.

2. No song could be uploaded without the copyright owner's permission. This problem poses an instance of copyright infringement. This use of others' works without the permission of the copyright owners would not be "fair use" because it is not a clearly permissible purpose (criticism, comment, news reporting, teaching, scholarship, or research) and it would not otherwise pass a court's scrutiny—particularly as this use would undercut the market for the copyrighted work.

Chapter 15

True-False Questions

1. F. A mechanic's lien involves real property. An artisan's lien or an innkeeper's lien involves personal property.

2. F. This is prohibited under federal law. Garnishment of an employee's wages for any one indebtedness cannot be a ground for dismissal of an employee.

3. T

4. T

5. F. This is the most important concept in suretyship: a surety can use any defenses available to a debtor (except personal defenses) to avoid liability on the obligation to the creditor. Note, though, that a debtor does need not to have defaulted on the underlying obligation before a surety can be required to answer for the debt. Before a *guarantor* can be required to answer for the debt of a debtor, the debtor must have defaulted on the underlying obligation, however.

6. T

7. F. Any individual can be a debtor under Chapter 7, and any debtor who is liable on a claim held by a creditor may file for bankruptcy under Chapter 7. A debtor does not have to be insolvent.

8. T

9. F. Under Chapter 11, the creditors and the debtor formulate a plan under which the debtor pays some of the debts, the other debts are discharged, and the debtor is then allowed to continue the operation of his or her business.

10. F. Some small businesses—those who do not own or manage real estate and do not have debts of more than $2 million—can choose to avoid creditors' committees under Chapter 11. Those who choose to do so, however, are subject to shorter deadlines with respect to filing a reorganization plan.

Fill-in Questions

contract of suretyship; surety; surety; guaranty contract; guarantor

Multiple-Choice Questions

1. B. The creditor in this problem can use prejudgment attachment. Attachment occurs at the time of or immediately after commencement of a suit but before entry of a final judgment. The court issues a writ of attachment, directing the sheriff or other officer to seize property belonging to the debtor. If the creditor prevails at trial, the property can be sold to satisfy the judgment. (A writ of execution can be used after all of the conditions represented by the answer choices in this problem have been met.)

2. D. The creditor can use garnishment, a collection remedy directed at a debtor's property or rights held by a third person. A garnishment order can be served on the employer so that part of debtor's paycheck will be paid to the creditor.

3. C. The debt is $200,000. The amount of the homestead exemption ($50,000) is subtracted from the sale price of the house ($150,000), and the remainder ($100,000) is applied against the debt. Proceeds from the sale of any nonexempt personal property could also be applied against the debt. The debtor gets the amount of the homestead exemption, of course.

4.   B. A guarantor is secondarily liable (that is, the principal must first default). Also, in this problem, if the officer were, for example, the borrower's only salaried employee, the guaranty would not have to be in writing under the main-purpose exception to the Statute of Frauds. A surety is primarily liable (that is, the creditor can look to the surety for payment as soon as the debt is due, whether or not the principal debtor has defaulted). Usually, also, in the case of a guarantor, a creditor must have attempted to collect from the principal, because usually a debtor would not otherwise be declared in default.

5.   C. A guarantor has the right of subrogation when he or she pays the debt owed to the creditor. This means that any right the creditor had against the debtor becomes the right of the guarantor. A guarantor also has the right of contribution, when there are one or more other guarantors. This means that if he or she pays more than his or her proportionate share on a debtor's default, the guarantor is entitled to recover from the others the amount paid above the guarantor's obligation. This problem illustrates how these principles work.

6.   C. The first unsecured debts to be paid are domestic support obligations, subject to certain administrative costs, and then other administrative expenses of the bankruptcy proceeding. Among the debts listed in this problem, the order of priority is unpaid wages, consumer deposits, and taxes. Each class of creditors is fully paid before the next class is entitled to anything.

7.   D. Claims that are not dischargeable in bankruptcy include the claims listed in the other answer choices: claims for back taxes accruing within three years before the bankruptcy, claims for domestic support, and claims for most student loans (unless their payment would result in undue hardship to the debtor, as stated in the correct answer choice). There are many other debts that are not dischargeable in bankruptcy.

8.   A. Other grounds on which a discharge may be denied include concealing property with the intent to defraud a creditor, fraudulently destroying financial records, and refusing to obey a lawful court order. Having obtained a discharge in bankruptcy within the eight previous years is also a ground for denial. The other choices represent individual debts that are not dischargeable in bankruptcy, but they are not grounds for denying a discharge altogether.

9.   D. Under Chapter 11, creditors and debtor plan for the debtor to pay some debts, be discharged of the rest, and continue in business. Under Chapter 13, with an appropriate plan, a small business

debtor can also pay some (or all) debts, be discharged of the rest, and continue in business. A petition for a discharge in bankruptcy under Chapter 11 may be filed by a sole proprietor, a partnership, or a corporation; a petition for a discharge under Chapter 13, however, may be filed only by a sole proprietor, among these business entities, subject to certain debt maximums.

10.   D. Most corporations can file for bankruptcy under Chapter 7 or 11. The same principles that govern liquidation cases generally govern reorganizations as well. Corporate debtors most commonly file petitions for bankruptcy under Chapter 11. One important difference between the two chapters is that in a Chapter 11 proceeding, the debtor can continue in business.

GamePoints

1.   Creditors who make improvements to real property can place mechanic's liens on the property if the creditors are not paid for their labor, services, or material. Creditors who repair personal property can place artisan's liens on the property for the same reason, but the creditor must have possession of the property. With either lien, the creditor can sell the property to satisfy payment of the debt. The proceeds are used to pay the debt and the costs, with any remainder paid to the debtor. Both a mechanic's lien and an artisan's lien requires the lienholder to give notice of legal action to the debtor before the debtor's property is sold to satisfy the debt.

2.   Yes, the accounting firm in this problem can file an involuntary Chapter 11 bankruptcy petition against you. Involuntary petitions are permitted under Chapters 7 and 11 only. An involuntary petition is commenced by its filing with a bankruptcy court. A single creditor may file the petition if the debtor has fewer than twelve creditors and the unsecured portion of the creditor's claim is at least $12,000. These conditions are met by the facts here—you have ten unsecured creditors and the accounting firm has an unsecured claim for $15,000.

Cumulative Hypothetical Problem for Unit Three—Including Chapters 9–15

1.   B. Intellectual property law protects such intangible rights as copyrights, trademarks, and patents, which include the rights that an individual or business firm has in the products it produces. Protection for software comes from patent law and from copyright law. Protection for the distinguishing trademarks on the software comes from, of course, trademark law.

2. D. An offeror can revoke an offer for a bilateral contract, which is what this offer is, any time before it is accepted. This may be after the offeree is aware of the offer.

3. C. The modification would not be considered a rejection. Under UCC 2–207, a merchant can add an additional term to a contract, with his or her acceptance, as part of the contract, unless the offeror expressly states otherwise.

4. D. Of these choices, the firm most likely violated tort law, which includes negligence and strict liability, both as distinct torts and as a part of product liability. Negligence requires proof of intent. Strict liability does not. These firms may also have breached their contracts and their warranties, topics that are categorized as contract law and sales law.

5. B. Only a debtor can file a plan under Chapter 11, but for the court to confirm it, the secured creditors must accept it. There is another condition that the plan must meet. It must provide that the creditors retain their liens and the value of the property to be distributed to them is not less than the secured portion of their claims, or the debtor must surrender to the creditors the property securing those claims.

Questions on the Focus on Ethics for Unit Three—The Commercial Environment

1. A. If a contract is unconscionable, it is so unfair and one-sided as to "shock the conscience" of a court and be unenforceable. Unconscionability, which represents an attempt by the law to enforce ethical behavior, is a common law concept that is not precisely defined. UCC 2–311 refers to the UCC's pervasive concepts of good faith and commercial reasonableness, but does not define unconscionability. Even UCC 2–302, which adopts the doctrine, does not define the term with specificity. Instead, it is the prerogative of the courts to determine its application in contract cases.

2. B. This problem presents a question involving a cybergriper. A cybergriper uses another's trademark to protest, or otherwise complain about, in good faith and usually without profit, the owner's product or policy. Courts have held that this use of a mark is protected by the freedom of speech. The business's mark is not infringed because the public is not likely to be confused by the cybergriper's use.

3. A. The bankruptcy laws—including the automatic stay provision, and the provisions as to which and how much debt can be discharged—can make a creditor's secured or unsecured obligation worthless, while enhancing the debtor's position by freeing secured assets from the obligations that they secure.

This situation and the ease with which debtors can file for bankruptcy underlies the attempt of the bankruptcy laws to make it less easy for debts to be discharged by directing debtors to debt-counseling classes and funneling petitions into Chapter 13 (subject to the "means test"). Under Chapter 13, many debts may be paid according to a five-year plan and a budget imposed on a debtor, rather than going unpaid and being discharged.

Chapter 16

True-False Questions

1. F. This is the definition of loan flipping. Steering and targeting occur when a lender manipulates a borrower into accepting a loan product that benefits the lender but is not the best loan for the borrower.

2. F. This is a definition of a mortgage. A mortgage is also defined as a written instrument that gives a creditor an interest in real property being acquired by a debtor as security for the debt's payment. A recession occurred following the collapse of the housing market and the financial crisis that accompanied it in the second half of the first decade of the twenty-first century.

3. F. When all disclosures required under federal law are provided, a borrower's right to rescind a mortgage is limited to three business days (not including Sunday) after a loan is finalized. If the lender fails to provide material required disclosures, the borrower has a right to rescind the transaction for up to three years.

4. T

5. T

6. F. This is almost the definition of the average prime offer rate, which is the rate offered to the best, or most qualified, borrowers as established by a survey of potential borrowers. The annual percentage rate, or APR, is the actual cost of a loan on a yearly basis.

7. T

8. F. A Higher-Priced Mortgage Loan, or HPML, is subject to an amendment to Regulation Z enacted by the Federal Reserve Board. A lender cannot make an HPML based on the value of the borrower's home without verifying an ability to repay the loan. Part of the process involves a review of the borrower's financial records, including the borrower's other credit obligations. This is only one of the additional protections that consumers receive under this regulation.

9. F. To initiate foreclosure on a mortgage, the lender records a notice of default, or NOD, with the appropriate county office. The borrower is then on notice that a foreclosure sale is possible and can act to cure the default. If the loan is not paid within a reasonable time after a notice of default, the borrower will receive a notice of sale. This is also posted on the property, recorded with the county, and published in the newspaper.

10. T

Fill-in Questions

a fixed-rate; an adjustable-rate; an interest-only subprime mortgage; hybrid mortgage; home equity loan

Multiple-Choice Questions

1. B. A mortgage is a loan that a lender provides to enable a borrower to buy real property. It is a written instrument that gives the creditor an interest in, or lien on, the property being acquired by the debtor as security for the payment of the debt.

2. A. A fixed-rate mortgage is a standard mortgage with a fixed, or unchanging, rate of interest. Payments in the same amount are due periodically for the duration of the loan, which normally ranges from ten to forty years. The rate depends on a number of factors, including the borrower's credit rating. With adjustable-rate and interest-only mortgages, the amount of the payments can increase over time.

3. A. Under the Truth-in-Lending Act of 1968, a lender must disclose the terms of a loan in clear, readily understandable language for a potential borrower to make rational choice. Among the terms that must be disclosed is the annual percentage rate (APR). The APR is what the answer says—the annual cost of a loan on a yearly basis. Like other disclosures, the APR must be based on a uniform formula of calculation.

4. D. As the example in this problem illustrates, steering and targeting occur when a lender manipulates a borrower into accepting a loan product that benefits the lender but is not the best loan for the borrower. This a predatory lending practice that is often at the heart of a violation of real estate financing laws.

5. A. Federal law primarily regulates mortgage terms that must be disclosed in writing. Congress and the Federal Reserve Board imposed a number of these requirements on lenders as a consequence of the real-estate financing bubble that occurred in the early years of the twenty-first century. Many of the new disclosures were included in the provisions of the Truth-in-Lending Act of 1968 and the Federal Reserve Board's Regulation Z.

6. D. Recording a mortgage in the appropriate county office protects the creditor's rights in the property against later good faith purchasers for value and others. If the debtor defaults, a creditor who has *not* recorded his or her interest may have only the priority of an unsecured creditor.

7. A. An amendment to Regulation Z that the Federal Reserve Board enacted created a category of expensive loans known as Higher-Priced Mortgage Loans, or HPMLs. To qualify as an HPML, a loan must be secured by the borrower's principal residence and the annual percentage rate, or APR, of the mortgage must exceed the average prime offer rate for a comparable transaction by at least 1.5 percentage points if the loan is a first lien or at least 3.5 percentage points if the loan is a subordinate lien. The average prime offer rate is the rate offered to the best qualified borrowers.

8. C. The Home Affordable Modification Program (HAMP) offers incentives to lenders to change the terms of certain loans. The purpose of HAMP is to modify mortgages to, as the answer states, reduce the monthly payments to levels that borrowers can reasonably afford to pay. This amount is specifically estimated to be no more than 31 percent of an individual's borrower's gross monthly income.

9. C. Foreclosure is a process that allows a lender to repossess and auction the property that secures a loan. A lender has the right to foreclose on real property securing a mortgage if a homeowner defaults, or fails to make the payments on the mortgage. Before a foreclosure sale, the borrower has a right to buy the property by paying the full amount of the debt, plus interest and costs—this is the equitable right of redemption. A short sale is a sale of the property for less than the balance of the mortgage loan, and forbearance is the postponement for a limited time of part or all of the payments on the loan. A lender might opt for either of these choices to avoid foreclosure, which can be expensive and time consuming.

10. A. If the amount on a sale of property in foreclosure is not enough to cover the amount of the loan, a lender can ask a court for a judgment against the borrower for the amount of the debt remaining unpaid. This is a deficiency judgment. The borrower is required to make up the difference to the lender over time. Some states do not permit deficiency judgments for mortgaged residential real estate.

GamePoints

1. The mortgage is a residential loan, and thus the Truth-in-Lending Act (TILA) applies. The loan is a first mortgage but the APR exceeds the interest rate on Treasury bonds of comparable maturity by only 2 points and the fees are not more than 8 percent of the loan. Thus, the Home Ownership and Equity Protection Act (HOEPA)—which covers mortgage loans that carry a high rate of interest or impose high fees on borrowers—does not apply. The mortgage is a first lien secured by the borrower's home, but the APR does not most likely exceed the average prime offer rate for a comparable transaction by 1.5 percentage points or more. Thus, the loan is not a Higher-Priced Mortgage Loan (or HPML). The U.S. Treasury Department's Home Affordable Modification Program (HAMP) encourages private lenders to modify mortgages to lower the monthly payments of borrowers in default. But The borrower is not in default, so the loan is not eligible for HAMP.

TILA imposes disclosure requirements on lenders. When all required disclosures are provided, a borrower's right to rescind is limited to three business days (not including Sunday) after a loan is finalized. If a lender fails to provide material required disclosures, the borrower has a right to rescind the transaction for up to three years. So, if Blockhead did not give Carlotta all of the required disclosures, her right to rescind extended to three years. Otherwise, she is too late.

2. Blockhead's options include forbearance, a workout agreement, a U.S. Department of Housing and Urban Development (HUD) loan, a short sale, a sale and leaseback arrangement, the U.S. Treasury Department's Home Affordable Modification Program (HAMP), a deed in lieu of foreclosure, and a prepackaged bankruptcy. Foreclosure is also an option.

In these facts, because the market value of Edgar's home has declined, it would be unlikely to bring enough on a short sale or a foreclosure sale to recover the unpaid amount of the loan. A deficiency judgment would be necessary. The best option here, however, would most likely be forbearance or a workout agreement. Blockhead could ask for proof of Edgar's upcoming job and agree to delay Alpha's efforts to collect the next six payments on the mortgage. This option would save both parties time, expense, and the negative consequences of some of the other choices.

Cumulative Hypothetical Problem for Unit Three—Including Chapters 9–16

1. B. Intellectual property law protects such intangible rights as copyrights, trademarks, and patents, which include the rights that an individual or business firm has in the products it produces. Protection for software comes from patent law and from copyright law. Protection for the distinguishing trademarks on the software comes from, of course, trademark law.

2. D. An offeror can revoke an offer for a bilateral contract, which is what this offer is, any time before it is accepted. This may be after the offeree is aware of the offer.

3. C. The modification would not be considered a rejection. Under UCC 2–207, a merchant can add an additional term to a contract, with his or her acceptance, as part of the contract, unless the offeror expressly states otherwise.

4. D. Of these choices, the firm most likely violated tort law, which includes negligence and strict liability, both as distinct torts and as a part of product liability. Negligence requires proof of intent. Strict liability does not. These firms may also have breached their contracts and their warranties, topics that are categorized as contract law and sales law.

5. B. Only a debtor can file a plan under Chapter 11, but for the court to confirm it, the secured creditors must accept it. There is another condition that the plan must meet. It must provide that the creditors retain their liens and the value of the property to be distributed to them is not less than the secured portion of their claims, or the debtor must surrender to the creditors the property securing those claims.

Questions on the Focus on Ethics for Unit Three—Ethics and the Commercial Environment

1. A. If a contract is unconscionable, it is so unfair and one-sided as to "shock the conscience" of a court and be unenforceable. Unconscionability, which represents an attempt by the law to enforce ethical behavior, is a common law concept that is not precisely defined. UCC 2–311 refers to the UCC's pervasive concepts of good faith and commercial reasonableness, but does not define unconscionability. Even UCC 2–302, which adopts the doctrine, does not define the term with specificity. Instead, it is the prerogative of the courts to determine its application in contract cases.

2. B. This problem presents a question involving a cybergriper. A cybergriper uses another's trademark to protest, or otherwise complain about, in good faith and usually without profit, the owner's product or policy. Courts have held that this use of a mark is protected by the freedom of speech. The business's mark is not infringed because the public is not likely to be confused by the cybergriper's use.

3. A. The bankruptcy laws—including the automatic stay provision, and the provisions as to which

and how much debt can be discharged—can make a creditor's secured or unsecured obligation worthless, while enhancing the debtor's position by freeing secured assets from the obligations that they secure. This situation and the ease with which debtors can file for bankruptcy underlies the attempt of the bankruptcy laws to make it less easy for debts to be discharged by directing debtors to debt-counseling classes and funneling petitions into Chapter 13 (subject to the "means test"). Under Chapter 13, many debts may be paid according to a five-year plan and a budget imposed on a debtor, rather than going unpaid and being discharged.

Chapter 17

True-False Questions

1.   F. A sole proprietorship is the simplest form of business organization. In a sole proprietorship, the owner and the business are the same. Anyone who creates a business without designating a specific form for its organization is doing business as a sole proprietorship.
2.   T
3.   T
4.   F. A franchisor can exercise greater control in this area than in some other areas of the business, because the *franchisor* has a legitimate interest in maintaining the quality of the product or service to protect its name and reputation.
5.   F. There is state law covering franchises, and it is very similar to federal law on the subject, requiring certain disclosures, limiting termination without cause, and so on. State deceptive practices acts and UCC Article 2 may also apply to franchises.
6.   F. Federal laws covering franchises include the Automobile Dealers' Franchise Act of 1965, the Petroleum Marketing Practices Act (PMPA) of 1979, the federal antitrust laws, and the Franchise Rule of the Federal Trade Commission (which requires certain disclosures and a meeting between the parties to a franchise agreement).
7.   T
8.   F. General partners are subject to personal liability for the debts and obligations of a partnership. This is true whether or not they have participated in its management. On the firm's dissolution, its creditors (partners and non-partners) have the highest priority in the distribution of the firm's assets. If those assets are not sufficient to pay the creditors, the general partners are liable for the difference.

9.   T
10.   F. Unless it is set out otherwise in the partnership agreement, profits are shared equally, and losses are borne in the same proportion as the profits, under the UPA.

Fill-in Questions

are; one or more; obligation; is not; does not release

Multiple-Choice Questions

1.   D. There are no limits on the liability of the owner of a sole proprietorship for the debts and obligations of the firm. A sole proprietorship has greater organizational flexibility, however, than other forms of business organization.
2.   B. Antitrust laws are most likely to be violated if the franchisor requires the franchisee to purchase exclusively from the franchisor. A franchisor's setting of prices at which products may be sold may also violate antitrust laws.
3.   A. Under a contract between the franchisor and the franchisee, the latter may be required to pay a fee for the franchise license, fees for products bought from or through the franchisor, and a percentage of advertising and administrative costs.
4.   B. Of the choices here, again the franchisor can set the terms. There may be little for a franchisee to negotiate with some franchises, but perhaps the chief advantage of a franchise is that the franchisee is obtaining the opportunity to profit from the sales of a proven product or service.
5.   C. Franchise agreements typically provide that the franchisor can terminate a franchise for cause. If no set time for termination is provided, a reasonable time will be implied. A franchisor cannot usually terminate a franchise without notice.
6.   A. A disadvantage of the sole proprietorship form of doing business is that the ability to raise capital while maintaining control, and retaining the same form, is limited chiefly to borrowing funds. The trade off in this situation is that a sole proprietorship provides greater organizational flexibility—no one needs to be consulted in making business decisions. Bringing in partners would convert the business to a partnership. Issuing stock would require incorporating or establishing another form of business. Selling the business would of course sacrifice all control.
7.   C. The dissociation of a partner from a partnership is not necessarily the end of the firm's business, which may be continued by the remaining partners. The partner's interest in the firm must be bought out, however, according to the UPA's rules. Also, to avoid potential liability on a theory of ap-

parent authority, a partnership should file a statement of dissociation in the appropriate state office.

8. B. Under a partnership by estoppel theory, a person who is not a partner, but who represents himself or herself as a partner, is liable to a third person who acts in reasonable reliance on that representation. If one of the actual partners had consented to the misrepresentation, however, the firm would also be liable.

9. A. This arrangement for the payment of an employee (a base wage and a sales commission) does not make the employee a partner in the employer's business. There are three attributes of a partnership: sharing profits, joint ownership of a business, and an equal right in the management of the business. None of these are present here.

10. B. A newly admitted partner is liable for previous debts and obligations of the partnership only to the extent of his or her capital contribution to the firm. In other words, as far as a new partner is concerned, existing partnership debts can be satisfied only from the assets of the firm. Previous partners may be fully, and personally, liable, however.

GamePoints

1. At its inception, a small, undiversified business with few, or no, employees and little profits and is most likely to exist as a sole proprietorship. This is in part because a sole proprietorship is easier and less expensive to start than other forms. As the owner, you can make decisions without consulting others. Taxes are paid on the business's income as the owner's personal income. One advantage to this form is its organizational flexibility—you can operate the enterprise without formality. An important disadvantage is there are no limits to your liability for business debts and obligations. A second disadvantage is the ability to raise capital without losing control. The sole option may be to borrow.

2. Agreements to form a partnership can be oral or implied by conduct, but sometimes they must be in writing to be enforceable under the Statute of Frauds. In this problem, the partners agree to pursue their venture for five years, which by this term is to continue for more than one year. Thus it must be in writing under the one-year rule of the Statute of Frauds to be enforceable. Practically speaking, even if the one-year rule did not apply, the agreement might be better in writing to make proof of the profit sharing provision easier. In the absence of proof of an agreement to the contrary, it is assumed that partners agreed to share profits and losses equally.

Chapter 18

True-False Questions

1. F. State law applies to the formation of limited liability companies (LLCs). Like the formation of a corporation and other forms of limited liability organizations, the formation of an LLC requires that articles of organization be filed in the state of formation. Otherwise, an LLC will not be held to exist, and its members will not enjoy the features that they wanted.

2. T

3. F. One of the chief advantages of a limited liability company (LLC) is that it offers the limited liability of a corporation. Because an LLC also offers the tax advantages of a partnership, many businesses are using this form of organization.

4. T

5. T

6. F. Unless it is set out otherwise in the partnership agreement, profits are shared equally, and losses are borne in the same proportion as the profits, under the UPA.

7. F. The death of a limited partner will not dissolve a limited partnership, nor will a limited partnership dissolve on the personal bankruptcy of a limited partner.

8. F. A feature that makes a limited liability partnership attractive is that its partners can avoid liability for any partnership obligation, whether in contract, tort, or otherwise. Of course, each partner is liable for his or her own wrongful acts.

9. F. The liability of the *limited* partners in a limited partnership is limited to the amount of their investment in the firm, but the liability of the *general* partners is the same as that of the partners in a general partnership (unlimited).

10. T

Fill-in Questions

members; limited liability company; members *or* shareholders; joint stock company

Multiple-Choice Questions

1. B. A limited liability company (LLC) can be taxed as a partnership, a sole proprietorship (if there is only one member), or a corporation, but electing to be taxed as a partnership is often preferable. The income can be passed through to its members without being taxed at the company level. Generally, there is no particular advantage to being taxed as a corporation. In fact, avoiding the double corporate tax is one reason for forming an LLC.

2. B. Normally, the members of a limited liability company are liable for the debts of their company only to the extent of their investment in the firm, like corporate shareholders or limited partners. Sole proprietors and general partners, in contrast, may be personally liable for the full amount of their firms' obligations.

3. C. One of the advantages of the limited liability company (LLC) form of business organization is that its members are not personally liable for the debts of their firm regardless of the extent of their participation in management (unlike a limited partnership). In fact, unless agreed otherwise, an LLC's management will be considered to include all members. Another advantage is that there is generally no limit on the number of members that a firm can have (unlike an S corporation).

4. D. It is expected that eventually, state laws governing limited liability companies (LLCs) will be made relatively uniform. As for the other choices, the members are not subject to personal liability for the firm's obligations and can participate in the management of the firm to any extent. Also, unlike corporate income, LLC income can pass through the firm and be taxed only once.

5. C. In a manager-managed limited liability company (LLC), the members designate a group of persons (members or not) to manage the firm. These managers owe the fiduciary duties of loyalty and care to the LLC and its members.

6. D. Ordinarily, limited partners are liable for the debts of their limited partnerships only to the extent of their capital contributions to the firms. A general partner, in contrast, may be held personally liable for the full amount of the firm's obligations. Similarly, a limited partner, unlike a general partner does not have a right to control the partnership.

7. D. Limited partnerships may be dissolved by many causes but not by any of these choices. Partners may expressly agree to dissolve their partnership, or dissolution may be caused by the withdrawal, death, or mental incompetence of a general partner (unless the others agree to continue the business). A general partner's death or bankruptcy causes the firm to dissolve, as would an event that makes it impossible to operate the partnership lawfully. Dissolution can also result from a court decree.

8. C. Professionals, and others, who organize as a limited liability partnership can avoid personal liability for the wrongdoing of other partners. In that circumstance, they may have only the same liability as a limited partner in a limited partnership.

9. B. A partner (general or limited) pays personal income taxes on his or her share of the firm's income, regardless of whether or not it is distributed to him. The other partners pay taxes on their shares of the firm's income. Note that each partner is liable for a pro rate share of the taxes even if they are not distributed.

10. B. Besides this requirement, the partners must sign a certificate of limited partnership. This certificate must then be filed with the appropriate state official, usually the secretary of the state in which the partnership is formed.

GamePoints

1. According to the principles discussed in the chapter, the firm would be taxed as a partnership unless it elected to be taxed as a corporation. In other words, the profits would pass through the firm to its owners, who would declare the amounts as personal income and pay taxes accordingly. The members of a limited liability company (LLC) can be its managers, but a non-member can also manage the day-to-day business of the firm. Because an LLC offers its members the limited liability of a corporation—the owners are liable for the obligations of the firm only to the extent of their investment in it—a member of an LLC is not likely to be held fully liable for the acts of another member or employee.

2. According to the principles discussed in this chapter, your firm may be bound to the contract. The chief factor to determining the liability is what the third party knew and when. The apparent authority of a partner to bind a partnership in dealing with a third party cannot be limited by an agreement between the partners of which the third party is unaware. Every partner is an agent of the partnership and can bind the firm to a contract with a third party. Only if the third party is aware that a partner's authority is limited will the liability of the firm be limited.

If your firm is bound to this contract, as a general partner, you are personally liable to the full extent. At first risk is the amount of your capital contribution. Once the partnership's assets have been exhausted in meeting the firm's obligation, your personal assets may be reached by the firm's creditor to make up any deficiency. But a limited partner who participates in the management of the firm is just as liable as a general partner to a creditor who transacts business believing, based on the limited partner's conduct, that the limited partner is a general partner. Thus your cousin Melvin is as obligated as you are.

Chapter 19

True-False Questions

1. T
2. T
3. T
4. F. Preemptive rights consist of preferences given to shareholders over other purchasers to buy shares of a new corporate issue in proportion to the number of shares that they already hold. This allows a shareholder to maintain his or her proportionate ownership share in the corporation. Generally, these rights are granted (or withheld) in the articles of incorporation.
5. T
6. F. Any damages recovered in a shareholder's derivative suit are normally paid to the corporation on whose behalf the shareholder or shareholders exercised the derivative right.
7. T
8. F. Officers and directors owe the same fiduciary duties to the corporations for which they work. They both owe a duty of loyalty. This duty requires them to subordinate their personal interests to the welfare of the corporation.
9. F. The business judgment rule immunizes directors (and officers) from liability for poor business decisions and other honest mistakes that cause a corporation to suffer a loss. Directors are not immunized from losses that do not fit this category, however.
10. T

Fill-in Questions

promoters; unless; an incorporator; need not

Multiple-Choice Questions

1. D. State incorporation laws vary, so looking for the state that offers the most favorable provisions for a particular firm is important. There are some principles that states commonly observe, however. For example, in all states a firm can have perpetual existence, but cannot do business under the same, or even a similar, name as an existing firm.
2. A. Corporate directors manage the business of a corporation. The directors normally employ officers, who oversee the daily operations. The directors may be initially designated by the incorporators or promoters, but are later elected by the shareholders (the owners of the corporation).
3. A. This firm has the characteristics of a close corporation. A close corporation is also generally allowed to restrict the transfer of its stock. Firms represented by the other answer choices could also be close corporations. To be a professional corporation, a firm must be a corporation formed by professionals (and the firm is designated by "P.A." for "professional association," or some other appropriate abbreviation). S corporations and nonprofits corporations have other requirements.
4. A. Other factors that a court may use to pierce the corporate veil include that a party is tricked or misled into dealing with the firm rather than the individual, that the firm is too thinly capitalized (not overcapitalized), and that the firm holds too few (not too many) shareholders' meetings.
5. D. The other choices do not represent proper purposes for which a shareholders' derivative suit may be filed. A shareholder's derivative suit is a claim filed on behalf of the corporation. Such a suit may allege, for example, that officers or directors misused corporate assets. Of course, any damages that are awarded must be paid to the corporation.
6. C. Cumulative voting can often be used in the election of directors to enhance the power of minority shareholders in electing a representative. In calculating a shareholder's votes under the cumulative voting method, in this problem, Mary's number of shares is multiplied by the number of directors to be elected.
7. B. Unless a state statute provides to the contrary, a quorum of directors must be present to conduct corporate business, such as the declaration of a dividend. A quorum is a majority of the number of directors authorized in the firm's articles or bylaws. The rule is one vote per director.
8. C. Under their duty of loyalty, directors cannot compete with their corporation or have an interest which conflicts with the interest of the corporation. Owning the stock of a competitor would also constitute an interest which conflicts with the interest of the corporation on whose board a director serves.
9. D. A corporation's board of directors hires the firm's officers and other executive employees and high-level managers. These employees' contracts with the corporation define the individuals' rights.
10. A. There is no such right. This is also not a right of directors, except as specified in the articles of incorporation. The ownership of a corporation by shareholders also does not include rights of actual ownership of specific corporate property.

GamePoints

1. Under the business judgment rule, if a corporate officer or director makes a serious but honest mistake in judgment, he or she is not normally liable to the firm. To avoid liability, the officer or director must have acted in good faith and in a rea-

sonable manner. The officer or director may reasonably rely on information provided by corporate employees. Thus, if there is a reasonable basis for a corporate decision, a court is not likely to interfere even if the firm suffers. Under this rule, it is not likely that the directors of the corporation in this problem would be personally liable for the drop in the price of its stock.

2. A shareholder can sue on a corporation's behalf to redress a wrong suffered by the firm when those in control of it—the directors—fail to sue in the corporate name. To maintain a shareholder's derivative suit, a wrong must have been done to the corporation. This is particularly useful when the wrong is caused by a corporate officer or, as in this problem, a director. In such a case, any damages recovered are paid to the corporate treasury. One likely defense to the suit is the business judgment rule, under which a director or officer is immune from liability when a decision within managerial authority complies within the individual's fiduciary duties.

Cumulative Hypothetical Problem for Unit Four—Including Chapters 17–19

1. A. A partnership is an association of two or more persons who manage a business and share profits. Here, the partnership began when the parties combined their assets and commenced business. Before that time, there was no sharing of profits, no joint ownership of a business, and no equal right in the management of a business (because there was no business). The execution of a formal partnership agreement is not necessary, nor is the consent of creditors.

2. B. Unlike general partnerships, which can come into existence even when the parties do not intend to form a partnership, a limited partnership can only be created pursuant to the provisions of a state statute. This statute sets out exactly what partners must do to form a limited partnership, which must include at least one general partner who assumes personal liability for the debts of the firm.

3. D. The information that each state requires to be in articles of incorporation differs somewhat, but the information represented by the choices in this problem is generally required. It is not necessary to name the initial officers in the articles. Other information that might be required includes the number of authorized shares. Other information that is not required includes quorum requirements.

4. B. Directors' main right is their right to participate in board meetings. Directors also have a right to inspect corporate books and to be indemnified in defense of some lawsuits (regardless of the outcome

of the suit). Rights that directors do not have include a right to compensation. That is, directors may be compensated for their efforts, but they have no inherent right to it. "Preemption" is not a right.

5. A. Dividends may be paid from any of the other of sources in the answer choices. Note that there is no right to a dividend. Its payment is subject to the discretion of the board of directors.

Questions on the Focus on Ethics for Unit Four—Ethics and the Business Environment

1. D. This duty arises from the legal principles of agency, and applies to all corporate officers, managers, and directors. When personal interests conflict with the interests of the corporation, the corporate party must not act against the interest of the corporation. If an officer usurps a corporate opportunity by, for example, setting up a competing firm to take advantage of an opportunity that might have otherwise been utilized by his or her corporation, a successful claim against the individual can result in the individual giving up an interest in the new company to the shareholders of the corporation.

2. D. Corporate directors have a fiduciary duty to exercise care when making decisions that affect their corporations. Fiduciary duties may, in some extraordinary circumstances, be owed to other directors, officers, or the firm's creditors, particularly if a director's corporation is nearly insolvent. In normal situations, however, the duty of care extends chiefly to the corporation's shareholders, and may include a duty to implement a program to uncover and prevent wrongdoing by corporate personnel.

3. B. When a franchisor's control over the operations of its franchisee is too extensive, the franchisor may be held liable for the torts of the franchisee's employees under agency principles. This may occur even if the franchise agreement between the parties specifies that the individuals are independent contractors, or otherwise.

Chapter 20

True-False Questions

1. T
2. T
3. T
4. T
5. F. An agent is liable for his or her own torts, but a principal may also be liable under the doctrine of *respondeat superior*. The key is whether the tort is committed within the scope of employment. One

of the important factors is whether the principal authorized the act that constituted the tort.

6. T

7. F. The parties to an agency may always have the *power* to terminate the agency at any time, but they may not always have the *right*. If a party who terminates an agency does not have the right to do so, he or she may be liable for breach of contract.

8. T

9. F. An e-agent is a semi-autonomous computer program that is capable of executing specific tasks, including responding to e-messages or other e-actions without review by a human being.

10. F. One of the main attributes of an agency relationship is that the agent can enter into binding contracts on behalf of the principal. When an agent acts within the scope of his or her authority in entering a contract, the principal is bound, whether the principal's identity was disclosed, partially disclosed, or undisclosed to the other party to the contact.

Fill-in Questions

performance; notification; loyalty; obedience; accounting

Multiple-Choice Questions

1. A. Agency law is essential to the existence of most business entities, including corporations, because without agents, most firms could not do business. A corporate officer who serves in a representative capacity, as in this problem, is an agent. The corporation is the principal. For a contract to be binding on the firm, it needs only to be signed by the agent and to be within the scope of the officer's authority.

2. A. There is a long list of factors that courts can consider in determining whether an individual is an employee or an independent contractor, and all of the choices in this question are among those factors. The most important factor, however, is the degree of control that the employer has over the details of the work.

3. B. In performing an agency, an agent is expected to use reasonable diligence and skill, which is the degree of skill of a reasonable person under similar circumstances. If an agent claims special skills, such as those of in this problem, he or she is expected to use those skills.

4. A. An agent's duties to a principal include a duty to act solely in the principal's interest in matters concerning the principal's business. This is the duty of loyalty. The agent must act solely in the principal's interest and not in the interest of the agent, or some other party. It is also a breach of the duty of loyalty to use a principal's trade secrets or other confidential information (but not acquired skills) even after the agency has terminated.

5. D. Implied authority can be conferred by custom, inferred from the agent's position, or inferred as reasonably necessary to carry out express authority. In determining whether an agent has the implied authority to do a specific act, the question is whether it is reasonable for the agent to believe that he or she has the authority.

6. A. Until an agent is notified of the principal's decision to terminate the agency relationship, the agent's authority continues. Similarly, third parties with whom the agent deals must be informed of the termination to end the agent's apparent authority, as regards those third parties. Unless an agency is in writing, in which case it must be terminated in writing, an agent can learn of a termination through any means.

7. B. When an agent enters into a contract within the scope of his or her authority, the principal is liable, whether or not the principal's identity was disclosed. The agent is also liable as a party to the contract when neither the identity of the principal nor the fact of the agency is disclosed.

8. A. Apparent authority exists when a principal causes a third party reasonably to believe that an agent has the authority to act, even if the agent does not otherwise have the authority to do so. If the third party changes positions in reliance on the principal's representation, the principal may be estopped from denying the authority. Thus, here, the principal could not hold the customers liable for failing to pay.

9. C. An agent (or employee) is liable for his or her own torts, whether or not they were committed within the scope of a principal's employment. The principal is also liable under the doctrine of respondeat superior when a tort is within the scope of the employment. One of the important factors in determining liability is whether the agent was on the principal's business or on a "frolic of his or her own."

10. D. An agency relationship can be created only for a legal purpose. An agency relationship created for an illegal purpose, such as a scheme to defraud, is unenforceable. Also, it should be kept in mind that although a principal must have contractual capacity, an agent does not need it. Even a person who is legally incompetent can be an agent.

GamePoints

1. Of course, an agency relationship can only be created for a legal purpose, and one created for an illegal purpose is unenforceable. Assuming an agency relationship exists, an agent can enter into binding contracts on behalf of the principal. When an agent acts within the scope of his or her authority in entering into a contract, the principal is bound, whether the principal's identity was disclosed, partially disclosed, or undisclosed to the other party to the contact. The agent is also bound if the principal's identity was only partially disclosed or not disclosed to the other party. Thus, in this problem, you are bound to all three contracts and your agent is also bound to the second and third contracts (but not the first).

2. Under the doctrine of *respondeat superior*, a principal is liable for any harm caused to another through an agent's negligence as long as the agent was acting within the scope of his or her authority at the time of the harmful act. Here, you instructed your agent to "loot the universe," which he was doing when his negligent escape from the asteroid caused an injury to the Cyclops. Thus, the Cyclops could recover from you for the harm.

Chapter 21

True-False Questions

1. T
2. F. Employment "at will" means that either party may terminate the employment at any time, with or without good cause. There are many exceptions to this doctrine, enacted by state legislatures and Congress, or created by the courts. These include exceptions based on contract or tort theories, or public policy.
3. F. Employers are free to offer employees no benefits. Federal and state governments participate in insurance programs designed to protect employees and their families by covering some of the financial impact of retirement, disability, death, and hospitalization.
4. T
5. F. A "whistleblower" is one who reports wrongdoing. Whistleblower statutes protect employees who report their employers' wrongdoing from retaliation in the form of discharge, and sometimes other adverse employment conditions, on the part of those employers.
6. F. The Electronic Communications Privacy Act prohibits the interception of telephone (and other electronic) communications. Some courts recognize an exception for employers monitoring employee business-related calls, but monitoring personal conversations is not permitted.
7. F. These laws do not cover all employees. Although statutes vary in their coverage from state to

state, they often exclude domestic workers (such as maids), agricultural workers, temporary employees, and employees of common carriers (such as trucking companies).
8. T
9. F. Under the Fair Labor Standards Act, minors (persons under the age of eighteen) cannot work in hazardous occupations.
10. T

Fill-in Questions

either; unless; may; Some; A few states; may not

Multiple-Choice Questions

1. A. Child-labor, minimum-wage, and maximum-hour provisions are included in the Fair Labor Standards Act (also known as the Wage-Hour Law), covering virtually all employees. The employer may also be subject to the other laws given as choices in this problem, but those laws concern other rights and duties of employees and employers.
2. B. Investigating theft is the only circumstance in which an employer may require polygraph tests. Drug tests are prohibited by some states, and restricted by others or by collective bargaining agreements. Their use may also be subject to tort actions for invasion of privacy. An employer may monitor employees' *business* phone conversations but not their *private* ones.
3. B. Intentionally inflicted injuries are not covered by workers' compensation. Many states cover problems arising out of preexisting conditions, but that is not part of the test for coverage. To collect benefits, an employee must notify the employer of an injury and file a claim with the appropriate state agency.
4. C. Under the Fair Labor Standards Act, employees must be paid no less than one and a half times their regular pay for all hours that they work over forty in a week. Various categories of workers, including executives, administrative employees, professional employees, outside salespersons, and computer employees, are exempt if their pay exceeds a certain amount, their duties do not include certain types of work, and they meet other requirements.
5. C. The Federal Unemployment Tax Act of 1935 concerns the system that provides unemployment compensation. The Employee Retirement Income Security Act (ERISA) of 1974 concerns the regulation of private pension plans. There is no "Employee Payments Act" that covers any of these subjects.
6. B. The Employment Retirement Income Security Act (ERISA) covers such employers. The Labor

Management Services Administration of the U.S. Department of Labor enforces ERISA. Most of the other laws mentioned in the choices in this problem regulate other areas of retirement and security income. There is no "Employer Payments Act" that covers any of these subjects.

7. B. Under the Family and Medical Leave Act (FMLA) of 1993, employees can take up to twelve weeks of family or medical leave during any twelve-month period and are entitled to continued health insurance coverage during the leave. Employees are also guaranteed the same, or a comparable, job on returning to work.

8. C. Under the Consolidated Omnibus Budget Reconciliation Act (COBRA) of 1985, most workers' medical, optical, or dental insurance is not automatically eliminated on termination of employment. The workers can choose to continue the coverage at the employer's group rate, if they are willing to pay the premiums (and a 2 percent administrative fee).

9. C. When an employment relationship is "at will," either the employer or the employee may terminate it at any time—and for any reason. An employment relationship is at will when there is no contract and no law to otherwise restrict its duration or other conditions of its termination.

10. B. Depending on the particular state, and the rulings of the courts in the state, some state constitutions effectively prohibit private employers from testing for drugs. There are also state statutes that restrict drug testing by private employers. Other sources of limitation on the use of such tests include collective bargaining agreements and employee tort actions for invasion of privacy.

GamePoints

1. The Fair Labor Standards Act requires covered, nonexempt individuals who work more than forty hours in one week to be paid overtime wages of no less than 1.5 times their regular pay rate for the hours worked beyond forty. In two of the weeks noted in this problem—the first and second weeks—you played the game for more than forty hours and would be entitled to overtime pay if, of course, this game-play was work. That you played less than forty hours in the other weeks has no effect.

2. State workers' compensation laws allow compensation to be paid to workers whose injuries occur on the job or in the course of their employment. Under those laws, an employee who receives workers' compensation cannot successfully maintain a suit against his or employer for negligence to recover for the same injury. Thus, in this problem, Derek is entitled to recover workers' compensation because

he was an employee of the service, and the injury was accidental and occurred in the course of employment. Derek could not then, however, successfully sue the service on a negligence theory because he was the service's employee and would be recovering workers' compensation.

Chapter 22

True-False Questions

1. T

2. F. An employer may be liable even though an employee did the harassing, if the employer knew, or should have known, and failed to take corrective action, or if the employee was in a supervisory position and took a tangible employment action against the injured employee.

3. F. Just as an employer may be liable for an employee's misconduct, the employer may be liable for harassment by a nonemployee, if the employer knew, or should have known, of the harassment and failed to take corrective action.

4. T

5. T

6. T

7. F. If the Equal Employment Opportunity Commission (EEOC) decides not pursue a claim, the victim can file a suit against alleged violator. The EEOC can pursue a claim in federal district court, however, in its own name against alleged violators (and this is true even if the employee has agreed to submit the dispute to arbitration). The EEOC can also intervene in a suit filed by a private party.

8. F. Title VII covers only employers with fifteen or more employees, labor unions with fifteen or more members, labor unions that operate hiring halls, employment agencies, and federal, state, and local agencies. In other words, small employers are generally exempted from the application of this federal statute.

9. T

10. T

Fill-in Questions

can; may sue if a settlement between the parties is not reached; reinstatement, back pay, and retroactive promotions

Multiple-Choice Questions

1. C. Here, the employer would seem to have a valid business necessity defense. It appears reasonable that administrative assistants be able to type.

An employer can insist that, to be hired, a job applicant possess the actual skills required for a job. Except for an applicant's willingness or unwillingness to acquire certain skills, the other answer choices might be legitimate defenses in other circumstances.

2. C. The Equal Pay Act of 1963 prohibits gender-based discrimination in wages for equal work. Different wages are acceptable because of any factor but gender, including seniority and merit.

3. A. The other choices would not subject the employer to liability under the Age Discrimination in Employment Act (ADEA). Discrimination is prohibited against persons forty years of age or older, even if the discrimination is unintentional. Mandatory retirement may be instituted, but not on account of an employee's age, and an employee may be discharged for cause at any age. This question and answer are based on a question that appeared in the CPA exam in 1996.

4. C. An employer who is subject to the Americans with Disabilities Act cannot exclude arbitrarily a person who, with reasonable accommodation, could do what is required of a job. A disabled individual is not required to reasonably accommodate an employer. Also, the standard is not "significant additional costs," to either the employer or the disabled individual.

5. C. Title VII prohibits employment discrimination on the basis of race. This includes discriminating against members of a minority with darker skin than other members of the same minority. Title VII also prohibits using physical characteristics that are typical of some races to distinguish applicants or employees.

6. A. Before filing a lawsuit, the best step for a person who believes that he or she may be a victim of employment discrimination is to contact a state or federal agency to see whether the claim is justified. The appropriate federal agency is the Equal Employment Opportunity Commission. Most states have similar agencies that evaluate claims under state law.

7. C. Title VII prohibits showing a preference for members of one minority over members of another. Title VII also prohibits making distinctions according to the race of a person's spouse, friends, or other contacts. The other laws mentioned in the answer choices prohibit discrimination on the basis of age and disability, respectively, as suggested by their titles.

8. A. The Age Discrimination in Employment Act (ADEA) of 1967 requires, for the establishment of a *prima facie* case, that at the time of the alleged discrimination, the plaintiff was forty or older, was qualified for the job, and was discharged or otherwise rejected in circumstances that imply discrimination. The difference between a *prima facie* case under the ADEA and under Title VII is that the ADEA does not require a plaintiff to show that someone who is not a member of a protected class filled the position at the center of the claim.

9. C. The employer's best defense in this problem would be that being able to pass the tests is a business necessity—it is a necessary requirement for the job. Discrimination may be illegal even if it is not intentional, and whether or not all men pass the tests is not relevant to whether there is discrimination against women. If the employer hires some women for the job, it could not argue successfully that gender is a BFOQ for the job.

10. A. Sexual harassment occurs when, in a workplace, an employee is subject to comments or contact that is perceived as sexually offensive. An employer may be liable even though an employee did the harassing. If the employee was in a supervisory position, as in this problem, for an employer to be held liable, a tangible employment action may need to be proved. Here, the employee's pay was cut.

GamePoints

1. Under the Americans with Disabilities Act, a disabled person qualified for a given job is protected from employment discrimination on the basis of his or her disability. A disabled person is not unqualified for a job simply because the employer would have to make a reasonable accommodation. In fact, employers are required to reasonably accommodate the needs of persons with disabilities. Thus, here, the employer has apparently engaged in discrimination by choosing not "to make changes to accommodate this guy." For that reason, the disabled person could recover damages.

2. Title VII of the Civil Rights Act of 1964 prohibits job discrimination against employees on the basis of race. To recover on this ground, the employee must show that (1) the employee is a member of a protected class, (2) the employee applied and was qualified for the position in question, (3) the employer rejected the employee, and (4) the employer continued to seek applicants or hired someone not of a protected class. In this problem, the employee applied and was qualified for the promotion (a year's driving experience and a specific license). The employer clearly rejected the employee on the basis of race ("whites are lazy"). And the employer most likely continued to seek applicants and may have hired "someone not of a protected class." The chief difficulty in concluding that this problem presents an instance of employment discrimination under these standards is the employee's race.

"Whites" have not been historically discriminated against so that Sam could qualify as a member of a "protected class."

Chapter 23

True-False Questions

1. F. Secondary boycotts, including hot-cargo agreements, which are described in the question, are illegal.
2. F. It is the central legal right of a *union* to serve as the bargaining representative of employees in negotiations with management, not the other way around, as set out in this question.
3. F. An employer is required to evaluate job applicants, and their documents, fairly and consistently (for example, proof of qualifications or citizenship cannot be asked of some individuals and not others). But it is illegal for an employer to hire for work in the United States a person who is not authorized to work here.
4. F. Employees' right to engage in collective bargaining through elected representatives, like their right to organize and their right to engage in concerted activities for those and other purposes, was established in the National Labor Relations Act.
5. T
6. T
7. T
8. F. A lockout is a shut down to prevent employees from working. An employer cannot use this tactic to break a union or to pressure employees into decertifying it.
9. F. A private individual who claims injury as a result of an employer's illegal hiring of noncitizens may sue the employer under the Racketeer Influenced and Corrupt Organizations (RICO) Act. The individual may also complain to federal agencies empowered to enforce or otherwise act on immigration employment laws and regulations, including the U.S. Immigration and Customs Enforcement, the U.S. Department of Justice, the U.S> Department of Labor, and others.
10. T

Fill-in Questions

Norris-LaGuardia; National Labor Relations; Relations; allows; prohibits

Multiple-Choice Questions

1. D. It is not a violation of any of these laws *not* to pay workers for time spent on union activities (going to meetings, soliciting support, canvassing co-workers, and so on). In fact, paying workers for participating in union activities is an unfair labor practice because it is considered to be giving support to the union.
2. A. It is illegal to hire for work in the United States a person who is not authorized to work here. The principal responsibility to verify an individual's identity and eligibility to work rests with the employer. The U.S. Citizenship and Immigration Services supplies a form that an employer must complete within three days of hiring an employee (and retain for three years). An employer has some defenses against alleged violations but is otherwise subject to penalties for illegally employing noncitizens.
3. A. Among these choices, an employer may hire a noncitizen who is a lawful permanent resident (as proved by an I-531 Alien Registration Receipt, or "green card"). Subject to certain strict requirements, an employer may apply for a "green card" for a noncitizen. But under no circumstances can an employer legally hire a noncitizen who is in the United States unlawfully. Also, an immigrant employee's ability to stay in the United States and to switch jobs here is limited
4. D. An employer cannot refuse to negotiate in good faith, during collective bargaining, over either of these terms and conditions of employment. They are mandatory subjects for collective bargaining. Because an employer must agree to talk about these subjects does not mean that the employer must accept the union's position on the topics, however.
5. A. Management is not required to bargain with a union over a decision to close a facility—although an employer may bargain over this topic if it chooses to do so. (Economic consequences of the decision must be bargained over, however.) On the other hand, the procedure for employee grievances is an appropriate subject for the bargaining table.
6. B. The National Labor Relations Act protects employees who engage in union activity and prohibits employers from refusing to bargain with employees' designated representative. Firing workers for supporting or joining a union is an unfair labor practice, as is refusing to recognize and bargain with the union.
7. C. It is an unfair labor practice to ask employees to declare their views on a union without anonymity. An employer can poll its employees during a unionization campaign, or any time, only if their identities are protected.
8. A. Persons who immigrate to the United States to work include those with special skills, such as the individual in this question. To hire such an individual who is not otherwise authorized to work here,

an employer must petition the U.S. Citizenship and Immigration Services, or CIS. The employer can obtain a visa for a person to work in the United States in a highly qualified, specialty occupation as part of the H-1B visa program. ICE is the U.S. Immigration and Customs Enforcement, which enforces immigration laws and rules. RICO is the acronym for the Racketeer Influenced and Corrupt Organizations Act, under which a private individual who claims injury as a result of illegal hiring may sue an employer.

9. D. It is an unfair labor practice for an employer to threaten employees with the loss of their jobs if a union wins a scheduled union election. What can be difficult is determining what constitutes a threat. Explicit statements, such as "if the union wins, you're all fired," are obvious violations. Less clear is whether such a statement as "if the union wins, we will lose business to our competitors" is a violation. The point, however, is that an employer cannot require rejection of a union as a condition of employment. The other choices are, of course, not unfair labor practices.

10. D. An employer can hire permanent replacement workers during an economic strike. After the strike, the replacement workers do not have to be fired to make way for the strikers. Temporary replacement workers may be hired during any strike.

GamePoints

1. It is illegal to hire for work in the United States a person who is not authorized to work here. Thus, under no circumstances can an employer legally hire a noncitizen who is in the United States unlawfully. But an employer may hire a noncitizen who is a lawful permanent resident. The principal responsibility to verify an individual's identity and eligibility to work rests with the employer. The U.S. Citizenship and Immigration Services (CIS) supplies a form—Form I-9, Employment Eligibility Verification—that an employer must complete within three days of hiring an employee (and retain for three years). An employer has some defenses against alleged violations but is otherwise subject to penalties for illegally employing noncitizens. Lawful permanent residency can be proved by an I-514 Alien Registration Receipt, or "green card."

Subject to certain strict requirements, an employer may apply for a "green card" for a noncitizen. Persons who immigrate to the United States to work include those with special skills, such as an individual who might qualify to fill the job with Palace in this question. To hire such an individual who is not otherwise authorized to work here, an employer must petition the CIS. The employer can

obtain a visa for a person to work in the United States in a highly qualified, specialty occupation as part of the H-1B visa program.

2. There are a number of steps that Periwinkle might legally take on Palace's behalf to attempt to avoid the unionization of its employees. Firing Danica is not one of those steps, however, nor is threatening the employees with discharge. These acts would be considered unfair labor practices by the National Labor Relations Board (NLRB), which would likely order the employees' reinstatement with back pay. And if the employees want to unionize, Palace or any other employer cannot completely, legally thwart their wishes, except by going out of business. Palace can actively campaign against unionization without offering the union an opportunity to rebut. Palace can limit union solicitation on its premises. Palace can quickly oppose any illegal steps that the union might take by appealing to the NLRB. And if unionization does occur, Palace can urge its employees to decertify the union.

Cumulative Hypothetical Problem for Unit Five—Including Chapters 20–23

1. B. The requirements for recovery under state workers' compensation laws include the existence of an employment relationship and an accidental injury that occurs on the job or within the scope of employment. Accepting benefits precludes an employee from suing his or her employer, but it does not bar the employee from suing a third party for causing the injury.

2. D. The Social Security Act of 1935 provides payments for persons who are retired or disabled. The Social Security Administration is a federal agency that also administers the Medicare program. Unemployment benefits, however, are part of a state system created by the Federal Unemployment Tax Act of 1935.

3. D. One of the agent's fiduciary duties to the principal is the duty of loyalty. This means that the agent must not engage in conflicts of interest, and the agent cannot compete with the principal without informing the principal of the conflict of interest and obtaining the principal's consent.

4. A. Title VII of the Civil Rights Act of 1964 covers many forms of discrimination, including discrimination based on gender, race, religion, color, and national origin. But Title VII does not prohibit discrimination based on age, which is the subject of the Age Discrimination in Employment Act of 1967.

5. B. The Age Discrimination in Employment Act of 1967 prohibits discrimination against persons aged forty or more. This includes mandatory retirement of such individuals. In most circumstances, however, an employer can discharge an employee for cause, regardless of his or her age, without running afoul of this, or any other, federal anti-discrimination law.

Questions on the Focus on Ethics for Unit Five—The Employment Environment

1. D. The conduct stated in the answer choices is permitted by legal and ethical considerations. Other actions that may be proscribed by ethics include secretly profiting from the agency relation, and failing to disclose the agent's interest in property that the principal is buying.

2. C. Agents and principals owe each other fiduciary duties. The law mandates for a principal duties of compensation, cooperation, and reimbursement of agency-related expenses. A principal is not legally bound to a duty of loyalty, however, although a sense of loyalty may be based on ethical obligations.

3. D. When an innocent party must suffer a loss, the party in the best position to prevent the loss is generally held to bear its burden, even if that party was also innocent with respect to the loss. In an employment relationship, that party is the employer, who, when the situation involves an employee and a third party, is in a better position to control the employee. The employer may also have insurance or some other form of "deep pockets" from which to cover a loss or injury.

Chapter 24

True-False Questions

1. T

2. T

3. F. Under certain circumstances, consumers have a right to rescind their contracts. This is particularly true when a creditor has not made all required disclosures. A contract entered into as part of a door-to-door sale may be rescinded within three days, regardless of the reason.

4. T

5. F. A consumer can also include a note in his or her credit file to explain any misinformation in the file. Under the Fair Credit Reporting Act, consumers are entitled to have deleted from their files any misinformation that leads to a denial of credit, employment, or insurance. Consumers are also entitled to receive information about the source of the misinformation and about anyone who was given the misinformation.

6. T

7. F. The Fair Debt Collection Practices Act applies only to debt collectors that attempt to collect debts on another party's behalf. Typically, the collector is paid a commission—a percentage of the amount owed or collected—for a successful collection effort.

8. F. The Federal Trade Commission (FTC), the Federal Reserve Board of Governors (Fed), and other federal agencies regulate the terms and conditions of sales. For example, the FTC issues regulations covering warranties and labels, and the Fed regulates credit provisions in sales contracts.

9. F. One who leases consumer goods in the ordinary course of their business must disclose *all* material terms in writing—clearly and conspicuously—if the goods are priced at $25,000 or less and the lease term exceeds four months. The Consumer Leasing Act of 1988 requires this.

10. T

Fill-in Questions

$50; before; prohibits; from billing; if

Multiple-Choice Questions

1. C. Under the Fair Debt Collection Practices Act, once a debtor has refused to pay a debt, a collection agency can contact the debtor *only* to advise him or her of further action to be taken. None of the rest of these choices would be legitimate possibilities.

2. D. The FTC has the power to issue a cease-and-desist order, but in some cases, such an order is not enough to stop the harm. With counteradvertising (also known as corrective advertising), an advertiser attempts to correct earlier misinformation by admitting that prior claims about a product were untrue.

3. B. A regular-size box of laundry soap, for example, cannot be labeled "super-size" to exaggerate the amount of product in the box. Labels on consumer goods must identify the product, the manufacturer, the distributor, the net quantity of the contents, and the quantity of each serving (if the number of servings is given). Other information may also be required.

4. B. Under certain circumstances, consumers have a right to rescind their contracts. In a door-to-door sale, a consumer generally has at least a three-day cooling-off period within which to rescind the transaction. Salespersons are required to give consumers written notice of this right.

5. B. This is required under Regulation Z (which was issued by the Federal Reserve Board under the Truth in Lending Act) and applies to any creditor who, in the ordinary course of business, lends money or sells goods on credit to consumers, or arranges for credit for consumers. The information that must be disclosed includes: the specific dollar amount being financed; the annual percentage rate of interest; any financing charges, premiums or points; the number, amounts, and due dates of payments; and any penalties imposed on delinquent payments or prepayment.

6.   D. When contracting parties are subject to the Truth-in-Lending Act (TILA), Regulation Z applies to any transaction involving an installment sales contract in which payment is to be made in more than four installments. Normally, such loans as those described in this problem require more than four installments to repay. In any transaction subject to Regulation Z, the lender must disclose all of the credit terms clearly and conspicuously.

7.   C. The Fair Packaging and Labeling Act requires that products include a variety of information on their labels. Besides the information specified in the answer to this problem, manufactures must identify themselves and the packager or distributor or the product, as well as nutrition details, including how much and what type of fat a product contains.

8.   B. Under the Smokeless Tobacco Health Education Act of 1986, packages of smokeless tobacco products must include warnings about the health hazards associated with the use of smokeless tobacco similar to warnings contained on cigarette packages.

9.   A. The Consumer Product Safety Commission (CPSC) has sufficiently broad authority to remove from store shelves any product that it believes is imminently hazardous and to require manufacturers to report on products already sold. Additionally, the CPSC can ban the make and sale of any product that the CPSC deems to be potentially hazardous. The CPSC also administers other product safety legislation.

10. D. The Truth-in-Lending Act includes rules covering credit cards. There is a provision that limits the liability of a cardholder to $50 per card for unauthorized charges made before the creditor is notified, and exempts a consumer from liability if the card was not properly issued. When a card is not solicited, it is not "properly issued," however, and thus a consumer, in whose name unauthorized charges are made, is not liable for those charges in any amount.

GamePoints

1.   No, the lender in this problem has violated the provisions of the Truth in Lending Act (TILA), which requires the disclosure of credit and loan terms to enable borrowers to shop for the best financing arrangements. The TILA applies to those who lend money in the ordinary course of their business, which of course a credit union does. (There is an exception for installment loans of fewer than four payments, but that is an unlikely schedule for an auto loan.) Under the TILA, all of the terms of a credit instrument must be fully disclosed even if "it would take too long."

2.   With respect to food, the general legal standard is that it contains no substance that could cause injury to health. Most statutes involving food are monitored and enforced by the Food and Drug Administration and the Food Safety and Quality Service of the U.S. Department of Agriculture. Various federal laws specify safe levels of potentially dangerous food additives—which cannot be carcinogenic—create classifications of food and food advertising, and provide for the inspection of meat and poultry.

Chapter 25

True-False Questions

1.   F. Common law doctrines that were applied against polluters centuries ago may be applicable today. These include nuisance and negligence doctrines.

2.   T

3.   F. There are different standards for different pollutants and for different polluters. There are even different standards for the same pollutants and polluters in different locations. The standards cover the amount of emissions, the technology to control them, the notice that must be given to the public, and the penalties that may be imposed for noncompliance.

4.   F. The Toxic Substances Control Act of 1976 regulates substances that the production and labeling of substances of that potentially pose an imminent hazard or an unreasonable risk of injury to health or the environment. The Comprehensive Environmental Response, Compensation, and Liability Act (CERCLA) of 1980 regulates the clean up of leaking hazardous waste disposal sites.

5.   T

6.   T

7.   F. To penalize those for whom a violation is cost-effective, the EPA can obtain a penalty equal to a violator's economic benefits from noncompliance. Other penalties include criminal fines. Private citizens can also sue polluters. It is generally more eco-

nomically beneficial for a business to comply with the Clean Air Act.
8. T
9. F. Under CERCLA, a party who transports waste to a hazardous waste site may be held liable for any and all of the cost to clean up the site. There is a variety of "potentially responsible parties" who may also be held liable, including the party who generated the waste, and current and past owners and operators of the site. A party assessed with these costs can bring a contribution action against the others, however, to recoup the amount of their proportion.
10. T

Fill-in Questions

federal; federal; environmental impact that an action will have; environment; an action might cause to the environment; and reasons

Multiple-Choice Questions

1. A. An environmental impact statement (EIS) must be prepared when a major federal action significantly affects the quality of the environment. An action that affects the quality of the environment is "major" if it involves a substantial commitment of resources and "federal" if a federal agency has the power to control it.
2. C. Under the 1990 amendments to the Clean Air Act, different standards apply to existing sources and major new sources. Major new sources must use the maximum achievable control technology (MACT) to reduce emissions from the combustion of fossil fuels. Other factories and businesses must reduce emissions of hazardous air pollutants with the best available technology.
3. D. Sport utility vehicles are now subject to the same standards for polluting emissions as automobiles. If new motor vehicles do not meet the emission standards of regulations issued under the Clean Air Act, the EPA can order a recall of the vehicles and a repair or replacement of pollution-control devices.
4. C. A polluter can be ordered to clean up the pollution or to pay for the clean-up costs, and other penalties may be imposed. For example, fines may be assessed and imprisonment ordered.
5. B. Under the Resource Conservation and Recovery Act, producers of hazardous waste must properly label and package waste to be transported. Under the Comprehensive Environmental Response, Compensation, and Liability Act, the party who generated the waste disposed of at a site can be held liable for clean-up costs.

6. B. Under the Resource Conservation and Recovery Act of 1976, the EPA monitors and controls the disposal of hazardous waste. Under the Comprehensive Environmental Response, Compensation, and Liability Act, the EPA regulates the clean up of hazardous waste sites when a release occurs.
7. B. An action that affects the quality of the environment is "major" if it involves a substantial commitment of resources. Minor landscaping does not qualify because it does not involve such a commitment. The landscaping in this problem is "federal," however, because a federal agency controls it, and any landscaping can affect the quality of the environment.
8. C. Under the 1990 amendments to the Clean Air Act, different standards apply to existing sources and major new sources. Major new sources must use the maximum achievable control technology to reduce emissions from the combustion of fossil fuels. Other factories and businesses must reduce emissions of hazardous air pollutants with the best available technology.
9. B. One of the goals of the Clean Water Act is to protect fish and wildlife. In part, this goal is met by protecting their habitats, such as swamps and other wetlands. Protecting these areas can also protect navigable waters into which wetlands drain and other surrounding resources. Before dredging and filling wetlands, a permit must be obtained from the Army Corps of Engineers.
10. B. Any potentially responsible party can be charged with the entire cost to clean up a hazardous waste disposal site. Potentially responsible parties include former owners and may, under certain circumstances, include a lender to the owner. Of course, a party held responsible for the entire cost may be able to recoup some of it in a contribution action against other potentially responsible parties.

GamePoints

1. Under the National Pollutant Discharge Elimination System (NPDES) of the Clean Water Act of 1972, the trash removal service may be able to dispose of some of its waste in the ocean, providing it meets the NPDES requirements. The Marine Protection, Research, and Sanctuaries Act, also known as the Ocean Dumping Act, regulates the transportation and dumping of pollutants in ocean waters, and provides permit programs for some materials. But dumping of chemical warfare supplies and high-level radioactive waste, as well as other radiological, chemical, and biological wastes, into the ocean is prohibited. Civil penalties and criminal fines are possible up to $50,000 each. Imprisonment for up to a year and an injunction may also be ordered. The oil refinery may be liable under the Oil Pollution Act of 1990 for discharging oil into navigable waters or onto the shore. Sanctions include the clean-up costs, which can be considerable, as well as damages for the harm to natural resources, private property, and the local economy.

2. The Comprehensive Environmental Response, Compensation, and Liability Act of 1980 regulates the clean up of hazardous waste disposal sites. Any potentially responsible party can be charged with the entire cost to clean up a leaking hazardous waste disposal site. Potentially responsible parties include the person who generated the waste, the person who transported the waste to the site, the person who owned or operated the site at the time of the disposal, and the current owner or operator of the site. Sludge most likely qualifies at least as a party who owned or operated Toxin at the time of the disposal, and possibly its leak, and may have been the party who generated or transported the waste, even if Sludge does not own Toxin now. A party who generates only a fraction of the waste can be held liable for the entire clean-up cost. (Of course, whoever is held liable for the cost can bring a contribution action against any other person who is, or who may be, liable for a percentage of the expense.)

Chapter 26

True-False Questions

1. T
2. F. The owner of a life estate has the same rights as a fee simple owner except that the value of the property must be kept intact for the holder of the future interest.
3. F. An easement merely allows a person to use land without taking anything from it, while a profit allows a person to take something from the land.
4. T
5. F. The government has the power to take private property, but the purposes for which such property may be taken must be *public*.
6. T
7. T
8. F. Under the Fifth Amendment to the U.S. Constitution, when taking private property, the government is required to pay the owner just compensation.
9. F. To be entitled to a variance, a landowner must show that a granting of the variance would *not* substantially alter the essential character of the zoned area.

10. T

Fill-in Questions

warranty; special warranty; quitclaim

Multiple-Choice Questions

1. C. A *profit* is the right to go onto land in possession of another and take away some part of the land itself or some product of the land. In contrast, an easement is a right to make limited use of another person's land without taking anything from the property. A license is a revocable right to come onto another person's land.
2. A. This action would meet all the requirements for acquiring property by adverse possession: the possession would be (1) actual and exclusive; (2) open, visible, and notorious; (3) continuous and peaceful for the applicable statutory period; and (4) hostile, against the whole world, including the original owner. The owner's filing a suit would undercut the peaceful and exclusive elements. Occupying the property without the owner's awareness would affect the open and hostile requirements. The state's permission would normally have no effect on this issue.
3. B. The rights that accompany ownership in fee simple include the right to sell the land or give it away, as well as the right to use the land for whatever purpose the owner sees fit, subject, of course, to the law's limitations.
4. D. This is an exercise of the power of eminent domain. The proceeding is known as a condemnation proceeding. The government cannot acquire land in this manner without paying for it, however. A later proceeding is held to determine the fair value of the property. The government pays this price to the owners of the land.
5. A. Besides a legally sufficient description of the property and the price, a valid deed must contain the names of the grantee (buyer) and grantor (seller), words evidencing an intent to convey the property, and the grantor's (and usually the spouse's) signature.
6. C. An easement is a right to make limited use of another's real property without taking anything from it. In this problem, it is an easement by necessity—the owner needs access to his property. The right to take something from the property is a profit. A revocable right to come onto the property is a license.
7. C. A general development plan provides information about growth in a community. This plan may be supplemented by specific area plans that indicate special requirements. Zoning ordinances

relate to particular land uses and include building and use restrictions and requirements. Other sources of relevant local policy and law include growth-management ordinances. Warranty deeds and restrictive covenants are *private* documents.

8. C. As a parcel of land is developed, it needs such public services as streets and sewers. When the land is developed for residential use, new schools and other public facilities, such as parks, must often be built. To meet these needs, subdivision development typically takes shape in a process of give and take between a developer and local authorities. Sometimes, a developer is asked to dedicate land to public use, or to otherwise contribute to the cost of public facilities.

9. A. What the local authorities have done is to have effectively confiscated the developer's property. In this developer's case, it does not matter that the surrounding undeveloped property was zoned for use as a nature preserve only. If the developer sues the county, the regulation will likely be held unconstitutional and void unless the county pays for its effective confiscation of the developer's land.

10. C. Most zoning laws provide means by which a property owner may be granted a variance from the laws. Factors for granting a variance include that the owner finds it impossible to realize a reasonable return on the land as zoned, that the adverse effect of the ordinance is particular to the person seeking the variance and not of similar effect on other owners within the zone, and that granting a variance will not substantially alter the character of the zone. The most important of these criteria is the effect of the variance on the character of the neighborhood.

GamePoints

1. When the trees were growing, they constituted real property, which is defined as land and things permanently attached to it, including plant life. The felled forest of trees became personal property when they were no longer attached to the land, and turning them into lumber refines them as personal property but does not change that status. The change comes when they are built into a structure and they again become real property. If the land had been sold before the trees were downed, the sale of the real property would have included the trees (unless otherwise specified). If the trees had been sold by themselves, however, they would have been considered personal property, and the sale would have been a sale of goods.

2. To be valid between a buyer and seller of real estate, a deed must contain the names of the grantee (buyer) and grantor (seller), words evi-

dencing an intent to convey the property, a legally sufficient description of the property, and the grantor's (and usually the spouse's) signature. And of course the deed has to be delivered. To meet these requirements, the deed must be in writing, but it does not have to include the sales price, the source of the funds for its purchase, or the signature of the buyer. Thus, in this problem, assuming the other requirements have been met, the only "last-minute act" actually needed to make the deed valid is its delivery.

Chapter 27

True-False Questions

1. T

2. T

3. T

4. F. Antitrust law is intended to promote business competition: the sort of competition that is believed to benefit society. It is thought that competition in the marketplace leads to better products and lower prices, which benefit consumers, as well as business owners and their employees.

5. F. A firm that can substantially ignore its competitors in setting a price for its product, or that can otherwise limit competition in its market, has considerable market power.

6. T

7. F. Attempted monopolization *is* an antitrust violation. To constitute a violation, an action must be specifically intended to exclude competitors and garner monopoly power. It must have a "dangerous probability" of success, but it need not have actually succeeded.

8. F. Under the Clayton Act, no person can be a director in two or more corporations at the same time *if* elimination of competition between or among the corporations would violate any of the antitrust laws (which include a requirement that any of the corporations have capital, surplus, or undivided profits aggregating more than a certain limit).

9. T

10. F. Under the Clayton Act, a private party can sue for *treble* damages and attorneys' fees, and may obtain an injunction if the violation hurt business activities protected by the antitrust laws.

Fill-in Questions

A restraint of trade; Monopoly power; monopoly power

Multiple-Choice Questions

1. A. The elements of the offense of monopolization include monopoly power and its willful acquisition. Market domination that results from legitimate competitive behavior (such as foresight, innovation, skill, and good management) is not a violation.

2. D. Of course, a U.S. firm is subject to the jurisdiction of a U.S. court. For a U.S. court to hear a case against a foreign entity under U.S. antitrust laws, the entity's alleged violation of the law must have a substantial effect on U.S. commerce (or be a *per se* violation). In other words, foreign and domestic firms may be sued for violations of U.S. antitrust laws.

3. C. Market power is the extent to which a firm can raise prices without concern for its competitors' response, or the extent to which a firm can otherwise exclude competition. Restraints of trade include agreements between suppliers in a market to limit output. Agreements between business firms that reduce competition are exercises of market power, but the agreements are not legitimate. They are generally restraints of trade that are against public policy and that violate the antitrust laws. An agreement that does not promote competition is not considered economically efficient or socially beneficial.

4. C. Selling a product or a service at a price substantially below cost is predatory pricing. Even if the result is to drive some competitors from the market, predatory pricing is not an antitrust violation if the firm that engages in the practice is attempting to gain access to an established market and the firm is unlikely to obtain monopoly profits in the future.

5. A. Determination of the relevant market is required to determine whether a firm has monopoly power. The relevant market has two parts: the relevant product market and the relevant geographical market. The product market consists of all products with identical attributes and products that are sufficient substitutes for each other. The geographical market is limited to the area in which a firm and it competitors sell those products.

6. B. Similar exemptions from the antitrust laws include cooperative research among small business firms, and joint efforts by businesspersons to obtain legislative, judicial, or executive action. Exporters that cooperate to compete against similar foreign associations are also exempt from the antitrust laws, as long as the activity does not restrain trade in the United States or injure other U.S. exporters. Other exemptions include labor activities, agricultural associations, fisheries, insurance companies, oil marketing, and professional baseball.

7. A. The elements of the offense of monopolization include monopoly power (market domination) and its willful acquisition. Conduct is considered to be anticompetitive if it is intended to obtain monopoly power and it is engaged in willfully. Market domination that results from historical circumstances, a superior product, or business acumen (which may involve foresight, innovation, skill, and good management) is not considered to have been acquired unlawfully.

8. D. A seller charging different buyers different prices for identical goods is a violation of the Clayton Act's price discrimination provision. (The effect of the price discrimination must also be to substantially lessen competition.) It is *not* a violation of the act if the different prices are due to different production and transportation costs. Of course, it is also not a violation to charge different prices for different goods, or if the situation involves no more than one buyer buying different kinds of goods, or no more than one price at a level no less than that charged by competitors. Price discrimination is discussed in more detail in Chapter 28.

9. C. The U.S. Department of Justice can prosecute violations of the Sherman Act as criminal or civil violations, but can enforce the Clayton Act only through civil proceedings. The Federal Trade Commission can also enforce the Clayton Act (and has sole authority to enforce the Federal Trade Commission Act). A private party can sue under the Clayton Act if he or she is injured by a violation of *any* antitrust law.

10. B. Illegal tying arrangements violate the Clayton Act. Although violations of the Clayton Act are not criminal, the U.S. Department of Justice can enforce its provisions in civil proceedings. The Federal Trade Commission can also seek civil sanctions under the Clayton Act, and private parties (such as the customers in this problem) can seek civil remedies for their injuries.

GamePoints

1. Yes. The term monopoly is used to describe a market in which there is a single seller. Having monopoly power is not a violation of the antitrust laws if it results from business acumen, historical circumstances, a superior product, or a product that more consumers want to buy. A monopoly, or an attempt to monopolize, is a violation of the law only if anticompetitive conduct is involved.

2. Yes. The set of facts in this problem presents an attempt to monopolize. Such an attempt is illegal under the Sherman Act if it (1) is intended to exclude competitors and garner monopoly power and (2) has a dangerous probability of success. Business firms enter into exclusive or favored agreements every day. To have a "dangerous probability of success," the party making the attempt must possess some degree of market power. In this problem, the game maker has and uses its monopoly power to affect competition. The marketplace injury consists of an increase in the prices of the maker's products and the decreasing market shares of the maker's competitors.

Chapter 28

True-False Questions

1. F. This is a vertical restraint.
2. F. This is a horizontal restraint.
3. F. Exclusive dealing contracts are those under which a seller forbids a buyer from purchasing products from the seller's competitors.
4. F. Price discrimination occurs when sellers charge competitive buyers different prices for identical goods.
5. F. This is a *vertical* merger. A horizontal merger is a merger between firms that compete with each other in the same market.
6. F. This is a *horizontal* merger. A vertical merger occurs when a company at one stage of production acquires another company at a higher or lower stage in the chain of production and distribution.
7. T
8. T
9. F. The opposite is true. If an agreement is *not* deemed a *per se* violation of Section 1 of the Sherman Act, a court analyzes its legality under what is referred to as a rule of reason.
10. T

Fill-in Questions

1. horizontal, horizontal, may, or; 2. vertical, vertical, vertical.

Multiple-Choice Questions

1. A. An agreement to set prices in the manner described in the problem is a price-fixing agreement, which is a restraint of trade and a *per se* violation of Section 1 of the Sherman Act.
2. D. Territorial or customer restrictions, like the restriction described in the problem, are judged under a rule of reason. The rule of reason involves a weighing of competitive benefits against anticompetitive harms. Here, the manufacturer's restriction on its dealers would likely be considered lawful because, although it reduces *intra*brand competition, it promotes *inter*brand competition.
3. D. In applying the rule of reason, courts consider the purpose of the conduct, the effect of the conduct on trade, the power of the parties to accomplish what they intend, and in some cases, whether there are less restrictive alternatives to achieve the same goals.
4. D. Price discrimination occurs when a seller charges different buyers different prices for identical goods. To violate the Clayton Act, among other requirements, the effect of the price discrimination must be to substantially lessen competition or otherwise create a competitive injury.
5. D. If a merger creates an entity with more than a small percentage market share, it is presumed illegal. In determining market share, the factors include market concentration. Other factors include the relevant market's history of tending toward concentration, economic efficiency, and the factors that are part of the correct answer to this problem.
6. D. A contract under which a seller forbids a buyer from buying products from the seller's competitors is an exclusive-dealing contract. Subject to the rule of reason, under Section 3 of the Clayton Act, these agreements are prohibited if their effect is "to substantially lessen competition" or to "tend to create a monopoly."
7. A. Conduct subject to the rule of reason is unlawful if its anticompetitive harms outweigh its competitive benefits. Conduct typically subject to a rule of reason analysis includes trade association activities, joint ventures, territorial or customer restrictions, refusal to deal, price discrimination, and exclusive-dealing contracts.
8. A. An important consideration in determining whether a merger substantially lessens competition and hence violates the Clayton Act is market concentration (the market chares among the firms in the market). If a merger creates an entity with more than a small percentage market share, it is presumed illegal.
9. D. An agreement between a manufacturer and a distributor or retailer in which the manufacturer specifies the retail prices of its products is a resale price maintenance agreement. These agreements were once considered *per se* violations of the Sherman Act, but are now subject to the rule of reason.
10. C. Conduct that is blatantly anticompetitive is a *per se* violation of antitrust law. This is the most important circumstance in determining whether an action violates the antitrust laws. If an action un-

dercuts competition, a court will not allow a party to undertake it. Such conduct typically includes price-fixing agreements, group boycotts, and horizontal market divisions. The U.S. Department of Justice can prosecute violations of the Sherman Act as criminal or civil violations, but can enforce the Clayton Act only through civil proceedings. The Federal Trade Commission can also enforce the Clayton Act (and has sole authority to enforce the Federal Trade Commission Act). A private party can sue under the Clayton Act if he or she is injured by a violation of *any* antitrust law.

GamePoints

1. Contracts, combinations, and conspiracies that restrain trade and monopolize are prohibited under the Sherman Act. Price-fixing is an agreement among makers or sellers to increase or maintain a price level with the purpose of blocking free trade. A price-fixing agreement among competitors is so blatantly and substantially anticompetitive as to be considered *per se* illegal. This is true even if the price is reasonable. In this problem, the agreement among the competitive sellers fits the definition of price-fixing and is thus *per se* illegal. There is no need to determine whether the agreement actually injures market competition.

2. This agreement appears to be a tying arrangement. The legality of a tying arrangement depends on the purpose of the agreement, the agreement's likely effect on competition in the relevant markets (the market for the tying product and the market for the tied product), and other factors. Subject to the rule of reason, these agreements are illegal if their effect is "to substantially lessen competition" or to "tend to create a monopoly." Tying arrangements for commodities, but not services, are subject to the Clayton Act. Tying arrangements for services can be agreements in restraint of trade in violation of Section 1 of the Sherman Act.

Chapter 29

True-False Questions

1. T
2. T
3. T
4. T
5. F. Rule 506, issued under the Securities Act of 1933, provides an exemption for these offerings, if certain other requirements are met. This is an im-

portant exemption, applying to private offerings to a limited number of sophisticated investors.
6. T
7. T
8. F. *Scienter* is required for liability under Section 10(b) of the 1934 act and under SEC Rule 10b-5. For either criminal or civil sanctions to be imposed under these provisions, the violator must have acted with an intent to defraud or with the knowledge of his or her misconduct. This can be proved by false statements or a wrongful failure to disclose material facts.
9. F. Anyone who receives inside information as a result of an insider's breach of his or her fiduciary duty can be liable under SEC Rule 10b-5, which applies in virtually all cases involving the trading of securities. The key to liability is whether the otherwise undisclosed information is *material*.
10. F. Most securities can be resold without registration. Also, under Rules 144 and 144A ("safe harbor" provisions), there are specific exemptions for securities that might otherwise require registration with the SEC.

Fill-in Questions

prosecution; triple; twenty-five; may

Multiple-Choice Questions

1. A. A corporate officer is a traditional inside trader. The outsider in this problem is a tippee who is liable because the tippee knew of the officer's misconduct. Liability here is based on the fact that the information was not public. Liability might be avoided if those who know the information wait for a reasonable time after its public disclosure before trading their stock.
2. D. Under the Securities Act of 1933, a security exists when a person invests in a common enterprise with the reasonable expectation of profits derived primarily or substantially from the managerial or entrepreneurial efforts of others (not from the investor's own efforts).
3. A. This purchase and sale is a violation of Section 16(b) of the Securities Exchange Act of 1934. When a purchase and sale is within a six-month period, as in this problem, the corporation can recover all of the profit. Liability is strict liability—proof of neither *scienter* nor negligence is required.
4. A. Because of the low amount of the issue, it qualifies as an exemption from registration under Rule 504. No specific disclosure document is required, and there is no prohibition on solicitation. If the amount had been higher than $1 million but

lower than $5 million, this offer might have qualified for an exemption under Regulation A, which requires notice to the SEC and an offering circular for investors.

5. D. The amount of this offering is too high to exempt it from the registration requirements except possibly under Rule 506. This issuer advertised the offering, however, and Rule 506 prohibits general solicitation. Thus, without filing a registration statement, the issuer could not legally solicit *any* investors (whatever it may have believed about the unaccredited investors).

6. D. This issue might qualify under Rule 505 except that the issuer advertised the offering, which it cannot do and remain exempt from registration. In other words, the amount of this offering disqualified the issuer from advertising it without filing a registration statement.

7. B. Of course, the offering must be registered with the SEC before it can be sold, and this requires a registration statement. Investors must be given a prospectus that describes the security, the issuing corporation, and the risk of the security.

8. A. Most resales are exempt from registration if persons other than issuers or underwriters undertake the resales. Resales of restricted securities acquired under Rule 505 or Rule 506 may trigger registration requirements, but the original sale in this problem came under Rule 504.

9. B. A registration statement must supply enough information so that an unsophisticated investor can evaluate the financial risk involved. The statement must explain how the registrant intends to use the proceeds from the sale of the issue. Also, besides the description of management, there must be a disclosure of any of their material transactions with the firm. A certified financial statement must be included.

10. B. Under the Securities Exchange Act of 1934, the Securities and Exchange Commission all of the other duties and more, including regulating national securities trading, supervising mutual funds, and recommending sanctions in cases involving violations of securities laws. This question and answer are based on a question that was included in a 1996 CPA exam.

GamePoints

1. If the SEC files a suit against this firm on the basis that its offering was not exempt from registration, the SEC will likely win, and the firm will be required to forebear sanctions. The problem is that the offering complies with all of the requirements for an exemption from registration but one—the offering is advertised to the general public online

and the stock is sold to too many unaccredited investors (including, of course, your avatar). A private, noninvestment company offering for less than $5 million in any twelve-month period may be exempt under Rule 505 of Regulation D if it is sold to no more than thirty-five unaccredited investors (any number of accredited investors is okay), it is not generally advertised or solicited, and the SEC is notified of the sales. This offering does not qualify.

2. Minor misstatements or ill-phrased puffery is not of much concern to serious investors. Like others, you and your avatar would most likely want to know only facts that illuminate the business condition of an issuer—such things as fraud, an important change in a firm's finances, or a new discovery or product, as well as a firm's liability, loans to officers or directors, and pending lawsuits. This type of information could affect a decision to invest in the firm. And false statements or omissions of such information could subject the firm to liability under the securities laws. That would be material.

Cumulative Hypothetical Problem for Unit Six—Including Chapters 24–29

1. D. Advertising that consists of vague generalities is not illegal. This is also true of advertising that includes obvious exaggerations. Advertising that may lead to sanctions by the Federal Trade Commission is deceptive advertising: advertising that misleads consumers.

2. A. An administrative agency has a number of options to determine whether a manufacturer is complying with the agency's rules, but the agency may not use its powers arbitrarily or capriciously or abuse its discretion. The options that an agency may choose include those in the other answer choices, such as obtaining a search warrant to search the premises for a specific item and return it to the agency.

3. A. Under the Comprehensive Environmental Response, Compensation, and Liability Act of 1980, any "potentially responsible party" can be charged with the entire cost to clean up a hazardous waste disposal site. Potentially responsible parties include the party who generates the waste, the party who transports the waste to the site, and the party who owns or operates the site.

4. C. It is price discrimination when a seller charges different buyers different prices for identical products. Price discrimination is a violation of the Clayton Act if the effect of the pricing is to substantially lessen competition or otherwise create a competitive injury.

5. D. Other information that must be included in a registration statement, under the Securities Act of

1933, includes a description of the issuer's business, a description of the security, the capital structure of the business, the underwriting arrangements, and the certified financial statements.

Questions on the Focus on Ethics for Unit Six—The Regulatory Environment

1. D. Of course, this outcome is debatable, and the issue is contentious. The questions, which do not have certain answers, concern the extent to which the government goes in regulating individuals and businesses in the interest of protecting the environment. At what point are the costs of environmental regulations too much for an individual, a business, or society as a whole to bear? How much are we willing to sacrifice to ensure that future generations have a healthful world?

2. C. Pollution does not stop at a nation's political border (as illustrated by the federal government's involvement in a problem that was once left to the states). The world is a global community. A single standard for the emission of pollutants might be desirable, but given the competing political and economic interests at stake, it might be nearly unattainable.

3. A. What the local authorities have done is to have effectively confiscated the developer's property. In this developer's case, it does not matter that the surrounding undeveloped property was zoned for use as a nature preserve only. If the developer sues the county, the regulation will likely be held unconstitutional and void unless the county pays for its effective confiscation of the developer's land.